# Cybercrime

As technology develops and internet-enabled devices become ever more prevalent new opportunities exist for that technology to be exploited by criminals. One result of this is that cybercrime is increasingly recognised as a distinct branch of criminal law. This book is designed for students studying cybercrime for the first time, enabling them to get to grips with an area of rapid change.

The book offers a thematic and critical overview of cybercrime, introducing the key principles and clearly showing the connections between topics as well as highlighting areas subject to debate. Written with an emphasis on the law in the UK but considering in detail the Council of Europe's important *Convention on Cybercrime*, this text also covers the jurisdictional aspects of cybercrime in international law. Themes discussed include crimes against computers, property, offensive content and offences against the person, and recent controversial areas such as cyberterrorism and cyber-harassment are explored.

Clear, concise and critical, this text offers a valuable overview of this fast-paced and growing area of law.

**Alisdair A. Gillespie** is a Professor of Criminal Law and Justice and Head of the Law School at Lancaster University.

# Cybercrime

## Key Issues and Debates

Alisdair A. Gillespie

Taylor & Francis Group

LONDON AND NEW YORK

First published 2016
by Routledge
2 Park Square, Milton Park, Abingdon, Oxon, OX14 4RN

and by Routledge
711 Third Avenue, New York, NY 10017

*Routledge is an imprint of the Taylor & Francis Group, an informa business*

© 2016 Alisdair A. Gillespie

*British Library Cataloguing in Publication Data*
A catalogue record for this book is available from the British Library

*Library of Congress Cataloging-in-Publication Data*
Gillespie, Alisdair, author.
Cybercrime / Alisdair Gillespie.
pages cm
Includes bibliographical references and index.
ISBN 978-0-415-71221-7 (hbk : alk. paper) – ISBN 978-0-415-71220-0 (pbk
: alk. paper) – ISBN 978-1-315-88420-2 (ebk : alk. paper) 1. Computer
crimes–Great Britain. 2. Internet–Law and legislation–Great Britain–
Criminal provisions. I. Title.
KD7990.G55 2015
345.41'0268–dc23
2015002452


ISBN: 978-0-415-71221-7 (hbk)
ISBN: 978-0-415-71220-0 (pbk)
ISBN: 978-1-315-88420-2 (ebk)


Typeset in Times New Roman by
Servis Filmsetting Ltd, Stockport, Cheshire

# Contents

**PART 4**
**Offences against the person** 255

# Preface

This is not a usual textbook. It does not purport to be the definitive book on the issue of cybercrime, even if such a thing was possible. Cybercrime, as will be seen, is not easy to define and covers a breadth of subjects. A difficulty with trying to write the 'definitive' book on cybercrime is that something is bound to be missed out. Trying to cover everything also tends to mean that there is a breadth of coverage but without depth, partly because publishers (not unreasonably) want books to be of an appropriate (readable!) length.

What this book does is to highlight some of the key issues of debate that exist in respect of cybercrime, including what cybercrime is. You will find many of the key areas within this book and perhaps a couple that are not always considered. Each topic follows the same format: the behaviour is discussed critically and an analysis is made of whether the law can solve the behaviour and, if so, how.

One area that is not considered is the detection and investigation of cybercrime. This is because the focus of the book is about the criminal law and not how it is enforced (in the same way that a criminal law textbook will not ordinarily discuss how crimes are investigated). This is not to minimise this issue, because the investigation of cybercrimes, including digital evidence and investigatory techniques, are of crucial importance. However, the book has to have a focus and for this one it is the criminal law. If you are interested in the investigation of cybercrimes then, whilst dated, Walden (2007) remains the benchmark for these issues, although there is an increasing library of texts and articles dedicated to the subject.

There can be little doubt that cybercrime has now emerged as a sub-species of criminal law. Whilst it will be seen that some behaviours exist both online and offline, there are undoubtedly particular forms of behaviour that can only take place either through, or facilitated by, the internet. This poses challenges for the law, as the law prefers tangible actions that it can see. Where the behaviour is less clear and seems to involve the manipulation of data then it does not always understand either the behaviour or the consequences. This book will demonstrate a number of examples where either the law has not developed adequately or has reacted to a threat in a way that it did not need to.

The book is presented in such a way that you can read each chapter individually, so that if you are interested in a particular area it is not necessary to read the whole of the book before understanding that concept. That said, there are two chapters that are relevant to the whole of the book. These are the first two chapters. Chapter 1 introduces the concept of cybercrime, including identifying what makes cybercrime different and how it operates. The second chapter is on jurisdiction. One part of the internet is known as the 'World Wide Web' and the first two Ws – 'World Wide' – are of crucial importance here. The internet is a truly global resource. It does not really care about national borders, which is the opposite of how the law operates. At the heart of law is the concept of territorial sovereignty, with laws generally only applying within the territorial borders of a state. The internet challenges this position and thus all crimes discussed in this book are subject to the discussion on jurisdiction that is set out in Chapter 2.

I should like to thank a number of people. First of all, I would like to thank Emma Nugent who commissioned this book. Emma has now sadly left Routledge but she was very helpful in getting the project going. I would also like to thank Laura Muir who took over as the editor in the final stages of this book. I would like to thank those whom I have worked with in the past on these issues, including Professor Suzanne Ost, Dr Bela Chatterjee and Dr Catherine Easton of Lancaster University, and Professors Gavin Dingwall and Michael Hirst of De Montfort University. I would also like to thank the various people I speak with as part of my work with the EU TAIEX (Technical Assistance and Information Exchange) programme. In particular Laviero Bueno, Albena Spasova, Cormac Callahan, Professor Ian Walden and Professor Marco Gercke. I would also like to thank Esther George for the help she has offered over the years.

Finally, this book is dedicated to Suzanne and to my baby daughter Elin. The latter was responsible for the significant delay in this book being published. I had hoped to finish the manuscript before her birth but, once born, entertaining a baby seemed much more fun than writing a book!

Whilst the law is generally correct as of December 2014, it was possible at the proofs stage to make brief amendments in chapter 9 to reflect the introduction of the offence referring to revenge pornography.

*AAG*
*Lancaster*
*January, 2015*

# Chapter 1

# Cybercrime

This chapter will place the rest of the chapters into context. It is necessary to consider what we mean by cybercrime, which as will be seen is a phenomenon that is not easy to define, and to consider what its characteristics are. The chapter will also briefly introduce the primary international instrument on cybercrime, the *Council of Europe Convention on Cybercrime* which will be considered throughout this book.

## What is cybercrime?

The first issue to consider is the definition of cybercrime. Whilst there are numerous arguments over its features and its definition it should be noted at the outset that the very term 'cybercrime' is controversial.

### 'Cybercrime' or 'computer crime'?

Whilst this book has been deliberately called *Cybercrime* and there are many references to 'cybercrime' in other literature, including the mass media, the term itself is contested. If you look at other books and articles you will see reference not only to cybercrime but also to 'e-crime', 'computer crime', 'hi-tech crime' and 'digital crime'. Indeed the topic is not necessarily as new as some may think. In 1991 Martin Wasik published his seminal book *Crime and the Computer* (Wasik, 1991) at a time when the internet as we know it now was unheard of (see Wasik, 2010, for an illuminating history of computer crime). Does cyberspace (meaning in this context the internet) alter what the subject matter is?

Walden argues that cybercrime is a subset of computer crime (Walden, 2007:19) and this must be correct. A computer need not be connected to cyberspace (in this context meaning the internet) and thus if we are looking at internet crime then we will be looking at something narrower than computer crime, although some computer crimes will be relevant. Similarly it has been argued that 'digital' and 'hi-tech' crime are also broad labels that do not necessarily require connection to the internet whereas 'e-crime' and 'cybercrime' do (Hunton, 2009:529).

Of course it could be questioned whether the distinction between 'computer crime' and 'cybercrime' continues to be relevant in the modern era of ubiquitous internet connections, particularly with the advancement of mobile technologies. When the internet was first introduced into the consumer market there was a clear distinction between the 'online' and 'offline' worlds. In order to connect to the internet it was necessary to directly connect to an ISP through a modem connected to the telephone system (ISP stands for Internet Service Provider and is the company that allows you to connect to the internet, either through broadband (telephone), cable or satellite). This would tie-up the telephone line and would provide a slow connection to the internet. Internet usage was invariably metered, so people would be careful as to how much time they spent on the internet. The development of broadband revolutionised this concept. It was no longer necessary to 'dial' up an ISP, broadband was 'always on' and was not metered in terms of duration (although it sometimes was in terms of the amount of traffic that was allowed to be downloaded and uploaded). 'Always-on' broadband meant that people could look at the internet in a way they had not done before, but it still did not lead to it becoming a ubiquitous tool.

Mobile technologies have revolutionised the way that we access the internet. This was initially through the mobile telephone, which quickly ceased to be an instrument that was used only to make a telephone call and became a computer in its own right (discussed below). Indeed, for many, the ability to make telephone calls is perhaps one of the least-used functions of the mobile phone. Again, mobile technology went through phases of development. The first telephones were analogue, and then the so-called second-generation mobiles (2G) became digital. Developments of digital technology (sometimes known as 2.5G and 2.75G to reflect the fact that they were not really new generations but rather developments) allowed users access to data through GPRS and EDGE technologies. This allowed people to have (slow) access to the internet. The third generation (3G) provided much faster data connection and 'smartphones' such as the iPhone were developed to fully exploit this. Again, providers started to offer consumer packages that provided unlimited data meaning that people could connect to the internet whenever they wanted. Companies such as Blackberry and Apple placed great emphasis on the fact that emails could be delivered instantly through 'push' technology, meaning that a person would never miss an email. The latest development is 4G (fourth generation) where broadband-like speeds for mobile technology are being delivered.

Coupled with the advances of broadband and mobile technologies was the development of wireless technology, so-called 'wi-fi'. Whilst many wi-fi providers are commercially operated (providing so-called 'hotspots' through which people can connect) many providers (particularly BT) realised that numerous domestic customers were not using their full broadband capabilities. They encouraged users to become hotspots themselves, meaning that users suddenly find it possible to get high-speed internet use almost anywhere, although public places such as shops, restaurants and hotels remain the most stable and popular hotspots.

This coupling of wi-fi and mobile technology (particularly the development of tablet technologies which even 10 years ago were only within the imagination of science fiction movie and television prop developers) has meant that we no longer distinguish between the 'online' and 'offline' worlds. We switch between them frequently. How many times have you been debating an issue with someone and decided to resolve the matter by 'googling' the answer on a mobile telephone? We no longer think 'oh, I will go onto the internet and find this out' we just do it. Indeed the term 'googling' which is a derivative of the verb 'to google' has entered the popular lexicon. We have almost forgotten that the company 'Google' did not exist before 1998. Like Hoover before it, it has now ceased to be thought of as a company and it is now arguably a behaviour.

People have started to refer to this era as the 'converged environment', i.e. a situation where we co-exist the online and offline worlds and where both interact easily with each other. That being the case, does it mean that the distinction between 'computer crime' and 'cybercrime' is now pointless? Arguably not. There are still examples of situations where there can be a computer crime that does not constitute a cybercrime. For example, A sneaks into an office and downloads confidential information from B's computer to a USB stick. He then sells this information to C, B's competitor. Whilst this could have been done as a cybercrime – instead of sneaking into B's office, A could have hacked A's computer – nothing that A did involved the internet. It was all done offline. Whilst investigators may still need to investigate the matter in the same way (which is why police often refer to themselves as having 'hi-tech' crime units rather than cybercrime units) and whilst it may be prosecuted in the same way, it is not strictly speaking cybercrime.

This provides the first limitation of this book. The book concentrates on cybercrime and not computer crime. Accordingly, the internet is at the heart of this book. It is concerned with crimes that are committed on, or facilitated by, the internet. It will not differentiate between how access to the internet is made – be that through a computer or mobile technology – but the internet is the limiting factor. It is for that reason that the book continues to be called *Cybercrime* and not *Computer crime*.

### Classifying cybercrime

Whilst the term 'cybercrime' is to be used, what does this mean? Are all crimes against, or using the internet, cybercrimes? If so, does that mean they are all treated the same and can be classified the same? It is generally thought that the answer to that is 'no' because cybercrime is an overarching term that covers a wide range of crimes and behaviours. However, identifying how cybercrime should be defined is something that many have struggled with.

A popular distinction is to draw a divide between 'computer-assisted' crime and 'computer-focused' crimes. This distinction operates on the basis that in some instances the computer simply facilitates crimes that are already known to the law. Classic examples of this would include theft and the distribution of child pornography. Both of these crimes pre-dated computers and certainly pre-dated the internet. However, cyberspace has allowed the crimes to be committed in new ways – phishing (for example) or the hacking into a bank account or the publishing of illicit material to a webpage. Computer-focused crimes, however, are different and are those crimes that came into existence because the computer is an intrinsic part of the conduct. A classic example here would be hacking. There was no crime of hacking before a computer because hacking requires a computer – something has to be hacked.

A criticism that can be levelled at this broad categorisation is that technological advancements have arguably blurred the distinction between assisted and focused. It is for this reason that some have suggested a slightly more nuanced distinction, containing three categories:

- Traditional criminal activities that are expanded *or enhanced* by the internet.
- Traditional criminal activities that are *generalised* and 'radicalised' by the internet.
- Criminal activities that are *created* by the internet.

(Sandywell, 2010:46)

This provides a useful understanding of cybercrime, that in many instances it is not that there is new criminal behaviour but rather there are new ways of committing existing behaviour. A good example of the first category would be credit card fraud. Credit card fraud has existed since the development of credit cards (by duplicating receipts, placing 'traps' in ATM machines, etc.) but the internet and the growth of e-commerce has led to a transformation in this type of crime. A good example of the second category would be bullying. Whilst bullying has always existed, the use of communication technologies allows the crime to not only flourish but to develop in a more harmful way; a victim could hide from a traditional bully but it is now almost impossible to hide from a cyber-bully because of our use of mobile technologies. The first two categories therefore demonstrate that existing crimes have been given new life by the internet, but obviously some forms of crimes did not exist before the establishment of the internet (the classic example being hacking).

For some the emphasis should not be on the technology but rather the focus should be on the offender's behaviour. Thomas and Loader suggest three categories:

- Hackers and phreaks (those that seek to exploit the technology).
- Information merchants and mercenaries (those that trade data).
- Terrorists, extremists and deviants.

(Thomas and Loader in Walden, 2007:20)

The advantage of an offender-based approach is that it is not technology-dependent. Accordingly, it is not necessary to try and 'fit' new technologies around old definitions. However, a disadvantage of perpetrator-based definitions is that they perhaps lose some of what is unique about cybercrime. Some of the labels would fit behaviours both online and offline, perhaps confusing the issues. In terms of Thomas and Loader's definition, they argue that the first group are curious persons who seek ways of finding information that others would prefer them not to. The second group are those who have a financial motivation for their crime. Interestingly, offenders in the first and second categories could be carrying out the same behaviour but for different motivations. So, for example, X who hacks into the computer system of D Ltd to see what confidential information they hold, would probably be placed in the first category. Where Y hacks into the computer system of D Ltd to gain the same confidential information but with the intention of selling it to E Ltd, the major competitor of D Ltd, then this falls within the second category. This illustrates the conflation that exists between the categories because arguably the behaviour does not differ remarkably, at least in terms of the cyber-nature of the crime, although the punishment may well be very different.

The third category identified by Thomas and Loader would be those who are engaged in illegal political or social activity (Walden, 2007:20). This would be an extremely large category and indeed it could be argued that it is simply too broad. Few would believe that the motivation of a terrorist would be the same as that of a sex offender or a cyber-bully. Of course that is a criticism of the categorisation used by Thomas and Loader and not of the principle itself. It would be possible to have as many sub-categories as are necessary. However, would this tell us anything? It may assist in understanding the offender – and therefore the motivations for their actions – but it probably does not assist in understanding what a crime is.

It would seem, therefore, that there needs to be a mix of both offender and technology behaviour. Wall, one of the earliest authors to study cybercrime, managed to do this in part when he put forward a four-fold classification system. He suggested that cybercrimes could be categorised as follows:

- Cyber-trespass (the invasion of a person's space, including hacking, etc.).
- Cyber-deceptions and theft (stealing money and property).
- Cyber-pornography (illicit material that is created or distributed).
- Cyber-violence (stalking, hate speech, etc.)

(Wall, 2001:3–7)

This classification borrows much of the offender-focus model by looking at some aspects of what the person is trying to do (cyber-violence for example) but it is premised very much on the basis that this is cyber-behaviour. The model is arguably closer to the traditional method of identifying and classifying criminal offences (where we have labels such as fatal offences, non-fatal offences, crime against property, etc.). Rather than consider, at least in the labelling of offences, *why* the offender acted in the way that he did, the categorisation adopts the approach of considering what the end-result is.

There are difficulties with this approach. It does not allow us to readily identify what crimes are new (in the sense that technology has created them) and which are new forms of existing offences (because technology has provided new ways of committing the offence). However, it has been questioned whether that is necessarily a helpful distinction, particularly as technology continues to advance. Does it matter why the offence is in existence so long as it covers the relevant behaviour?

A more pertinent criticism of the classification is that it misses some of the newer forms of cybercrime, although this should not realistically be called a criticism because the forms did not exist at the time it was formulated. Good examples of this would be both cyberwarfare and cyberterrorism, neither of which necessarily easily fit into the classification. Perhaps, therefore, the criticism is that the classification system does not necessarily keep up with technological advancements. However, given the pace of development this is perhaps not surprising and it is relatively easily remedied, new categories can be developed as necessary.

Some believe cybercrime is not a single type of offence and is instead best thought of as a broad range of behaviour *and* technologies that are always evolving (Urbas and Choo, 2008:5). If that is true then classifications on the basis of technology and offender behaviour will always be in a state of flux. That therefore returns us to the initial classification of simply looking at how the crime takes place. Clough believes that the most common distinction is between one of three categories:

- Crimes in which the computer or computer network is the target of the criminal activity (including, for example, hacking).
- Existing offences where the computer is a tool used to commit the crime (for example, child pornography, harassment, etc.).
- Crimes in which the use of the computer is an incidental aspect of the commission of the crime but may afford evidence of it.

(Clough, 2011:672)

The third category is perhaps the most interesting because it returns us to one of the earlier discussions about what is, or is not, a cybercrime. Clough recognises that whilst a crime may not be a cybercrime *per se* it is quite possible that an investigation would need to proceed as though it were a cybercrime.

We are accustomed to the police routinely examining the computers and mobile telephones of missing persons because the messages and websites they have visited may provide clues as to their whereabouts. In the converged environment it is quite likely that this will be increasingly common even with what would appear to be 'traditional' crimes. Let us take an example:

> Alfred and Betty plan to rob a bank. They enlist Charlie to act as the getaway driver. Alfred sends a map of the area including the bank to both Betty and Charlie, and the day before the robbery, Betty sends an SMS message to both Alfred and Charlie saying 'tomorrow'. Charlie is the getaway driver. He waits in a side-street away from the bank so as not to arouse suspicion. Betty sends an SMS message saying '2 minutes' and he drives around to the front of the bank, picking Alfred and Betty up who entered the bank with guns and stole a significant amount of money.

Is this a cybercrime? It would be difficult to argue that it was. The principal crime in the example is the physical robbery of a bank. Few would label this a cybercrime. However, an investigator may well investigate certain parts of the evidence – the emails, SMS messages, etc. – as though it were a cybercrime. The proliferation of modern technologies means that investigations in many spheres will now require the interrogation of technologies. That does not make the crimes cybercrimes but is perhaps simply a reflection of our converged environment.

It is clear that there is no simple method of identifying and classifying cybercrimes. Each system of identification has both advantages and disadvantages. Does it matter? Arguably yes. It is not just criminological curiosity that requires us to know what cybercrime is and how it can be identified, it is also important for understanding its prevalence, something discussed below. When giving written evidence to the Home Affairs Select Committee, Peter Sommer – a leading expert on e-crime – noted that the absence of an agreed definition 'directly impacts assessments of extent' (HAC, 2013:Ev101). In other words, if we don't know what cybercrime is then how can we understand how often it is committed, whether it is a problem and how we are going to tackle it?

This book adopts an adaptation of Wall's categorisation. The book concentrates on themes of identifiable conduct that can be seen as cybercrime. The categories used here are:

- Crimes against computers. That is to say, crimes that were not in existence before the internet and where the computer is the target of the crime. Chapters 3–5 inclusive consider this.
- Crimes against property. This is where the object of the cybercrime is to obtain property (be that financial or intellectual) from another. Chapters 6 and 7 consider this.

- Crimes involving illicit content. This is where the crime relates to the posting, hosting or accessing of objectionable content. Chapters 8–10 inclusive consider this.
- Crimes against the person. This is where technology is used as a 'weapon' against an individual, with the potential of causing harm to that person. Chapter 11 considers this.

As with any classification system this can be subject to criticisms, not least in respect of cyberterrorism, which is considered a crime against computers but which could easily be considered a crime against property since, in many instances, the object of the cyberterrorism is data, which could be considered by some to be intellectual property. However, this classification allows for the presentation and exploration of the key themes.

### Characteristics of cybercrime

Regardless of how cybercrime is defined, it is perhaps easier to identify some of its characteristics and, in particular, the challenges that it can pose to law. Clough (2010) believes that there are five key issues.

- **Scale**. The large number of persons using the internet and related communications means that the potential number of victims and offenders is immense.
- **Accessibility**. The internet continues to reach areas of the world where it has not traditionally been found, and this is particularly true in respect of, for example, Africa and certain parts of the Middle East where mobile technology is more widespread than fixed broadband internet. This provides opportunities for offenders to meet people who share their desires.
- **Anonymity**. Unlike most traditional crime where it is relatively difficult to hide your identity, on the internet it is possible. Whilst there will be some that doubt true anonymity is possible (something that will be discussed elsewhere in this book) it is relatively easy to mask one's identity so that the average person/investigator does not know who you are.
- **Portability and transferability**. The growth in storage media means that it is increasingly difficult to find the results of the crime or an electronic trace of it. This is particularly true of so-called 'cloud computing' which is often said to involve data being stored in the internet itself (although it is not quite that simple, as the information is stored on servers which must, themselves, be located somewhere; but cloud content moves between servers rapidly as most cloud providers will rent space). This can pose significant challenges to investigators who may find that the evidence they require is held outside of their jurisdiction.
- **Global reach**. One of the issues that will be discussed later in this chapter is the fact that the internet is a global resource, and this poses significant

challenges in terms of jurisdiction which has a direct impact on whether countries are able to enact laws governing behaviour and whether investigators can gain access to evidence.

These are powerful challenges and demonstrate the difficulties that cyber-crime can cause. Two practical examples can be given of one of these elements – scale – to place it into context. It will be seen from Chapter 5 that the internet remains a powerful tool for committing fraud. There are many different types but one of the more popular remains phishing. This is where a person sends emails that purports to come from a bank or store and requests all the log-in credentials for the bank or credit card. This then allows them to take money from the victim's bank account. Ordinarily, where someone commits theft a report would be made to the local police. However, the scale of internet fraud means the police would not be able to cope and UK government policy has been to shift reporting such matters away from the police towards the banks (HAC, 2013:24). In essence this has privatised internet fraud and small-scale fraud is dealt with as a civil rather than criminal matter. The police ultimately created a national reporting helpline for internet fraud (www.actionfraud.police.uk) although there are concerns about whether reports are investigated or whether they are simply recorded, in essence ignoring a large volume of crime.

The second practical example concerns child pornography, something discussed in Chapter 8. During the 1990s the US Postal Inspection Service arrested two people who were responsible for *Landslide Productions*, a website portal that allowed access, *inter alia*, to child pornography. When arrested the service found the list of subscribers to the site (including credit card details). This list covered people from all over the world and the list was thus passed to law enforcement authorities in each country. The UK list contained over 7,000 names (from a world-wide list of nearly 400,000 names). Never before had the UK police suddenly been presented with a situation where a single crime involved several thousand suspects. The systems in place to investigate such crimes quickly began 'creaking at the seams' (Jewkes and Andrews, 2005:49) and that was before the list was passed to local forces. Many local police forces had small cybercrime units and were not prepared for investigating several hundred individuals for such crimes. To put this in context, at that time it was said that 'it could take one officer the whole of his working career to thoroughly investigate the contents of a 10 gigabyte hard drive' (Jewkes and Andrews, 2005:52). Most offenders had significantly more than one device and storage has expanded exponentially since then, with personal storage devices in the terabytes now being considered commonplace. The impact of this investigation (*Operation Ore*) is arguably outside the scope of this book (but see Gillespie, 2012, for a discussion on this) but it is a useful example of Clough's point: the scale of suspects involved in a single operation was more than the police service could cope with at that time. This means new methods of investigating cybercrime needed to be developed, including police forces co-operating to pool their resources and the development of automated analysis.

## Advancement

Whilst Clough's challenges are important there is perhaps one missing, that of technological advancement. An undoubted challenge of cybercrime is the fact that technology advances so quickly. This is not just in terms of the physical technology (e.g. computer power, data storage, mobility) but also in terms of the architecture of the internet itself. As this changes, so does the pattern of use and it has been suggested that this can pose challenges for combatting cybercrime, not least in terms of victimisation.

Perhaps one of the most notable advances in terms of the architecture of the internet is in respect of the shift from Web 1.0 to Web 2.0. Unlike with mobile technologies discussed above, this was not technically a physical upgrade as such (which, for example, required software updates) but was rather a shift towards different methods of functionality. Web 1.0 is commonly said to be the first type of web content which was, in essence, one-dimensional. The information was created by a user and it was placed on the web so that other users could see it. To an extent many web pages continue to operate on the Web 1.0 platform because some pages are all about presenting information. Web 2.0 was where the functionality of the web changed to allow two-way generation of material. It became easier for people to collectively interact with each other in the production of material. Classic examples are blogs, comment pages and perhaps most notably *Wikipedia*, which allows users to edit the information displayed so that a collective agreement as to content is reached (although, of course, the success of this is questionable in controversial topics where users will have different views that they present as 'facts').

Yar believes that cybercrime has evolved in the same way. He labels the initial behaviour of cybercrime as Ecrime 1.0 (2012:209) and notes that it, in essence, replicates much of Web 1.0. He includes crimes such as the distribution of illegal pornography, the commission of fraud and the downloading of copyright material as being examples of this. His point is perhaps that there is no need for user generation in these aspects. They are, in essence, one-directional crimes that were propagated by an individual doing something, such as actively downloading content that was placed there by others, or accepting a communication request from someone not known to them (e.g. malware allowing for the hacking of a computer, etc.). He believes that the growth of Web 2.0 has led to the development of 'Ecrime 2.0' which targets the way users of Web 2.0 present themselves and he summarises it thus, '[c]entral to my argument is the connection between one's *visibility* and one's *vulnerability* to criminal predation or exploitation' (Yar, 2012:210; original emphasis). As Yar himself notes, the connection between visibility and vulnerability is something that is known to criminologists in other (offline) crimes but it is arguably stronger for some types of crime when it is placed in the online context. This is perhaps particularly true with certain offences against the person, and in Chapter 11 the phenomenon of 'cyber-bullying' will be discussed, which is undoubtedly facilitated, in part, because of the visibility of the victim. The same is true of grooming (which will also be discussed in Chapter 11) which is where, *inter alia*, an adult befriends a child with the intention of later sexually assaulting them.

### Individual, corporate and state behaviour

Yar has noted that an interesting characteristic of cybercrime is that we are most comfortable with criminalising individuals rather than corporate entities. Whilst corporate liability exists in respect of some offences, most notably in respect of content-based offences, the majority of attention appears to be placed on the individual. Yar has noted that this brings about a significant distinction between the actions of the individual on the one hand and large corporations and states on the other (Yar, 2012:214).

Something that will be addressed throughout this book is the question about why some types of conduct are criminal but others are not. It will be seen in a number of the chapters that invasions of privacy can act as a trigger for some offences. Yet arguably some of the major breaches of privacy aspects are conducted by states (who are increasingly seeking to conduct surveillance on the internet, with media reports in 2013 discussing the extent to which the US and UK state security services actively target internet traffic) and corporations. Again, media reports have been full of corporations that have gathered information about users without necessarily being clear as to why this is. Google was perhaps one of the more notable examples of this when it was reported that their 'google maps' vehicles (that drive around providing street-level photography of roads, paths, etc.) were also gathering wi-fi data (Richmond, 2010). Similarly, Facebook – one of the largest collection of online users – has faced criticism over the way that it gathers data, uses data and makes changes to user-based privacy settings (Barnett, 2011). This corporate behaviour has always been considered to be a matter for the civil law (even where administrative penalties have been imposed) but it undoubtedly raises questions about the ethics of their behaviour.

Yar believes that corporate misconduct can also be classified as a 'cybercrime' (Yar, 2012:215), meaning that cybercrime does not only encompass behaviour that breaches laws but also encompasses behaviour that is considered to be inappropriate or morally wrong. However, for the purposes of this book – which, unlike most of Yar's work which adopts a sociological and criminological perspective, is a law book – the term 'cybercrime' will be used to discuss behaviour that breaches laws. Accordingly, behaviour such as that discussed here in respect of corporations will not be considered in detail in the book although, as noted, the extent of the criminal law (including considering *why* some matters are criminal) will be discussed.

### 'Computer'

Before leaving the definition and characteristics of cybercrime it would be prudent to pause briefly to consider the meaning of 'computer'. It has been noted several times already that our use of technology has been transformed over the years and this includes what we understand 'computer' to mean. Even a decade ago when one talked about a computer most people would conjure up the idea of a traditional computer: a desktop consisting of usually three components: a central processing unit (a box that was either on the desk or on the floor as a 'tower' which contained most of the components of the computer), a monitor and a keyboard. Whilst laptops certainly existed they were not as popular as now, partly because they were less powerful than desktops and also because battery life was short.

In modern times what we mean by 'computer' has changed. Whilst traditional computers still exist, as do laptops, they have been joined by lots of other devices, particularly mobile technologies. Most smartphones these days have significantly more processor power than NASA would have ever dreamed of when first initiating the space programme. If you think about your own smartphone and compare it to a computer is there much difference? Whilst the functionality may be different, it is highly likely that you will have some games on the phone, and you will be able to check your emails and browse the web. You can send communications to others, including sending files such as video, pictures, etc. Whilst we still refer to the device as a 'phone' the reality is that they could be considered small computers. Tablet technology is perhaps even closer to what we think of as a computer.

In respect of domestic law, it is perhaps interesting to note that 'computer' is not defined anywhere in the *Computer Misuse Act 1990* notwithstanding the fact that 'computer' is in the short title of the Act. In fact, this was a deliberate decision by Parliament as it was thought that if computer was to be defined it would quickly be overtaken by technological advancement. This is perhaps true, because if in 1990 a person was asked to define what was meant by computer it is unlikely that they would have ever conceived of an iPhone, iPad or other tablet technology. However, it does not assist us in knowing what a computer is, although it arguably has not caused any problems for the law in that there has not, to the author's knowledge, been any case that has considered whether a piece of technology was, in fact, a computer.

Not every instrument fails to define a computer. The *Convention on Cybercrime* – which will be introduced below – does provide a definition of 'computer system'. Article 1(a) defines it as 'any device or a group of interconnected or related devices, one of more of which, pursuant to a program, performs automatic processing of data'. The final words of the provision

– automatic processing of data – are the most important and it means the definition is not based on the physical architecture of the machine but rather its capabilities. This would also accord with the definition commonly used in science which requires the automatic storage, retrieval and processing of information (data) to be the precursor to classifying a machine as a computer.

Despite the fact that the definition of 'computer system' is relatively straightforward, the Cybercrime Convention Committee found it necessary in 2012 to provide clarification about what the meaning of 'computer system' was (see T-CY, 2012:21). The point of this explanation was because there was some doubt as to whether PDAs, tablets and smartphones constitute 'a computer'. Having referred to the original explanatory notes the Committee note the key question is whether data is automatically processed and note this includes the input, output and storage of data (T-CY, 2012:21 at 3). In the context of communication devices the Committee notes that they have 'the capacity to produce, process and transmit data, such as accessing the Internet, sending e-mail, transmitting attachments, upload contents or downloading documents' (T-CY, 2012:21 at 4). This supports the assertion that when we consider cybercrime we should consider devices other than traditional computers but include all those devices that, *inter alia*, connect to the internet.

### Problem of cybercrime

It is sometimes tempting to downplay cybercrime, painting it as always being the actions of lone individuals, but whilst this is true of some crimes the reality of cybercrime as a whole is very different. E-crime is now considered to be a major problem, with a government report in 2011 suggesting that cybercrime was estimated to cost the UK some £27 billion per year (Detica, 2011:24) although there are perhaps question marks over the reliability of some of the assumptions this was based on (see HAC, 2013:12). This figure includes the cost to citizens (£3.1 billion), the cost to government (£2.2 billion) and the cost to business (£21 billion). Even if the assumptions used vary, it is beyond doubt that cybercrime will cost several billion pounds a year in the UK alone. The 'benefits' from cybercrime are such that it is now thought that several thousand organised gangs/groups are dedicated to cybercrime (Choo, 2008) The rewards for even simple cybercrime can be immense for what is relatively little effort (through, for example, the use of botnets – a type of malware that will be discussed more extensively in Chapter 3 – and spam).

Some caution that there is a danger that there are moral panics surrounding cybercrime (Thierer, 2013) and certainly one must be careful of this. However, the advancement of technology will almost certainly lead to a transformation of cybercrime which is why, as was noted previously, some prefer to think of cybercrime as an ever-changing set of behaviours. Whilst we must be careful not to over-estimate the potential harm of cybercrime it is clear that as we become more dependent on technology it becomes easier to conceive ways that cybercrime could evolve to bring about new problems. Whilst so far when we talk about cybercrimes against the person we tend to mean psychological harm, it may not be too far off before physical harms become at least potential. We tend to think of a computer killing a human as the product of science fiction such as the infamous HAL computer in *2001: A Space Odyssey* but it was reported in late 2012 and early 2013 that it was possible to hack a pacemaker, in essence allowing someone to kill at a distance.[1] It is necessary to note that this is purely speculation and it can be how moral panics begin, but it must be remembered that technology is essentially dumb. Therefore, where technology can be programmed to be beneficial it can equally be programmed to be harmful. Advances in medical technologies could mean that this becomes more realistic although, of course, the developers will spend considerable effort trying to perfect protection arrangements.

### Prevalence of cybercrime

In order to understand what the problem of cybercrime is, it is perhaps necessary to understand its prevalence. However, this leads us to an immediate problem. There is no accurate way of understanding how prevalent cybercrime is. There are a number of reasons for this, some of which may be surprising in the context of ordinary crimes.

The first issue is that there are very few statistics on cybercrime. It was noted above that there was some scepticism when the UK government purported to quantify the cost of cybercrime. There is no easy way to identify how many people have been arrested or convicted of a cybercrime. That is partly because of the way that the law works. There appears to be a belief that the principal statute to criminalise cybercrime attacks – the *Computer Misuse Act 1990* – is seen as a 'stopgap' where alternative legislation exists (HAC, 2013:24). This may appear strange but it perhaps reflects the need for the Crown Prosecution Service to consider what the most appropriate charges are, including reflecting on what would give the sentencing judge the most suitable powers of disposal in the event of a conviction. So, for example, someone hacking into a computer, stealing the log-in credentials of a person's e-banking system and transferring £10,000 from their account could be dealt with under the *Computer Misuse Act 1990* (CMA 1990) but it may be more appropriate to charge the offender under the *Fraud Act 2006*, not least because the maximum sentence for the conduct will differ (five years for computer misuse (s.2(5)(c), CMA 1990 or ten years for fraud (s.1(3), *Fraud Act 2006*)). Of course both offences could be theoretically be charged but as it is unlikely that consecutive sentences would be imposed – because all

---

1 The person who made this claim (Jack Barnaby) died shortly before explaining how this could occur, which inevitably led to conspiracy theories.

offences occurred from the same transaction – what would the point of that be? It could be argued that it better reflects the conduct of the offender but if it would not alter the disposal of the offender, it could be considered by the prosecutors as over-complicating an indictment and leading to longer trials for no real purpose. However, the significant disadvantage of this decision is that the current approach to criminal justice statistics could not identify whether this was a cybercrime or not, making it virtually impossible to state how many cybercrime prosecutions there are in any given year.

Of course prosecutions are not the only measure of cybercrime and it has been noted that surveys, including the British Crime Survey, have shown that there is an increase in people considering themselves to be victims of cybercrime (HAC, 2013:14). However, there are two serious difficulties with this kind of survey (as compared with 'traditional' crime); whether people consider themselves to be a victim and whether they know they are a victim.

In terms of the first – whether people consider themselves a victim – this does at least have parallels in some other forms of crime. However, it is perhaps more pertinent in cybercrime. Let us take an example of a single type of cybercrime, phishing. Whilst this will be defined and discussed in detail in Chapter 5, it can be summarised here as a fraudulent attempt to persuade someone to part with their credit-card details or log-in credentials for internet payment services. Technically the sending of the emails trying to influence people to enter their details is illegal but almost everyone with an email address will have received an email asking them to 'confirm' their bank details. However, how many of those who received the email would consider themselves to be the victim of a crime?

The more difficult issue in identifying victims of cybercrime are those situations where a person does not know they have been victimised. Most users of computers will be aware of the need to install firewall and anti-virus software. The vast majority of the time these just reside in the background and do their own thing, it is comparatively rare for someone to be told that the program has stopped (as distinct from deleting) a virus or potential hack. Symantec, one of the leading software firms that operates anti-virus and firewall packages, reported that in 2011 there had been an 81 per cent increase in malicious attacks that they had identified (HAC, 2013:15), with their estimate of attacks being placed at over 5.5 billion. Of course not every single attack is necessarily a single crime because it will be seen in Chapter 3 that a popular form of attack is to use bots to launch an attack using multiple computers. However, it should also be noted, of course, that Symantec are only one of a small number of leading anti-attack software developers and so their figures will not account for users who use alternative software. At the very least it demonstrates the fact that cybercrime attacks are an almost routine form of criminality and most internet users are likely to face an attack on almost a daily basis but perhaps do not realise this because they rely on automated protection systems.

## Cybercrime Convention

The final part of this chapter will introduce the *Council of Europe Convention on Cybercrime*. This is an important international instrument and was the first international treaty to specifically consider these issues. Whilst there are criticisms of the Convention (discussed briefly below) it arguably retains its position as the leading international instrument tackling cybercrime.

As the first, and arguably most important, international instruments to consider the issue of cybercrime, the Convention will be considered throughout this book. Many of the key themes that are discussed in this book are contained within the Convention, although it should be noted that not all are. One of the criticisms of the Convention is that it is starting to age and some of the newer forms of cybercrime, particularly those that could be classed as against the person, are not contained within the Convention. However, in respect of other parts of this book the Convention remains important and much of the UK domestic law has been shaped by its provisions.

In this section a brief introduction to the Convention is given. It is not intended to discuss in depth the contents of the Convention because these will be picked up in the individual chapters. However, the reader should have an understanding of the Convention and where it stands today.

### Drafting of the Convention

The Cybercrime Convention was opened for signature in Budapest in 2001 (and it is therefore sometimes also known as the 'Budapest Convention' which follows the trend in international law to name treaties after the place they are signed). It was the culmination of several years drafting and unusually for a Council of Europe instrument it had always been intended to be an instrument that would be used by people outside of Europe.

The Cybercrime Convention was arguably ahead of its time with its direct genesis being attributed to a 1985 committee of experts looking at computer crime (Walden, 2007:329). To put this into context, the Apple Mac had only just been released in 1984 and the state-of-the-art computers at the time were the Atari ST and Commodore Amiga, both of which cost nearly £1,000. The following year Amstrad released the first home/office PC at what was considered to be a reasonable price. So this was the very early stages of computing entering the consciousness of the public. Following the report of these experts the Council of Europe began work to examine the practical difficulties of prosecuting cybercrime (Walden, 2007:330) and eventually turned their attention to the development of an international treaty that would seek to harmonise laws across signatory states, the *Convention on Cybercrime*.

Whilst the Council of Europe is a European initiative – and indeed is the oldest grouping, with it being set up in the aftermath of World War II to address issues relating to human rights – there was recognition that combatting cybercrime would require the support of countries and geo-political blocks beyond Europe. During its drafting a number of countries, most notably the USA, Canada, Japan and South Africa were given 'observer' status (Keyser, 2003:297) and it is interesting to note that they have all now signed the Convention.

## The provisions of the Convention

Whilst the detail will be left to subsequent chapters (where relevant) it is obvi-ously important that there is a brief understanding of what the Convention's principal provisions are. The Convention is divided into four chapters, although these are themselves subject to significant sub-divisions. The four chapters are:

- Use of terms (Chapter I).
- Measures to be taken at the domestic level (Chapter II).
- International co-operation (Chapter III).
- Final provisions (Chapter IV).

Chapter I is, in essence, simply the definitions chapter and includes only Article 1 that sets out the various terms used within the Convention. Chapter IV simply deals with the formalities of the signing and ratifying of the Convention and the tabling of derogations, etc. This leaves Chapters II and III as including the key 'working' elements of the Convention.

### Measures to be taken at the domestic level

Chapter II is the larger of the two chapters and contains Articles 2 through to 22. The chapter is broken up into three sections, each of which is then sub-divided. The three sections are:

- Substantive criminal law (section 1). This is the area that this book will concentrate most attention on. It contains Articles 2 through 13 and broadly encompasses offences relating to the integrity of computer sys-tems and data, computer-related offences such as fraud, content offences and offences relating to intellectual property.
- Procedural law (section 2). In recognition of the fact that cybercrime recognises no borders the Convention attempts to harmonise many of the procedural laws so that the offences contained within section 1 can be investigated and prosecuted effectively. This section contains Articles 14 through 21. It discusses standard ways of securing evidence, producing evidence and the collection of data. By ensuring a harmonised approach to such matters it is to be hoped that this will facilitate co-operation in combatting transnational crime (discussed in Chapter III).

- Jurisdiction (section 3). Article 22 details the provisions of jurisdiction. Whilst cybercrime does not recognise international borders most countries still adopt the approach of adopting rules relating to territorial borders. This is an issue that will be considered in depth during Chapter 2.

### International co-operation

The principal purpose of harmonising the laws across the signatory states is to facilitate cross-border co-operation. Where there are agreed terms and procedures it becomes easier to co-operate, not least because some countries operate the principle of dual-criminality in respect of extradition and indeed some investigations. Dual criminality is where there is a requirement that an act is criminalised not only in the country where the suspect is but also the country that is seeking assistance or the custody of the individual. Again this will be discussed further in Chapter 2.

As with Chapter II of the Convention, this part of the Convention is subdivided into a number of sections, which are:

- General principles (section 1). This sets out the key principles of basic co-operation and includes consideration of extradition and the basic standards of mutual assistance.
- Specific provisions (section 2). Whilst section 1 provided overarching principles guiding co-operation, section 2 considers specific issues where co-operation should be facilitated. This would include the preservation of stored data, expedited disclosure of data, facilitating access to the data and the collection or interception of data. An important provision is Article 35 which creates an international network of 'single point contacts'. This provides a system where there is the possibility of contacting each national authority 24 hours a day so that urgent cases can be resolved.

We will be spending less time on these issues because this book concerns crime rather than the procedural aspects of investigating and prosecuting the offences. Walden (2007) remains the pre-eminent book that considers these wider issues and whilst it is beginning to show its age, the detailed provision of the Cybercrime Convention obviously does not alter, and the book continues to provide an excellent introduction and overview of the general principles that apply in this area.

## The Convention today

The Convention has almost universal acceptance across the Council of Europe. Only two member states of the Council of Europe (Russia and San

Marino) have refused to sign the Convention. Of the remaining 44 countries, nine have not ratified it but have signed it. As noted above, the Convention was never intended simply to be a European instrument and this is reflected by the fact that the USA was one of the first countries to sign the Treaty and ultimately ratified it five years later. In terms of non-European countries there are six states that have both signed and ratified the Convention (including Australia, Japan and the USA) and two further countries have signed it (Canada and South Africa).

The list of signatories, whilst impressive, is not the only story since the Convention has been used as a model for other international instruments, most notably by the Commonwealth (formerly known as the 'British Commonwealth') who developed model cybercrime laws that were based on the Cybercrime Convention. This dramatically increases its reach as the Commonwealth includes a number of African, Asian and Caribbean countries. Other geo-political groupings have taken the Cybercrime Convention but then built upon it. A good example of this is the African Union whose 'Draft African Union Convention on the Establishment of a Credible Legal Framework for Cybersecurity in Africa' has the potential to become one of the most comprehensive international documents.

However, not all countries consider the Cybercrime Convention to be the ideal standard and there is a tension between what used to be called the 'Western' and 'Eastern' powers. Russia and China, who have emerged as major economic powers, have called for more control over the governance of the internet and they reject the approach of expanding the reach of the Cybercrime Convention, in part because they were not involved in the drafting of the Convention (although there are also some who consider that they do not agree with a number of the terms of the Convention, particularly in respect of data interception and intellectual property rights). They want a new international treaty to be drafted, ideally under the auspices of the United Nations, but the Western powers do not want this and believe it would involve unnecessary expenditure and effort which would be best spent ensuring there were global minimum standards. Whilst the Cybercrime Convention is not perfect there is a belief that it contains useful minimum standards and therefore it should be used as the standard.

This dispute is likely to continue, not least because it is part of the geo-political bickering that now exists since the re-emergence of Russia and China as superpowers. So far there is an impasse and it is notable that major powers continue to sign the Cybercrime Convention (e.g. Australia, Canada, Japan and South Africa) which would suggest that they agree that the creation of a new global instrument is not desirable. However, if some geo-political areas do refuse to become involved and extend this to countries within their sphere of influence then it may be difficult to get true global reach, which may cause complications in the fight against cybercrime.

## *Protocol to the* Convention on Cybercrime

Before leaving the Convention it should be noted that in 2003 a Protocol to the Convention (*Additional Protocol to the Convention on Cybercrime*, concerning the criminalisation of acts of a racist and xenophobic nature committed through computer systems) was opened for signature. During the drafting of the original convention there had been concerns about the proliferation of race-hate material through the internet but many countries found the tackling of such behaviour difficult because of laws and principles governing free speech. It was therefore decided to include this within an additional Protocol that countries could decide to sign if they so wished. As of 2014, 36 countries within the Council of Europe have signed this although only 20 have ratified it. Of the non-Council-of-Europe countries, only two (Canada and South Africa) have signed it and neither has ratified it.

The UK has neither signed nor ratified the additional Protocol and has traditionally decided that it is not necessary to sign this because UK law is sufficient (see, for example, *Hansard Written Answers*, vol 471, 29 Jan 2008, col 209W). That said, the Protocol remains an important instrument and it will be discussed in Chapter 8.

## Suggested further reading

Clough, J. 'Cybercrime' (2011) 37 *Commonwealth Legal Bulletin* 671–680
*Clough is one of the leading commentators on cybercrime and this introductory piece sets out many of the core concepts of cybercrime in an easy to understand way.*

Wall, D. 'Cybercrimes and the internet' in Wall, D. (ed.) *Crime and Internet* (2001, Abingdon: Routledge).
*This is one of the earlier pieces on cybercrime by one of the first people in the UK to study this behaviour. It is a useful introduction to some of the criminological concepts involved in cybercrime.*

Weber, A.M. 'The Council of Europe's Convention on Cybercrime' (2003) 18 *Berkeley Technology Law Journal* 425–446.
*Whilst written from a North American perspective this remains an excellent introduction to the Cybercrime Convention, which also provides a history of its development and overview of its content.*

Yar, M. 'E-crime 2.0: the criminological landscape of social media' (2012) 21 *Information and Communications Technology Law* 207–219.
*This is a very important article that demonstrates how criminality has developed to take account of technological advancements.*

# Chapter 2

# Jurisdiction

One concept that will be returned to throughout this book is that of jurisdiction. It will be remembered from Chapter 1 that one of the challenges of cybercrime is the fact that it can transcend physical borders. The difficulty is that the law of jurisdiction still tends to depend on territorial borders and thus this chapter will consider how this can be reconciled.

## Concept of jurisdiction

Whilst the term jurisdiction is bandied around quite frequently there is sometimes a lack of consideration about what this actually means. Brenner argues that it encompasses 'three distinct concepts: jurisdiction to prescribe, jurisdiction to adjudicate and jurisdiction to enforce' (Brenner, 2006:190). These three concepts are sometimes conflated but they are technically separate.

Perhaps the easiest to define is the first: jurisdiction to prescribe. A sovereign state can prescribe any law that it sees fit. It has long been argued under English law that the UK Parliament, as a sovereign body, could pass a law that makes smoking on the streets of Paris illegal. Whilst this is true, there would be difficulties in adjudicating and enforcing the law, not least because a state cannot enforce its own laws on the sovereign territory of another state without the permission of that country (Brenner, 2006:192).

The same principle is true of cyberspace: a country could decide to prescribe what it wishes but enforcing it would be another matter. Perhaps the classic illustration of this is the Yahoo! litigation. Yahoo! ran an internet auction site that people from all over the world could access (very similar to eBay). Some of the items that were for sale included Nazi memorabilia which it is illegal to sell in some countries. Two campaign groups – *La Ligue Contre le Racisme et L'Antisemitisme* (LICRA) and *L'Union des Etudiants Juifs de France* (UEJF) – objected to the fact that Nazi memorabilia were listed on the site and demanded that Yahoo! France remove hyperlinks to the website that housed the items. Yahoo! stated that the French courts had no jurisdiction over these matters and the matter proceeded to the *Tribunal de Grande Instance de Paris*.

The court stated that France did have jurisdiction and they required Yahoo! to prevent French citizens accessing the site, required users of Yahoo! France to be told that certain items were illegal, to explain at a later date what measures had been taken and to pay 10,000 francs each day to each of the campaign groups (Meehan, 2008 provides a good summary of the litigation). In November 2000 the court rejected an appeal by Yahoo! complaining that it was technically impossible to do the matters required and also that to comply would infringe its rights under the First Amendment to the US Constitution, where the server was based. Yahoo! petitioned the US District Court for a declaration that the French judgment was unenforceable because it would violate the First Amendment. The District Court agreed although this was later reversed – for technical reasons – by the Ninth Circuit Court of Appeals (see *Yahoo! Inc v La Ligue Contre le Racisme et L'Antisemitsme (Yahoo! IV)* 433 F.3d. 1199 (9th Cir, 2006), and see Meehan, 2008:352), although the reversal did not make the order enforceable.

The Yahoo! litigation was a civil matter but it showed that whilst France purported to exercise jurisdiction in a particular way it could not enforce its judgment in a foreign state. Criminal matters proceed on the same basis. Whilst a state can exert jurisdiction it can only enforce the jurisdiction if the state secures jurisdiction over the individual. This is something that will be returned to.

### The bases of jurisdiction

The first issue to consider is under what circumstances a country can claim jurisdiction. Whilst it has been noted that theoretically a state can claim whatever jurisdiction it wishes, international law (and custom) ordinarily restricts what a state will do. There are two principal bases upon which a state will exercise jurisdiction: territorial jurisdiction and extraterritorial jurisdiction.

Territory is at the heart of jurisdiction, both domestically and in international law (Hirst, 2003:45). It is for this reason that territorial jurisdiction is the general rule. Territorial jurisdiction is where a state has jurisdiction over a crime because it occurs within its geographical borders, although Hirst notes that identifying what a state's borders are is not particularly easy (Hirst, 2003:7) even though it is now commonly thought to be prescribed by international law. It should also be noted that international law prescribes special rules for state-flagged ships, state-registered aircraft, military vehicles and embassies (Hirst, 2003:52–54). Of course the fact that some crimes can be cross-border has meant that the territorial principle has to be adapted. This is not just in the context of cybercrime but more broadly. Let us take an example:

> X is standing in country A but on the border with country B. He points a gun at Y, who is standing in country B, and shoots her dead.

Has X committed a crime in country A or country B? Or indeed in both? It would depend on how each country defines the laws and, for example, whether a killing occurs where a person dies or where the events occur that lead to the death. The fact that crimes can take place across borders means that rules have evolved to deal with cross-border crimes, at least in part. The territorial principle of jurisdiction is now taken to mean that a country can claim jurisdiction where a crime occurs within its territory, either in whole or in part. Accordingly, if we return to our example above, this would mean that country A may claim jurisdiction because the discharge of the gun occurred in its territory but, perhaps more likely, country B will seek to claim jurisdiction because the result of the actions (the death of Y) took place within their jurisdiction. We will return to this concept later because it poses significant challenges when the internet becomes involved.

As noted above, whilst a state will primarily seek to exercise jurisdiction on a territorial basis, it can also exercise jurisdiction on an extraterritorial basis, i.e. state that its law applies outside of its national borders. It is commonly accepted that there are four grounds upon which extraterritorial jurisdiction can be exercised:

1. Universal jurisdiction.
2. Protective principle.
3. Active personality principle.
4. Passive personality principle.

Universal jurisdiction is a particular form of jurisdiction that can be exercised by any state (that claims the right to do so). It is reserved for the most serious of offences (Aust, 2005:46) and is a reflection of their gravity. The idea is that some crimes are so heinous that any country should be able to prosecute them without extraditing the culprits to the state of their nationality or the place the crime took place. By doing this it means theoretically there is no place to hide for those who commit those most serious offences.

The protective principle allows states to seek extraterritorial jurisdiction in order to safeguard the security of the state or an important state interest (Aust, 2005:45). Potentially this could be of relevance to some types of conduct in cyberspace as it could include cyber-attacks on military infrastructure or government listening outposts situated around the world. This is not strictly relevant to many of the crimes considered within this book and so no more will be said on this, although it will be considered in passing in Chapter 5.

The active and passive personality principles are two of the most common forms of extraterritorial jurisdiction and are based on nationality but differ in terms of whom the national has to be. The active personality principle is based on the nationality of the offender (Hirst, 2003). There is sometimes an extension (particularly in respect of child sexual exploitation) to this, which is sometimes referred to as 'active plus' and which encompasses not only nationality but the place of habitual residence. Thus, for example, if X is a citizen of France but lives in England (and has done so for ten years) then he may be considered to be within the active personality principle of the UK where it extends to residence. The passive personality principle is similar but it relates to the nationality of the victim rather than the offender (and, as with the active personality principle, can occasionally be extended to include habitual residence).

Whilst some authors do discuss extraterritorial jurisdiction in the context of cybercrime, the reality of the matter is that most matters can be dealt with under the territorial basis rather than an extraterritorial principle. This is because the territorial principle is commonly considered to apply when conduct takes place *in part* within the territory of a country. For the majority of crimes that are discussed in this chapter this will suffice, and how this works in practice will be discussed below. Extraterritorial jurisdiction will be rarely invoked in many cybercrimes although an exception to this is the issue of child sexual exploitation where extraterritorial jurisdiction could be useful. For example, in Chapter 11 the crime of grooming will be discussed and it is possible that some countries would wish this to be extended under the passive personality principle (so that their citizens were protected). A different use of extraterritorial jurisdiction could be in respect of child pornography. Let us take the following example:

> D, a citizen of the UK, visits Sri Lanka where he pays two children to engage in sexual activity with each other. He records this footage on a digital camera and uploads the material to the internet.

If territorial jurisdiction was used here then only Sri Lanka would have jurisdiction to try D. However, countries may decide that in order to tackle child sexual exploitation they could justify the use of extraterritorial jurisdiction to try the offender in the 'home' jurisdiction (in the context of English law see s.72, *Sexual Offences Act 2003*).

Apart from these few instances the more likely application of jurisdiction is in respect of the territorial principle and this will be the focus of the remainder of this chapter.

### Cyberspace and jurisdiction

How does the internet affect jurisdiction? This is probably one of the most contested issues in the regulation of cyberspace. As will be seen, some contend that the internet is a unique structure and should be treated as a new dimension in law. However, the counter-argument is that the internet is nothing special; it has a physical presence in countries, as the internet is merely a network of servers and computers. Those servers and computers must be physically located somewhere and if they are within the territory of a country then it can be argued that the territorial principle will apply.

### Cyberspace as a new dimension

When the internet was first developed there was a belief by some that this created a new world order, that cyberspace represented a new dimension through which national laws could not apply. The idea was that it created a space that could be claimed as a place of freedom, and certainly since its very inception there has been an attempt to divorce the regulation of cyberspace from traditional rules of sovereignty operated by states (Reidenberg, 2005:1952).

The rationale behind classifying cyberspace as a new dimension is that the internet is unlike any other space. The architecture of the internet and the fact that content is copied, cached and stored, together with the speed of modern communication technologies means that it is as easy to access a file hosted in America as it is to access a file hosted in Australia. Indeed the way that the internet and, in particular, 'cloud technology' works is such that the data requested may not be in one location but instead is spread out across multiple locations. It has been argued that this means that it simply becomes impractical to apply national laws to an infrastructure that is spread out across the globe (Rahman et al., 2009).

Those that recognise this argument suggest that cyberspace should be recognised as a new international space. Whilst geographical borders normally define jurisdictional borders, there are three existing international areas: Antarctica, the high seas and outer space. In each of these areas no single country can exercise jurisdiction and instead international law applies. To those who advocate that the internet become a fourth international area the rules governing the existing three areas serve as a precedent that could be followed. International law would apply to the internet, meaning that the differences in national laws would end (Rahman et al., 2009).

However, it is not clear what law would apply. International Criminal Law is not applicable to cybercrime as its focus is on crimes against humanity. Whilst other laws do exist, none are codified in such a way that they apply to the internet, and thus new laws would be required. Theoretically that is possible, because an international treaty would be required to establish the internet as a new international area, and so the laws could be contained within that treaty. Even if this could happen, however, it does not take away the fact that cyberspace is not like the existing spaces. Antarctica, the high seas and outer space do not interfere with the territorial borders of any state. They exist outside of those borders. It has already been noted that this is not the case for cyberspace. The internet exists within servers based in countries. Therefore, an international area for cyberspace would require states to surrender sovereignty over what happens within their own country. Why would any country do that?

### International court for cyberspace

Even if cyberspace were to be recognised as a new form of international space the question would then arise as to how cybercrimes would be tried? One solution that has been proposed is to extend the jurisdiction of the International Criminal Court (ICC) to adjudicate cybercrime issues (discussed in Rahman, 2012a:407). However, this would be a significant change from what the ICC ordinarily does. The principal jurisdiction of the ICC is in respect of what can be termed crimes against humanity (Schabas, 2011). Whilst the United Nations Security Council can refer matters to the ICC it was never intended that this would be used for what is really quite low-level crime.

Of course a solution to this would be to create a sub-committee of the ICC (Rahman, 2012a:409) but this would suffer from exactly the same issues. Whilst it is accepted that it would allow the court to shed the 'crimes against humanity' tag, an international court could simply not cope with the workload that would be imposed on it. There are tens of thousands of cybercrimes each day and it is improbable that a single international court could exercise jurisdiction over so many crimes. There is also the difficulty that the ICC is considered to have concurrent jurisdiction with those states where the crime took place (Schabas, 2011) and so why should a state surrender their jurisdiction to the ICC? Most of the evidence would be within the territorial borders of the country and so it would seem more logical for the national courts to try these matters.

A solution would perhaps be to allow 'satellite' courts of the ICC, i.e. create a system of national courts that sit under the ICC jurisdiction, but what would the point of that be? A better solution would simply be to decide that each country adopts the same standard of criminal laws. The advantage of this is that it would mean that there would be no need for the ICC but also it would mean that there would be no problems with competing jurisdictional claims. If more than one country claims jurisdiction (which, as noted above, is likely) then there would be no need to extradite a person from country X to country Y because the law would be the same in both countries meaning that extradition would be pointless. However, this would also require a global treaty on cybercrime to create these specific laws and removed the right of a state to strengthen them beyond that which was agreed.

### Domestic laws apply

It was noted above that there have been calls for a new global treaty, either to designate cyberspace as a new international area or to create a harmonised set of laws that would apply to the internet. However, the reality is that this will never happen. It is inconceivable that every country will agree to the same laws being introduced as there will be differences of opinion in terms of penalties and even the concept of deciding what should be illegal would be problematic. There are major differences between countries on, for example, copyright infringements and even what constitutes child pornography. It is perhaps notable that the *Convention on Cybercrime* – which does not even pretend to standardise laws (in that it prescribes a minimum standard and leaves a lot to the discretion of signatory states) – has not achieved universal agreement, with a number of countries being unwilling to sign (Rahman, 2012a:411). The Cybercrime Convention is the closest instrument we have to a global treaty on cybercrime and the compromises inherent within it demonstrate that the idea of a universal treaty is simply unrealistic. Whilst it may be attractive from a theoretical stance, it is simply impossible to implement in reality.

That state-based jurisdiction is the most appropriate basis is perhaps illustrated by the Cybercrime Convention itself. The convention addresses jurisdiction (Article 22) but it is clear that it considers the territorial principle to be the default position and it has been suggested that this is not accidental (Brenner and Koops, 2004:10). Article 22 requires signatory states to adopt measures to criminalise acts that take place within the territory of the state. It then encourages states to extend this to include ships flagged, or aircraft registered, in their territory and also to consider extraterritorial jurisdiction on the basis of the active personality principle, but unlike the rules relating to territorial jurisdiction it is clear that this is optional and there is no requirement on signatory states to do so (see Article 22(2)).

It would seem, therefore, that domestic laws continue to apply to the internet. However, that does not erase the difficulties of jurisdiction. Even if we accept for the moment that states are entitled to regulate the internet, this does not negate the problem identified by Reidenberg that 'network boundaries intersect and transcend national borders' (2005:1951). This returns us to our notion of cross-border crimes and the fact that many argue that as the internet does not recognise state territorial boundaries neither can the law. However, Trachtman makes the point that actually this is something that is not unique.

> Did the telephone, telegraph, television, or mail [not] do so? Are they different from cyberspace, other than in terms of frequency, velocity and cost? Conduct still occurs in territory ... Thus, while cyberspace may be a 'supraterritorial' phenomenon that fractures both conduct and effects, supraterritoriality is not new, and conduct and effects have been fractured in the past.
>
> (Trachtman, 1998:568)

This is an interesting point that is missed by some commentators. Radio waves have, for example, challenged territorial jurisdiction for some time. Whilst many readers will be too young to remember this (and, I should hasten to add, so is the author!) the launch of BBC Radio 1 was preceded by 'pirate radio' whereby DJs would operate on a ship based outside what was thought to be the territorial limits of England and Wales, and who would broadcast radio when the state would not provide a broadcasting licence (Robertson, 1982, provides a good summary of these issues). The telephone also potentially raises challenges for jurisdiction. For example: A telephones B and says, 'I am outside your front door, as soon as I hang up, I'm going to come in and beat you up'. Let us assume B does not know where A is, but B is in England and A is in Spain. Has A committed a criminal offence? Following the decision in *R v Ireland* [1998] AC 147 it is clear that words alone can cause the commission of the crime of assault. As a result, the crime of assault would take place where B is located, meaning that in the situation discussed above the law would already have to deal with the jurisdictional issues.

However, it could be argued that Trachtman underplays the significance of the internet. Whilst it may be true that other technologies raise territorial issues, none perhaps do so as easily as the internet – where a few keystrokes will suffice (Meehan, 2008:345) – and where the ubiquitous nature of it means that frequency is exponential compared to the technologies that he mentions. Whilst in terms of the theory of jurisdiction this may not raise any issues, there is undoubtedly a difficulty in terms of practice, and this is perhaps the point made by those authors who suggest that the internet poses jurisdictional challenges even if some use language that suggests (incorrectly) that traditional conceptions of jurisdiction will not work on the internet.

### Cross-border crimes

The fact that the internet transcends physical borders means that we return to the issue of cross-border crime. Where a crime transcends the physical borders of a country, this creates a position whereby multiple countries could claim jurisdiction. Let us take a very brief example. A, a resident of country X, sends a virus that infiltrates the machine of B, in country Y, and the machine of C, who resides in country Z. It has been seen already that countries X, Y and Z may seek to claim jurisdiction. Country X will claim jurisdiction on the basis that the virus was created in their territory and distributed from within their borders. Countries Y and Z are also likely to claim jurisdiction because, although the virus was not created within their territory, a computer within their borders was affected, meaning they have a territorial claim.

Podgor notes that there is no coherent system to decide who should exercise jurisdiction and notes that even the *Convention on Cybercrime* does not address this problem (Podgor, 2009:733). The Convention states that where there is a disagreement 'the parties involved shall, where appropriate, consult with a view to determining the most appropriate jurisdiction for prosecution' (Article 22(5)) but it does not state what factors should be taken into account. Presumably this is a pragmatic approach because the drafters realised that identifying consensus on which order any prosecutions should occur in would be difficult to achieve.

This is a point taken up by others who have tried to consider what factors would be taken into account. An important consideration is the fact that we are likely to be talking about multiple jurisdictions rather than concurrent jurisdiction. In most legal systems – including international law – there is ordinarily the principle of double jeopardy which states that a person cannot be tried for the same crime twice. However, this would not apply in the example above because A has not committed a single crime, he has committed *separate* crimes in countries X, Y and Z, so there is no issue of prosecuting him multiple times for the same offence, they are different offences.

However, realistically it is unlikely that an offender would be tried by all three countries – so who decides the order in which the prosecutions will occur? Perhaps the most obvious factor is who has custody of the person. It will be remembered that jurisdiction is not only about a state claiming jurisdiction, it is about enforcing it. Where a state has the custody of the individual then they can more easily exercise jurisdiction. Let us take another example:

> D is a citizen of, and resident in, England and Wales. Using internet-based chatrooms he starts to bully X, another resident of England, and Y, a resident of the USA. X suffers severe anxiety as a result of the bullying and is prescribed medication. Y similarly suffers effects and attempts suicide, although she is found before dying.

It will be seen in Chapter 11 that D would be guilty of an offence under English law for his treatment of X and the same would be true of US law. Both England and the USA could claim jurisdiction. England on the basis that the whole crime took place within its territory, and the USA on the basis that the effect of the crime took place there.

Assuming that the English police have arrested D then it is quite possible that England will decide to prosecute D first. Whilst the USA may be able to argue that a more serious crime took place in its country, it does not have custody of the offender and thus it is unable to prosecute D unless England decides to extradite him, but that would mean, in essence, suspending the decision to prosecute him in England. Of course the position is more complicated where neither party has custody. Let us assume that instead of being English, D was German and that the bullying took place when D was in Germany. Whilst it is possible that Germany could claim jurisdiction, it is more likely that they will decide that England or the USA is a more suitable venue because a citizen of their country was the victim. Neither England nor the USA have physical custody of the perpetrator so neither can prosecute him immediately. Both will require Germany to extradite D to them and the choice of which country to send him to is likely to be left to Germany, with both England and the USA making representations.

The fact that there are multiple jurisdictions can cause controversy when it comes to deciding whether to surrender custody of the individual. Perhaps one of the most controversial cybercrime cases in recent years was that of Gary McKinnon, a Scot resident in England, who hacked into the US Pentagon system allegedly looking for evidence of aliens. The US authorities alleged that he had not only viewed sensitive files but that he also deleted a number of files which prevented certain parts of the US defence network from functioning. He also allegedly left a message on a part of the network saying 'your security is crap'. McKinnon never admitted deleting any files but did admit (although not in court) to the hacking.

The US government sought his extradition to face various charges relating to cybercrime. McKinnon sought to prevent his extradition, initially arguing that a plea bargain offered to him by US officials amounted to undue pressure and an abuse of process. The House of Lords ultimately rejected this argument (*McKinnon v United States* [2008] 1 WLR 1739). Further attempts to prevent extradition then occurred based on two arguments: the first that he suffered from autism and that extradition to the USA would amount to ill-treatment within the meaning of Article 3, ECHR (which was again rejected: *R (on the application of McKinnon) v Secretary of State for Home Affairs* [2009] EWHC 2021 (Admin)) and the second basis was that he could be prosecuted in England for his crimes.

Ultimately, whilst the courts decided that McKinnon could lawfully be extradited, the Home Secretary decided in 2012 not to order extradition (something that she was legally entitled to do). Whilst the Home Secretary is a senior politician, in these instances she is supposed to act in a quasi-judicial manner. Whether it was a political or legal decision is not relevant to this discussion but what is notable is that McKinnon was undoubtedly correct to state that he could have been tried in England.

The *Computer Misuse Act 1990* specifically addresses the issue of jurisdiction in terms of, *inter alia*, hacking but this does not mean that the USA did not have jurisdiction too. As noted above, both England and the USA could claim jurisdiction and therefore the question arose who should go first. Supporters of McKinnon argued that he should be prosecuted in England *instead* of the USA, but that would not be an accurate summary of the position because he was arguably accused of separate offences in England and the USA and so could theoretically have been tried in both, although another reading of the law would be that it was the same crime.

The most obvious reason for McKinnon being initially prosecuted in England was custody of the individual – McKinnon was in England and could easily be tried there. However, counting against that was the fact that he had not committed any damage to machines in England. The alleged damage was to servers based in the USA, so it could have been (legitimately) argued that America had a stronger case for prosecuting him. It is worth questioning whether England would wish to try someone from, for example,

Vietnam who hacked into Ministry of Defence computer systems in England causing damage.

The English and US prosecutors discussed the fact that there were competing jurisdictional claims and they decided that the USA would be the most appropriate venue for the following reasons:

1. The harm occurred in the USA.
2. An investigation had already been launched in the USA.
3. There were a large number of witnesses, most of whom were located in the USA.
4. All of the physical evidence was in the USA.
5. The US prosecutors were able to bring a case that reflected the full extent of McKinnon's alleged criminality.
6. The bulk of the unused material was located in the USA.

Against that was, in essence, the fact that McKinnon's supporters simply did not want him extradited because they did not like the US cybercrime laws. The offences he was charged with carried a maximum sentence of ten years' imprisonment compared to two or five years' imprisonment (depending on the offence charged) in England. Whilst oppressive punishments must be a factor that is taken into account in extradition (see, perhaps most notably, *Ahmad v United Kingdom* (2013) 56 EHRR 1) it does not follow that this was the case here, and the mere fact that country X does not like the punishment given in country Y must be a smaller factor.

In 2012, after the Home Secretary reached her decision, the Director of Public Prosecutions announced that the reasons for electing to proceed in the USA had not changed and McKinnon would not be prosecuted in England. This was partly because there were doubts as to whether the USA would co-operate with any prosecution. Whilst England had custody of the suspect all the evidence was located in the USA. Whilst the USA had the evidence they had no suspect. This demonstrates the simple difficulty of multiple claims of jurisdiction, that if a compromise is not reached then it is likely no prosecution will be brought.

Of course the US charges have not disappeared and the mere fact that McKinnon will not be extradited by England does not mean that he can never be tried. If he were to enter the territory of the USA, or another country with an extradition treaty with the USA, then he could be arrested (and, if necessary, extradited) to stand trial.

## Jurisdiction in practice

The internet, as has been seen, poses practical difficulties for the law when it comes to jurisdiction, although these are not, as some authors contend, unique. However, there are undoubtedly problems with overlapping jurisdictional claims and it is notable that no instrument has sought to try and resolve these issues, perhaps recognising that it is likely to be easier to decide this on a bilateral basis. The difficulty with this, of course, is the old adage that 'difficult cases make bad law', meaning that it is quite possible that a solution to situation X works perfectly well but it cannot easily be transposed to situation Y.

The most important issue in terms of jurisdiction in practice is securing the custody of the individual. Most countries will seek to claim jurisdiction where harm occurs within their territorial borders, but without custody of the individual that claim is, to an extent, meaningless. It would undoubtedly be easier if the world adopted the same legal standards in respect of the internet as that would mean that there would be less need for competing claims, but the reality is this will not happen. International treaties, particularly global treaties, rarely provide sufficient detail to ensure universal agreement. Even the agreement that set up the International Criminal Court and prescribed the key forms of war crimes does not have universal acclaim, and yet it is dealing with a very small subset of crimes, including those that are arguably amongst the worst an individual can commit. How likely is it that more low-level crimes, particularly those relating to speech and content, could ever be agreed? Thus the call by some for cyberspace to be recognised as an international space is an empty one: it will not happen. That being the case, extradition and securing the custody of a suspect becomes crucial in exercising jurisdiction.

## England and Wales internet jurisdiction

Having considered the theoretical basis for exercising jurisdiction and some of the difficulties involved, the remaining part of this chapter will consider the English approach to securing jurisdiction over cybercrimes. The approach adopted will differ depending on the offence that is alleged to have been committed. The *Computer Misuse Act 1990* makes specific reference to jurisdiction although this only applies to the offences in that Act. Where another offence is being alleged then unless a statute says to the contrary then the ordinary principles of jurisdiction apply.

### Computer Misuse Act 1990

The first issue to consider is how the *Computer Misuse Act 1990* (CMA 1990) approaches jurisdiction. The offences contained in the Act will be examined in more detail in Chapter 3 but it suffices to note here that it creates four offences:

- Unauthorised access to computer material (s.1).
- Unauthorised access with intent to commit or facilitate commission of further offences (s.2).

- Unauthorised acts with intent or recklessness to impair operation of a computer (s.3).
- Making, supplying or obtaining articles for use in an offence above (s.3A).

Sections 4–9 of the Act then expressly deal with jurisdiction. Section 9 is perhaps the simplest to deal with, which states that in respect of any proceedings under the Act, the fact that the suspect is not a British citizen is completely irrelevant. At first sight this may appear an unusual statement because citizenship is not ordinarily relevant to territorial jurisdiction (it being relevant to some forms of extraterritorial jurisdiction). However, it is placed into context by the earlier sections which widen jurisdiction over these offences beyond the territorial borders of the UK.

Section 4 of the CMA 1990 states that in any proceedings under ss.1 and 3, it is immaterial whether the act, or any other element of proof required for conviction, occurred in the home territory or whether the accused was in the home country at the time of such an act (s.4(1)). 'Home territory' in this context means, for our purposes, England and Wales (see s.4(6)). However, for s.1 there must be at least one 'significant link' to the home territory, which is defined in s.5(2) as:

(a) that the accused was in the home country concerned at the time when he did the act which caused the computer to perform the function, or
(b) that any computer containing any program or data to which the accused by doing that act secured or intended to secure unauthorised access, or enabled or intended to enable unauthorised access to be secured, was in the home country at that time.

Let us take two examples to illustrate this.

X is a resident of Durham, England, and he hacks into a computer based in Austria to access files held by a company that he has a vendetta against.

Y is a resident of Serbia and he hacks into a computer based in London to access files held by the government.

In both of these examples the English courts could claim jurisdiction. In the first example there would be questions over whether England or Austria had jurisdiction (although as noted earlier it is likely that both do) but s.1, when read in conjunction with ss.4 and 5, would be infringed by X and so he could be prosecuted.

In the second example Y could also be liable under s.1 because, although he is based outside of the jurisdiction, he has attacked a computer within the territory and this suffices as a result of ss.4 and 5. To an extent this is understandable because it fits within the ordinary understandings of the territorial jurisdiction since the attack was directed towards a computer in England. Of course the difficulty in this second example is obtaining custody of Y but that does not preclude the English courts claiming jurisdiction to try him.

The same principle applies to s.3 (see s.5(3)) but the position is significantly different for s.2 and indeed the distinction has been described as 'complex and obscure' by one of the leading authorities on jurisdiction (Hirst, 2003:196). As Hirst notes, s.2 is, in essence, an aggravated form of section 1 and so it could be thought that the same principles should apply. However, s.4(3) disregards the requirement for the 'significant link' that would otherwise be required for s.1, which creates something of a paradox. The ulterior intent required for s.2 must still be an offence that is punishable in England by at least five years' imprisonment but as Hirst notes, if that offence is itself extra-territorial (as a number of sexual offences are), then there is no requirement for any link for the matter to be prosecuted under s.2 (Hirst, 2003:196). Let us take an example:

> D is a British citizen currently living in the USA. He gains access without authority to a computer based in Germany which he knows stores images that constitute child pornography. He intends to take those images and send them to X who lives in England who he believes will be able to sell them.

Section 2 would apply to this example and therefore D could be tried in an English court. Whilst the 'hack' takes place in either the USA or Germany it is still an unauthorised access within s.1, and s.4(3) disregards the territorial link for the purposes of s.1. Paragraph 1(d) of Schedule 2 to the *Sexual Offences Act 2003* (SOA 2003) prescribes s.1 of the *Protection of Children Act 1978* (PoCA 1978) as an offence to which s.72, SOA 2003 applies (sexual offences committed outside of the UK). Thus D has gained unauthorised access to a computer with intent to commit an offence under s.72 which is punishable by up to ten years' imprisonment and thus all the requirements for s.2, CMA 1990 are satisfied even though the whole crime takes place outside the territorial borders of England (especially if the images are never sent). Why should the UK assert jurisdiction in this example since it would seem more appropriate to leave this to the courts of the USA or Germany? Yet the CMA 1990 permits D to be tried which seems, at best, odd.

It has been noted that the s.3A offence, which was introduced by the *Police and Justice Act 2006*, does not attract the extraterritorial provisions in ss.4–9 (Walden, 2007:301) because s.3A is not listed. Walden argues that extending jurisdiction could have been achieved had the offence been classed as a communications offence but this may not be necessary. Section 3A applies, *inter alia*, where a person 'supplies or offers to supply' a relevant article. Whilst 'supplies' may imply not only the transmission of any article but also its receipt (in which case both would arguably have to be within the territory for ordinary principles of jurisdiction to apply) the same is not true of 'offers to supply'. An offer is just that, the willingness to supply. Thus there is no need for the transaction to proceed or for the offer to be accepted. That being the case, then so long as the person making the offer is within the territory of England then it is irrelevant that the offer was to someone outside of the territory. Where Walden would seem to be correct is where the positions are reversed, i.e. someone from outside the territory offers to supply a prohibited article to someone in England. The relevant territorial link would not appear to be satisfied under those circumstances.

It may be argued that the absence of s.3A from the CMA 1990 jurisdiction principles simply means that the common-law rules on jurisdiction could be invoked but it is a clear principle that statutory law overrules the common law. Parliament has obviously deliberately refrained from including s.3A within ss.4–9 and this must be an indication that it did not intend for s.3A to apply beyond the territorial borders.

### Other offences

The CMA 1990 provisions apply only to those offences contained within the Act. What of other offences? For reasons of space it will not be possible to consider the position in respect of all specific offences considered in this book, although it should be noted that some do specifically make reference to jurisdiction (see, for example, the discussion of fraud in Walden, 2007:302). Instead what will be examined are some of the general principles of jurisdiction.

Traditionally the approach to jurisdiction adopted in England and Wales was that of the terminatory theory, meaning that the 'last act' of a crime had to take place within the territory of England and Wales to constitute an offence (for a detailed analysis see Hirst, 2003:115 et seq.). This was a legal rather than factual analysis so it meant, for example, that it was the last element of the *actus reus* that was important rather than the last factual act. This could be important with certain crimes, for example, blackmail. The last legal act would be where the demand was made and not where it was received, meaning that a demand from a computer in England would constitute blackmail even if the victim lived abroad (Hirst, 2003:115).

Eventually there was a move away from the terminatory approach, as it was recognised that identifying where the last act took place was becoming increasingly difficult, especially in the context of the internet. The courts began to shift away from this, with perhaps the most decisive shift being in *R v Smith (Wallace Duncan) (No 4)* [2004] QB 1418 where the Court of Appeal held that 'when substantial activities constituting a crime takes place in England the court shall have jurisdiction' (at 1434).

Thus English courts have now adopted the more nuanced approach to territorial jurisdiction adopted in international law, i.e. that it is not necessary for the whole of a crime to take place within the territory so long as some part of it does. *Smith (Wallace Duncan)* raises the threshold by requiring there to be 'substantial activities' but this continues to be a more practical test than the terminatory theory. Whilst there was some doubt as to whether *Smith (Wallace Duncan)* was an accurate reflection of the law (see Hirst, 2009:337), the position now seems settled by the decision in *R v Sheppard and Whittle* [2010] 1 WLR 2779 where the principal ground of appeal was that 'substantial activities' was not appropriate for securing jurisdiction over the internet.

*Sheppard and Whittle* is a useful case to demonstrate how the English courts now approach this issue of jurisdiction. Sheppard operated a website that was hosted on servers in California. The website contained racially inflammatory material that was written both by himself and, in part, by Whittle. A police officer based in England accessed the material that had been posted and which included the ability to order some of the material in hard copy. Both defendants were charged with an offence under s.19, *Public Order Act 1986*, which concerns publishing written material which was threatening, abusive or insulting with intent to stir up racial hatred. Sheppard was also charged with the distribution of such material.

Both defendants attempted to argue, *inter alia*, that as the material was hosted in California any publishing of the material took place there, meaning the courts had no jurisdiction to try them. The Court of Appeal held that the correct test for jurisdiction was the 'substantial activities' test put forward in *R v Smith (Wallace Duncan)* and indeed went so far as to say that counsel would need to identify reasons why *Smith (Wallace Duncan)* should not apply (at 2787) thus reinforcing the fact that this has now become the accepted rule. The Court noted that the material had been written in England, edited in England, uploaded from England and, as was clear from the text of the website, intended primarily for an English audience. The Court stated therefore that, 'the only "foreign" element was that the website was hosted by a server in ... California, and ... the use of the server was merely a stage in the transmission of the material' (at 2788).

The Court was undoubtedly correct to say that the vast majority of the activity took place in England and Wales but it has been noted by some that they dealt with the issue in an unusual way. The Court acknowledged that there were three general theories that could be applied to the internet ([2010] 1 WLR 2779 at 2788) but decided that it was unnecessary to deal with these because *Smith (Wallace Duncan)* applied. It has been noted that whilst this is probably true, the court could have explained in further detail why it believed that this applied (Dyson, 2010:8). It also leaves some uncertainties. For example, what does 'substantial activities' mean? Is the fact that the material was written in England and uploaded from here determinative? The answer would seem to be 'no' if one looks at how jurisdiction has been dealt with in respect of obscene articles, which raises similar issues (i.e. content).

In *R v Waddon* (2000, unreported) the Court of Appeal held that publishing occurred when a person either downloaded or uploaded material (at [12]). Hirst notes that this was a comment that was made *in obiter* by the court, partly because of the facts of the case whereby the defendant had admitted that he had transmitted the material from England, something that would satisfy the *Obscene Publications Act* (OPA 1959) requirements for 'publish' (see Hirst, 2003:189). However, this dicta was then adopted by the Court of Appeal in the later case of *R v Perrin* [2002] EWCA Crim 747 where a French citizen resident in England was found culpable for publishing an obscene article even though the material was hosted in the USA and the prosecution called no evidence to suggest that the material had been prepared in England. Instead the prosecution contended, applying *Waddon*, that the fact that 'publish' includes downloading material meant that material that is accessible to people resident in England is published, and if the material is obscene, culpability then arises. The Court of Appeal accepted this logic. Hirst disapproves of the ruling, suggesting that it imposes English law on foreign citizens (Hirst, 2003:190) although this is not a view that is universally supported (see Gillespie, 2012:169).

If the ruling in *Perrin* is correct then it would seem that the 'substantial activities' required by *Smith (Wallace Duncan)* could be that a substantial part of the crime takes place within England, including publishing. If this were applied to *Sheppard and Whittle* then it may not matter that the material was prepared in England so long as it was directed towards or accessible in England. It could be argued that this creates an extremely broad ambit for the offences (Dyson, 2010:8–9), but it probably fits within the principles of international law that deem that the territorial principle applies where *part of* the crime takes place within the territory of the state asserting jurisdiction, an approach adopted by other countries (discussed in Gillespie, 2012).

When countries adopt this approach it raises difficulties for those who publish material on the internet because they are potentially liable for publishing material that is perfectly lawful in the country they reside in, but which is illegal in countries that it is accessible from. In essence this returns us to the very start of this chapter and the logic adopted in the Yahoo! litigation. This perhaps supports the argument of those who call for a global standard. By allowing each country to adopt their own rules when exercising jurisdiction there is undoubtedly conflict, especially when it comes to illicit content which has historically seen major variations in the way that countries adopt regulations. However, recognising this as an issue does not overcome the practical difficulties of identifying this global standard, most notably the fact that there will never be a global consensus on laws. This means that the current approach will undoubtedly continue even though it has its flaws.

## Suggested further reading

Brenner, S.W. and Koops, B. 'Approaches to cybercrime jurisdiction' (2004) 41 *Journal of High Technology Law* 1–46.
*Whilst written from a North American perspective this provides a very useful summary of many of the key arguments that surround jurisdictional challenges over the internet.*

Gillespie, A.A. 'Jurisdictional issues concerning online child pornography' (2012) 20 *International Journal of Law and Information Technology* 151–177.
*In this piece I seek to show how jurisdiction is applied in cyberspace by reference to one particular issue, child pornography. The article includes an overview of competing arguments surrounding jurisdiction and then culminates in an analysis of how international and domestic instruments tackle child pornography.*

Hirst, M. *Jurisdiction and the Ambit of the Criminal Law* (2003, Oxford: Oxford University Press).
*Whilst this is now over twelve years old it remains probably the most important reference work on issues of jurisdiction within England and Wales. It sets out the history and development of the jurisdiction as applied by the criminal courts in England and Wales*

Rahman, R. 'Legal jurisdiction over malware-related crimes: From theories of jurisdiction to solid practical application' (2012) 28 *Computer Law and Security Review* 403–415.
*This article provides a good summary of the arguments as to why individual states should surrender jurisdiction over the internet and a new global treaty be introduced to tackle cybercrime.*

# Part I

# Crimes against computers

# Chapter 3

# Targeting the technology

We are now moving our analysis onto the different types of behaviour that can constitute cybercrime. It was noted in Chapter 1 that there are numerous types of cybercrime but that one of the most common is that behaviour which relates to the targeting of technology. The most obvious example of this is known as 'hacking', which will be discussed extensively in this chapter, but so too will other aspects of this behaviour, including the production and distribution of malware as this undoubtedly targets technology.

This chapter is focused on computers but it was noted in Chapter 1 that the term 'computer' is not defined and that many forms of technology could also be considered to be a computer, including mobile telephones. In recent years there has been very public recognition that mobile telephones can be hacked but this is something that will be explored in the next chapter (offences relating to data) as the issues raised are better considered within that chapter.

## Hacking of computers

The first form of behaviour to discuss is the unlawful accessing of a computer, a phenomenon that is more commonly referred to as hacking. Hacking is an interesting phenomenon because it is an issue that is in the consciousness of most computer users and it carries with it a particular stigma, a belief that it is one of the more ominous forms of cybercrime. Yet the reality is that it is a relatively small number of people who have experienced hacking (McGuire and Dowling, 2013:8) although that will depend on the definition. Whilst it is probably true in respect of computers being infiltrated, if the question was broadened to asking who had experienced the infiltration of their email (including the 'taking over' of the account and changing the password) or social media (e.g. Facebook) then it is likely that the number of victims would rise. Where hacking is perhaps more prevalent is in respect of corporate or government bodies and it is probably true to say that the majority of 'typical' hacking remains directed towards corporations and governments rather than individuals.

The public perception of hacking is undoubtedly affected by media atten-tion and whilst some believe that 'hacking has become one of the most rec-ognised and feared threats in cyberspace' (Furnell, 2010:174) others believe that there could be a moral panic surrounding hacking (discussed in Yar, 2013:24). Certainly there does seem to be some evidence that hacking is presented in a way that is disproportionate to the harm that occurs. Perhaps this is because the notion of controlling machines is something that goes to the heart of science fiction (one of the earliest examples being *Neuromancer* by Gibson, 1984) and then entered the mainstream entertainment environ-ment. *War Games* was a very popular film in the 1980s that implied a teenage hacker almost started thermonuclear warfare by hacking into the Pentagon system. As a plot for a movie it was quite good and was perhaps no more outrageous than other films from the 1980s including *Space Camp* (where a group of teenagers are accidentally launched into space) but it was (obvi-ously) a complete distortion of reality, including what the potential effects of hacking could be.

We are used to movies 'pushing the envelope' of reality but Yar notes that the press has, in the past, used similar stories, including a '17-year-old com-puter hacker who, while ensconced in his bedroom, had supposedly broken into US military systems and had "his twitching index finger hover[ing] over the nuclear button"' (Yar, 2013:24). The reality, of course, is very different and it is inconceivable that the hacker mentioned in the story came anywhere close to being able to do anything with nuclear weapons. Sensationalism is of course common with tabloid newspapers but it can also affect the percep-tions of the public. The complaint of some is that it can influence people to believe that hacking is more dangerous than it actually is, although others will strongly disagree and point to the commercial losses that can be inflicted on companies.

### What is hacking?

Before considering how the law tackles those who hack computers it is first necessary to consider what hacking is. One of the first points to note is that hacking is not restricted to cyberspace. If, as will be argued, hacking is con-sidered to be improperly accessing to a computer, then this need not take place on the internet. Indeed, switching on a computer that one does not have authority to use could be considered unlawful access, as would reading or deleting files on a computer already switched on. However, the internet has revolutionised the way that hacking takes place. As the internet is a network of connections it means that people can exploit those connections and gain access to a computer no matter where it is hosted.

Hacking is a term that has gone through a degree of metamorphosis. Originally 'hacker' was a term of pride applied to those that had superior computer skills. Of course, it could be argued that the same is true now and that self-styled hackers are making claims about their skills. However, where the terms diverge is that hackers originally did not try to do something that was unauthorised, it was simply the demonstration of programming skills. Hacking quickly took on its current definition, the action of gaining unauthorised access to computers (and later servers, websites, etc.). However, terminology continues to be problematic and some hackers seek to draw a distinction between those who simply look at information and those who access computers with the intention of doing something malicious. The latter they seek to label 'crackers' although that term has not really captured the public's attention.

In public consciousness, a hacker is quite often presented as the lone 'geek'; a teenager or young person who stays in their bedroom and tries to access various computers and servers. Admittedly this does appear to be borne out by the limited research that exists. The vast majority of hackers do seem to be male and young (Yar, 2013:35–36), with older hackers viewed as becoming 'beyond it'. That said, of course, older hackers do exist but it is perhaps notable that many do appear to be young.

Ascertaining why hackers do as they do is more problematic. Yar noted that one of the difficulties here is that hackers will often present themselves as rebels who act against a traditional society (Yar, 2013:35) and he points to the 'Hackers Manifesto' (Mentor, 1986) which attempts to argue that hacking is about curiosity and a response to the greed, wars and lies of governments and major corporations. That said, Furnell makes the point that to many this is simply a 'flag of convenience' that can be used to try to justify activities that they know to be wrong and which they are deliberately undertaking (Furnell, 2010:175).

### White hat, black hat and grey hat

One of the more popular ways of distinguishing hackers is by 'hats'. Commonly there are said to be three 'hats':

- White hat (the use of hacking techniques to test security measures).
- Black hat (an overtly malicious hacker who will not only look around but who will also seek to damage or steal files, servers or websites).
- Grey hat (perhaps the least-clear definition but considered to be someone who is somewhere between the other two).

These terms are only approximations and are open to some debate. For example, the term 'white hat' is the subject of some dispute. Most agree that it is synonymous with 'ethical hacking' but there is disagreement as to whether this means that it is authorised or not. Ethical hacking has existed for some time and it has been said that 'the ethical hacker possesses a high level of specialized knowledge combined with a belief in the ethics of freedom of access' (Wall, 2007:55). This is then expanded upon by reference to the fact that they 'tested systems and forced code writers to achieve higher standards of quality' which implies that their activity was legitimate, but Wall then identifies three types of ethical hackers; 'gurus' (who are experts), 'wizards' (who are renowned for their knowledge) and 'samurais' who are the only group who would 'hire themselves out to undertake legal cracking tasks, legitimate or justified surveillance' (Wall, 2007:55). In other words the other forms of ethical hacking are based on the beliefs of the hackers themselves, that they were not doing any harm and that their skills showed organisations that they needed to improve security since otherwise someone else would do so.

Where there is no authorisation, can it be said that this is truly considered to be either ethical hacking or white hat hacking? Furnell points out that one of the flaws in the 'improving security' concept is what happens to the information gained in the attack. Where the information is provided to that company quietly and discreetly this may imply ethical standards but where, as is not uncommon, the hackers announce the security breach to the world then it is difficult to classify this as ethical (Furnell, 2010:176) because, in essence, it draws everyone's attention to the flaw and *de facto* invites the world's hackers to exploit this hack, including those who may wish to cause damage.

However, Furnell also challenges the idea that even where disclosure is made discreetly it can be said to be ethical. He is dismissive of the argument that people who only look but do not act can be said to be ethical. He makes the point that 'while a hacker could well pop in and out of my system, without changing or disrupting anything, they may still have seen something that I would consider personally private or commercially sensitive, and therefore harm has been done even though the data remains unaffected' (Furnell, 2010:177). This is a key point: how can the hacker know what is harmless and what is not? What one person considers to be harmless another may consider to be a gross invasion of privacy.

Furnell develops this concept of harm by drawing an analogy to a house (a somewhat common analogy). He makes the very valid point that people would not consider it appropriate if a person decided to take an uninvited look around the house and 'arguments that the door was open (or didn't require much of a push) would hardly be expected to justify it' (Furnell, 2010:177). This is undoubtedly true, although this raises the interesting question about whether we consider the 'real world' differently to that of cyberspace. We would probably consider an invasion of our house to be particularly distressing whereas we may not feel the same about our presence in cyberspace (although this may not be true in respect of emails, social media sites, etc.). However, where there is a major difference is that entering a house is not by itself illegal. Clearly where the entry is with the intention of stealing, causing criminal damage or to cause grievous bodily harm then it is illegal in England and Wales (see s.9(1)(a), *Theft Act 1968*) but merely entering the property is a civil matter and not a criminal matter. As will be seen below, however, this is not true of hacking, where even gaining unauthorised access is sufficient to establish criminality.

Given the status of the law (which will be outlined below) it is likely that accessing a system without authorisation – but without any intention of damaging anything – should be considered an example of grey hat hacking. White hat hacking should be restricted to those situations where there is authority, either specific or general. Certainly there has in recent years been an increased acceptance by industry of authorised white hat hacking, and indeed it is sometimes thought to be the only way that one can truly test online security systems (Caldwell, 2011). However, there must be a difference between those who participate in authorised activities and those who act on their own initiative.

Of course a difficulty with these descriptions is they do, to an extent, rely on self-identification, i.e. we only know why they did something because of what the hacker said. This has led some to note that it is difficult to separate out what their motivation was before they acted from the justification they provide afterwards (Yar, 2013:34). That said, this is perhaps not as problematic as one may believe, as hackers will not infrequently talk about their conduct.

Whether the hats remain a useful manner of classifying hackers is perhaps more open to question. Partly this is because in recent years hacking has been used as a political tool. In other words, some hackers will seek to gain unauthorised access to computers, servers or websites as part of a campaign (for example, against corporate greed). Given that one of the aims of such hacks is to cause damage and disruption, most would probably classify such behaviour as 'black hat' hacking, but it is more likely that the hackers would consider themselves grey hats, because they believe they are undertaking the hack for (what they see as) legitimate or ethical purposes. Chapter 5 will consider this behaviour in more detail but it does perhaps demonstrate the difficulty of classifying the behaviour, especially in deciding whether it is an objective or subjective view of what hat a hacker is wearing.

## Taxonomy of hacking

The fact that hacking involves a broad range of behaviour has meant that some believe a more scientific approach to defining hacker behaviour is required. One of the earliest proponents of this was Rogers who, as part of a graduate study, developed a 'hacker taxonomy' (Rogers, 2000) that was later refined and was developed into nine categories (2006:98):

1.  Novice (a person new to hacking who tends to rely on the programs of others to assist in the hacking).
2.  Cyber-punks (a person more technologically astute than the novice and who tends to undertake low-level malicious acts).

3. Internals (a disgruntled employee or ex-employee who uses the authorisations he has been given to maliciously damage or leak content).
4. Petty-thieves (a person who uses his hacking skills not for notoriety and to gain access to damage sites, etc., but rather to steal money).
5. Virus Writers (a person who creates viruses and spreads them through hacking).
6. Old Guard Hackers (a person who does not have any overtly malicious intentions and is hacking to show skill or to look for information).
7. Professional Criminals (a person who belongs to a professional (organised) gang and who uses hacking to make significant financial gains).
8. Information Warriors (a person who uses hacking to launch attacks on command and control activities of a state).
9. Political Activist (a person who uses hacking for political purposes).

This is an interesting taxonomy and whilst some have quibbled over the terminology (Hald and Pederson, 2012) the changes suggested have been relatively minor. The taxonomy perhaps shows the variety of different hacking activities and certainly it is more nuanced than the 'hat' system. That said, it is perhaps notable that there is no 'ethical hacking' or 'white hat' equivalent in the taxonomy, which is perhaps a little surprising. This is possibly because the author has concentrated on illegal activities, but it would be more appropriate to have considered all forms of hacking and therefore this would include the ethical hacker. The exception to this being category 8 – information warriors – who may not be acting illegally. Information warriors are considered to be those who launch or defend against attacks and Rogers specifically states that '[t]his group includes traditional and non-traditional state sponsored technology based warfare' (Rogers, 2006:99), in other words so-called cyberwarfare. This will be considered more extensively in Chapter 5.

The taxonomy is broadly based on a continuum of novice to information warrior, the idea being that the skills broadly increase as one rises through the taxonomy. Political activist is separate from this and 'was included as it balances the circumplex and may increase the overall usefulness of the classification model' (Rogers, 2006:99). In other words it sits outside of the other nine but was included because it was thought that the political motivation separates it from others. It must be questioned whether this is true, and it is probably comparable to categories 2, 4 and 6. Indeed, it could be argued that these categories could have been better articulated to take account of either maliciousness or political activism. This is perhaps particularly true of category 6 (old guard hacker) who may not act maliciously *per se* but would be prepared to undertake illegal activity in order to push a particular political standpoint. It is perhaps for this reason that Hald and Pederson, for example, believe that the term 'grey hat hacker' should be used instead of 'old guard hacker' (Hald and Pederson, 2012:82) although that then raises the question of where the other 'hats' fit into the taxonomy.

The taxonomy is certainly useful in presenting the spectrum of behaviour that hacking can entail. As noted at the beginning of this chapter, it is some-times tempting to believe that hacking is a simple form of behaviour but the taxonomy shows that people will undertake hacking for very different reasons.

### What do hackers do?

Whilst hacking may be considered to be illegally accessing a computer system, which may raise issues of privacy, some hackers will go beyond this, particularly the grey hat and black hat hackers. Yar believes that there are six activities that most commonly occur:

1.  Theft of computer resources (including storing files on the hacked server, etc.).
2.  Theft of proprietary or confidential information.
3.  Sabotage, alteration and destruction of systems (or indeed files).
4.  Website defacement.
5.  Denial of Service attacks.
6.  Distribution of malicious software.

(Yar, 2013:28–31)

Of these six types, categories 2 to 4 inclusive will be considered in the next chapter because they primarily relate to data attacks. The remaining three categories can be considered briefly in this chapter.

### Theft of resources

The first type of activity identified by Yar relates to the theft of resources. This is different from the theft of data, which is discussed in Chapter 4, and refers to activity where the object of the hack is to use some or all of the resources of the hacked computer. Yar notes that this can include illegal or undesirable material and cites a case in Sweden where a hacked server was used to store illegal music files (Yar, 2013:28). It can also refer to the stealing of wi-fi bandwidth which may have repercussions for the owners of the wi-fi connection who could incur additional costs, but perhaps more seriously be thought liable for illegal activity that occurs over their wi-fi connections. For example, if illegal material (e.g. child pornography) was distributed via the hacked wi-fi connection then if the distribution was traced by law enforce-ment it would show the owners' IP address, leading law enforcement to believe that they, not the hackers, were the distributors.

Hacking into a computer to store material would contravene the *Computer Misuse Act 1990*, but can the storing of the files constitute an offence in its own right? The most obvious would be theft – the argument being that a

person has 'stolen' the space on the drive. There would seem to be no difficulty in deciding that a person has appropriated property belonging to
another. Appropriation, as is well known, is defined as the appropriation
of the rights of the owner (s.3, *Theft Act 1968* and see *R v Gomez* [1993] AC
442) and only the owner of the storage space has the right to store data there,
so at least one right of the owner has been usurped. There must be property
because ultimately files are stored on a physical storage device (hard disc,
server hard disc, etc.) and this belongs to another. However, the difficulty
would be that the storage space has not been taken in its entirety. Nothing is
physically removed, the space is simply being used in a way that the owner is
not aware of. Where the files are identified they can be removed and the space
recovered. Thus instead of a permanent removal, what is in essence occurring
is that the space is being 'borrowed' albeit without permission. On that basis
s.6(1), *Theft Act 1968* becomes relevant which states:

> A person appropriating property belonging to another without mean-
> ing the other permanently to lose the thing itself is nevertheless to be
> regarded as having the intention of permanently depriving the other of
> it if his intention is to treat the thing as his own to dispose of regardless
> of the other's rights, and a borrowing or lending of it may amount to so
> treating it if, but only if, the borrowing or lending is for a period and in
> circumstances making it equivalent to an outright taking or disposal.

As the property is not being disposed of only the words 'borrowing or lend-
ing' are relevant. It cannot be said that the circumstances are the equivalent
of the outright taking or disposal of the property because ultimately the space
can be recovered. Indeed that is the whole point of storage devices, they
can store data and overwrite that data several times over. It is clear that the
enjoyment of a possession cannot constitute theft (Ormerod, 2011:833) and
this rule would apply here.

What of the 'stealing' of wi-fi? That raises separate issues. A wi-fi signal
is unlikely to be considered property within the meaning of the *Theft Act
1968* because electricity is not and thus, for example, making a telephone
call cannot amount to theft (*Low v Blease* [1975] Crim LR 513). There would
seem to be no reason why, by analogy, the same should not be true of wi-fi
signals. However, liability can be found under the *Communications Act 2003*.
Section 125 criminalises dishonestly obtaining electronic communications
services. Wi-fi would amount to an 'electronic communications service' (see
s.32, *Communications Act 2003*) and thus liability could be established.

The theft of resources could also relate to the use of a computer as a
'zombie' for a 'bot attack'. Whilst this can be used to do a number of things,
including downloading or distributing material, they are commonly used for
Denial of Service attacks and thus will be considered further below. Liability
for making a computer a 'zombie' would be under the CMA 1990.

*Denial of Service attacks*

Whilst hacking was once solely about the infiltration of a computer (and indeed this remains the case in many instances) it is also being increasingly used to undertake Denial of Service (DoS) and Distributed Denial of Service (DDoS) attacks.

A DoS attack is where a server or website is targeted with the aim of over-loading it, in effect making it unusable. Servers and websites can only handle a certain amount of traffic. Bandwidth is expensive and therefore companies will normally estimate the likely number of users that will access their services at any one time and tailor their requirements accordingly. It is possible to over-whelm a server and either slow it down or cause it to crash. Think of popular sporting events or pop concerts. When a popular event is advertised it is some-times said that a ticketing site 'crashes' because too many people are trying to buy tickets at the same time. A DoS attack works on the same principle.

One of the more typical forms of DoS is to simply send too much traffic to the server. Another variant is to trick the server into forming an ever-growing queue of people that it is seeking to communicate with. Clough summarises how this works:

> A networked system such as the Internet relies upon protocols to allow computers to communicate with one another and to ensure that the data requested arrives at its destination. The client computer sends a request to the server, which then responds and identifies itself. Once the client computer receives this identification, data can be transferred ... the attacker may use a spoofed address to send the request to the server. The server duly identifies itself and waits to hear back. However it will never hear back because it has been given the wrong or a non-existent address. If enough messages are sent the server is paralysed by waiting.
>
> (Clough, 2010:38)

A DDoS operates in the same way as a DoS attack but it involves multiple computers. Sometimes this will be a concerted effort of people who will com-municate through peer-to-peer networks which allow an attack to be made, and for the attack to be varied as the targeted computer tries to evade the attack. In other examples it will use what are called 'zombies' or 'bots'. This is where a hacked computer is 'taken over' by the hacker and instructions passed to the computer. This can be to launch a DoS attack. With multiple bots it means that the attacks can take place from different computers and IP addresses making it more difficult for the operator of the attacked server to respond to the attack, since as they block one IP address another can simply take over.

It has been said that DDoS attacks against computers based in the UK are relatively uncommon (McGuire and Dowling, 2013:16), although this could be more to do with where websites and servers are based. For example, just because a company is British does not mean that its servers or websites are based in the UK rather than another country, in which case an attack would be classed as occurring elsewhere. DoS and DDoS attacks are popular tools of so-called 'hacktivism', i.e. where hacking is used for a political object as part of a protest. This link can be seen from the typical victims of DDoS attacks, which were online shopping (25 per cent), banks and stock exchanges (23 per cent) and gaming sites (20 per cent) (McGuire and Dowling, 2013:16). However, there have also been high-profile examples of political or governmental websites being attacked to make political points, something that will be discussed in Chapter 5.

It may seem that DoS attacks are more matters of inconvenience rather than damage, but that is not necessarily the case. Where the site or server is, for example, a bank or e-commerce site then a DoS attack will cost it the value of lost transactions together with reputational damage. Even where there is no immediate pecuniary damage there is still the cost of stopping the attack and trying to prevent future attacks. A good example of this can be seen from *R v Martin* [2013] EWCA Crim 1420 where a DoS attack was launched, *inter alia*, on the website of Oxford University and where the university estimated that 'nearly two weeks' of man hours were expended in dealing with these attacks' (at [11]). There is a cost to such remedial work and this shows that DoS attacks are not merely matters of inconvenience. This will be explored in more depth in Chapter 5 which explores so-called cyberterrorism.

## Malware

The second principal attack that takes place against technology is that of malware, i.e. software that targets computers for malicious purposes. The most obvious example of this is a 'virus' but, as will be seen, this is only one type of malware and others exist. Whilst hacking has garnered a lot of public attention, malware is by far the more likely negative experience people will have suffered online, with it being noted that it has 'dominated the scene since mass adoption of the Internet began' (Furnell and Ward, 2006:28). Certainly, anti-virus software is now considered to be essential equipment and basic versions are now regularly included in operating systems, and most email services (particularly those used by the major ISPs) will include virus detection software.

### What is malware?

As with hacking, it is first necessary to consider what malware is. As noted already the term 'virus' has almost taken on a social definition to encompass all forms of malware but there are differences. Furnell and Ward argue that there are three principal categories:

- Viruses.
- Worms.
- Trojans.

(Furnell and Ward, 2006:28)

Although they note that some will use different terminologies and there will be different variants of this. For example, a 'time bomb' is not infrequently a virus that will not 'destruct' until a certain time point or period of time after completion. A 'logic bomb' is similar but it is 'triggered' by a particular process or event. Others believe that in addition to these categories 'bots' (which have already been considered in respect of DDoS attacks) and 'spyware' should be added. The latter is certainly something that has become prevalent in recent years and is worthy of inclusion.

A virus is perhaps the oldest of the types of malware and certainly existed before the inception of the internet where it would be spread through users swapping infected files or through the use of infected media, for example floppy discs (and later USB drives). It is for this reason that many corporate and governmental computers will not allow the use of removable storage, believing that cloud-based storage is more secure (in part because cloud service providers will normally include virus protection in the file transfer process fearing a virus could compromise the whole of the cloud).

A virus is a self-replicating program that seeks to spread itself by attaching itself either to a particular file or storage medium. When it detects that it has been placed into a new device it will embed itself there. Sometimes the virus is programmed to increase the likelihood of someone opening it. In 1999 a virus called 'Happy 99' was created which, when opened, produced a fireworks display on the screen. Whilst harmless it was passed on by people choosing to open the message because they thought it was a greeting. A more sinister example was the 'ILOVEYOU' virus which was passed through email. The virus would garner contacts from a person's email system and then generate a love-letter email to persons within the contacts. If the person opened the email attachment (which was likely due to curiosity) then their machine would be infected and the virus would repeat the action.

A worm is similar to a virus in that they are self-replicating but they are also autonomous (Furnell and Ward, 2006:29). Whilst a virus would attach itself to a file or a storage device and be spread in that way, a worm exploits the connectivity of the internet. Its source code allows it to access the internet protocol of an infected machine and it will then exploit any weaknesses in computers that are connected to the internet. Worms are particularly problematic in local networks (e.g. companies, universities, etc.) because the nature of the network means that it can spread across computers quickly.

Viruses and worms are problematic in part because of what is sometimes called their 'payload'. This is an interesting term and it is semantically linked to bombs or missiles where the destructive part is known as the 'payload' with the delivery system being the actual missile. The varieties of payloads for viruses and worms are almost limitless as this will be down to the creativity of the designer, but will commonly include the deletion of certain files or the corruption of an operating system. A more recent example is extortion. Files are encrypted and a message is sent to the owner of the infected machine demanding payment in return for the key to de-encrypt the files. Of course the reality is that, as with most forms of extortion, it is unlikely that this promise would be kept. Not all payloads are necessarily harmful, some are simply annoying or, as in the 'Happy99' virus, just silly.

A Trojan is a variant of a virus and is quite often the payload of a virus or worm. Unlike a virus or worm it is not self-replicating, which is why it is sometimes attached to a virus since this will permit replication to occur. Named after the Greek ploy to enter the city of Troy, the Trojan virus is the electronic version. A user will allow the file to be installed because they believe it is doing a particular task but in fact it will be performing a very different function. Sometimes this will be to make the computer a 'bot', facilitating DDoS attacks. Other frequent examples would include the distribution of spam from the computer, theft of files or data, or placing software such as 'keylogging' onto the computer. This would allow the person controlling the machine to monitor what was typed into the machine, including passwords, bank IDs, etc.

A Trojan permits a person to have remote access to the computer and therefore they could, for example, clone the computer or see what is happening on the screen. More than this, however, they can take over functions of the computer. This could include, for example, the webcam, meaning that a person could watch and record the user. This could then be used, for example, to blackmail an individual for money or to gain sexually explicit photographs.

### Spyware

Spyware 'often finds itself separated from other malware on the basis that while its guises may vary they all share the same overall objective of invading privacy' (Furnell, 2010:185). This recognises that not everyone will necessarily consider spyware to be malware, although this will partly depend on how it is defined.

Spyware differs from viruses, worms and Trojans in part because its focus is on the invasion of privacy rather than causing damage to systems or the direct stealing of financial information. The problem with spyware is that it carries a broad definition. It has been suggested that, for example, the use of keyloggers, pop-ups and website monitoring can amount to spyware (Clough, 2010:36), but where it facilitates remote access this could equally be classified as a Trojan.

Further complications arise from the fact that whilst viruses, worms and Trojans are likely to be developed by individuals, spyware could arise from legitimate companies. Many large companies and websites will engage in using spyware and, for example, Google, Microsoft and Apple have all been accused at one time of using spyware. Another classic area of confusion is in respect of cookies. Cookies are a small piece of data that are downloaded upon the first visit to a website. On subsequent visits the cookie is sent back to the server and can provide information on what the user has been doing or how they have been accessing a particular site. Cookies are used, for example, by online shopping portals to 'remind' you of what you have looked at before.

Tracking cookies – i.e. those that track the usage of a user – undoubtedly raise issues of privacy. The use of spyware, including tracking cookies, can be very big business with companies prepared to pay a lot of money for information about how users act (Klang, 2004:197). The implications for privacy have meant that cookies have been regulated for some time but those regulations have increased in recent years. In the context of the UK, the regulation of cookies can be traced through EU law. The first regulation was introduced by the so-called 'e-privacy Directive' (more properly *Directive 2002/58/EC of the European Parliament and of the Council … concerning the processing of personal data and the protection of privacy in the electronic communications sector* [2002] OJ/ 201) and this was amended by EU Directive 2009/136/EC which required users' consent to store and disseminate details. This Directive required Member States to incorporate these changes within two years, with the UK doing so by *The Privacy and Electronic Communications (EC Directive) (Amendment) Regulations 2011* (SI 2011/1208). These regulations are responsible for the statements that you will now commonly find on websites that state that by continuing you agree to the site's privacy rules.

Spyware is perhaps a good example of the debate that exists over whether cybercrime, or certain aspects of it, should be dealt with as a matter of civil law rather than criminal law. Generally, spyware is not destructive in the way that other malware is, it is annoying and raises concerns about privacy but does that by itself make it a cyber*crime* rather than a civil wrong? Where it is harvesting information concerning wi-fi passwords, bank log-in credentials, etc., then that perhaps raises different issues, but that is more akin to a Trojan than ordinary spyware and otherwise it should be a matter best left to the civil law. For that reason the rest of this chapter will omit discussion about spyware and concentrate on the three traditional forms of malware identified above.

### Motivation for malware

Why do people create malware? This is an area of some dispute and it seems to follow some of the logic of what was discussed in respect of hacking. As with the earliest hackers, it would appear that the initial creators of malware were motivated by the technical challenge rather than any desire to be malicious (Gordon, 2006:68). However, it would be a mistake to believe that all early creators were benevolent since there were people who sought to cause damage.

The analogy to hackers can also be seen in some of the *ex post facto* justifications put forward by some. For example, it has been noted that some have argued that they could only do what they want because others – Microsoft or Apple – have written bad software and left open security flaws (Gordon, 2006:69). Whilst this attempts to put forward the belief that malware writers are somehow 'noble crusaders' the reality is that, as with hacking, there are better ways of identifying security flaws. Certainly, the idea that the damage that can be caused by malware (for example, the corruption of a storage device or the permanent deletion of data) can be justified by 'illustrating' security flaws is simply not credible.

Later developments appear to be the subject of dispute. Whilst some believe that 'malware writers are now actually key members of real criminal gangs, tasked with the role of writing new malware' (Cluley, 2010:8) others believe that this is not true and that there are 'many young people, such as university students [who] continue to experiment with computers in ways considered to be antisocial' (Gordon, 2006:70). To an extent it probably depends on what the purpose of the virus is. It would be easy to see how Trojans or viruses that encrypt data for extortion could be valuable to criminal gangs, but it is perhaps less easy to see what justification there is for criminal gangs to become involved in those viruses that just seek to attack the infected computer by corrupting or deleting files.

As with hackers, where it will be remembered that the taxonomy included an 'insider', one of the challenges with malware is the person who exploits personal knowledge of a system to produce malware. Most users will employ anti-malware software and this is particularly true of corporations. However, where malware is tailor-made to attack a particular system then it is more difficult to respond to this and it is more likely that an attack will succeed (Furnell, 2010:188). As with hacking, the motivation for such attacks is likely to be personal, with the most probable culprit being a disgruntled employee. This makes them more difficult to identify and prevent an attack before it begins.

## Legal responses

What are the legal responses to the behaviour considered above? Whilst the majority of the discussion will be focused on the position within England and Wales, it is necessary to consider the international context since, as will be seen, this has influenced the English legal response.

### Cybercrime Convention

One of the principal reasons for drafting the Cybercrime Convention was to provide a legal framework for attacks against computers. Title 1 of Chapter II of the Convention sets out five provisions:

- Illegal access (Article 2).
- Illegal interception (Article 3).
- Data interference (Article 4).
- System interference (Article 5).
- Misuse of devices (Article 6).

Whilst all of these could arguably apply, Articles 3 and 4 are more properly considered to be relevant to the behaviour considered in Chapter 4 (offences relating to data) and therefore they will be examined in that chapter. The remaining three will be discussed here.

#### Illegal access

The first article of relevance is Article 2 which relates to illegal access and which states:

> Each party shall adopt such legislative and other measures as may be necessary to establish as criminal offences under its domestic law, when committed intentionally, the access to the whole or any part of a computer system without right. A party may require that the offence be committed by infringing security measures, with the intent of obtaining computer data or other dishonest intent, or in relation to a computer system that is connected to another computer system.

It is notable that the reference here is to *access* which is very similar to how the *Computer Misuse Act 1990* is drafted too. Thus, in its basic form, there is no requirement that any actual damage is caused, simply accessing the computer system without authority will suffice. That said, some countries were concerned that this could make the offence over-broad and thus the second half of the article allows signatory states to put limitations on this offence, most notably the requirement that either it involves infringing security measures (so, for example, simply switching on a computer would not suffice – cf. the position in domestic law discussed below) or with ulterior intent (either obtaining data or some other dishonest intent).

The Article is based on the premise that it is conducted 'without right' and thus it is not intended to regulate those circumstances where a person accesses the computer either with permission or because there is a legal right to do so (e.g. because domestic law provides law enforcement with a power to do so). Whilst the basic offence deals with the accessing of a system, this is also the most relevant offence where, for example, the person is taking rather than damaging information. Thus, for example, a hacker who steals information (including identity data) would be culpable under this offence. The explanatory notes to the Convention also suggest that electronic access (through a bot or cookie) would also apply and so the offence does not simply apply to someone who directly accesses the system themselves (at [41]).

It has been questioned whether it is necessary to gain working control of the machine to fall foul of this article, or whether trying, but failing, to access the machine would suffice (Clough, 2010:59). The argument here is that where a person interacts with a computer and is asked for a password, that computer has been accessed (as it is performing a function) even though there is not yet any control over the machine. Whilst the Convention is silent on this, it would seem that this is more likely to be an inchoate offence and that access would seem to mean accessing the machine in a way that allows interaction rather than just the request for a password.

### System interference

Article 5 of the Convention tackles system interference and it states:

> Each party shall adopt such legislative and other measures as may be necessary to establish as criminal offences under its domestic law, when committed intentionally, the serious hindering without right of the functioning of a computer system by inputting, transmitting, damaging, deleting, deteriorating, altering or suppressing computer data.

The explanatory notes to the Convention make clear that the primary aim of this article is to tackle the sabotage of systems (at [65]) by hindering them. 'Hinder' means actions that 'interfere with the proper functioning of the system' (at [66]) and this would therefore include programs that slow a computer down to the point of being ineffective and DDoS attacks. The terms of the article require that the hindering be 'serious', but this is not defined and thus signatory states will adopt their own standards to this which could cause problems in terms of transnational crime.

The explanatory notes state that the sending of spam could be within the provisions of this offence but only where 'the communication is intentionally and seriously hindered' (at [69]); however, they do say this is, in part, because signatory states are entitled to take other measures to combat this behaviour, and this perhaps reflects the fact that the Cybercrime Convention was not intended to be a comprehensive treaty but rather a basic set of agreed standards.

The other classic example of behaviour that would be caught by this article is that of malware, particularly viruses. The payload of most viruses is the impairment of the system and therefore they would be captured by this article. Malware also features in the next article and thus a distinction is perhaps drawn between those who deploy malware (Article 5) and thus who create and sell malware (Article 6).

## Misuse of devices

The last article of particular relevance to this behaviour is contained in Article 6, which states:

(1) Each party shall adopt such legislative and other measures as may be necessary to establish as criminal offences under its domestic law, when committed intentionally and without right:

  (a) the production, sale, procurement for use, import, distribution or otherwise making available of:

    (i) a device, including a computer program, designed or adapted primarily for the purpose of committing any of the offences established in accordance with Articles 2 through 5;

    (ii) a computer password, access code, or similar data by which the whole or any part of a computer system is capable of being accessed,

  with intent that it be used for the purpose of committing any of the offences established in Articles 2 through 5; and

  (b) the possession of an item referred to in paragraphs a(i) or (ii) above, with intent that it be used for the purpose of committing any of the offences established in Articles 2 through 5. A Party may require by law that a number of items be possessed before criminal liability attaches.

(2) This article shall not be interpreted as imposing criminal liability ... is not for the purpose of committing an offence established in accordance with Articles 2 through 5 of this Convention, such as for the authorised testing or protection of a computer system.

(3) Each party may reserve the right not to apply paragraph 1 of this article, provided that the reservation does not concern the sale, distribution or otherwise making available of the items referred to in paragraph 1(a)(ii) of this article.

This is perhaps the most complicated of the provisions to be examined and certainly the most detailed. Certain parts of the provision appear superfluous, not least paragraph (2) which simply states that where the item is not to be used for criminal purposes then no such offence takes place, but this is already clear from paragraph (1) where it is made clear that ulterior intent is necessary for culpability. This perhaps reflects the compromises that are at times required in the drafting of international instruments where repetition is sometimes demanded for clarity.

The overall purpose of this offence is to criminalise the making and distribution of devices or access codes. Article 5(1)(a)(i) makes clear that 'device' includes a computer program and therefore it is not just physical tools but also computer programs, including malware and hacking tools. Article 5(1)(a)(ii) concerns the sale of passwords and access codes. Once these details are stolen during hacks it is not uncommon for them to be sold to others to exploit and this paragraph is seeking to tackle this trade. It is notable that paragraph (ii) is mandatory – it is not possible for signatory states to derogate from this (see Article 5(3)).

Article 5 is recognition that there is a black market in the trade of hacking tools, technologies and techniques and that in order to tackle computer misuse it is necessary not only to tackle those who deploy the attacks but those who enable them to happen. The explanatory notes make reference to the fact that this is something that occurs in respect of forgery and money counterfeiting (at [73]) and it is obviously intended that the same strategy should be adopted here. An interesting question arises, however, whether it is the tools or the techniques that is being criminalised. Whilst clearly tools and programs are caught within Article 5, there is a question as to whether detailed instructions on how to hack could be sold or distributed. Article 5(1)(a)(ii) makes reference to 'similar data by which the whole or any part of a computer system is capable of being accessed' and it may be thought that this would include details of how to hack but it has been suggested that this may not be true because the principle of *ejusdem generis* should apply and that would mean the similar data would be in the context of passwords or codes not instructions (Clough, 2010:121). That being the case, it does not seem that an instruction manual would be caught by the provision, which would seem odd as preventing their sale would be an obvious way of trying to stem the development of hacking (even if it would be difficult to police, but the same can be said of anything within Article 5).

An undoubted difficulty in this area is that a number of tools that can be used for hacking are also capable of being used for legitimate purposes (Sommer, 2006:68) and this raises practical difficulties. Exempting dual-purpose tools would leave a loophole but criminalising all tools capable of hacking would neuter legitimate security testing. Therefore, the compromise was to require a specific intent to commit a further relevant offence, which is defined as an act contrary to Articles 2 to 5 inclusive of the Convention. Specific intent will require positive proof of this ulterior motive and therefore legitimate security testing should be exempted.

### EU legislation

The EU has been involved in this area for some time, arguably dating back to 1999 where an agreement was reached to approximate laws in respect of cybercrime (Klimek, 2012:89). There is recognition that many critical economic systems are based in technology and that cyber-attacks are capable of interfering with the market economy. Prior to a Directive that was passed in 2013, the most significant piece of legislation was Framework Decision 2005/222/JHA on attacks against information systems. The purpose of this Framework Decision was to create a common set of legal definitions and offences across the EU and to improve the effective prosecution of offenders (Klimek, 2012:91). To do this, the Framework Decision put forward a definition (Article 1) and criminalised the illegal access to information systems (Article 2), illegal system interference (Article 3) and illegal data interference (Article 4). It also addressed issues of jurisdiction (Article 10) and attempted to facilitate the exchange of information between Member States (Article 11).

Theoretically a Framework Decision is legally binding (Article 34 of the (then) *Treaty on the European Union*) and Member States should have implemented the Decision by 2007 (Article 12) but there was no enforcement mechanism. The Court of Justice of the EU had no jurisdiction to enforce obligations under a Framework Decision and thus it was questionable whether Member States would adhere to their commitments. The Commission was required under Article 12(2) of the Decision to make a report on the implementation of the Decision and it did so (COM (2008) 448 Final). The Commission found that 'the [Decision] has been implemented in very different ways ... In most States, the wording of the national law is close to that used [in the Decision but] in others a more indirect and general method of implementation has been applied' (p.3). Given that one of the purposes of the Decision was to approximate wording that suggests this has not been as helpful as would have been hopeful. In respect of the particular matters, it was clear that there was not universal compliance, with only 16 out of 20 States having properly implemented Article 2 (p.4), 18 having implemented Article 3 (p.5) and 19 having implemented Article 4 (p.6) and only 11 out of 20 implementing Article 11 (p.9).

The fact that there was less than universal implementation led to concerns that there were gaps in the protection that the Decision was supposed to address. There was also concern by the Commission that new developments – particularly DoS and DDoS attacks – had meant that the Framework Decision was in danger of becoming ineffective (p.10) and thus it was decided new legislation was required.

The constitutional changes brought about by the Lisbon Treaty meant that the Framework Decision was replaced by a Directive, an instrument that is both legally binding and enforceable. Directive 2013/40/EU on attacks against information systems ((2013) OJ L 218/8) repeals Framework Decision 2005/222/JHA. The Lisbon Treaty provides opt-outs for this type of legislation to the UK, Ireland and Denmark (contained in the Protocols to the Treaty on the Functioning of the European Union) but the UK and Ireland stated that they wished to opt-in to the Directive (paragraph 31 of the recital) and thus it becomes binding.

In common with most EU instruments the Directive intends to harmonise laws in order to ensure that there are no 'gaps' within the framework of laws across the EU. The recital to the Directive notes that 'significant gaps and differences in Member States' laws … in the area of attacks against information systems may hamper the fight against organised crime and terrorism and may complicate effective police and judicial cooperation in this area' (paragraph 27). Whilst many EU Member States are signatories of the Cybercrime Convention it has been noted already that this is not legally enforceable or binding whereas the EU Directive is. Accordingly, the level of protection should be better, not least because Member States have no choice but to accede to this Directive, including those who have chosen not to sign the Cybercrime Convention.

The Directive harmonises the laws in a number of ways. One of the simplest is by ensuring that there are common definitions for certain terms. Article 2 provides standard definitions for 'information system', 'computer data', 'legal person' and 'without right'. The advantage of this approach is that the laws of the Member States should be based on the same definitions and thus there should be no question in respect of dual criminality where that is required in respect of jurisdiction. 'Information system' is given a wide definition and includes, 'a device or group of inter-connected or related devices, one or more of which … automatically process computer data, as well as computer data stored, processed, retrieved or transmitted by that device' (Article 2(a)). This definition is wide enough to encompass the various communication devices that are in common use.

The main thrust of the Directive is through the introduction of criminal offences. Six offences are created:

- Illegal access to information systems (Article 3).
- Illegal system interference (Article 4).
- Illegal data interference (Article 5).
- Illegal interception (Article 6).
- Production, sale, procurement, importing, distributing or making available tools that permit an offence above (Article 7).
- Inciting, aiding and abetting or attempting an offence above (Article 8).

This covers a broad range of material. Each of the offences must occur 'without right' which is defined in Article 2 as 'not authorised by the owner or by another right holder of the system or part of it, or not permitted under national law'. Thus it accepts that some forms of hacking activity may be permissible (security testing). Illegal access is committed when 'the whole or any part of the system' is intentionally accessed without right (Article 3) and this will cover the hacking activities discussed above. System interference is criminalised where someone *seriously* hinders or interrupts 'the functioning of an information system' including by 'inputting computer data, transmitting, damaging, deleting, deteriorating, altering or suppressing data' (Article 4), meaning that cyber-damage will be culpable.

The Directive does not simply require the establishment of criminal offences but also addresses the penalties that should be imposed. It puts forward a series of minimum, maximum sentences that must be imposed. That is to say, the Directive does not set out what the absolute maximum term *has* to be (that is a matter for Member States) but it sets out a minimum level for that maximum term of imprisonment. The default position is that Member States should ensure that the maximum sentence for a crime under Articles 3 to 7 is no less than two years' imprisonment (Article 9(2)). Where a 'significant' number of information systems have been affected then this rises to three years' (Article 9(3)) and where it is 'aggravated' it rises to five years (Article 9(4)). The circumstances of aggravation are:

- Where it is committed by a criminal organisation within the meaning of Framework Decision 2008/841/JHA.
- The attack causes serious damage.
- The attack is committed against a critical infrastructure information system.

It is interesting to note that the offence has variable maximum sentences although, of course, some countries will deal with this by setting a single maximum sentence but issuing sentencing guidelines to deal with the aggravating circumstances. One issue of note is that 'significant', 'serious' and 'critical infrastructure information system' are not defined and thus it will be left to Member States which may mean that there are different definitions, although as this relates to penalty rather than the substantive offence this difference may not matter.

A result of harmonisation is that jurisdiction and extradition may be simpler. As noted in Chapter 2, many countries adopt a 'dual criminality' requirement for extradition and extraterritorial jurisdiction. Since Article 2 provides common definitions of 'information system', 'computer data', 'legal person' and 'without right' these terms will become harmonised across the EU. Whilst Member States will be able to include other definitions within their domestic instruments, the definitions within Article 2 will be required as a minimum.

Jurisdiction is considered in Article 12. Whilst jurisdiction was considered in Chapter 2 and therefore it is not necessary to rehearse many of the issues again here, it is perhaps worth noting a couple of points. The default position is that jurisdiction should be secured in respect of the territorial principle (Article 12(1)(a)) or alternatively extraterritorial jurisdiction on the basis of the active personality principle (Article 12(1)(b)). It was noted that the territorial rule is subject to interpretation when it applies to the internet. However, this Directive specifically addresses this when it states that activities take place within the jurisdiction (whether whole or in part) when the offender commits the offence when physically present in the territory (Article 12(2)(a)) or where 'the offence is against an information system on its territory' (Article 12(2) (b)). This reinforces the fact that an attack directed from outside of the territory is justiciable within the territory where the object of the attack is within the territory. This is an important principle although, as noted in Chapter 2, this does mean that several countries could presumably claim jurisdiction in respect of the same attack. Unfortunately, the Directive does not direct how this should be resolved, presumably it being thought that it best to leave the matter to the discretion of Member States.

Article 13 mandates Member States to ensure 'an operational national point of contact' and that this contact point is maintained 24 hours a day. Clearly it is designed to recognise the speed at which some attacks occur and the short window of opportunity that may arise to arrest persons involved in an attack, thereby disrupting it. This is a welcome step and if implemented properly should ensure cross-border co-operation, something it has been suggested could be more important than the substantive offences the Directive introduces (Collis, 2013:723).

Wong reports that some questioned the need for the Directive and complained that instead of introducing new laws there was a need for more policing of cybercrime (2013:34). Whilst the lack of policing is undoubtedly a problem, it would be wrong to say that there is sufficient law. Whilst this may be true in some Member States, the EU Commission itself noted that a number of Member States had not complied with their obligations under Framework Decision 2005/222/JHA, meaning that there were countries that had insufficient legal instruments and this could have consequences. In that regard, the Directive should be welcomed.

### England and Wales: the Computer Misuse Act 1990

The primary legislation in England and Wales is the *Computer Misuse Act 1990* (which was amended by the *Police and Justice Act 2006*). Its genesis was a report and consultation paper by the Law Commission. In their final report, the Law Commission noted that 'the criminal law does not generally protect confidentiality or privacy, or provide sanctions against the removal of information' (Law Commission, 1989:11). This is correct and was noted briefly earlier when it was questioned why the unauthorised access to a virtual space should be considered a crime. In many other instances this would be considered to be a tort and not a crime. The Law Commission believed that computers were unique. Writing in 1989 – before the internet as we now know it was invented – they said that the justification for criminalising computer misuse was the costs involved in dealing with security invasions, the fact that it could be inchoate action and that repeated computer misuse act may militate against people using computers which would be against the public interest (Law Commission, 1989:12). It is perhaps inconceivable to think about not using computers now but in 1989 this was perhaps more realistic: the age of the typewriter was still alive and most data was stored physically.

The government accepted the premise of the Law Commission report and the *Computer Misuse Act 1990* (CMA 1990) was quickly passed. Some have argued that indeed it was passed too quickly (MacEwan, 2008:956) and that part of its rationale was undermined quickly. The Law Commission had recommended that 'it should be made clear in any legislation that neither an unauthorised modification of a computer's memory or computer storage medium, nor any resulting impairment of computer operations or data, should be capable of amounting to criminal damage under the [Criminal Damage Act 1971]' (Law Commission, 1989:31). This did not happen and the courts in *R v Whiteley* (1991) 93 Cr App R 25 reached the opposite conclusion.

In *Whiteley* the appellant gained access to JANET (the academic network that connects higher education establishments and research councils, etc.). Once he had gained access he then added, amended and deleted files that were stored on one of the network servers. In other instances some of the servers needed to be closed down temporarily so remedial action could be taken. He was charged with several offences of criminal damage (s.1, *Criminal Damage Act 1971*) and the prosecution put forward two possible rationales for conviction. The first was that criminal damage was caused by bringing about a temporary impairment in the servers' performance by causing them to be shut down, and the second was that the data (which was stored magnetically on the discs) was damaged when it was deleted or amended. The jury acquitted the defendant of all charges based on the first rationale but convicted him on the second.

He appealed stating that the judge had misunderstood the technology and whilst the intangible data stored on the data had been damaged the physical storage device had not (at 27). The argument was based on s.10(1) of the Act which defined property as 'property of a tangible nature, whether real of personal'. However, the Court of Appeal rejected this contention. They stated, '[w]hat the Act requires to be proved is that tangible property has been damaged, not necessarily that the damage itself should be tangible' (at 28). They concluded that

> any alteration to the physical nature of the property concerned may amount to damage ... Whether it does so or not will depend upon the effect that the alteration had had upon the legitimate operator ... where ... the interference with the disc amounts to an impairment of the value or usefulness of the disc to the owner, then the necessary damage is established.
>
> (at 29)

The decision was welcomed by Smith, arguably the leading commentator on criminal law at that time, as being 'entirely desirable' (1991:437). Some have argued the decision proves that the CMA 1990 was premature as the law was capable of tackling hacking (MacEwan, 2008:956), but this misses an important distinction. Criminal damage requires proof of damage. *Whiteley* does not contradict this central point and the Court of Appeal expressly held that a hacker 'whose actions do not go beyond, for example, mere tinkering with an otherwise "empty" disc' would cause no damage ((1991) 93 Cr App R 25 at 29). Accordingly, such a person could not be guilty of an offence under the CDA 1971. However, the CMA 1990 does not require damage, it simply requires unauthorised access. The Law Commission believed that this by itself was appropriate for criminalisation and thus the CMA 1990 would still have been required. *Whiteley* simply demonstrates that there was not necessarily a loophole in the law and that hacking before the CMA 1990 was culpable where it caused damage. In addition, the Law Commission's proposal was that legislation should clarify that this did not amount to criminal damage but that was partly to ensure there was no overlap between offences. That did not happen but it is not uncommon for there to be overlap between offences even when it would be preferable that there was none.

When originally passed, the CMA 1990 consisted of three offences but the amendments brought about by the *Police and Justice Act 2006* mean that there are now four:

- Unauthorised access to computer material (s.1).
- Unauthorised access with intent to commit or facilitate the commission of further offences (s.2).
- Unauthorised acts with intent to impair, or with recklessness as to impairing, operation of computer, etc. (s.3).
- Making, supplying or obtaining articles for use in offence under s.1 or s.3 (s.3A).

As was noted previously, whilst the Act refers to 'computer' it does not define it. This was a deliberate decision, as to define computer 'would give rise to a danger that future changes in technology might invalidate the definition and enable criminals to exploit the changes to circumvent the letter of the [A]ct' (Walton, 2006:40). Clearly, as noted in Chapter 2, the pace of technology has meant that this has proved to be a correct decision. Quite what amounts to a computer and, perhaps more importantly, what does not, is open to serious debate and a definition contained within primary legislation could quickly prove cumbersome, requiring primary legislation to amend it, meaning that any response would invariably be slow.

A good example of this development is in respect of social networking sites and websites. Whilst we may not think of those as being computers *per se* they are obviously stored on a computer or, in respect of social networking sites, several computers (servers). Hacking into a person's profile is obviously different to the type of hacking that one envisages from an attack based on a specific computer, where the object is to gain access to a particular device and from there access all the files included in it. Hacking into a social network-ing site profile is different and may not involve 'classic' hacking techniques but could include, for example, subterfuge. However, it is clear that gain-ing unauthorised access to a social networking site profile is contrary to the CMA 1990 (see, for example, *R v Crosskey* [2013] 1 Cr App R (S) 76 where the appellant hacked a celebrity's Facebook page) and this perhaps demonstrates the breadth of the CMA 1990.

## Section 1

The first section has been considered to be the 'base' offence, with ss.2 and 3 being considered aggravated forms of behaviour. When first passed the offence under s.1 was a summary-only offence, but the *Police and Justice Act* 2006 (PJA 2006) amended this and it is now triable either-way with a maxi-mum sentence of two years' imprisonment (s.1(3), CMA 1990).

The key elements of the offence are set out in s.1(1):

(a) he causes a computer to perform any function with intent to secure access to any program or data held in any computer, or to enable any such access to be secured;
(b) the access he intends to secure, or to enable to be secured, is unauthorised; and
(c) he knows at the time when he causes the computer to perform that function that is the case.

Section 1(2) states that the requisite intent required by s.1(1) need not be directed at a particular program or data, a program or data of any particular kind, or a program or data held in any particular program. The consequences of s.1(2) are that it is not necessary to prove that person D intended a specific attack and it is sufficient to prove that the access would be to a computer or data.

What does securing access mean? In s.17(2) it is said that it means causing a computer to:

(a) alter or erase the program or data,
(b) copy or move it to any storage medium other than that in which it is held or to a different location in the storage medium in which it is held,
(c) use it, or
(d) have it output from the computer in which it is held (whether by having it displayed or in any other manner).

This makes the offence extremely broad, not least because reference to 'using' it or to displaying it will cover most forms of access with more malicious types being covered by reference to alterations, erasure and duplication.

The PJA 2006 amendments widened it even further by including not only attacks that led to immediate access but also to modifications that enabled later access to be secured. This has been summarised as 'broadening ... the offence to encompass ... "opening the door" to unauthorised access without stepping through it' (Fafinski, 2008:56). It would include, for example, the placing of a Trojan virus onto a machine with the intention of later using it to gain access to the computer. In essence this can be considered to be a form of unproblematic inchoate liability. There is still conduct: the computer has been altered to allow later access (to, for example, turn it into a zombie for a DoS or DDoS attack) but it is not necessary to wait for the attack to take place before culpability arises.

Whilst clearly the principal mission of the CMA 1990 was to tackle hacking, it is notable that the term 'hacking' is not used anywhere in the Act and its short title refers to computer *misuse* not, for example, hacking or unauthorised access. In *Attorney-General's Reference (No 1 of 1991)* [1993] QB 94 the question was raised whether there needed to be more than one computer. Hacking, as has already been discussed in this chapter, is ordinarily thought of as using one computer to gain access to another. Is that necessary? In the Attorney-General's reference the acquitted person had gained access to a computerised till and keyed in a sequence that provided him with a 70 per cent discount on a purchase that he made. He was charged, *inter alia*, with s.2 which, as will be seen momentarily, builds on the liability of s.1. The judge at first instance upheld a submission of no case to answer on the basis that s.1(1) required a computer to access any other computer. At that time the prosecution had no right of appeal (now see s.58, *Criminal Justice Act 2003* explained in brief by Gillespie, 2013a:473–477) but the Attorney-General sought permission to refer the case to the Court of Appeal (s.36, *Criminal Justice Act 1972*) as a potential error of law. The Court of Appeal agreed that the Crown Court had erred, noting that the phrase 'any computer' within s.1(1)(a) had to be given its ordinary meaning and that it was not possible to read in the word 'other' to restrict it to at least two computers. Lord Taylor CJ, giving the judgment of the Court, felt this conclusion was supported by the fact that not to do so would create a loophole whereby 'there would be nothing in the Act to meet ... industrial espionage or obtaining information as to security details or other confidential information' ([1993] QB 94 at 100).

Clearly the decision in *Attorney-General's Reference* is correct and to rule otherwise would have undermined the offence. As noted at the beginning of this chapter, it should not make any difference if D accesses a file on a computer in a person's office physically or by remotely hacking it. However, that does raise more interesting questions in respect of the term 'authorised'. It will be remembered that s.1 requires access to be unauthorised but the fact that it can be to a single computer does mean that questions can be raised about situations where a person has the right to access the computer for purpose X but does so for purpose Y (see *R v Bow Street Metropolitan Stipendiary Magistrate ex parte Government of the USA* [2000] 2 AC 216). However, this will be discussed in the next chapter as this circumstance usually applies in respect of data.

The *mens rea* element is twofold. Section 1(1)(a) states that the causing a computer to perform a function must be with *intent* to secure access to any program or data held in the computer or to enable any such access to be secured. Thus there is intention to secure access either immediately or in the future. The second form of *mens rea* is found in s.1(1)(c) where it is said that D must *know* at the time he causes the computer to function that this was unauthorised. Accordingly, there must be knowledge. It has been stated that

> if ... D could readily ascertain the nature and extent of his authority but chooses not to do so and decides to take the risk that his access is authorised, and his access is in fact unauthorised, it may be that he does not *know* his access is unauthorised but this is only because he does not want to know. ... wilful blindness of this kind is enough to constitute knowledge.
>
> (Ormerod, 2011:1050)

This must be correct as it is a standard rule within criminal law that you cannot avoid knowledge by closing one's mind to the obvious.

## Section 2

Section 2 of the CMA 1990 builds upon s.1. It states:

> A person is guilty of an offence under this section if he commits an offence under section 1 above with intent
>
> (a) to commit an offence to which this section applies; or
> (b) to facilitate the commission of such an offence (whether by himself or by any other person) ... (s.2(1)).

It can be seen that s.2 can be both a substantive offence (s.2(1)(a)) or an inchoate crime that facilitates the (later) commission of such an offence (s.2(1)(b)). An 'offence to which this section applies' is defined in s.2(2) as an offence for which the sentence is fixed by law which currently means only murder (which has the mandatory sentence of life imprisonment) or an offence for which a person aged over 21 with no previous convictions may be sentenced to imprisonment for a term of at least five years (s.2(2)(b)). The *Criminal Justice and Court Services Act 2000* amended this to reduce the age to 18 (Schedule

7, paragraph 28) but this has never been brought into force and it is not clear that the government intends to do so. However, it is unlikely in most practical circumstances to make any difference.

Section 2 is clearly an aggravated form of s.1 and this is reflected in the sentence, with the maximum sentence being five years' imprisonment (s.2(5)). The *actus reus* of the offence is to commit the offence under s.1 but the *mens rea* contains the additional offence of intending to commit or facilitate the commission of the relevant offence. The list of offences that meet this threshold (five years' imprisonment) is very wide and it would take too long to list them here. However, it is worth noting that in the context of cybercrime it would include blackmail (14 years), theft (seven years), fraud (ten years) together with some sexual offences. That said, it does not include all potentially relevant offences. So, for example, voyeurism (s.67, *Sexual Offences Act 2003*) is punishable only by two years' imprisonment and would not meet the threshold. There has been some concern that people may install software onto a computer that allows, for example, the built-in webcam to be accessed (Kisiel and Osborne, 2013). If this was done for sexual purposes then it may meet the definition of voyeurism but the initial access with the intent to do so could not infringe s.2 because it does not meet the threshold (although an offence under s.1 would be committed).

One final point to note is that as the offence relates to the *intent* to commit the further offence then it does not matter whether that further offence takes place. More than this, however, it is clear from s.2(4), CMA 1990 that it does not matter if it was impossible to commit that later offence. Liability still arises and a direct parallel to this can be drawn to other forms of inchoate liability where impossibility is not a defence (see most notably s.1(2), *Criminal Attempts Act 1981*).

### Section 3

Section 3 is the offence that was most heavily amended by the PJA 2006 which also introduced a new offence (s.3A). Section 3 differs from the other offences in that instead of simple access to a computer or access with intent to commit a further offence, s.3 tackles the unauthorised access to a computer with intent or recklessness to impair the operation of a computer. In other words, s.3 is designed to tackle those attacks where a person is seeking to damage a computer system or heavily impede it.

The revised wording of s.3 is:

(1)  A person is guilty of an offence if

(a)  he does any unauthorised act in relation to a computer;
(b)  at the time when he does the act he knows that it is unauthorised, and
(c)  either subsection (2) or subsection (3) below applies.

(2)   This subsection applied if the person intends by doing the act

    (a)   to impair the operation of any computer;

    (b)   to prevent or hinder access to any program or data held in any computer;

    (c)   to impair the operation of any such program or the reliability of any such data; or

    (d)   to enable any of the things mentioned in paragraphs (a) to (c) above to be done.

(3)   This subsection applies if the person is reckless as to whether the act will do any of the things mentioned in paragraphs (a) to (d) of subsection (2) above.

Section 3 is more serious than either ss.1 or 2 and this is reflected by the fact that it is punishable by a maximum sentence of ten years' imprisonment (s.3(6)). Whilst ss.1 and 2 were designed to tackle hacking, it has been said that the principal purpose of s.3 was to tackle malware, particularly viruses (Fafinski, 2006a:434) although it would seem to be wider than this.

The *actus reus* of the offence is based on the fact that a person does an unauthorised act in respect of a computer. This is a significant departure from the original wording of the legislation and was brought about by the PJA 2006 reforms. As originally drafted, there was a requirement that there was an 'act which caused unauthorised modifications of the contents of any computer', which is significantly broader since it would have been necessary to prove what modifications had occurred. The PJA 2006 reforms mean that, in essence, the focus of the offence shifted from the modification of a computer to the mere impairment of one. The central focus of the *actus reus* is whether D does an unauthorised act. Section 3(5) states that 'act' includes reference to causing an act to be done (s.3(5)(a)) and 'act' includes a series of acts (s.3(5)(b)).

The *mens rea* is more complicated. There must always be the knowledge that at the time of doing the act it was not authorised (s.3(1)(b)) but it must then be accompanied either by the intent to do an act within s.3(2) or reckless-ness as to whether that will happen. When originally passed, the legislation related only to intention and it was the PJA 2006 reforms that introduced the concept of recklessness, something that will be discussed below.

One of the primary reasons for introducing the reforms of the PJA 2006 was the fact that there was uncertainty as to whether s.3 (as originally enacted) would apply to DoS/DDoS attacks. This uncertainty was evident, at the time of the passage, in the proceedings against David Lennon. Lennon was an employee of an insurance company and when he was sacked he used his credentials (which allowed him access to the computer system) to download and install a 'mail-bombing' program. Approximately half-a-million email messages were then sent to the company, which caused the mail server to become compromised. After being identified, he was charged under s.3,

CMA 1990 and tried in the Youth Court (as he was 16 at the time of the offence). The District Judge hearing the matter held that there was no case to answer because a person consents to an email being sent and therefore there was no unauthorised modification.

The prosecution appealed by way of case stated to the High Court (*DPP v Lennon* [2006] EWHC 1201 (Admin)) who quashed the decision. Jack J, giving the lead judgment, stated that whilst there may be consent to receive an email, this consent 'plainly does not cover emails which are not sent for the purpose of communication with the owner, but are sent for the purpose of interrupting the proper operation and use of his system' (at [9]). He went further and stated that if the defendant had asked the recipient if he could send her half-a-million messages she would have said 'no' (ibid.). The court also drew an analogy with a letterbox – a house owner would not consent to having their letterbox jammed up with junk – but it has been suggested that this is a false analogy because clogging up a letterbox is not a criminal act (Fafinski, 2006b:476). Two responses can be made to this. The first is that this is not what the Divisional Court used the analogy for; it was not about guilt or innocence, it was about whether the act was authorised. The second response is that depending on why the letterbox was clogged up, it could amount to a criminal offence (see *Protection from Harassment Act 1997*).

The case was remitted to the Youth Court because the trial had only been part-heard. However, the Court gave a very particular steer on what the judge should consider:

> [o]ne test which the District Judge might consider applying is the answer which Mr Lennon would have expected had he asked [the company] whether he might start Avalanche ... I mention that because it seems to me that it points to the reality of the situation, something which ... has been rather missed in this case thus far.
>
> ([2006] EWHC 1201 (Admin) at [13])

Perhaps unsurprisingly following such a statement, the defendant decided to plead guilty when the matter was reverted.

MacEwan believes that the fact that Lennon pleaded guilty after the Divisional Court remitted the matter to the magistrates' court means 'legal clarity remained elusive' (2008:960), although it is not clear why. The Divisional Court was very clear as to the argument about consent – realistically the only argument that could have been put forward by Lennon – and was positively scathing about the suggestion that implied consent to five million emails could properly be advanced. In this context it was undoubtedly clear but it was believed that a change was required because of international obligations. At that time, the principal obligation was Council Framework Decision 2005/222/JHA. Whilst some commentators have suggested the UK was also obligated to act under the Cybercrime Convention (e.g. Fafinski,

2008:53) the UK had not ratified the Convention at that time (it did not do so until 2011) and so it was not legally binding on the UK.

The effect of the PJA 2006 reforms is, as has been noted already, that impairment effectively becomes the central issue within s.3. Fafinski dislikes the term because he believes it is too much of a subjective concept: 'the threshold at which a transient decline in system performance crosses the boundary into "temporary impairment" is likely to trouble the courts' (2007:9). He believes that the deterioration should only be culpable if it 'is noticeable to the senses' (Fafinski, 2008:59) although it is less than clear why it should be noticeable to the senses given the processing speed of computers. It is difficult to know whether Parliament intended the threshold to be relatively high, but impairment, if given its ordinary meaning, would not necessarily suggest this. Impairment, according to the *Concise Oxford English Dictionary*, means 'to weaken' and, accordingly, it would seem that any reduction in performance would satisfy the test, although that would make the offence extremely wide.

One of the difficulties here is that the international instruments do include a threshold but the CMA 1990 does not. The *Convention on Cybercrime* requires 'serious hindering' (Article 5) and the Framework Decision required action where the interference was 'not minor' (Article 3), the same wording to be found in the EU Directive (Article 4). In this context perhaps the EU legislation is more relevant as it is, in essence, incorporating a *de minimis* rule, something that it not uncommon in law. The EU Directive specifically leaves identifying what is minor to the Member States (paragraph 11 of the recital). The CMA 1990 does not include a *de minimis* rule although this is perhaps what Fafinski is requesting (although it is unlikely in this context that *de minimis* would equate to a speed differential noticeable to the senses).

There is no case-law indicating whether a *de minimis* rule applies and it is notable that the Crown Prosecution Service prosecution guidance does not make any reference to this either, although where it was truly *de minimis* then it is unlikely to meet the prosecutorial tests set out in the Code for Crown Prosecutors. The fact that impairment can be temporary (s.3(5)(c), CMA 1990) could be construed as meaning that Parliament was not intending to require substantial impairment since temporary impairment without damage is culpable, and yet this is perhaps a good example of less than serious impairment.

The second principal change brought about by the PJA 2006 reforms was the introduction of recklessness as a form of *mens rea* to a charge under s.3. Recklessness is only permitted in respect of s.3, it is not to be found in either ss.1 or 2. MacEwan believes that it could lead to some 'questionable attempts at prosecution' (2008:964) although there is no clear evidence that this has happened. He also complains that the move is contrary to the international obligations in that neither the Framework Decision (now the EU Directive) nor the Cybercrime Convention require the criminalisation of recklessness. Whilst this is true, it is important to remember that these treaties simply set out minimum standards and therefore there is no reason why individual states cannot go further. Fafinski appears less troubled by recklessness but notes that it would mean that in *Lennon* the 'realisation that there was a possibility that the unauthorised email bombardment might impair the operation of the target computer would suffice' (Fafinski, 2008:58). Given that the unauthorised act is still required, coupled with knowledge of the fact that it was unauthorised, it is perhaps not unreasonable to decide that a person should think about the consequences of their unauthorised act. That said, it is highly likely that most activities will involve intent rather than recklessness.

### Section 3A

Along with amending the law, the PJA 2006 introduced a new offence into the CMA 1990, known as s.3A:

(1) A person is guilty of an offence if he makes, adapts, supplies or offers to supply any article intending it to be used to commit, or to assist in the commission of, an offence under section 1 or 3.
(2) A person is guilty of an offence if he supplies or offers to supply any article believing that it is likely to be used to commit, or assist in the commission of, an offence under section 1 or 3.
(3) A person is guilty of an offence if he obtains any article with a view to its being supplied for use to commit, or to assist in the commission of, an offence under section 1 or 3.

The offences are punishable by a maximum sentence of two years' imprisonment (s.3A(5)) and 'article' is defined to include 'any program or data held in electronic form' (s.3A(4)).

Fafinski believes that this new offence was probably envisaged as the e-equivalent of 'going equipped', i.e. the use of legitimate tools could be culpable where it was proved that they were to be used for an improper purpose. As he notes, the difficulty with this approach is that in cyberspace there is no carrying anything in public, everything can be done from the same remote location meaning the analogy becomes more difficult to sustain (Fafinski, 2008:60).

The offence under s.3A(1) is perhaps not problematic. It tackles those that supply, etc., an article intending that it is to be used to commit, or facilitate the commission of, a crime under either s.1 or s.3. In other words the supplier has intent that it should be used in an illegal way. The same can be said for the offence under s.3A(3) which criminalises those who obtain an article 'with a view to it being supplied for use to commit or to assist in the commission of' an offence under s.1 or s.3. This criminalises procurement, but again procurement where there is the intention for it to be used in a criminal way as that must be the natural meaning of 'with a view to'. However, the offence under s.3A(2) is perhaps more problematic.

Section 3A(2) is, to an extent, simply a derivative of s.3A(1) but it applies where a person supplies an article 'believing that it is likely to be used to commit' an offence. 'Belief' is considered to be more than mere suspicion but less than knowledge (Ormerod, 2011:1056) and is therefore significantly less than intent. The requirement of mere belief could cause problems in respect of cybercrime. The principal difficulty is that many tools that can be used to either hack or create malware can also undertake legitimate tasks. These are the so-called 'dual-purpose tools'. Sommer, an expert in computer forensics, notes that 'many hacking tools are indistinguishable from utilities that are essential for the maintenance and security of computers and networks' (Sommer, 2006:68). This means that it can be very difficult to know why a person has sourced a particular tool. Given the low benchmark of 'belief', there was the thought that this could mean that sellers could potentially face culpability in circumstances where they were unsure as to why a person was procuring the tool. Where the transaction takes place over the internet it may be more difficult to identify the reasoning and therefore the position was perhaps even more uncertain.

Rahman, building on Fafinski's point concerning 'going equipped', draws an analogy with s.3A to that of knives and guns (Rahman, 2012b:95). By this he means that knives are generally (although not always) lawful to possess whereas a gun is not. The analogy is meant to show that s.3A could have been better drafted. So that those tools that are obviously malicious could be prohibited easily (a point also made by Sommer, 2006:69) but that other tools should only be culpable with ulterior intent (in essence, s.3A(1)) and not where there is mere belief (s.3A(2)). Fafinski concedes that the difficulty with this is that for dual-purpose tools it would be difficult to prove the necessary ulterior intent because it would always be open to a defendant to say that he was an ethical hacker who was conducting a security test (Fafinski, 2008:61). This is a valid point but by itself it cannot justify criminalising those who possess tools for innocent purposes. Perhaps the better solution would have been to create a reverse burden of proof for the possession of a tool that could be used for malicious purposes. This would require the prosecution to prove that D knowingly possessed (or sold) a tool that was capable of being used maliciously. At that point the defendant would be required to prove (on the preponderance of probabilities) that the tool was for legitimate purposes. This would be easily done by legitimate forensic examiners, security testers etc. (the cause of some concern). It may be more difficult to do so for ethical hackers but ultimately that would be for the jury to decide, taking into account the questions raised earlier in this chapter whether ethical hacking is in any event as ethical as it is portrayed. Whilst reverse burdens of proof are controversial (for an outline see Ormerod, 2011:28–30) they are now a feature of the English criminal law and a reverse burden of proof would be preferable to the offence contained within s.3A(2).

## Suggested further reading

Furnell, S. 'Hackers, viruses and malicious software' in Jewkes, Y. and Yar, M. *Handbook of Internet Crime* (2010, Cullompton: Willan Publishing).
*This is a good overview of the different types of hackers and the behaviours that they demonstrate.*

Klimek, L. 'Combating attacks against information systems: EU legislation and its development' (2012) 6 *Masaryk University Journal of Law and Technology* 87–100.
*It was noted in this chapter that the EU has become increasingly active in seeking to tackle cybercrime and this article sets out the history of its action and provides an overview of the latest EU Directive.*

MacEwan, N. 'The Computer Misuse Act 1990: lessons from its past and predictions for its future' [2008] Crim LR 955–967.
*This is a good critique of the Computer Misuse Act 1990. Whilst it will be remembered that the author of this book does not agree with all of the arguments contained within this article, it is important that you read all points of view and this is a good piece of work that questions the development of the law.*

Chapter 2 of Yar, M. *Cybercrime and Society* (2nd ed.) (2013, London: Sage Publishing).
*This is a useful summary of the criminological literature surrounding the issue of hacking and computer misuse. It tracks the development of this behaviour.*

# Chapter 4

# Offences relating to data

The previous chapter examined the issue of those who hack computers. Its focus was on those who gained access to a computer or produced malware. However, directly related to this are attacks on the integrity of data. Sometimes the two issues are the same, e.g. a hacker who accesses a system to look at data (in which case realistically the primary liability will relate to the hacking) but in other instances there will be differences. It is this behaviour that will be examined in this chapter. Four issues will be examined although they do overlap to an extent. The issues are:

- Destroying data.
- Inappropriate access to data.
- Unlawful disclosure of data.
- Interception of data.

The first three types of behaviour are to an extent linked whereas the fourth is probably separate.

## Destroying, disclosing and accessing data

The first type of behaviour to consider is that which relates to the destruction, disclosure or accessing of data. Accessing has been considered quite extensively in the previous chapter but there are other offences that can be relevant and these will be briefly discussed in this chapter. Realistically there are two ways in which the destruction, access or disclosure of data can occur. The first is where a person gains unlawful access to a computer system and either destroys, accesses or discloses the data that they have found (or, in respect of destroying data, infects a computer with malware) and the second is where someone who is authorised to access the computer then subsequently destroys or discloses data (without authority). In respect of the first method the liability would be based on the unlawful access or the creation of malware. This was already discussed in Chapter 3 and reference should be made to that chapter.

The second method of committing these crimes is linked by the concept of 'authorised'. It will be remembered from Chapter 3 that the CMA 1990 is based on unauthorised access and therefore it is necessary to initially consider what authorisation means.

### Authorisation

As noted already, the key to crimes under the CMA 1990 is whether the access or act is unauthorised. What does this mean, however? Section 17(5), CMA 1990 defines unauthorised as where:

(a)  he is not himself entitled to control access of the kind in question to the program or data; and
(b)  he does not have consent to access by him of the kind in question to the program or data from any person who is so entitled.

The words 'of the kind in question' have caused problems as will be seen momentarily. There are two limbs to this test but this is simply to reflect reality. The first limb concerns those who have the right to set the access parameters. Clearly, those who have the right to decide who can, or cannot, access the computer must themselves be authorised. Whilst we may think of that person as being the senior member of an IT company it is not as simple as this, not least because it does not necessarily need to be a person. In one respect it will include the owners of a computer or a system. Thus, for example, if I own a laptop then I am entitled to decide who is able to access it. At the other end of the spectrum will be companies that operate multi-level computer systems. The company itself (probably through a senior member of staff but more likely through procedures and practices) will decide who has access to the system and therefore will be the person within limb (a).

The second limb is that where a person does not fall within limb (a) then they are acting in an unauthorised way where he does not have the consent of that person. Going back to the example of my laptop, a person who comes into my study and switches it on will fall within this definition. She is not the person who decides access (limb a) and she will know that she is not authorised to do so without my express permission. Similarly in a company, people will be aware whether they are allowed to access equipment.

Where issues have become complicated is where the purpose of the access is called into question. This is particularly problematic with so-called 'internals', i.e. those who are employed to access a system but for specific purposes. One of the key cases in this area is *DPP v Bignall* [1998] 1 Cr App R 1 which concerned police access to the Police National Computer (PNC). The two appellants were serving police officers of the Metropolitan Police. Following

the breakup of an earlier marriage, a dispute arose concerning the ownership of cars held by the new partner of the first appellant's former wife. On
six occasions the appellants directed police operators access the PNC and
information about the car registration numbers and ownership details but the
information was used for personal rather than police use.

Counsel put two diametrically opposed submissions forward. Counsel for
the Crown argued that whilst a police officer is authorised to gain access to
the PNC, the access is limited by the data controller (the Commissioner of the
Metropolitan Police) to access required for police purposes. Counsel for the
defendants argued the contrary and stated that the purpose of the CMA 1990
(under which they were charged) concerned the integrity of the computer
system and not the information on it. Therefore, if they were authorised to
access the computer then it was an authorised access irrespective of whether
they were authorised to access the specific data.

The Divisional Court examined s.17(5), CMA 1990 which states that access
is unauthorised, *inter alia*, where a person is not entitled to control, or has no
consent to, access *of the kind in question*. Astill J concluded that the wording
'kind in question' meant it was a general rather than specific question and
concluded 'the respondents had authority to access even though they did
not do so for an authorised purpose' (at 12). The court held that this did not
create a lacuna because a police officer who gains access for improper purposes would be subject to disciplinary action and/or action under the *Data
Protection Act 1984* (at that time).

Smith criticised the decision believing that it was doubtful that there was
authority to access the computer system. 'If I give you permission to enter
my study for the purpose of reading my books, your entering to drink my
sherry would surely be an unauthorised "access" to the room as well as to
the sherry' (Smith, 1998:54). Of course the counter-argument to this is these
are very different forms of access. If I said you could gain access to my study
to read book X but you know that I also have book Y in my study, could
it truly be said that you have unauthorised access to my study if you read
book Y? Certainly it is plausible but it would seem somewhat harsh. Smith is
perhaps on stronger grounds when he believes that the court were influenced
by the fact that the *Data Protection Act 1998* criminalised improper access (to
be discussed below) but, as Smith notes, the two Acts are for very different
purposes.

The reasoning in *Bignall* was questioned in *R v Bow Street Metropolitan
Stipendiary Magistrate, ex parte Government of the USA* [2000] 2 AC 216.
This was an extradition case, but in most extradition cases the principle of
dual criminality applies. This principle means that extradition will only occur
where the resident has been charged with an offence that is criminal in both
the country that he is resident of and the country seeking extradition. The
USA sought extradition of the suspect on the basis of conspiracies to commit
fraud against American Express. A third-party (Ojomo) was an employee of

American Express where she was employed as an analyst. She was given the technical access to any account although she was only supposed to access those records of customers who had been assigned to her. She accessed other records and the allegation was that she then passed these details to, amongst others, the suspect who used the information to defraud American Express of US$ 1 million.

The basis of the charges was, in essence, that the suspect conspired with Ojomo for her to gain unauthorised access to the American Express computer system, which would be an offence contrary to the CMA 1990. The District Judge hearing the extradition requests refused the application of two out of three charges because he felt bound by the Divisional Court decision in *Bignall*. Applying the reasoning of *Bignall* (above) then Ojomo was entitled to access the American Express computer system meaning that although she accessed records that she was not authorised to, the actual access to the system was lawful and therefore there would be no liability under the CMA 1990 meaning the principle of dual criminality would also fail.

The matter eventually reached the House of Lords because the USA sought to judicially review the decision of the District Judge not to extradite on those charges (which, according to international treaties, would mean the suspect could not be tried on those offences but only on the third charge where extradition was authorised) and the suspect also sought to appeal the decision to extradite him at all. Lord Hobhouse gave the sole speech in the House and he held that the Divisional Court erred in *Bignall*. His Lordship held that the CMA 1990 was 'concerned with authority to access the actual data involved' and not the general principle of accessing the system ([2000] 2 AC 216 at 225). The logic underlining this is that s.17(5)

> identifies the two ways in which authority may be acquired – by being oneself the person entitled to authorise and by being a person who has been authorised by a person entitled to authorise. It also makes clear that the authority must relate not simply to the data or program but also to the actual kind of access secured.
>
> (at 224)

The implication of this was that the person who is entitled to authorise access can do so in a way that limits the access. For example, a chief constable could decide that access can only be for police purposes. Thus the question is not whether a person was authorised to access a computer system but rather whether he was authorised to access the particular data he sought access to.

Lord Hobhouse believed that the eventual decision in *Bignall* was correct but based on false logic. The reasoning behind this is that the operators accessed the system correctly – they were not authorised to access the system unless asked to do so by a police officer, and thus the police officers could not be culpable of the crime through complicity. However, Smith disagrees. Whilst it is true to state that the operators accessed the system properly (when asked by a police officer) there is no evidence to suggest that they knew or believed what the true purpose of the request was. Accordingly, Smith believes that it would be more appropriate to construe the operators as innocent agents (Smith, 1999:971). Innocent agents are people who, whilst undertaking the *actus reus* of a crime, do not have the *mens rea* because they do not know the circumstances of the crime (Ormerod, 2011:189). Where the *actus reus* takes place via an innocent agent then the participant whose activity is most proximate to the cause will be deemed to be the principal offender. Applying it to this case, Smith is arguing that the police operators were innocent agents because they did not know the improper circumstances of the request and thus, applying the rule in *ex parte USA*, the defendants should have been convicted as they caused the PNC to be accessed for an improper purpose. The logic of Smith is cogent and it is submitted that Lord Hobhouse was wrong: *Bignall* was wrongly decided but also its decision was ultimately wrong too.

A number of police officers have been convicted for accessing the PNC for personal reasons because chief constables have made clear that they are not authorised to use it for those purposes[1] but it is less than clear that this rule applies to all situations and it perhaps relates to what controls have been put in place. For example, Mahomet – an employee of BT – was acquitted for sending ex-directory telephone numbers to a journalist. Mahomet argued he was doing this to evidence a security flaw but this would not provide a defence under the CMA 1990 and, indeed, would arguably demonstrate the *mens rea* for s.1 as it would show that he knows the act was unauthorised. The District Judge held that there was no case to answer because he was entitled to access the records that he had in fact accessed. This differs from the employee Ojomo in the *ex parte USA* case where it was clear that she accessed records she was not authorised to access. That said, the *Mahomet* case precedes the judgment in *ex part USA* and it is quite possible the District Judge would reach a different decision today. According to Lord Hobhouse, access can be for a particular purpose. Assuming that BT permitted access to service-related issues it is quite likely that accessing the system so that the details can be passed to a journalist would fall within this ruling, meaning that the access was not, in fact, authorised. However, there does appear to remain a lack of clarity over what 'authorisation' means. It also potentially widens the use of the CMA 1990 into areas that would ordinarily be dealt with by the civil law. Setting aside police officers for a moment – where the offence of misconduct in a public office would probably criminalise unlawful access irrespective of whether it amounted to an infringement of the CMA 1990 – the ruling of Lord Hobhouse means that if an employee provides

---

1    A partial list can be found here: www.computerevidence.co.uk/Cases/CMA.htm.

restrictions on what can be accessed then exceeding these limits becomes an offence punishable by up to two years' imprisonment (the sentence imposed by s.1). It will be remembered from Chapter 3 that there is no requirement for the user to do anything other than access the system and, accordingly, merely looking at records they are not authorised to examine would be culpable. Is this really something that should be dealt with by the criminal law? It would seem a classic example of when employment law and/or civil law should be used. Whilst the notion of criminalising invasions of privacy was discussed in Chapter 3 this was in the context of a third-party accessing the system. Different issues are arguably raised by internals and it must be questioned whether the use of the criminal law is appropriate. If such conduct was exempted from s.1 (for example, by returning to the logic of *Bignall*), there would still be liability where data was destroyed or disclosed but the actual access would not be culpable.

### Destroying data

As noted above, authorisation links the various types of conduct. It is now necessary to consider what the liability would be for the data issues discussed at the beginning of the chapter. The first of these is the destruction of data.

Where a third-party has accessed the system and destroyed the data – either through personally deleting files or through the deployment of malware – then the liability discussed in Chapter 3 would apply. The destruction of data undoubtedly impairs the system and so it would amount to an offence contrary to s.3, CMA 1990. Is there other liability?

It will be remembered from the previous chapter that the *Criminal Damage Act 1971* has been used in respect of the deletion of data (see, most notably, *Cox v Riley* (1986) 83 Cr App R 54 and *R v Whiteley* (1991) 93 Cr App R 25). In principle this would appear an easier offence to use. Whilst the CMA 1990 requires proof that a person undertook an act that was unauthorised (and that he knew it was unauthorised) the offence under s.1, CDA 1971 is much simpler. All that is required is that damage is intentionally or recklessly caused to property belonging to another without lawful excuse (s.1(1), CDA 1971).

It will be remembered that the Law Commission had recommended that the CDA 1971 should not be used in hacking cases and the CMA 1990 – which was proceeding through Parliament during the hearing of *Whiteley* – incorporated this belief into the law. Section 3(6), CMA 1990 (as initially drafted) included a provision that for the purposes of the CDA 1971 'a modification of the contents of a computer shall not be regarded as damaging any computer or computer storage medium unless its effect on that computer or computer storage medium impairs its physical condition'. This has the effect of, in essence, statutorily overruling *Whiteley* because the court specifically held there that the physical condition of the storage device was not affected: 'the computers and the discs cannot be damaged by the sort of interference perpetrated by the defendant' ((1991) 93 Cr App R 25 at 27). That being the case then s3(6) would now preclude the use of the CDA 1971.

As noted in Chapter 3, the entirety of s.3 was replaced by the PJA 2006 and s.3(6) was not replicated in the new s.3 but was transferred to the CDA 1971 itself. Schedule 14, paragraph 2 of the PJA 2006 inserts a new s.10(5) into the CDA 1971 which uses the same wording of s.3(6). Accordingly, the defendant in *Whiteley* could not now be convicted under the CDA 1971. That is not to say that there would be no liability of course. A person doing the same actions would now be caught by the (revised) s.3, CMA 1990. Interestingly, the PJA 2006 reforms which included recklessness mean that s.3, CMA 1990 now has a similar *mens rea* requirement to the CDA 1971 (which has always permitted recklessness) although it will be remembered this inclusion was controversial.

It would seem, therefore, that the destruction of data is now primarily based within the CMA 1990. Article 4 of the Cybercrime Convention requires that member states 'take the necessary measures to ensure that the intentional deletion, damaging, deterioration, alteration, suppression or rendering inaccessible of computer data' is punished as a criminal offence. Section 3, CMA 1990 probably covers this requirement although it is notable that Article 4 is based on the premise of doing something 'without right' rather than without authorisation as the CMA 1990 requires. 'Without right' is arguably closer to the provisions of the CDA 1971 and whilst *ex parte USA* did clarify what is meant by 'without authorisation' there is still a degree of uncertainty. It would be preferable to use a concept such as 'without right' as this is simpler to define and apply. The terms of Article 4 (deletion, damaging, deterioration, alteration and suppression) will undoubtedly all be covered by the term 'impairment' given the expansive way that this is likely to be construed by the courts.

### Access or disclosing

The next two forms of behaviour are arguably best considered together. This is partly because access has been considered already in the most part (both in Chapter 3 and in the analysis of 'authorised' at the beginning of this chapter). Whilst third-parties may inappropriately access a system simply to look around, this will ordinarily be as a hacker and the discussion in Chapter 3 applies. Where it is an internal person then, save where they are seeking to damage the data, it is perhaps more likely that they would wish to access the data in order to inappropriately disclose the data to a third-party. Whilst some of the liability will be based on the CMA 1990 (through the s.1 access offence) this does not necessarily capture the entirety of the behaviour and alternative liability can be found.

## Data Protection Act 1998

Given that we are focusing on data, it may be thought that offences under the *Data Protection Act 1998* (DPA 1998) would be a natural starting point. The DPA owes its origins to European law (Walden, 2007:102) and this continues to influence the way in which the law must operate. The growth of the internet has meant that the amount of personal data that is now available is considerable. Companies and public bodies are almost universally requiring us to conduct transactions on the internet meaning that our digital presence is increasingly rapidly. The same is true of public records including tax and health details. Such data has significant commercial value (as it allows companies to profile potential customers) and it is perhaps not surprising therefore that there have been incidents of people seeking to access and improperly disclose such data.

At the heart of the DPA 1998 is the concepts of 'data' and 'personal data' which are defined accordingly:

'data' means information which

(a) is being processed by means of equipment operating automatically in response to instructions given for that purpose,

(b) is recorded with the intention that it should be processed by means of such equipment,

(c) is recorded as part of a relevant filing system or with the intention that it should form part of a relevant filing system,

(d) does not fall within paragraph (a), (b) or (c) but forms part of an accessible record as defined by section 68 [which governs certain public records],

(e) is recorded information held by a public authority and does not fall within paragraphs (a) to (d).

'personal data' means data which relate to a living individual who can be identified

(a) from those data, or

(b) from those data and other information which is in the possession of, or is likely to come into possession of, the data controller,

and includes any expression of opinion about the individual and any indication of the intentions of the data controller or any other person in respect of the individual.

(s.1(1), DPA 1998)

Thus it can be seen that it is an extremely wide definition. Certainly the definition of 'personal data' would include things as simple as a person's name and address (see, for example, *R v Rooney* [2006] EWCA Crim 1841 and *Corporate Officer of the House of Commons v Information Commissioner* [2008] EWHC 1084 (Admin) at [41]) but it would equally include employment data, health data, insurance data, banking details, etc. However, the over-arching test that needs to be employed is whether it is *personal* and therefore it should fall within their private or family life, home, correspondence or working life. Where a person cannot be identified then it would not be personal data as s.1(1) is very clear that it must relate to an individual who can be *identified*. Similarly, it is clear that the data protection applies only to the living and thus data protection laws cease to apply post-mortem although alternative civil actions could potentially be pursued by the estate (where, for example, a disclosure amounts to a breach of confidence).

Whilst much of the DPA 1998 is civil in operation and is designed to ensure that there are safeguards in the manner in which it is processed (for a general overview see Carey, 2009), there are also a number of offences created under the Act. Some are in respect of inappropriate processing of data (see, for example, s.54, DPA 1998) but these do not concern us. The more relevant to us are the offences contained in s.55, DPA 1998.

The basic elements of the offence are contained in subsection (1) which states:

> A person must not knowingly or recklessly, without the consent of the data controller
>
> (a) obtain or disclose personal data or the information contained in personal data, or
> (b) procure the disclosure to another person of the information contained in personal data.

There are then different ways of committing this offence. The simple offence is committed under s.55(3) which states that a person who breaches s.55(1) commits an offence. A person who sells the information is guilty under s.55(4) if he obtains the information in contravention of s.55(1). A person can also be guilty of offering to sell the data if:

(a) he has obtained the information in contravention of subsection (1), or
(b) he subsequently obtains the data in contravention of that subsection (s.55(5)).

Advertising the data for sale constitutes an offence under s.55(5) (see s.55(6)). It is interesting to note that the Act differentiates between the disclosure of and the selling of information, and presumably this should be reflected in sentencing although, as will be seen, the penalty for these offences cannot be considered anything other than lenient.

Section 55(1) is therefore the more important provision. The *actus reus* of the offence would seem to be:

- Obtaining or disclosing personal data (or the information contained in the data) without the permission of the data controller.
- Procuring the disclosure to another person of the information contained in the personal data.
- The above acts must be without the permission of the data controller.

The terms 'obtains' and 'discloses' should be given their natural meaning and the definition of personal data has already been noted. The term 'procuring' is one that is well known to the criminal law and it is intended to cover situations where third-parties are involved. Let us take an example:

> A works in a credit-control agency in their computer department. B needs to know the address of V (a customer of that agency) and he arranges with C, a friend of both him and A, to obtain the information for him by asking A to send it to B.

In this instance A will disclose the data (to B) but C, by asking A to disclose the information, will procure that disclosure. Thus she will be liable under s.55 even though A is the one who has access to the data and will ultimately be disclosing the data.

Whether the data controller gives permission will be a question of fact on each case. The term 'data controller' is defined 'as a person who (either alone or jointly or in common with other persons) determines the purposes for which and the manner in which any personal data are, or are to be, processed' (s.1(1), DPA 1998). In other words the controller is the person who controls how the data should be managed, for what purposes and who can be involved. Presumably it is necessary for the data controller to know the circumstances of the obtaining or disclosing for permission to be effective. Let us consider two examples:

> D is employed in the customer services team of a company. He, and other employees, are told to access the computerised records regularly to identify the last item a customer has purchased and/or identify patterns of purchases. They should then pass on this information to a member of the sales team.

> D is employed in the same capacity above. D realises that V has recently purchased a number of specialist tools. He contacts Y who runs a competing business and recommends that he contacts V to offer a particular set of tools. They agree that if V purchases them, D will be given a job.

D undoubtedly has permission to access the computerised records and pass on that information to another. However, in the second example it is unlikely that if the employer knew that D was going to pass on the information to a rival that they would give permission for this to happen. Does that mean that it is without authority? Obviously if there is something in the employment manual that prevents disclosure to someone outside of the company then the answer must be 'yes'. What if there is no express instruction? It has been held in other contexts that if a person would not grant permission if they knew the true purpose of their act then this negates permission (*R v Jones and Smith* [1976] 1 WLR 672, a case concerning burglary). It is not yet known whether the same rule would apply here and it is for this reason that most companies will have explicit rules on the dissemination of data.

The *mens rea* of the offence is to intentionally or recklessly undertake the *actus reus*. It would have made more sense if the *mens rea* was addressed to the issue of consent but the syntax of the section does not appear to suggest that this is the case. Thus the intention or recklessness would also be addressed to the issue of whether data was obtained (which may be more difficult to envisage) or disclosed (which is perhaps easier to understand; for example, it could be that a person recklessly leaves sensitive data in a public place or forgets to encrypt the information online).

The main difficulty with s.55, DPA 1998 is the penalty. The maximum penalty for an offence under s.55 is a fine. It must be seriously questioned whether this is sufficient penalty for a disclosure offence given that the consequences of disclosing confidential data can be significant (as it could leave the victim open to other forms of cybercrime). The *Criminal Justice and Immigration Act 2008* (CJIA 2008) introduced a reserved power to the Secretary of State to increase the penalty to two years' imprisonment (s.77, CJIA 2008) but this has never been implemented and currently there are no plans to do so. At the very least it is submitted that it would be appropriate to introduce this penalty in respect of those who sell the data. The DPA 1998 specifically considers the commercial exploitation of data and this should be reflected by an appropriate penalty. A financial penalty does not provide any deterrence to selling information and thus persons who have access to data may be prepared to 'chance' selling the data given that there is no potential loss of liberty under the DPA 1998.

The lack of appropriate penalties has led the courts to consider alternative offences to tackle those who unlawfully disclose data and this is particularly true where the person who inappropriately discloses the data is a public official.

### Misconduct in a public office

Another offence that is not specifically categorised as a cybercrime but which, as will be seen, is relevant to cybercrime, is the common law offence of misconduct in a public office. Recent years have seen the issue of misconduct become relevant to issues relating to cybercrime. The existence of phone hacking by *News of the World* journalists led to the establishment of *Operation Weeting* and information provided to that led to two spin-offs, *Operation*

*Elveden* (which looked at corruption) and *Operation Tuleta* (which concerned computer hacking). *Operation Elveden* is relevant here because some of the allegations were that the police (and others) would disclose confidential information to journalists and this could include information that was gathered by accessing relevant computer systems. At the time of writing, several suspects have been charged with misconduct in a public office or conspiracy to do the same but verdicts have not yet been returned and so no more will be said about that specific operation, but it does demonstrate the importance of the offence.

The offence of misconduct in a public office is a creature of the common law. It covers a wide form of behaviour but, as will be seen, it applies to the inappropriate access and disclosure of data by those operating computer systems. It is considered a serious offence and in *R v Keyte* [1998] 2 Cr App R (S) 165 the Court of Appeal noted its applicability to this sort of behaviour and was clear about its importance: 'the integrity of the police national computer is of absolutely vital importance and it goes without saying that the public must have faith and confidence in it and a belief that information relating to them will not be released by police officers for ulterior motive' (at 166 per Swinton Thomas LJ). It is submitted that these comments apply equally to any database held by a public body.

The elements of the crime of misconduct in a public office were discussed, albeit reluctantly, by the Court of Appeal in *Attorney-General's Reference (No 3 of 2003)* [2005] QB 73. The Court noted, with approval, the 'great variety of circumstances in which the offence of misconduct in a public office may be charged' (at 90). They noted that there were essential elements however, which include the fact that the defendant must be a 'public officer acting as such' (ibid.), something discussed below. After considering the authorities the Court concluded that the requirements were:

1. A public officer acting as such,
2. wilfully neglects to perform his duty and/or wilfully misconducts himself,
3. to such a degree as to amount to an abuse of the public's trust in the office holder, and
4. without reasonable excuse or justification.

([2005] QB 73 at 91)

The threshold of the offence is important and the Court were keen to emphasise step (3), that it must abuse the public trust, with the Court noting that 'a mistake, even a serious one, will not suffice' (at 90).

Whilst many of the cases have concerned police officers who hold a public office – that of the office of constable – the offence has a much wider reach. Within the civil law (and the tort of misfeasance in a public office is inextricably linked with the crime of misconduct in a public office) it was said that a public officer was 'every one [sic] who is appointed to discharge a public duty, and receives a compensation in whatever shape, whether from the Crown or otherwise' (*Henly v The Mayor and Burgess of Lyme* (1828) 5 Bing 92 at 1001 per Best CJ). This is of interest because it does not talk about an office but rather about someone who is appointed to discharge a public duty and implicit within this is the notion that they need not be an office holder. The closing words of the quote are also important where the Chief Justice is stating that the compensation (salary) can be from the Crown or otherwise, implicitly covering other public bodies.

The reasoning in *Henly* was adopted by the Court of Appeal in *R v Bowden* [1996] 1 WLR 98 where the defendant was a middle-ranking council employee who was accused of ensuring that home improvements were made to a house occupied by a friend of his even though they were not required. There was no doubt that the appellant was employed rather than holding an office *per se* but the Court of Appeal was clear that the offence of misconduct in a public office applied to his case.

The offence has been used successfully in a number of contexts, including DVLA employees (*R v Dickinson* [2004] EWCA Crim 3525), civilian employees of the police (*R v Iqbal* [2008] EWCA Crim 2066 and *R v Gallagher* [2010] EWCA Crim 3201) and nurses employed by the Prison Service (*R v Cosford* [2013] 3 WLR 1064). Thus the potential ambit of this offence is extremely wide. Indeed in *R v Cosford*, albeit in comments that must surely be *in dicta*, it was said that the court did not differentiate between a private prison and a publicly owned prison (at 1075). The basis of this statement is that the essence of the duty is to the public and not who the employer of the person is. A person working in a private prison still owes duties to the public (to keep prisoners incarcerated according to the rules, to uphold public safety, to protect prisoners, etc.) and this must be true of some other privatised state functions.

A notable feature of the offence is that it is based on misconduct. Accordingly it is not necessary to prove that a person has acted illegally, but merely done something that amounts to misconduct that undermines the public's trust in the holding of the office. Given the importance of the integrity of the computer system (as highlighted by Swinton Thomas LJ in *Keyte*) this would include inappropriate access to a computer system, especially where there has been the disclosure of information that should remain confidential (as this would be an offence under either the CMA 1990 or the DPA 1998). By focusing not on the authorisation (or lack thereof) of the access but rather whether it constituted misconduct it means that the debate about whether asking a third-party (who is authorised to access the system) to look at data constitutes an offence under the CMA 1990 becomes irrelevant. A good example of this is *R v O'Leary* [2007] 2 Cr App R(S) 51 where a serving police officer from Merseyside police accessed the computer system for inappropriate reasons but on other occasions asked others to access it (at 318). He was found culpable of both types of access and it was not necessary to differentiate between them.

The courts treat inappropriate disclosure that amounts to misconduct in a public office very seriously. In *Attorney-General's Reference (No 1 of 2007)* [2007] 2 Cr App R (S) 86 the then Lord Chief Justice warned '[i]t must be quite clear to police officers that if they commit this offence [by accessing a computer] they risk dire consequences' (at 552). Certainly the sentences that have been imposed by the courts have been significantly tougher than what could be expected under the CMA 1990 (in *Keyte* a sentence of two years' imprisonment was imposed after a plea of guilty, the circumstances being that a police officer disclosed details of motor vehicle checks to a private investigator). Where the access and disclosure leads to the hampering of police operations, significantly higher sentences will be imposed, see most notably *Attorney-General's Reference (No 30 of 2010)* [2011] 1 Cr App R (S) 16 where the disclosure of information over a five-year period to a drug dealer led to the defendant, a serving police officer, having his sentence increased to six years' imprisonment).

The fact that the offence is easier to prove than the CMA 1990 and attracts a more serious punishment means that this offence, whilst a relic of history, continues to have an important role to play in respect of even modern crimes using new technologies. Of course some will question whether this is just. Why should a person who discloses data obtained from a public database be at the risk of a much more significant punishment than someone who discloses data from a private database (where, it will be remembered from the preceding section, the punishment under the DPA 1998 is light). It is undoubtedly because, in the words of Swinton Thomas LJ, it goes to the heart of the trust that the public has in the integrity of its systems. That said, given the nature of many private databases it can be argued that the impact on a victim of any disclosure is likely to be equally severe and this perhaps serves as a further question mark over whether the CMA 1990 is in need of further reform (in that a tougher CMA 1990 could perhaps more appropriately deal with such matters).

## Intercepting data

The final issue to consider is that of intercepting data. This is an issue that has attracted some attention in recent years, partly because of the allegations levelled against certain tabloid newspapers, most notably the (now defunct) *News of the World* and the *Daily Mirror*. The allegations made against those papers were that mobile telephones had been 'hacked', allowing journalists to listen to voice messages left for users. However, interception is not restricted to this and can include the interception of data, including emails. These are issues that need to be discussed.

What will not be discussed here is the interception of data by government agencies. Whilst this is undoubtedly controversial, this is a book about cyber-*crime* and not simply a book on legal issues relating to the internet. This is not to undermine some of the legitimate questions that arise over whether there is too much interception but rather it is designed to reflect the reality of the book which is examining criminal conduct. Similarly therefore there will not be a discussion of the circumstances under which the state can intercept data, and whether this is effective (and reference should be made elsewhere: e.g. Walden, 2007, and for an interesting contemporary discussion see Stratford and Johnston, 2014).

## Convention on Cybercrime

The Interception of data is an issue that is specifically addressed by the Cybercrime Convention. Article 3 of the Convention states:

> Each party shall adopt such legislative and other measures as may be necessary to establish as criminal offences under its domestic law, when committed intentionally, the interception without right, made by technical means, of non-public transmissions of computer data to, from or within a computer system, including electromagnetic emissions from a computer system carrying such computer data. A party may require that the offence be committed with dishonest intent, or in relation to a computer system that is connected to another computer system.

Whilst Article 3 does not have any sub-clauses it is a complicated provision with a lot of detail packed into its provisions. It is clear that the overall purpose of Article 3 is to protect the privacy of communications (Clough, 2010:137) and the wording should be read in this context.

The wording of Article 3 is very particular. Reference to 'non-public transmissions' rather than a public or private network is meant to indicate that it is the message that is to be protected and not the method by which it is sent. Thus a private message that is sent over either a public or private network would be protected but a public message (e.g. a communication that was intended for all to see such as a Twitter feed without restriction) would not come within Article 3. This reinforces the fact that it is privacy that is being inherently protected.

'By technical means' is relatively self-explanatory and it is deliberately wide so as to include technological advancements. It is difficult to conceive how there could be an interception of computer data without technical means as manual actions would probably refer to illegal or inappropriate access rather than interception. Article 3 can be limited so as to ensure that it bites only when it is an intercept from one computer system to another. The objective of this limitation would be to exclude interceptions in private networks if a state so wished. Certainly there is an argument that, for example, a company intercepting email on its own private server is perhaps a less serious breach of privacy than intercepting messages that are sent over the internet (something reflected in domestic law by the lawful business practice regulations discussed below).

In terms of a fault element it is notable that Article 3 relates to interceptions that take place 'without right' which acknowledges that there will be circumstances in which it will be appropriate for an interception to take place (including for legitimate law enforcement purposes). Signatory states are also allowed to restrict the criminal offence to circumstances where there is a dishonest intent.

## Regulation of Investigatory Powers Act 2000

The principal piece of legislation that we need to be concerned with is the *Regulation of Investigatory Powers Act 2000* (RIPA 2000). This is an Act that is not particularly liked (Reid and Ryder, 2001) and arguably does not do what its short-title suggests. It does not regulate *per se* covert surveillance as it focuses (apart from the issue of interceptions) on public authorities, and even then it does not realistically provide any appropriate remedy where these powers are exceeded.

However, Part I of RIPA 2000 differs from the rest of the Act in that it applies to both public and private bodies. Section 1, RIPA 2000 creates two offences of interception:

(1) It shall be an offence for a person intentionally and without lawful authority to intercept in any place in the United Kingdom, any communication in the course of its transmission by means of

(a) a public postal service; or
(b) a public telecommunications system.

(2) It shall be an offence for a person

(a) intentionally and without lawful authority, and
(b) otherwise in the circumstances in which his conduct is excluded by subsection (6) from criminal liability under this subsection,

to intercept, at any place in the United Kingdom, any communication in the course of its transmission by means of a private telecommunications system.

The difference between a public and private communication system is not easily identified (Walden, 2007:186–187). However, for our purposes we can deal with this relatively simply. The two systems are defined in s.2(1), RIPA 2000. For our purposes a public telecommunications system is a service that uses services that are used in part by the public. This would include therefore the telephone network, fibre-optic data cables (for ultra-fast broadband), etc. Realistically for our purposes it will involve any access to the internet through an ISP, and there is a strong argument that the internet itself is a public communications network. A private network is one that is independent of a public communications network and would therefore have to be a completely stand-alone intranet system that does not use any part of the public communications network. As Walden has noted, the reality is that this would be somewhat rare (Walden, 2007:187).

The fact that both public and private communication systems are covered means that the essential essence of Part I, RIPA 2000 is, as with Article 3 of the Cybercrime Convention, to safeguard the privacy of communications. That said, the offences under s.1 would seem to be wider than those contained in Article 3 although it has been noted already that this is not unusual because treaties and conventions usually prescribe *minimum* levels of action and therefore there is nothing to stop domestic countries going further. As will be seen, however, the threshold for criminality is higher when it is a private telecommunications network rather than a public one.

## Interception

The key term to be defined is that of interception. Section 2(2) defines this as:

> a person intercepts a communication in the course of its transmission by means of a telecommunication system if, and only if, he
>
> (a) so modifies or interferes with the system, or its operation,
> (b) so monitors transmissions made by means of the system, or
> (c) so monitors transmissions made by wireless telegraphy to or from apparatus comprised in the system,
>
> as to make some or all of the contents of the communication available, while being transmitted, to a person other than the sender or intended recipient of the communication.

There are a number of points that must be made here. The first is that it should be noted that the interception must take place *in the course of its transmission* and this has caused some difficulties that will be discussed momentarily. The other point to note is that the essential issue with interception is that it makes the *contents* of the communication available. Thus the offences within s.1 do not seek to address the obtaining of communication data or IP address tracking (which, in essence, allows access to data concerning who sent the message, who received it and which websites were used, etc.), something that is covered elsewhere in RIPA in the context of law enforcement.

The technical processes of how a communication is intercepted (i.e. that covered under s.2(2)(a)–(c)) is less important than the consequences. The section is written broadly and thus it is clear that most forms of interception would be applicable. An example of (a) would be the telephone hacking system discussed below whereby a person tricked the voicemail system into believing that they were the user. Other obvious examples would be where, due to a program or through entering a new 'rule' into a computer system, emails are diverted into a location where they can be read.

### 'Is being transmitted'

Whilst a message must be intercepted, it must be intercepted whilst it is being transmitted. Whilst this may seem obvious it is not. In the context of telephones this means, for example, that listening to one side of a conversation via a listening device is not an interception (s.3(1), *Regulation of Investigatory Powers Act 2000*) because the communication – the voice – has already reached its recipient and therefore is not in the course of being transmitted.

It is perhaps more difficult in respect of computing and arguably the key authority on the meaning of interception in the course of transmission is *R (on the application of NTL) v Crown Court at Ipswich* [2003] QB 131. This is a slightly unusual case in that it concerned the production of material. The applicants – an ISP – had configured their email system (as many did) to automatically store messages on their servers. These were deleted shortly after being read but remained in the store until they were read. The police, who were investigating a complex fraud, sought to have these emails disclosed and in the interim made an order under s.9, *Police and Criminal Evidence Act 1984* requiring NTL to store the messages and not delete them. The applicants sought to discharge this notice and permission to delete the messages and they contended, in part, that by complying with the notice they would be committing an offence under s.1, RIPA 2000 as it would amount to an unlawful intercept.

An interception would occur because it was not possible to prevent the emails from being automatically deleted. Thus the only way that the material could be stored was if each email was automatically duplicated and that copy was sent to a storage area. Would this copying amount to an interception? The answer would seem to be 'yes' because s.2(7), RIPA 2000 extends the meaning of 'is being transmitted' to specifically include those situations where it is waiting in a store area pending it being accessed by the user. This would be a classic example of how web-based email services are used. Unless you have an email service that is 'always on' most people will access email by occasionally logging on to their service. Any emails that have been delivered wait in the 'box' until requested by the user (by selecting the message to read or to pull the messages down to the email client). Given the wording of s.2(7) this must mean that any accessing of those stored messages before they were read could be an interception, something confirmed by s.2(8) which states that an interception includes where a message is 'diverted or recorded so as to be available to a person subsequently' which is exactly what NTL were required to do. Thus NTL (a limited company and therefore a legal personality for the purposes of the criminal law) would have been guilty of an offence under s.1, RIPA 2000.

The Divisional Court decided that Parliament could not have intended to produce a section that would frustrate the objectives of the procedure under PACE 1984. This is not an unusual statement from the courts where they are invariably faced with conflicting pieces of legislation that Parliament forgot or otherwise decided to leave unreconciled. The Lord Chief Justice, presiding, held that the order under PACE 1984 was such as to provide lawful justification for what NTL were being asked to do and therefore any interception did not take place 'without lawful authority' (see [2003] QB 131 at 136).

Whilst this decision is pragmatically sensible it is somewhat unimpressive as a piece of law and it has been noted that the approach taken by the courts was an 'expedient' way of dealing with the matter rather than being one that was literally correct (Ormerod, 2002:973). However, it is a useful case in that it demonstrates unequivocally that duplicating a stored communication or re-routing the path of a communication would amount to an interception and thus be illegal if it occurs without lawful authority.

The correctness of this approach was challenged in respect of telephony in the case of *R v Coulson et al.* [2014] EWCA Crim 1119 which concerned preliminary rulings in respect of the phone hacking trial that ultimately took place during 2014. The circumstances of the case (or at least the parts relevant here) were that it was possible to access a user's voicemail using trickery. If a person was diverted to the voicemail service (because, for example, the caller was busy or did not answer) then by pressing a combination of keys (including a default PIN code) it was possible to access the voicemail service remotely and not just from the user's telephone. It was alleged that a number of journalists had done this (and indeed four pleaded guilty to charges relating to unlawful interception in respect of the phone messages) and a number of editors were accused of conspiracy to intercept messages, the essential allegation being that the editors encouraged the reporters to intercept the voicemail messages.

At a preliminary hearing the defendants raised the question about whether listening to the telephone messages amounted to an interception. Whilst they did not seek to minimise the ruling in *NTL* they argued that for telephones, interception must mean during the call and therefore unless the message was intercepted as the message was being left on the answerphone then this did not amount to an interception. In other words, listening to the message left did not amount to an interception because the transmission had been completed.

The Court of Appeal rejected this suggestion and noted that s.2(7) was not limited in time. There was nothing to suggest that any storage had to be transient or indeed that it could only be listened to once ([2014] 1 WLR 1119 at 1128). There followed a prolonged discussion on EU law because at least one reason for implementing Part I of RIPA 2000 was to comply with EU law (see *Directive 97/66/EC of the European Parliament and of the Council*

*Concerning the Processing of Personal Data and the Protection of Privacy in Telecommunications Sector* (1998) OJ L 24). The Court of Appeal noted, however, that the purpose of the EU legislation was to introduce *minimum* standards and there was no reason why states could not go further ([2014] 1 WLR 1119 at 1133). Thus the Court of Appeal upheld the trial judge's ruling that s.2(7), RIPA 2000 had the effect of applying to messages stored and awaiting delivery to the recipient (in the case of mobile telephones by ringing the voicemail messaging service and in the case of email through accessing it or calling the messages down to the email client) and thus accessing those stored messages amounts to an interception, and thus, if done without lawful authority, an offence under s.1, RIPA 2000.

### Without lawful authority

Both of the offences within s.1 require the interception to be 'without lawful authority'. Whilst the Act purportedly states that it is authorised only if it comes within ss.3 or 4 of RIPA 2000 or if it occurs following a warrant issued under s.5, it has been seen that is not necessarily true. In the *NTL* case discussed above it was decided that 'without lawful authority' would include those situations where other legislation required it.

In this section we will ignore interception by warrant since this is used where the interception is state-sanctioned and it has already been noted that we are not covering that. The main issue, therefore, is when non-warranted interceptions can be lawful.

Section 3(1) renders an interception lawful if both the sender and recipient consent to the interception, and s.3(3) permits interception by the provider of a communications service if it is necessary for the intercept to occur for the operation of that service or to enforce any legal obligation on the provider. Section 3(2) is less relevant to our circumstances as it applies to a public authority who listens with the consent of one of the persons communicating and a surveillance authority has been granted. Section 4 is not relevant to us as it concerns the interception of communications from outside of the country.

It can be seen, therefore, that in respect of public communication systems there are few ways of avoiding criminal liability for an interception. In *R v Coulson et al.* the editors sought to complain that RIPA 2000 does not, unlike the DPA 1998, provide a defence for legitimate journalistic exercises but this was quickly rejected by the Court of Appeal who thought nothing turned on this point ([2014] 1 WLR 1119 at 1135). It is submitted that this must be correct. The privacy of communications systems would seem a greater public interest factor than the possible use of such techniques by the press to expose wrongdoing. In any event, given the particular circumstances of that case it could be questioned whether any such defence would have assisted the editors' case.

What of private telecommunications systems? The same rules apply but there are additional ways of avoiding liability. One is through the *Lawful Business Practices Regulations* which will be discussed momentarily. The second is through an exception to s.1(2) which is introduced by s.1(6), RIPA 2000. This states:

> The circumstances in which a person makes an interception of a communication in the course of its transmission by means of a private telecommunication system are such that his conduct is excluded from criminal liability ... if:
>
> (a) he is a person with a right to control the operation or the use of the system; or
> (b) he has the express or implied consent of such a person to make the interception.

Where s.1(6) applies then an interception without lawful authority becomes a tort (civil wrong) rather than a crime (s.1(3), RIPA 2000). The question then becomes, of course, who has the right to control the operation or use of the private system? The leading authority on this point is *R v Stanford* [2006] 1 WLR 1554. The appellant co-founded a company with another person (and they served as deputy-chairman and chairman respectively). After a dispute the appellant resigned from the board of the company. The company operated its own communication system and a redirect was put on the victim's email system so that all emails sent to, or from, that address were copied to the appellant.

Whilst the appellant had access to the passwords, he claimed that an (unnamed) employee of the company had done the interceptions and that as that person had administrator access he had 'the right to control the operation ... of the system' meaning that any interception was not illegal (although he conceded it would be tortious). The rationale behind this argument was that, in essence, 'control' is like a switch: you are either in complete control or you are not. The difficulty with this approach is that it would mean that a rogue person who has been given such authority would be allowed to authorise anything that he wants without recourse. As the Court of Appeal noted, it was extremely difficult to believe that Parliament ever intended that (at 1560). Granting someone permission to control the system must suggest that there can be limits on the control, meaning the person (or legal entity) that grants control to a person must be able to either expressly or implicitly put limits on that control. In this instance, it is highly unlikely that the company would have said to the controller 'by all means intercept the chairman's emails and pass them onto the deputy-chairman who no longer works for the company'. To argue the contrary would drive a coach and horses through RIPA and, indeed, this was noted by the Court of Appeal who noted that if the legislation did not cover his activities then the 'legislation [would have] failed to achieve its object' (at 1561).

### Lawful business practices

The breadth of RIPA 2000 is extremely wide and this could pose problems for employers. As it applies to private networks it would mean that a company that creates an intranet system that is wholly private (and not connected to the internet) could not intercept communications if they so wished even though they created and administer the system. In addition, many employers will provide employees with an email address that will identify the company. The company may have a legitimate desire to ensure that these addresses are not used inappropriately. If they are granted by work and for work purposes, should they not be entitled to look at the contents since the company owns them? Let us take two examples:

> X works for Megabucks plc, a large bank, as a financial trader. To assure themselves that financial compliance rules are being followed all emails sent from X's work account to other people within the organisation are automatically directed to the compliance unit.

> Y works for Pile 'em High Ltd, a large retail organisation. Z, a fraud manager employed by the company, has legitimate reason to believe that Y is passing commercially sensitive information to a rival company. Z arranges access to the email account of Y to view the content of messages sent to or from Y's work email address.

In both of these instances there would seem *prima facie* to be a legitimate reason for the employer accessing the emails of their staff. It is not immediately clear that any of the exceptions contained within RIPA 2000 would apply to these situations which would render the actions of the companies illegal. However, the government recognised that there may be need for businesses to legitimately intercept communications for work purposes and so introduced the *Telecommunications (Lawful Business Practice) (Interception of Communications) Regulations 2000* (SI 2000/2699) which were designed to provide a further limited exception.

Regulation 3(1) states that an interception is authorised for the purposes of s.1(5), RIPA 2000 if it is with the consent of the system controllers and is for a legitimate purpose, namely:

(a) Monitoring or keeping a record of communications for a specific purpose (including complying with regulatory practices, quality assurance procedures, investigating inappropriate access to the system or the effective operation of the system).

(b) Monitoring the communications to see whether they are relevant to the business.
(c) Monitoring communications made to a confidential counselling or support telephony service.

However, the interception is only lawful if certain procedural steps are taken:

(a) The interception is solely for the purpose of monitoring (or where appropriate) keeping record of communications relevant to the system controller's business.
(b) The telecommunication system in question is provided for use wholly or partly in connection with that business.
(c) The system controller has made all reasonable efforts to inform every person who may use the telecommunication system in question that communications transmitted ... may be intercepted, and
(d) [certain procedural requirements that do not concern us].

(reg.3(2))

As these regulations potentially give a wide discretion to employers it would seem that there is a likelihood that they will be constructed tightly. In *A and others v Metropolitan Police Service* (2006, unreported) the Investigatory Powers Tribunal (a special tribunal that was created under RIPA 2000 and which has the powers equivalent to the High Court but which can, if it so wishes, sit in secret) held that the requirement to notify all users of the communication system that they could be recorded should be interpreted strictly. In that case the police commissioner could not show that he had taken reasonable steps to alert all employees and thus his reliance on the regulations was rejected (this was a civil rather than criminal case so the consequences concerned civil liability but the same principle would apply to criminal cases).

## Suggested further reading

Akdeniz, Y., Taylor, N. and Walker, C. 'Bigbrother.gov.uk: State surveillance in the age of information and rights' [2001] *Criminal Law Review* 73–90.
*This was a contemporary analysis of Part 1 of the Regulation of Investigatory Powers Act 2000 and offered an extremely good critique of its provisions.*

Chapter 4 of Clough J. *Principles of Cybercrime* (2010, Cambridge: Cambridge University Press).
*Whilst this is now starting to show its age slightly it remains a very useful overview of the behaviours relating to data attacks and how the law in various countries has sought to tackle them.*

Stratford, J. and Johnson, T. 'The Snowden "revelations": is GCHQ breaking the law?' [2014] *European Human Rights Law Review* 129–141.

*This is a very interesting piece that deals with an important issue, that of state-sanctioned interceptions. This was only touched upon in this chapter and this article provides a useful summary of the issues to allow a comparison to be drawn between national and international interceptions.*

Pages 183–201 of Walden, I. *Computer Crimes and Digital Investigations* (2007, Oxford: Oxford University Press).

*Again, this text is starting to show its age but it was one of the first books to examine in detail many of these provisions, including the Regulation of Investigatory Powers Act 2000.*

# Chapter 5

# Cyberterrorism and cyberwarfare

This chapter differs from the preceding – and indeed subsequent – chapters because it focuses on an issue that is not, strictly speaking, simply a legal issue. Indeed, unlike the other behaviours discussed in this book, there is doubt as to whether it actually exists. This chapter looks at the concepts of cyberterrorism and cyberwarfare, raising issues about whether such matters can exist in cyberspace.

It is intended to explore some of this debate but it will then take it further by presenting a continuum of behaviour. At one end of the continuum is ordinary hacking behaviour that was discussed in the previous chapters. As was noted already, the target of hacking could include companies or government bodies. Is that simple hacking or if it is for a political motivation does that make it something else? If you then go beyond this into sustained attacks on government infrastructure then this could be considered to be comparable to terrorism, but if it is state-sanctioned does this make it terrorism or warfare? Many terrorists will consider themselves to be 'at war' although, strictly speaking, war means something particular under international law. A question has been raised recently about whether warfare in cyberspace is possible. Each of these three aspects will therefore be considered although discussion of the first issue – hacktivism – will be relatively brief since it is based heavily on the preceding chapters.

## Hacktivism

There is undoubtedly a political side to the internet and it has been used as a tool of political resistance since the 1990s (Yar, 2013:46). There are different ways in which it can be used. It can be a way of facilitating offline political action, it can provide a secure communication system and can disseminate information. However, more than this it can be used as a method of conducting political activism. This could be through the creation of a website or through more direct political action.

Perhaps one of the most pointed examples of political activity is that which took place in connection with the so-called 'Arab Spring' where resistance movements across the Middle East took action and toppled a number of governments, most notably in Tunisia, Egypt and Libya. The internet facilitated much of this political activity by facilitating communications between individuals without state knowledge. More than this, however, there were sustained cyber-attacks, including sustained attacks on the infrastructure of governments and official websites, partly by those within the country but some from outside, including the group known as 'Anonymous' (Deseriis, 2013:44). However, there is an interesting question about whether this is hacktivism or whether it is something else. The governments that were overthrown would probably consider it terrorism, but would those who perpetrated it consider themselves to be hacktivists or people trying to assist a revolution?

Defining hacktivism is difficult. The etymology of the word is easy to understand in that it is a combination of 'hacking' and 'activism' but what does that mean? Yar believes that it is analogous to traditional civil rights movements but replicated in cyberspace (Yar, 2013:47) and that it involves four behaviours: virtual sit-ins, email bombs, website defacement and malware. Others believe it is more complicated and involves more actions:

- Website defacement.
- Information theft.
- Website parodies.
- Denial of Service (DoS) attacks.
- Virtual sit-ins.
- Virtual sabotage.

(Hampson, 2012:514, citing Samuel)

This is obviously a wider list and at first sight some of these inclusions may seem strange. For example, information theft and sabotage would appear to have negative connotations rather than the appearance of a civil rights movement. However, these are the tools of hacktivists. Think about Julian Assange. Regardless of what you may think of him as a person – and he is certainly a divisive figure – the WikiLeaks website could only be considered an example of information theft and yet it would also be difficult to classify the leaks as anything other than political activism. It should also be noted that this list does not include many issues that would be found within cyber-protests (for example, protest websites, consumer behaviour, donating money or online petitions: see Van Laer and Van Aelst, 2010) as these are not related to hacking but rather peaceful protests, something very different from the activities of the hacktivist.

If one looks at the examples of hacktivism above, many of them can be classed as criminal acts and this is something that will be picked up throughout this section of the chapter. What then is the difference between a hacktivist and a criminal? On the one hand, it could be argued that the answer is 'nothing' and that if the law is broken then a person is simply a criminal. However, others will argue that there is a difference and that hacktivism involves the perpetrator undertaking acts in pursuance of a political goal whereas the criminal hacker acts out of self-interest (Hampson, 2012:515). This is an interesting proposition but it does beg the question about who decides what a political goal is and whether it is legitimate or illegitimate. Does that even matter? Hacktivism is arguably even vaguer as a concept than the white hat hacker discussed in Chapter 3. The language is certainly interesting and it is noted that some refer to hacktivism as 'electronic civil disobedience' (Van Laer and Van Aelst, 2010:244), which is an interesting analogy to offline protests where people tend to talk about disobedience rather than criminality even though there is no such distinction in law.

It has been suggested that another key difference is the absence of violence (Hampson, 2012:514), which is an interesting proposition because it is not known what violence means in the context of cyber-attacks. Does it mean tangible offline violence? If so, this would limit the circumstances when attacks could be seen as violent. It may also allow a clearer distinction between hacktivism and cyberterrorism since, as will be seen, the latter is inextricably linked to violence. However, should violence be restricted to real-world violence? If, during a protest, people smashed shop windows or spray-painted graffiti onto buildings would we classify that as violence? Perhaps we need to reconsider what concepts are in the cyber-world in order to understand what permissible hacktivism is.

### Exploring the behaviours

It has been noted that hacktivism actually consists of a number of discrete behaviours and it is worth noting some of these.

The first, and perhaps most significant, is the 'virtual sit-in'. The language used here is interesting because it does provide a direct analogy to the civil rights movements where peaceful occupation of a building or space was a popular tactic (for an interesting discussion on this see Ledewitz, 1995). Virtual sit-ins are, in essence, where a site is 'occupied' by denying access to others. Unlike traditional sit-ins where the protesters would be visible (which is perhaps more akin to website defacement) there is no indication as to who the protesters are unless they unmask themselves. Some have suggested that virtual sit-ins are executed as part of a Distributed Denial of Service (DDoS) attack (Yar, 2013:47), although, as noted in Chapter 3, that tends to be a largely automated process. Others believe that virtual sit-ins take the form of mass direct action (Jordan, 2001; Hampson, 2012:520) and that instead of automated processes it is a mass collective of people acting in a way to flood a computer system. To an extent this could be considered to be two sides of the same coin but the latter arguably better shows a democratic/protest basis and does not, for example, rely on bots. It is perhaps closer to the ideal of the mass rally. From a technical point of view it also carries with it advantages, as it is more difficult to counter as there will be so many different IP addresses, each of which could take action to mask their actions or move to new IP addresses, frustrating the counter-actions.

Website defacement and website parodies are similar albeit discrete forms of behaviour. Defacement is where the actual webpage is defaced. Accordingly the content of the site is changed, often to say something provocative or which tallies with the political aim of the hacktivists. A good example of this is the work of Anonymous. In 2013 they defaced the website of MIT (Massachusetts Institute of Technology) on the anniversary of the death of Aaron Swartz. Swartz was a leading American programmer who was also a hacktivist and who committed suicide after being prosecuted for downloading academic journal articles and placing them into the public domain. Anonymous argued that MIT had supported the prosecution and the website defacement was designed to remind people that Anonymous had not gone away and that their action against those that they believed had harmed the internet would continue.

Website defacement is considered to be the most common type of hacktivist action (Hampson, 2012:519) and is considered by many to be the cyber-equivalent of graffiti. To an extent this is a reasonable analogy since there is no permanent damage. The site can normally be returned to its original state by the operators of the site in the same way that graffiti can (usually) be removed from the buildings that have been daubed.

Website parodies are where a website that gently mocks the original website is created. Using meta-data it is possible to ensure that the parody is displayed close to the original site in search engine returns. It is also possible to combine website parodies with hacking techniques to ensure that a person who seeks to access the official site will be diverted to the parody site. Most parody sites will mirror the look of the official site but will contain amended text to put forward the political message that the hacktivists wish to put forward.

Information theft has been discussed already in the context of WikiLeaks but it can be more widespread. The essence of the behaviour is that hacktivists will hack into a computer, site or storage medium and take information that will then (usually) be released into the public domain. Examples of this include the hacking of the San Francisco transport passenger database to protest against police action. Another example took place in November 2014 when Anonymous hacked into the Ku Klux Klan (KKK) database and publicly named those who belonged to the organisation and published their addresses.

Unlike other forms of hacktivism, information theft has consequences for individuals. Whilst a company may be embarrassed by having its customer list displayed, the list of names and passwords could compromise the individual customer. Also, during a DDoS attack on Sony by Anonymous it was alleged that other hackers (not thought to be linked to Anonymous) hacked into the Sony database and stole the details of its customers, compromising their safety (after passwords and payment details were then displayed). Sony state that their cyber-security experts were trying to prevent the DDoS attack meaning they were vulnerable to other attacks (although it should be noted that some believe that is not true). The KKK information disclosure potentially raises personal safety risks. Whilst the KKK is an odious organisation, membership is not illegal, and yet displaying the names and addresses of members during periods of high tension and civil disorder must undoubtedly place personal safety at risk.

### A lawful protest?

As has been noted already, some have drawn an analogy between some forms of hacktivism and the civil rights era, particularly in the USA. Indeed some have gone further and actively suggested that the law should recognise hacktivism, or at least some forms of it, as protest. In 2013 Anonymous presented a petition to the US government to recognise DDoS attacks as a form of legitimate protest akin to the peaceful occupation of land (Li, 2013:304). Perhaps not surprisingly this was rejected by the US government but it did demonstrate the more general question of whether hacktivism can be seen as a form of protest.

There is no doubt that many of the activities of the hacktivist will be considered criminal. The legality of DDoS attacks was considered in Chapter 3 and many of the other forms of activity, such as website defacement or information theft, would also be covered by the criminal law. Other forms are perhaps less certain. For example, a virtual sit-in achieved by DDoS attack would be illegal, but where it is facilitated by the co-ordinated action of thousands of persons all trying to access the same site (thus causing it to crash) it is probably not illegal as there is no unlawful access of the system: each user is doing what they are entitled to – try to access the site – they just happen to be doing it in such a way that will cause the site to crash.

If we accept that most hacktivist behaviour is *prima facie* criminal then it must be questioned whether it can be constructed as a legitimate form of protest. It is possible to state at the outset that some forms are unlikely to ever be so considered. For example, the use of malware or the theft of personal information are never likely to be considered to be anything other than criminal. That said, the theft of information raises more interesting issues. Let us take the WikiLeaks example. How many people would consider that this constituted a criminal offence? It undoubtedly is and Bradley Manning – the original source of the leak – was prosecuted for leaking the information, but many people probably thought it was in the public interest and therefore should not have led to criminal action. The issue of whistleblowing has always been contentious. There is a long history of people leaking documents to the press to make a particular point (an interesting summary is presented in Callahan *et al.*, 2004) and in many instances they are not prosecuted. The use of the internet should probably not make any difference but it is a very different proposition when a hacker has entered a system and taken the details for herself. That is no longer about leaking (even leaving aside the question about whether leaks can be in the public interest), this is a self-appointed individual who is deciding to hack into a system for their own (albeit political) purposes. It is highly unlikely that the courts would ever consider that this would be anything other than criminal.

What of other forms of hacktivism? Each of them has been seen to be disruptive but then again so are traditional forms of protest:

> Protests and demonstrations cause inconvenience, annoyance, and distraction; they can impede commerce and attract unwanted attention … the target of a permissible form of cyberprotest must generally tolerate the inconvenience caused by hacktivism. It is part of the price to be paid for the freedom of expression.
>
> (Hampson, 2012:540)

This an interesting point because it is extremely valid. If 300 people occupy or picket a shop in a particular location it is going to be incredibly annoying for the people close by or who are trying to use the site. However, that does not automatically make it illegal, so why should a virtual occupation be illegal? Of course the more interesting question is where the action goes beyond peaceful occupation. For example, in the offline world if a protest started to spray graffiti over property or smash windows then it is likely that it would be no longer classed as a peaceful protest and criminal action would be likely to follow. Perhaps the same model could apply online too, with website defacement being considered criminal? That said, the costs of repairing virtual defacement are perhaps significantly less than for offline graffiti, not least because most companies will have backups of everything that can be restored easily. However, the criminal law would not normally take such matters into account.

An area where virtual activity is arguably more draconian than its offline equivalent is in respect of entering. It was noted in Chapter 3 that if a person hacks into a computer even without any ulterior intent they commit an offence contrary to s.1, CMA 1990. However, in the offline world entering private property is rarely criminal. Could it be argued, therefore, that where a hacker accesses a site to make a political point that they should not be criminalised unless they cause damage? A person entering a corporate HQ and holding a protest sign would not be a criminal so why should the virtual equivalent be?

Where other forms of hacktivism are considered the position becomes even more difficult. Whilst it has been argued that DDoS attacks could be seen as a legitimate form of protest, it has been pointed out that (in the USA) the right to free speech would not normally permit the occupation of private property (Li, 2013:313), and the same would be true in England where it would be considered a tort. Perhaps more damaging, however, would be the fact that DDoS attacks could be considered to be the antithesis of what free speech/free expression guarantees. The aim of a DDoS attack is to cause a website or similar to crash. Therefore the information that would ordinarily be displayed on that site – which can only be considered to be speech or expression – could not be displayed. It has been postulated that in the US context it is unlikely that the US Constitution would recognise the right to prevent someone (including a corporate body) from exercising their constitutional right to free speech under the First Amendment (Li, 2013:321). In the European context it is likely that claiming the right to disrupt a website would be considered a breach of Article 17 of the European Convention on Human Rights (ECHR). Article 17 states that one cannot seek to rely on a convention right if to do so would damage the rights and freedoms of others, in this case Article 10 (Freedom of Expression).

Perhaps the principal difficulty is that the law does not really understand the concept of cyber-protests. This is understandable because although it is easy to say there is an analogy to civil rights protests, it is very different to actually draw that analogy. So, for example, it has been noted that

> there are no digital analogs to public sidewalks and adjoining the physical presence of the target of protest in cyberspace … speakers who wish to protest against an online-only business would be hard-pressed to find a public forum that would provide them with specific access.
>
> (Li, 2013:325)

This is an important point. In real life if a person wished to protest against a company they could stand outside their building (on public space) and protest. However, where is the public presence online? There is no way of creating a presence that people would have to see. If a person is outside the building then those who wish to attend the building have to pass that protest. They may not like it but the person protesting has that ability. In the online world there is no way to replicate this other than by doing something illegal – hacking the website (so that the message is displayed) or hacking the routing instructions so that instead of going straight to site X a message will be displayed first. Either of these, however, would constitute an offence under the CMA 1990. Thus hacktivists are always likely to fall foul of the law and can only rely on the vague hope that prosecutorial discretion may save them.

## Cyberterrorism

Beyond hacktivism is the issue of cyberterrorism. This marks a step up from hacktivism and can be said to be directed towards the state rather than individual corporations. Terrorism is generally seen as an attack against state interests (for an interesting discussion on defining terrorism see Ganor, 2002) even if it will sometimes be executed through attacks against private industry. Perhaps a good example of this was the terrorism inflicted as a result of the troubles in Northern Ireland. The Provisional IRA launched a number of attacks against private-sector targets – shopping centres and banks – rather than government infrastructure. However, there was no doubt that their 'message' was directed to the state rather than the private industry.

### Defining cyberterrorism

There is no doubt that since the events of September 11 there has been increasing attention paid to the issue of cyberterrorism (Yar, 2013:45), but what is perhaps less clear is whether cyberterrorism is either real or a credible threat. The term itself is easily understood, it is a conjoining of 'cyberspace' and 'terrorism' to produce the notion of terrorism that takes place either in, or through, the internet. Of course the difficulty with this is that both 'cyberspace' and 'terrorism' are terms that are themselves sufficiently vague (see Chapter 1 for a discussion of cyberspace and Yar, 2013:50 for a useful summary of the difficulty of the term 'terrorism').

It is necessary to differentiate terrorism from other forms of acts and this is not always done. So, for example, some incidences of disruption can be identified but invariably these have been intended to gain respect through 'beating the establishment' and therefore cannot be recognised as terrorism *per se* (Hinde, 2003:188). Similarly, other attacks – for example, Stuxnet (which will be discussed later but which can be summarised as a malware attack that led to physical damage being caused to an Iranian nuclear facility) – which would appear to have many of the elements of a classic terrorist attack have turned out to be more akin to cyberwarfare rather than cyberterrorism, partly because of the identity of the perpetrator.

If cyberterrorism is to exist in its own right then how is it to be defined? An emotive definition is 'hacking with a body count' (Iqbal, 2004:397, citing Ames) but this really does not tell us very much about what cyberterrorism is and would seem designed to try and startle rather than be a serious definition in its own right. It would also be somewhat limiting. For example, a sustained attack on the financial industry could be seen as terrorism (subject to the motivation for the attack) because affecting the financial stability of a country's economic system is undoubtedly a key attack on the state. However, it would not cause bodily harm or death so there would be no 'body count'. Indeed, the requirement that there has to be a 'body count' would mean that only extreme attacks would constitute cyberterrorism. Not only is this problematic in the sphere of cybercrime, it divorces itself from the reality of terrorism. For example, during the troubles in Northern Ireland it was not unusual for terrorist organisations to plant an explosive device but then provide a warning that would allow the area to be evacuated. Were the device to explode then it is quite likely there would be no casualties but few would suggest, therefore, that there was no terrorism (although it must be conceded that the analogy suffers from the fact that there was always the potential for casualties, including among those who would inevitably be sent to defuse the device).

We can therefore reject the notion of a body count, but how do you define cyberterrorism? The first thing to note is that cyberterrorism must be something different from terrorists simply using the internet. There can be no doubt that terrorists use the internet and this will be discussed below. However, the mere use of the internet cannot by itself constitute cyberterrorism. The concept of cyberterrorism is terrorism on, or facilitated by, the internet, rather than terrorists merely using the internet. To an extent this mirrors the debate in Chapter 1 where it was noted that not everything that involves the internet constitutes cybercrime, and the same is true of cyberterrorism.

However, if cybercrime does exist then it must presumably have a definition. Some have suggested that there are two methods of defining cyberterrorism. The first is effects-based, which is where the consequences of the cyber-attack are comparable to traditional forms of terrorism. The second definition is intent-based, which is where unlawful activity occurs with the intention to intimidate or coerce a government or people to 'further a political objective, or to cause grave harm or severe economic damage' (Stohl, 2006:229). These are interesting definitions but the inclusion of 'political objective' is interesting because it does raise the question again about the difference between hacktivism and terrorism. Perhaps this is simply because there is a continuum of behaviour from hacktivism through cyberterrorism to cyberwarfare.

A popular definition of cyberterrorism is the

> intentional use or threat of use, without legally recognised authority, of violence, disruption or interference against cyber systems, when it is likely that such use would result in death or injury of a person or persons, substantial damage to physical property, civil disorder, or significant harm.
>
> (Jones, 2005:4)

This is an interesting definition not least because it refers to concepts such as violence (which is difficult to envisage in the cyber-world) but also the tangible effects such as damage to physical property, civil disorder or significant harm. Property is examined elsewhere but it is known that as increasing numbers of physical objects are connected to the internet there is the possibility to cause physical damage. An engine that is linked to the internet could be told to switch off in an emergency, potentially causing damage to the pistons, etc. Perhaps an easier example would be to disable safety warnings and run technology beyond its tolerances (something seen from Stuxnet: see Langer, 2011).

### Reality of cyberterrorism

> The fact that it is possible for computers to cause physical damage means that cyberterrorism starts to capture the attention of authorities and the public. It has been suggested: 'The term "cyberterrorism" unites two significant modern fears: fear of technology and fear of terrorism'
>
> (Conway, 2011:26).

Fear is at the heart of terrorism but the point Conway makes is that our suspicion of the effects of technology coupled with our fear of terrorism can almost lead to greater anxiety, even though, as will be seen, there are serious concerns about its effectiveness. This fear has been affected by the entertainment industry and media in much the same way as hacking was. Movies and commentators put forward so-called 'doomsday scenarios'. There starts to be the suggestion that hackers could somehow launch nuclear missiles, crash telephone networks or cause air traffic control systems to direct aircraft in such a way as to cause mid-air crashes (Rathmell, 1997:42). Other popular scenarios include the power grid being switched off or the banking industry being crashed. However, a difficulty with this is that such networks are rarely connected to the internet and usually exist on private networks (Yar, 2013:55). Whilst this does not mean it is impossible for the systems to be hacked, it is difficult. Indeed the protection from hacking is the principal reason why these networks are not connected to the internet.

Identifying the likelihood of cyberterrorism is not easy. The public are sometimes told that cyberterrorism is inevitable. Emotive language is used, with a common analogy being to Pearl Harbour (Stohl, 2006:225). This is an interesting analogy because it remains a source of hurt to many Americans who recall the loss of life that was caused by the attack on the US Pacific Fleet. However, both within and outside of the USA, 'Pearl Harbour' has become synonymous with the notion of being unprepared for an attack. Rightly or wrongly, it is commonly thought that Admiral (later demoted to Rear-Admiral) Kimmel had not sufficiently prepared for the Japanese attack. The term 'Pearl Harbour' has entered common parlance as meaning that someone is almost deliberately minimising the potential for attack and not mustering the defences. The analogy is interesting in the context of cyberterrorism because it conjures up the notion of a physical attack and the destruction that can be brought by it. Such language can be used by those who claim we need to prepare more and those who believe additional powers or resources should be given.

Even where attacks can take place there have been some who question whether terrorists would bother. In respect of attacking, for example, the infrastructure of air traffic it has been noted that until cyber-attacks 'can be undertaken with less effort, the same chances of detection, produce the same results and have a greater likelihood of success' as a conventional attack then there is little chance of it happening (Stohl, 2006:233). This is perhaps key to one of the difficulties with cyberterrorism. It just doesn't necessarily have the 'wow' factor. One of the concerns has been that cyber-attacks could take down the power grid but people accept that power cuts happen from time to time even when they are widespread, including an incident in 2005 where 50 million people in America were left without power (Jones, 2005:4). If people merely accept the fact that there is disruption then it is difficult to see where the terror in cyberterrorism fits. That said, of course, there is a difference between accepting a relatively short-term power cut caused by natural events and the unpredictable consequences of a terrorist attack with indefinite outages.

The lack of a 'wow' factor has been recognised by others (Conway, 2011:28), and it undoubtedly does raise an issue. It is not enough that disruption can occur, there must be terror. In many instances it is difficult to see how that will apply to cybercrime. More than this, however, the point about effort is also telling. With traditional terrorism there was always the fact that even if a device did not explode, disruption was caused by sealing off the relevant area and the theatre of the bomb disposal. That does not happen in respect of cyberterrorism. The reality is that if the attack does not succeed then no-one outside of the targeted body would even know the attack has taken place. Therefore the cyberterrorists need to be sure that they will succeed, something that can rarely be guaranteed. The reality is that it is perhaps much easier to simply use traditional forms of terrorism.

Does that mean that cyberterrorism will never happen? No. It does, however, perhaps explain why despite a decade of discussion about cyberterrorism there have been few actual instances. There has been speculation that terrorists may seek to hire hackers, who advertise their skills on the black market, to undertake these attacks (Conway, 2007), and this would perhaps make the possibility more likely because the terrorists do not have to develop the necessary skills. However, there must be a major question mark over whether hackers would be prepared to work with terrorists and risk all the repercussions this brings, both in terms of legal risk (anti-terrorist legislation) and personal risk (would terrorists leave the hacker alive or would it be best to remove all evidence of who did what?). The alternative would be to try and recruit people who would then be sent to university to develop the necessary skills but that would take long-term planning, and few current terrorist groups operate on that basis as they have better chances of achieving publicity using traditional techniques.

### Use of the internet by terrorists

The discussion about cyberterrorism does mask one important issue, which is that terrorists are using the internet. However, as noted above, the fact that terrorists are using the internet does not make it cyberterrorism. Terrorists have used the internet for some time (for an early study see Furnell and Warren, 1999) and this is perhaps unsurprising because it is a cheap way of reaching a large audience. In Chapter 8 the use of the internet by hate-crime groups will be explored and similar issues arise in respect of terrorism.

The main uses of the internet by terrorists are:

- Propaganda/publicity.
- Fundraising.
- Information dissemination.
- Secure communications.

(Furnell and Warren, 1999:29–30)

In addition to this Yar argues that terrorists use the internet to gain intelligence (Yar, 2013:59), and this is something that should not be missed.

### Propaganda

The primary use would seem to be the issuing of propaganda/publicity and it is easy to see why the internet could be employed for these purposes. The internet, particularly after the advent of Web 2.0, is a very cheap way to get a message out. The message can also be presented in an uncritical way, something that would not occur through other media. In recent years the full extent of this has been seen through videos posted to YouTube (or equivalent sites) which have shown the beheading of hostages. Recruitment videos have also been placed which present a particularly distorted view of the objectives of the terrorist organisation to portray the belief that their activities are in some way just or appropriate (see Stohl, 2006:229). By hosting material in countries that prioritise free speech there is also the opportunity to ensure that the message is not easily blocked or censored, something not easily done in respect of mainstream media.

### Fundraising

The second principal use of the internet by terrorists is fundraising. Terrorism is an expensive business, and yet where it has a political goal that people are sympathetic to there will be people who will be prepared to contribute to 'the cause'. The internet allows this to occur in very different ways. First, it becomes much easier to have a 'global reach' because a fundraising site can simply be formed and then disseminated through email, social media and hyperlinks. Second, there are a number of online payment systems that would allow people to donate money. The internet also now allows for anonymous money transfers, which could be particularly attractive in the context of terrorism as it will allow people to donate money without fearing repercussions.

*Disseminating information*

This is subtly different to propaganda in that it is the dissemination of information that would be useful to 'the cause' rather than in regards to the specific group. So, for example, in the 1980s an American university publicised information regarding the movements of British troops in Northern Ireland (Furnell and Warren, 1999:30) which would be useful for those seeking to either attack or evade them. Similarly the internet has numerous examples of bomb-making instructions and terror manuals. The intention of this dissemination is not necessarily recruitment into a particular group but rather it is about trying to empower those who are sympathetic to the cause to develop their own strategies for causing terror. The dissemination of such information poses a real risk to society, as it allows people to produce improvised explosive devices cheaply for any cause, potentially widening the likelihood of an attack.

*Secure communications*

The internet provides a more secure system for communicating with one another. Simply from watching American crime movies we know how unsecure traditional telephony services are, and even mobile telephones can be intercepted. The internet, however, allows for entirely new ways of communicating. Everyone is now familiar with VoIP (Voice over Internet Protocol) software packages such as FaceTime and Skype. An advantage of this is that an anonymous email address can be created linked to an anonymous Skype address. Therefore the chances of the authorities being aware of the existence of the call may be remote.

More than this, however, technology allows for encrypted communications. So, for example, some providers will use encrypted data messaging (most notably Blackberry) which would mean that even if the authorities managed to intercept the content it would be meaningless. Simple encryption technologies allow emails to be sent without fear of their content being decoded and the security can be increased by using anonymous mailers. The growth of encryption technology has led some governments to consider the introduction of laws that are designed to require the production of either the key to decrypt the information or the plain information itself (Gillespie, 2014a). However, such laws are controversial as some argue they contradict the privilege against self-incrimination, but without such laws the ability to communicate securely is almost absolute.

*Intelligence*

Yar added the gaining of intelligence to the list of things that terrorists may use the internet for (Yar, 2013:59), and this is a point that is worth remembering.

We are now, to an extent, familiar with the fact that the authorities will conduct surveillance on the internet (it sometimes being referred to as 'open source intelligence' (Glassman and Kang, 2012)) and so it should not be a surprise to know that terrorists will do the same. There is vast amounts of data on the internet and terrorists can use publicly available information or information gathered through hacking to identify targets. So, for example, an official site might not state which clubs or societies a person belongs to but their social networking sites may. Personal sites can be useful in other ways too. For example, if it is known that target X's son participates in a football league it would not be difficult to find the schedule of matches, providing opportunities to target the individual.

Freely available resources can also assist in the preparation of an attack. We are all now accustomed to using things such as Google Earth or Google Street View. Instead of going out to a location to 'recce' it, which could carry the risk of detection or raise suspicions, it is possible to look at the area on computer. Indeed, modelling software can produce a computer representation so that issues such as line of sight, potential cover and escape routes can all be considered. This increases the chances a traditional attack will be successful.

### Legal responses

Terrorism is an area where the law is not slow to become involved. What follows is not a comprehensive analysis of terrorist laws (for which see Walker, 2011) but rather a brief explanation of the types of offences that cover some of the behaviour that has been discussed above.

The main legislation in this area is the *Terrorism Act 2000* (TA 2000) and the *Terrorism Act 2006* (TA 2006) and they introduce a series of offences that not only look at the substantive acts of terrorism (which for reasons discussed above may be difficult to prosecute in the context of cyberterrorism) but also ancillary offences (which are probably of more use).

At the heart of both the TA 2000 and the TA 2006 is the concept of 'terrorism' which is defined as:

> the use or threat of action where
>
> (a)  the action falls within subsection (2),
> (b)  the use or threat is designed to influence the government or an international governmental organisation or to intimidate the public or a section of the public, and
> (c)  the use or threat is made for the purpose of advancing a political, religious, racial or ideological cause.
>
> (s.1(1), TA 2000)

Thus at the heart of terrorism for these purposes is the use or threat of violence that is directed towards the state (including its citizens) for an ideological purpose. This chimes with much of the discussion above. What falls within subsection (2):

(a)  involves serious violence against a person,
(b)  involves serious damage to property,
(c)  endangers a person's life, other than that of the person committing the action,
(d)  creates a serious risk to the health or safety of the public or a section of the public, or
(e)  is designed seriously to interfere with or seriously to disrupt an electronic system.

Setting aside the discussion about whether cyberterrorism can lead to harm to an individual or the damaging of property, it is clear that s.1(2)(e) expressly contemplates cyberterrorism. That said, a peculiarity of the English laws on terrorism is that terrorism *per se* is not illegal, it is a series of activities surrounding it that is. Thus the TA 2006 contains offences relating to being a member or supporter of a proscribed organisation (ss.11–13, TA 2000), raising finance or money laundering (ss.15–22A) and offences relating to weapons training, etc. (s.54), but there is nothing within the TA 2000 that criminalises *per se* a cyber-attack that is designed to seriously disrupt an electronic system for political reasons.

The most likely terrorism offence for those purposes would be s.5, TA 2006, which criminalises preparatory acts. The offence is committed where a person 'engages in any conduct' in preparation for giving effect to the committing of acts of terrorism or assisting another to commit such acts (s.5(1), TA 2006). As terrorism includes certain cyber-attacks then a person who prepares to initiate such an attack could be prosecuted under s.5 so long as it constituted terrorism. It will be remembered that this would mean that any attack would have to be intended to influence the government or intimidate a section of the public and be conducted for, *inter alia*, an ideological reason.

As it has been noted that cyberterrorism itself is largely unproven it is worth discussing how the law reacts to some of the uses of the internet by terrorists, as that is behaviour that we know does exist and the law has sought to tackle this.

Section 56, TA 2000 criminalises someone who 'directs, at any level, the activities of an organisation which is concerned in the commission of acts of terrorism' and this could presumably include, for example, websites linked to the terrorist organisation. So, for example, if a site has been established to provide support for the group (including posting propaganda videos) or to raise finance for the group then presumably this must be an activity, and thus the person who creates or maintains that site could be liable under s.56.

In the context of cyberterrorism two important offences are those contained in ss.57 and 58, TA 2000. Section 57 creates the offence of possessing 'an article in circumstances which give rise to a reasonable suspicion that his possession is for a purpose connected with the commission, preparation or instigation of an act of terrorism', whereas s.58 criminalises:

(a) he [who] collects or makes a record of information of a kind likely to be useful to a person committing or preparing an act of terrorism, or
(b) he [who] possesses a document or record containing information of that kind.

(s.58(1))

Whilst these do not seem to be directly linked, they are, since it has been held that a document could constitute 'an article' for the purposes of s.57 meaning that there is undoubted overlap between the two provisions (*R v Rowe* [2007] QB 975). The Court of Appeal noted that the principal distinction between the two offences is their purpose. Section 57 requires possession for a specific purpose – it must be for a purpose to do with the commission, preparation or instigation of an act of terrorism, whereas s.58 criminalises, *inter alia*, the simple possession of material that is likely to be *useful* in committing or preparing an act of terrorism but there is no requirement that the person intends for that to happen.

It is clear that offences under ss.57 and 58 can be committed through, for example, downloading training manuals or videos (see, for example, *R v Y(A)* [2010] EWCA Crim 762), but for s.57 to apply the prosecution must prove that it was intended that this was to be used for a terrorist purpose. Where, for example, X downloads the manual and then orders the necessary components for an explosive device, that would meet the criteria. Section 58 is much wider as the download must merely be of use to a person preparing an act of terrorism and there is no need to prove that the defendant intended for it to be used for such purposes. A defence exists under s.58(3) if it can be shown that the defendant has a reasonable excuse for his possession. The wording of the defence should be noted. It is not that the person does not intend to use the article for terrorist purposes, it is that the person has a reasonable excuse for possessing it. Where, therefore, the person intends to use the article for a criminal (albeit non-terrorist) purpose then this would not be a 'reasonable excuse' and so the offence would apply.

One concern that has already been noted is that the internet could be used to disseminate material that could be of assistance to terrorists. This is partly covered by s.57, TA 2000, but that would require a positive intent to assist the commission, etc., of terrorism which can sometimes be difficult to prove. The *Counter-Terrorism Act 2008*, introduced a new specific provision that sought to tackle the obtaining of intelligence about designated persons. Section 58A, TA 2000 prohibits the eliciting (or attempted eliciting) of information about someone who is (or has been) a member of the military, police or intelligence services where that information would be useful to a person committing or preparing an act of terrorism (s.58A(1)(a)) or a person who publishes this information (s.58A(1)(b)).

Section 58A is very wide but clearly it would include, for example, information about the routes that certain military personnel take. It will be remembered from above that there could be concern that a person uses the internet to find out where, for example, a military officer's child plays football. If the person contacts the football club to find this out and to find the timing of training sessions so that this information could be passed over to terrorists then this could come within s.58A. Similarly, publishing the detailed schematics of an army base, including highlighting vulnerable areas would be covered. In *R v G* [2010] 1 AC 43 it was suggested that the addresses of serving military personnel (and by implication therefore, members of the intelligence services or police) would be paradigms of the type of information s.58A is concerned with.

What of propaganda videos? Could the posting of these videos constitute an offence? The most obvious offence would be s.1, TA 2006. This creates an offence of encouraging terrorism. It is quite ineloquently phrased:

> This section applies to a statement that is likely to be understood by some or all of the members of the public to whom it is published as a direct or indirect encouragement or other inducement to them to the commission, preparation or instigation of acts of terrorism.
>
> (s.1(1), TA 2006)

The offence is publishing such a statement either intending the public to be directly or indirectly encouraged, etc., or being reckless as to whether they will be so encouraged (s.1(2)). Allied to this is s.2, TA 2006, which is the dissemination of terrorist publications. As with s.1 this is in two parts.

Section 2(1) states that at the time of doing an act within s.2(2) he:

(a) intends an effect of his conduct to be an direct or indirect encouragement ... of terrorism,
(b) intends an effect of his conduct to be the provision of assistance ... in terrorism,
(c) is reckless as to whether his conduct has the effect in (a) or (b).

Section 2(2) proscribes the conduct as he:

(a) distributes or circulates a terrorist publication,
(b) gives, sells or lends such a publication,
(c) offers such publication for sale or loan,
(d) provides a service to others that enables them to obtain, loan, listen or look at such a publication, or to acquire it by means of a gift, sale or loan,
(e) transmits the contents of such publication electronically, or

(f)  has such a publication in his possession with a view to it becoming the subject of conduct within (a) to (e).

In the context of the internet, ss.1 and 2 clearly overlap. Both relate to documents that can encourage and in *R v Gul* [2013] 3 WLR 1207 it was made clear that propaganda videos, such as beheadings, are capable of coming within these provisions if their purpose is to encourage terrorism. The principal distinction would seem to be that s.1 requires a 'statement' whereas s.2 refers to publications, and thus it has been postulated that s.1 refers to the person who makes the statement whereas s.2 refers to those who distribute that statement (Hunt, 2007:443).

In essence these sections prohibit material and therefore this must raise a question over their compatibility with free speech and, in the context of the UK and Europe, Article 10 of the ECHR (freedom of expression). Article 10 encompasses material that is considered to be inappropriate, with it being pointed out that the freedom to say only inoffensive things is not worth having (*Redmond-Bate v DPP* [2000] HRLR 249 at 260 per Sedley LJ). However, Article 10 is not absolute and it is subject to Article 10(2), which provides that it is possible to interfere with free expression for a number of legitimate purposes, including national security, prevention of disorder or crime and the protection of morals. Such interferences must be proportionate and the clear link in respect of justifying the interference will be to link it towards terrorism. The Court of Appeal has noted that they 'do not consider it arguable that a publication which to the knowledge of the defendant carried a real risk that it would be understood [to be] encouraging the unlawful commission of terrorist offences ... is entitled to exemption [under Article 10]' (*R v Faraz* [2013] 1 WLR 2615 at 2635 per Pitchford LJ). However, the Court of Appeal was also aware of the dangers of the legislation when it noted that '[a] jury could not convict [a] defendant merely because his publication expressed a religious or political view, controversial or not' (ibid.), which shows that there is a line to walk on Article 10.

An interesting point about s.2 is that whilst the material must relate to terrorism there is no requirement that the person who is accused of breaching s.2 is a terrorist or acting for the purposes of terrorism. In *R v Brown* [2011] EWCA Crim 2751 the appellant sold online, for commercial rather than ideological reasons, copies of the 'anarchist cookbook' which provided details on how to manufacture explosive devices. He was tried and convicted under s.2. He sought to argue that he had the right under Article 10 to sell such material, noting that he was not inciting terrorism, but this was forcefully rejected by the Court of Appeal who noted that it would be difficult to argue Article 10 in respect of an offence that required the prosecution to prove an intention to encourage terrorism or, in the alternative, being reckless as to whether terrorism was encouraged.

A simple reading of s.2(2)(d) could leave open to question whether an internet service or content provider is at risk of liability for hosting propaganda videos. Theoretically there should not be any risk but the fact that the *mens rea* includes recklessness potentially raises this possibility. However, the risk is militated by the *Electronic Commerce Directive (Terrorism Act 2006) Regulations 2007* which implement the EU e-commerce directive by exempting service and content providers where they provide a mere conduit (further details on the implications of this Directive are found in Walden, 2007). However, it should be noted that the e-commerce directive does not apply where ISPs or Internet Content Providers (ICPs) have specific knowledge of the content. In respect of this, s.3, TA 2006 is notable. This section empowers a police officer to provide a notice to a relevant provider that material is considered to be terrorist material. If, after a period of two working days, the material has not been secured and rendered inaccessible to the general public then the provider is deemed to endorse the material and therefore would be liable for proceedings under ss.1 or 2. Section 3 details a number of ways in which this presumption will not apply, but it is obviously an attempt to ensure that ISPs or ICPs remove material that is known to constitute terrorist material. Of course this once again raises issues under Article 10, and it is notable that the notice is issued by the police rather than a court although the notice could be challenged by judicial review.

## Cyberwarfare

If hacktivism was the first part of a continuum then cyberwarfare is at the other end. This is arguably less about law and more about war but it is well known that international law prescribes rules for war (Shaw, 2008:1118 et seq.). Whilst some may question their applicability and the sense that law can in any way regulate war between two countries, it has been seen on numerous occasions that the international community has established tribunals to try those who break these rules. Perhaps the most notable of these were the Nuremberg trials after World War II where several Nazi leaders were tried for, *inter alia*, crimes against humanity. More recently there have been prosecutions arising out of the conflicts in the former countries of Yugoslavia and the African conflict in Darfur.

This section is speculative in places because there is no definitive instrument that puts forward the rules of cyberwarfare let alone having them recognised in international law. However, some believe that international law will have to react to and recognise cyberwarfare, including prescribing rules of war.

### Defining cyberwarfare

The first question to consider is what cyberwarfare is and whether it exists (or has existed). One issue is to differentiate between cyberterrorism and cyberwarfare. This is not necessarily an easy issue in some contexts. An obvious differential would be the fact that warfare usually involves states rather than individuals. This is not always the case as war can involve separatist groups, but we do not need to consider this here as this chapter does not pretend to give a comprehensive analysis of the meaning of war (for a discussion on this see Dinstein, 2011).

### State aggressors

For our purposes we can limit the analysis to state actors, i.e. a country acting as the aggressor. The problem that this immediately brings is the question of how one identifies whether it is the state rather than an individual that undertakes the act. In kinetic warfare (i.e. traditional warfare that involves bombs, bullets and traditional fighting) it is relatively easy to identify a state aggressor. Their warships, aircraft or tanks are fairly easily identified and they can be traced, even where a country denies it (as with, for example, the 2014 Crimean crisis where Russia denied allowing their military hardware to be used even though it was obvious they had). However, the position in respect of cyberwarfare is not as simple. The technology that allows others to hide can also be used by states. Thus whilst there may be suspicions that a state is responsible for an attack it can be very difficult to prove this.

Two examples can be adduced to show this difficulty, although it can be questioned to what extent they can be considered 'cyberwarfare'. The first is that of 'Moonlight Maze' which is often cited as an example of cyberwarfare (McGhee, 2013:66). The USA discovered that a number of its computer systems had been penetrated and systematic searches were taking place of their content. It is widely believed that Russia was behind the attack although it denies it and the US government has never formally accused Russia of the attack.

The second example is Stuxnet which is something that we will return to several times in this chapter. Stuxnet is malware that eventually led to physical damage in the Iranian nuclear enrichment programme by causing the computers controlling the centrifuges to run beyond their tolerance levels. It is widely believed that Stuxnet was created by the governments of the USA and Israel with the intention of it being used to damage the Iranian nuclear programme. However, this has never been proved and certainly neither the USA nor Israel have ever admitted that they are responsible for the attack.

Whilst in both cases there are, at the very least, suspicions as to who is responsible for the attacks, there is uncertainty and a lack of proof. Does this matter? It depends on what one thinks about the 'laws' of war. If one believes that armed conflict is regulated by international law (a position that not everyone certainly believes) then it is often said that military action can only be authorised as self-defence against the use of force or threatened use of force (Article 41, UN Charter) unless otherwise authorised by the UN.

Similarly, it is possible to bring allegations of improper use of force before the United Nations for censure, but a state only bears responsibility where it can be identified as being responsible (Schmitt, 2013:29). Whilst it is unlikely that proof to the degree required by courts is required, there would still need to be clear evidence of responsibility, something not easy to obtain in cyberspace. The very nature of the internet means, for example, that an attack need not be launched within the sovereign territory of the country launching an attack. It could be prepared there but the initial attack could take place anywhere there is an internet connection, further obfuscating responsibility.

It has been noted that one of the difficulties in identifying cybercrime is that states will often be reluctant to admit that they have been the victim of a (successful) cyber-attack (Dinniss, 2012:31). States do not want to appear weak nor will they necessarily wish to open themselves up to additional scrutiny through people 'testing' their security. For this reason, states are unlikely to accuse another state unless they have clear proof, meaning many cyber-attacks will mostly be behind the scenes. Of course it should be noted that this is not unusual. Countries engage in espionage and intelligence operations every day. These are hardly ever mentioned and so it should not be surprising that the same is true in the cybersphere.

### State as a victim

Whilst, for our purposes, we can decide that we need a state aggressor for cyberwarfare, does the victim need to be a state? It may seem an odd question but this perhaps demonstrates a (potential) difference between kinetic warfare and the cyber-world. In traditional warfare, if country X sends a naval warship to bombard the territory of country Y it does not really matter whether the building that is hit is a government building, a private factory or even a dwelling. It is the use of armed force on the territory of another state that is the key issue. What is the position in cyberspace?

The starting point must be jurisdiction. It will be remembered from Chapter 2 that jurisdiction is a complicated doctrine, but the general rule is that the state can control activities that take place on its territory. The same is claimed of the internet. The creators of the Tallinn Manual – an academic piece of writing that attempted to formulate the 'laws' of cyberwarfare – state that international law recognises the right of a state to control cyber-activities on its territories and cyber-infrastructure located on its territory (Schmitt, 2013:18). Perhaps an equally important rule is that it can apply the principles of extraterritoriality to the internet too. This was discussed in part in Chapter 2 but it could be important in the context of terrorism. Many countries claim the right to pursue extraterritorial jurisdiction in respect of either the passive personality principle (where the victim is a national of the state (and this would include a legal personality, i.e. company)) or through the protective principle (see Hirst, 2003 for a good overview of jurisdiction).

To put this into context, where the attack occurs on computers based within the territory of a sovereign country then that could be considered an attack on the state itself, as it would with kinetic warfare. Cloud storage makes the issue more complicated since it may mean that data is stored outside of the territory, and this is where extraterritorial jurisdiction would need to apply. Whether it does apply will depend on the domestic law of each country, as ultimately whilst international law permits states to exercise extraterritorial jurisdiction it is for each country to decide whether to do so.

Perhaps the best example to illustrate this point occurred in December 2014, just as this manuscript had been finished (requiring a hasty edit!). Sony Pictures had financed and made a film called *The Interview*, a comedy that involves two Americans being sent to North Korea to kill the leader. A cyber-attack was then launched against Sony which led to their security being compromised and a considerable amount of embarrassing information being released into the public domain, including email correspondence. This is classic hacking behaviour and has been discussed earlier in this chapter and indeed the preceding chapters. Interestingly, however, the US government stated that they believed the North Korean government was responsible for the cyber-attack.

The fact that a state publicly accused another state of perpetrating a cyber-attack raised questions about whether this was cyberwar? For reasons discussed momentarily it would seem the answer is 'no' but why was the US government involved at all? Sony is principally a Japanese company (although Sony Pictures is an American legal entity controlled by Sony) but the servers that were attacked were based in the USA. Therefore, it became a matter for the US government.

### Force

What separates cyberwarfare from other forms of cyber-attacks? Traditional warfare relies on the infliction of force but it is not clear how that relates to cyberspace. One of the issues is that the instruments governing force significantly predate the development of cyberspace. Article 2(4) of the *Charter of the United Nations* requires signatory states to 'refrain … from the threat or use of force' but it has never defined what force means. At the time the Charter was written it meant only kinetic force, but does that matter? One of the key decisions in this area is the *Nuclear Weapons Case*, which was a decision of the International Court of Justice (*Legality of the Threat or Use of Nuclear Weapons, Advisory Opinion, ICJ Reports 1996:226*).

The General Assembly of the UN passed a resolution (49/75K) to ask the International Court of Justice (ICJ) for a decision on whether nuclear weapons were lawful. There had been an argument that nuclear weapons were so destructive as to constitute a crime against humanity. There had also been a series of UN resolutions calling for the abolition of nuclear weapons and it had been argued that this produced a customary rule rendering nuclear weapons illegal. The ICJ, however, found to the contrary. They ruled that there was no prohibition on nuclear weapons and that the use, or threat of use, would be lawful if it came within Article 2(4). Whilst, by a majority, the ICJ conceded there was an argument that their use may be contrary to international humanitarian law (principally *jus ad bellum* which will be considered below), it held that it could not conclusively so rule because there may be extreme circumstances when the use of nuclear weapons would not violate these rules and that should not be adjudicated in advance.

What is the relevance of the *Nuclear Weapons Case* to us? The ICJ accepted that nuclear weapons – which were not contemplated when the Charter was written (whilst the US government had used nuclear weapons during World War II (the only time nuclear weapons have ever been used in war) it had not been contemplated that anyone else would develop a nuclear bomb and certainly not the thermonuclear bombs that superseded them) – came within the remit of the UN Charter. Therefore, as technology changes the instruments remain, but the concept of 'force' is defined to include the new developments.

It has been suggested that there is no reason why cyberwarfare cannot amount to 'force' (Schmitt, 2011; Dinniss, 2012) and it has been argued that there is no reason why a computer cannot be a 'weapon' (Schmitt, 2013:42). However, it does not follow that every cyber-attack amounts to force. For example, it has been noted that a cyber-attack that does not seek to threaten or damage but instead simply posts propaganda that seeks to undermine the leadership of a state cannot constitute 'force' (Schmitt, 2013:46).

The difficulty is in identifying when cyber-attacks can amount to the use of 'force'. The authors of the Tallinn Manual stated that where it was comparable to a kinetic attack – i.e. it causes death, injury or damage to property – then there is no doubt that it constitutes 'force' (Schmitt, 2013:48), but would other types of attack constitute force? Schmitt has argued that it is necessary to consider, *inter alia*, the severity and invasiveness of any attack (Schmitt, 2011:576). He argues, therefore, that DoS attacks that took place against Estonia during 2007 when it was in dispute with Russia (who were at the time commonly blamed for the attacks) could satisfy the criteria for cyberwarfare because they caused significant disruption to state activities (Schmitt, 2011:577).

However, others believe that it is not enough that the consequences are severe, they must also be considered something other than a 'frontier incident' (Dinniss, 2012:81). This implies that not even attacks that are comparable to kinetic attacks will meet the threshold, because in areas of disputed territory it is inevitable that there will be flashpoints, which could include the use of armed force. Article 2(4) requires proof that it is an attack by a state (Shaw, 2008:1133) and this presumably exempts minor skirmishes. Whilst easily applicable to kinetic attacks it does raise the question of what that means in the context of cyberwarfare.

It will be remembered that Stuxnet caused considerable damage to the Iranian nuclear programme and so it could be argued that this meets the threshold in that it could be considered comparable to a kinetic attack, but at least one commentator argues it did not (Dinniss, 2012:82), partly because it did not cause irreparable damage (presumably something that a kinetic missile strike probably would).

To some, the suggestion that damage must be comparable to a kinetic attack is an outdated concept and unrealistic (McGhee, 2013:72). The reasoning behind this argument is that it is possible for cyber-attacks to cause serious disruption but not in a way that replicates kinetic attacks, and that it would be better to consider the severity of cyber-attacks rather than trying to somehow compare them to kinetic attacks. McGhee uses the example of power disruptions to illustrate this.

It will be remembered that attacking national power grids or power stations was one of the 'doomsday scenarios' considered in the earlier section on cyberterrorism, but it must be conceded that such an attack is (theoretically) possible. If the electricity grid is disabled by a cyber-attack is that sufficiently severe as to be comparable to an armed attack? Certainly we know that graphite bombs have been developed to disrupt electricity power stations by, in essence, short-circuiting the power system, and so a cyber-attack could be considered comparable to a kinetic attack. However, McGhee makes the point that a kinetic attack would be likely to cause injuries to personnel and physical damage: the short-circuiting is likely to fuse circuits and even start fires. The cyber-attack need not do this. It could (theoretically) just shut down the station. Does that mean it is not severe as there is no harm or injury? If so, it would mean that such an attack would not breach Article 2(4) of the UN Charter, meaning it did not constitute armed force. As will be seen, that would not be accepted by a number of countries who have suggested that they will respond with (kinetic) force if they are the subject of a significant cyber-attack.

### Does cyberwarfare exist?

It will be remembered from the earlier section on cyberterrorism that there is some doubt as to whether cyberterrorism exists, and the same could be true of cyberwarfare. Does it exist? As noted above, this is perhaps a difficult question to answer because many cyber-attacks will not become public knowledge. It is therefore difficult to know whether it is a reality or not. Certainly governments are spending considerable resources developing national plans for cyber-security, including classifying them as a national security issue (Dinniss, 2012), and so there is the potential for cyberwarfare to exist.

It was noted above that 'Moonlight Maze', Stuxnet and the Sony attack are commonly adduced as examples of cyberwarfare but at least two of these do not meet the criteria above. 'Moonlight Maze' has the characteristics of espionage not warfare. Its overall objective was to allow the servers to be interrogated and so it cannot be said that this involved force. For similar reasons the Sony attack also does not meet this threshold: it was about embarrassing a company and not about using force against a state entity. Others point to DoS attacks that took place against Estonia and Georgia in 2007 and 2008 when there were tensions with Russia (Dinniss, 2012:2) but, as Dinniss points out, there was no damage caused by these attacks so it may be difficult to classify them as warfare. Had the DoS attacks disabled communications systems or caused damage to the operation of, for example, the military this might come close to the threshold, but the behaviour seen at that time cannot realistically be so-classified.

Stuxnet is perhaps the closest we have to a recognised form of cyberwarfare. It did cause significant damage to the nuclear laboratory. Whether it could be said to be comparable to a kinetic attack is perhaps more questionable. Whilst it caused damage, a kinetic attack through cruise missile or aircraft-launched weaponry would have caused permanent damage. Perhaps Stuxnet is best thought of as demonstrating the *potential* for cyberwarfare.

There can be little doubt that in times of war, cyberspace is likely to be a new frontier. Whilst kinetic battles are likely to remain the prominent type of force, it is highly likely that they will be accompanied by 'battles' in cyberspace. As Stuxnet demonstrates there is also the potential that actual damage could be caused by cyber-attacks and therefore there is also the potential that the opening 'shots' of a war could be by computer instead of missile. One of the early stages of most air wars is to disable the enemy radar and communication systems. If this can be done by computer rather than missile then it would be safer for the attacking country. Cyberwarfare is therefore entirely possible.

### The 'laws' of cyberwarfare

As noted already, international law scholars will argue that war is 'regulated' by law and the same is arguably true of cyberwarfare. Whilst this is controversial in that some will argue that it is almost impossible to enforce international law against the most powerful nations, in theory it is a sound argument. There is no international instrument that currently discusses cyberwarfare and instead reference is made to the ordinary rules of international law.

One of the most important secondary sources is the 'Tallinn Manual' (published as Schmitt, 2013). This is sometimes misunderstood. It is purely an academic publication following a symposium of experts brought together by the NATO Cooperative Cyber Defence Centre of Excellence in Tallinn. Perhaps because it contains the term 'NATO' it is sometimes thought of as an official publication (McGhee, 2013:82) even though the manual itself makes clear that it has no official status (Schmitt, 2013:11). To that extent it is simply an important secondary source, in much the same way as other commentaries are (most notably, Dinniss, 2012).

Whilst the rules cover many preliminary issues, such as those which were discussed above, the principal source of division for our purposes is between *jus ad bellum* (roughly translated as the right to initiate warfare) and *jus in bello* (the limitations of warfare).

### Jus ad bellum

If war is to be regulated then one of the key questions is under what circumstances armed force can be used. Under the Charter of the UN there are considered to be two grounds for authorising armed conflict. The first is the UN itself authorises the use of force (Article 42 of the UN Charter) and the second is the inherent right of a state to act in self-defence (Article 51 of the UN Charter).

Realistically it is the latter that is most important for us since there has been no indication that the UN would order cyberwarfare measures under Article 42, although that is presumably in part because the issue has not yet arisen. Interestingly the wording of Article 42 speaks of action by 'air, sea or land forces' which raises thought-provoking issues about where cyberwarfare would fit (although arguably it could come within 'land'). Where a country has the capability to engage in cyberwarfare such that the UN would contemplate invoking Article 42, it is likely that their cyber-infrastructure would be so developed that a cyber-attack would have limited success. More likely would be the use of kinetic strikes in order to stop the attack.

The principal question that needs to be answered is when Article 51 applies. The key is its relationship with Article 2(4) as it is considered to be a response to such force (Dinstein, 2011:189). Thus force can be used if armed force within the meaning of Article 2(4) is used against that state, and that includes the point above about proving a state attack and not a mere skirmish (Shaw, 2008:1133; Dinstein, 2011:201). It will be remembered from above that there are some circumstances when it was considered that cyber-attacks could be considered 'force' for these purposes and Article 51 could apply then. What of situations where the force is threatened? Some countries claim the right to pre-emptive self-defence and whilst this is probably valid, it undoubtedly applies only to imminent attacks and not to mere threats (Dinstein, 2011:199). Whether that applies to cyber-attacks is perhaps more questionable. How does one ascertain that an attack is imminent rather than merely threatened?

For our purposes the more interesting point is the self-defence argument under Article 51. Specifically the question arises whether, if a cyber-attack amounts to force, a state under attack can respond with kinetic force. It has been reported that a number of countries have stated that they would consider an attack on their cyber-infrastructure to be an act of aggression to which they would respond with direct military force (Dinniss, 2012:56–57). However, it has also been noted that NATO has previously decided that a cyber-attack is not something that would necessarily be considered a collective attack that would trigger Article V of the North Atlantic Treaty (i.e. the provision that states an attack on one member state is an attack on them all). What is notable is that Article 51 identifies a threshold and is silent as to weapons (Dinstein, 2011:212), and so in principle there is no reason why a state cannot respond kinetically. It will be for each country to decide so long as the threshold for Article 51 is satisfied, which includes the fact that it must be more than a 'frontier incident'.

### Jus in bello

When one refers to the 'laws' of war it is normally *jus in bello* that is being referred to. In brief, this is the concept that there are limitations about what can be done in war. Many of the principles will not apply in this context because, for example, they refer to the treatment of prisoners of war (Shaw, 2008:1167), but some do apply.

The principal distinction in this area is between the rules that apply to combatants and those that apply to non-combatants (Shaw, 2008:1170). It is this latter part that is most relevant to us. Perhaps the key principle can be summarised as 'the requirement to protect civilians against the effects of hostilities' (Shaw, 2008:1184). In other words, whilst it is accepted that conflict will invariably lead to actions that will cause death, injury or damage, those who are not directly involved should so far as possible be protected. With kinetic warfare this is obviously not always possible, and indeed the term 'collateral damage' was coined to explain the position whereby civilian injuries or deaths are caused as a secondary effect of a kinetic weapon.

A key principle in international law is that civilians should not be directly targeted: a distinction should be made between civilian and military targets (Shaw, 2008:1184). However, distinguishing between them is not easy, particularly in cyberspace. Some targets will be obviously military (for example, military installations, military air-traffic systems, etc.) and some will be obviously civilian (for example, schools or hospitals) but others will be less clear. For example, take a broadcasting tower. Is that a civilian or military target? Even if it is primarily used for civilian communications it can obviously be used for military communications too, and so is it classed as civilian or military? So-called 'dual-use' technology (where it can be used for either civilian or military purposes) poses a particular difficulty.

It has been suggested that a good example of dual-use technology would be the power grid (Dinniss, 2012:194). Obviously the primary purpose of the national power grid is civilian in nature but quite clearly it has a military use too. Military installations and technology require power, and therefore can such infrastructure be attacked? It has been suggested that a balancing exercise must take place to identify whether the technology is civilian or military (Shaw, 2008:1185), but not everyone agrees with that and it has been stated that it is the motivation of the attack that is relevant. So, for example, if the reason for disabling the dual-use technology is military in nature then it is a military target notwithstanding the fact that it could have civilian uses (Schmitt, 2013:134). If we think of the power grid then it may be justified to target a relay station or sub-station close to a military base where it is clear that this would cause significant disruption to the base's power even though it would also cause blackouts to civilians in the area.

A particular difficulty is that technology allows military and civilian use to be brought closer together. A classic example of this would be the GPS system (or its European equivalent, Galileo). The GPS system of satellites was developed by the US military but was licensed for civilian use when it was realised that there was over-capacity. However, it undoubtedly remains important for military purposes, and so if the satellites were the subject of attack (kinetic or, perhaps more likely, cyber) then would they be a civilian or military target? If it were done to disrupt military operations then they would be a military target. Where does that leave the internet itself? It will be remembered from the beginning of this book that the internet was initially conceived as a military communications system and it continues to be used for these purposes. If a country targets the cyber-infrastructure of another, does that constitute a military attack?

Some infrastructure is specifically protected under international law and this includes certain cultural objects (including religious buildings) but also those that 'are deemed indispensable to the survival of the civilian population' (Shaw, 2008:1186) and certain specific objects such as nuclear power stations (where, presumably, the risk to the general population from a nuclear event would be catastrophic). There is no reason why this should not apply equally to cyberwarfare since, as has been noted, the law does not generally differentiate between the 'virtual' and 'real' world. Accordingly, a cyber-attack that targeted a desalination plant that provided the majority of the drinking water for a country would be illegal as the plant is clearly linked to the survival of the civilian population.

However, where there is perhaps more uncertainty is what happens where the central infrastructure of a country reliant on technology is attacked? Dinniss provides the example of Taiwan and suggests that an attack that, in essence, 'shuts down' access to the internet there would be illegal because the consequences would be catastrophic, with it causing socio-economic meltdown and political instability (Dinniss, 2012:189). However, it is less than clear that this argument is correct. Whilst an attack that was designed to annihilate the cyber-infrastructure of a country would certainly be so significant that it would amount to 'cyberwarfare', that, by itself, does not mean that an attack after war has been declared would be illegal. Whilst Dinniss is correct to state that the political and economic consequences of such an attack would be catastrophic, that, by itself, is not sufficient to make it illegal. Wars are dirty. They are unpleasant. There is a danger that the nature of war is being misunderstood because it can now be fought 'by wire'. There is a perception that wars are 'surgical' or 'clean' (something that has been discussed in other contexts, most notably the use of armed drones; see Gregory, 2011 for an interesting discussion on this) and yet the reality is they are not. Wars target the political and economic infrastructure of a country because one of the fastest ways of winning a war is to remove the political and economic infrastructure of a country.

Would targeting the central cyber-infrastructure of the country pose a risk to the 'sustainability of the population'? It is submitted that it would not. The survival of a country is obviously not linked to the internet, something that was seen during the millennia that humankind existed before the development of the internet. Even where most of a country's logistics are handled by the internet it would be possible to strip this out. Food and water could be given to the population without the need for the internet. All food reserves could be requisitioned and distributed by the military, meaning the fact that the banking and economic system had collapsed would be irrelevant. It is submitted that only where there is systematic targeting of infrastructure that deliberately threatens the *survivability* of the population would international law be breached.

### Enforcing international law

Before leaving cyberwarfare a few short sentences should be spent on how these laws are enforced. It is perhaps this issue that leads to some questioning whether there is truly such a thing as 'laws' of war. The enforcement of international law is, by necessity, political rather than legal.

In terms of *jus ad bellum*, enforcement would ordinarily lie with the UN. The UN is empowered to uphold the peace (see Article 39 of the UN Charter) and so ordinarily the UN Security Council would decide what action should be taken against someone who (illegally) initiates armed conflict. This could include, for example, the use of sanctions (Article 41) but could also include military force (Article 42). The fact that the permanent members of the Security Council (China, France, Russia, the UK and the USA) wield a veto means that the position can become messy and the UN may be impotent to act. It is this which leads to a criticism of international law: that it does not really apply to the big countries or their principal allies.

The enforcement of *jus in bello* is more interesting. Again, the UN has ultimate responsibility but breach of many of the principles set out therein amounts to 'crimes against humanity' and therefore is also a legal matter. There is now a permanent International Criminal Court that has power to try those who are accused of war crimes (including political leaders). Not every country has agreed to its jurisdiction but *ad hoc* tribunals created by the victors of conflict show that it does not really matter whether jurisdiction is accepted: crimes against humanity are justiciable when enforced by international political leadership. Some countries also exercise so-called universal jurisdiction in respect of war crimes, meaning that they reserve the right to try *anyone* for a war crime regardless of territorial link (Shaw, 2008:668 et seq.), providing another potential enforcement mechanism.

Finally the reality of geopolitics should be noted. Whilst theoretically the UN is the competent body that adjudicates on these disputes, the fact that the Security Council is intrinsically political undoubtedly complicates matters. Where it cannot act because of a political impasse then others may sometimes act. Perhaps the classic example of this was when NATO undertook armed action in the former republic of Yugoslavia when, in essence, the country engaged in civil war. Yugoslavia was a socialist (Soviet) state that was, in effect, politically protected by the (then) Soviet Union and post-Soviet Russia. Essentially this meant the UN Security Council was impotent because of the veto, and so NATO claimed the right to act unilaterally.

Many argue NATO had no right to do so. Yugoslavia was not a NATO member nor had any of its forces sought to attack a NATO member (thus triggering Article V of the North Atlantic Treaty). However, there was clear evidence that crimes against humanity were taking place and NATO acted where the UN could not. This perhaps reinforces the point that international law is as much geo-politics as law. Ultimately the UN assumed authority but only after the NATO campaign and various concessions by the constituent republics. An action before the International Court of Justice to declare such action illegal (*Yugoslavia v Belgium* and the same against nine other NATO countries) ultimately failed due to a lack of jurisdiction. However, some have argued that the action could have been considered lawful because the force was ultimately used to safeguard humanitarian principles (discussed in Shaw, 2008:1156–1158).

## Suggested further reading

Coleman, C. *Hacker, Hoaxer, Whistleblower, Spy: The Many Faces of Anonymous* (2014, Brooklyn: Verso).
*This is an interesting book written by someone who has interviewed members of the Anonymous Collective. Whilst it is not an easy read, it does present the different ways that Anonymous work and details some of their key operations.*

Dinniss, H.H. *Cyber Warfare and the Laws of War* (2012, Cambridge: Cambridge University Press).
*This is a more academic text than the 'Tallinn Manual' and there is more critique than can be expected from the Manual. It is an easy-to-read book that explores the concept of law in the context of cyberwarfare.*

Hampson, N.C.N. 'Hacktivism: A new breed of protest in a networked world' (2012) 35 *Boston College International and Comparative Law Review* 511–542.

*This is an interesting introduction to hacktivism and whether this behaviour can be differentiated from criminal hacking. Whilst it is based on US law many of the concepts are directly applicable to the UK.*

Schmitt, M.N. *Tallinn Manual on the International Law Applicable to Cyber Warfare* (2013, Cambridge: Cambridge University Press).
*This is the 'Tallinn Manual' which was put together by a group of experts who were asked to theorise how the 'laws of war' apply to cyberwarfare. It is an interesting read as it demonstrates some of the difficulties in trying to wrap new technology in old laws.*

# Part 2

# Property

# Chapter 6

# Fraud

Now that we have left behind the attacks against technology we can begin to consider those crimes that use technology as part of their commission. Perhaps one of the most notable forms of this type of crime is that of fraud, which is sometimes known as cyber-fraud when it is committed online. There is a question as to whether referring to 'cyber-fraud' is at all helpful since it suggests that it is a type of fraud that occurs solely on the internet, when the reality is that fraudulent behaviour exists both online and offline but the internet provides new opportunities to use scams that have previously existed. To that extent it can be said to be an example of the radicalisation of pre-existing crimes (discussed further in Chapter 1).

There are dramatic differences in victimhood in fraud. It can range from an individual losing a small amount of money from buying a non-existent item on the internet to multi-national companies losing tens of millions of pounds. What is perhaps unusual about fraud on the internet is the fact that the same behaviour may lead to different results. For example, a simple phishing scam (where a person pretends to be from a bank) may lead to one individual losing only tens of pounds because, for example, their account is set up in a particular way. Yet in 2013 it was reported that the same scam cost St Aldhelm's Academy, a secondary school in Dorset, £1.1 million when a person pretending to be from their bank requested that they 'verify' their account details. It is this which is perhaps special about fraud: behaviours may not change very much but the amount of money a victim has could determine how 'successful' a scam actually is.

## Types of online fraud

As has been hinted at already, there are a variety of different types of frauds that are committed on the internet and indeed new forms are developed each year. Stabek *et al.* conducted some empirical analysis of frauds and suggested that there are seven distinct types (2010:44–45):

1. **Fraud through low-level trickery**. This would include such scams as advertising non-existent or bogus items for sale.

2. **Fraud through developed story-based application**. This is where a relation-ship is developed between scammer and victim. A good example of this would be '419 frauds'.
3. **Participation through employment-based strategies**. This could include the advertising of a job that requires the completion of a course or application that involves a fee to be paid in advance.
4. **Fraud through implied necessary obligation**. These types of scams require the user to respond in some way before the scam can work. It could include unintentionally subscribing to a particular site or requiring the user to ring a particular number (at a cost).
5. **Information gathering through apparently authentic appeals**. This would include the classic scams of phishing and spoofing.
6. **Financial gain through merchant and customer-based exploitation**. This would include most auction frauds.
7. **Financial gain through marketing opportunities**. This would include char-ity frauds, Ponzi schemes and get-rich-quick schemes which, of course, turn out to be false.

This is an interesting dissection and is clearly based on a careful analysis of the types of fraud that can be identified on the internet. Of course the flaw in this analysis is that it depends on visibility, and some forms of behaviour will not necessarily be known, but it is perhaps the most comprehensive analysis of fraudulent behaviour (particularly the descriptions of the 'scam genres' (see Stabek *et al.*, 2010:49–51)). For our purposes we can simplify the examination and we will look at a smaller number of more prominent types of fraud. The ones to be examined are:

- Auction frauds.
- '419 frauds'.
- Romance frauds.
- Phishing.

This is not to suggest that other types of fraud do not exist because clearly they do, but it is an attempt to present the most common types of fraud that exist and to allow examination of these issues. By concentrating on all the different types of fraud it would be difficult to give adequate analysis and so, as this book is based on themes, this approach will be adopted in this chapter.

### Auction frauds

The first issue to consider is that of auction fraud. As the name would sug-gest, this is fraud that takes place within an online auction environment. Online auctions are one of the more popular forms of e-commerce and eBay is probably the largest and best-known example of this genre, although others exist.

The potential for online fraud conducted through auctions is vast. In 2013 eBay facilitated US$212 billion of commerce globally (eBay Inc. website) with their own revenue amounting to upwards of US$19 billion. Some 128 million active users exist on eBay (both purchasers and sellers), meaning that even a very small percentage of fraud would equate to a large number of potential victims. eBay has developed a highly successful and sophisticated business model that allows people to sell items ranging from the extremely cheap to the very expensive. Cars, yachts and expensive antiques can, and are, traded on eBay meaning that the potential gains for fraud are immense. However, eBay also spends a lot of money countering fraud and has numerous pages dedicated to ensuring that fraud does not happen, including offering guarantees in certain circumstances.

The fact that eBay (and other sites) will co-operate with law enforcement and/or take civil action means that offenders will try to ensure that transactions do not take place through the site. It is not uncommon for people to offer to end an auction early for a 'good price' and they will try to justify this as ensuring a discount can be given because, for example, they can avoid paying commission to eBay. However, the real reason is often to ensure that there is no electronic trail through eBay that would tie the person to a fraud and also to ensure that protected payment systems can be avoided. In this way there is a greater chance that the fraud will be successful (a useful summary is presented by Aleem and Antwi-Boasiako, 2011:148, where they present emails from people who try to do this).

Whilst there are a variety of different types of fraud that can be conducted through auctions, the most common are:

- Shill bidding.
- Bid shielding.
- Non-delivery of goods.
- Goods that are not legitimate or as described.
- Overpayment.

There are, of course, many other types of fraud and it has been noted that another popular outlet for auction frauds is the 'fencing' of stolen goods (Yar, 2013:80). The large number of items available on a site such as eBay and the fact that it is no longer necessary to conduct an auction but instead the first person to bid can buy the item means that it would be very difficult for generic stolen items to be traced through auction sites. Whether this is a cyber-fraud *per se* is perhaps more questionable although arguably it is, not least because if the title to the item could ever be traced then the purchaser would be deprived of the item, probably without any refund.

*Shill bidding*

The first sub-category of auction fraud to consider is that of shill bidding. This is where the seller creates a (fake) profile in order to bid on the item that he himself has put up for auction (Snyder, 2000:457). Many auction sites, especially eBay, will allow users to place an automated 'highest bid'. This is where the site bids incrementally until the auction is won or until the maximum bid has been reached. By creating a fake bidder the winning bid will rise because the automatic bidding system will try to win. However, what is interesting about this type of fraud is the extent to which people would consider this to be a fraud. It almost certainly is, but it must be questioned how many people may contemplate doing this – even if they do not actually do so – or who would consider it to be a crime. Is it not likely that many people expect this happens in some cases and that is a disadvantage of an anonymous auction?

*Bid shielding*

Snyder argues that there is an opposite scam from shill bidding which he terms 'bid shielding' (Snyder, 2000:457). This is where two people work together to procure an item at a low price. Person X places the minimum bid to secure an item. Person Y then makes an absurdly high bid. As the winning bid is listed this dissuades people from making further bids but in the closing minutes this high bid is withdrawn meaning the only other (viable) bid is that made by person X. Not all auction sites would allow this scam to work since they will not display the highest bid but rather allow maximum bids to be placed so that there are incremental increases. However, those that display the full bids would be susceptible to such scams. Is this a fraud? The answer would seem to be 'yes' because it means that a person is able to secure the item for much lower than other people may be prepared to pay. However, the difficulty with this argument is that it is speculative. If there is no reserve then arguably the seller is prepared to sell the item for whatever money she is offered and in any event if bidders are put off by the large (fake) bid it is impossible to know whether anyone else would have bid and, if so, for what amount.

*Non-delivery of goods*

The most common type of auction fraud is where goods are never sent (Snyder, 2000:458) with it being suggested that 0.62 per cent of items bought through auctions are not being delivered (Yar, 2013:81). Given that millions of items are sold daily on eBay this will mean that tens of thousands of items will not be delivered each day.

The non-delivery of goods is arguably a very profitable fraud because, as will be noted below, a particular issue with fraud is under-reporting. If an item is for a relatively trivial amount (say £10) how many people will go through the hassle of reporting this as a fraud and contacting eBay to seek recompense? The chance is that whilst some will, it is likely a considerable number probably will not. If this scam is pulled off 100 times then a £10 fraud becomes a £1,000 fraud. Repeated even weekly this then becomes a significant fraud.

## Misrepresented goods

An offshoot of goods that are not delivered are those that are described inappropriately or in a misleading way. So, for example, it may be suggested that an item is genuine when it is fake (including counterfeit CDs or DVDs) or something may be described as new when it is in fact second-hand. A prominent example of misleading adverts was reported in December 2013 when a 19-year-old paid £450 for a picture of a games console believing he was buying the real thing (although the small print of the eBay advert did say that it was only offering a photograph of the console). In that instance eBay stepped in to ensure that a refund occurred but it does demonstrate the potential for this type of fraud to occur.

## Overpayment

A variation of an auction fraud is overpayment. Whilst this is facilitated by internet auctions the scam will normally be executed in person. A buyer will make a purchase of something, usually relatively valuable (e.g. £500) and usually something fragile. As it is fragile it will be collected in person and the 'buyer' will despatch a 'representative' to collect the goods and pay by cheque. However, the cheque will be made out for £800 instead of £500 due to 'confusion'. As the person collecting the item is only a representative he will claim that he will not be able to write out another cheque because only the purchaser can do this. As the item is needed quickly the representative and seller will arrange an easy compromise. The seller will take the £800 cheque and provide a post-dated cheque for £300 as the difference. The post-dating means (he believes) that it is a safe transaction (as he could stop the cheque). In fact, post-dated cheques are a myth and the bank can honour them regardless of the date. The £800 cheque turns out to be fake (or is stopped) meaning that the seller loses not only the item (which has been taken) but also £300.

## '419 frauds'

One of the most common types of frauds are those known as '419 frauds' or the 'Nigerian advanced fee scam'. The term 419 refers to the section of the penal code of the Nigerian Penal Code that criminalises this type of fraud, partly because for many years a large proportion of these frauds emanated from Nigeria (although they can now be found across the world).

419 frauds are perhaps the classic scam and one that many find it incredible that they work. A typical 419 scam involves a person pretending to be an official who needs assistance to move money that he claims is rightfully his out of a country to avoid a corrupt official. Variations of these will include winning a lottery in a foreign country even though the person never entered or an email saying that the recipient is the last-known descendent of a relative in another country and a large bequest has been left. Virtually everyone with an email address will, at some point, have received an email like this and most will simply have pressed 'delete' and wondered if anyone actually falls for these scams. The answer would seem to be 'yes' although it has been noted that there are no central statistics that quantify these losses. Media reports suggest that people continue to fall for the scams every day (see Anderson *et al.*, 2013:284).

That said, the fact that people are aware of 419 scams does appear to change the way that they now operate. Those that undertake the scams know that many people are aware of the scams, and indeed there are large repositories of information on the internet where people who have had contact with the scammers illustrate how they work (including, for example, displaying the various emails they have received). The effect of this is that 419 scammers now expect a number of potential victims not to be serious and there is some evidence to suggest that they will quickly decide to drop someone they believe is not likely to be co-operative (Glickman, 2005:467).

An interesting quirk of 419 frauds is that whilst they may be one of the most well-known examples of cyber-fraud, 419 frauds predate the internet by about 400 years. In the sixteenth century the 'Spanish prisoner' scam was used. The variations of this were usually that a prisoner had a beautiful sister in need of protection and a move to England, and who invariably was also the heir to a vast fortune or in possession of valuable diamonds. Correspondence would be entered into with a noble in England who would be persuaded that they needed to send an advance of gold in order to bribe the appropriate officials, book passage in a boat, etc. The 'classic' 419 frauds that began to emerge on the internet effectively adopted the same methodology.

It has been noted that 419 scams are normally linked by the concept of greed (Glickman, 2005:463), the greedy normally being the victim. The 419 scams normally suggest a way of doing something to get rich quickly or for free. This could, for example, be by using a bank account for a few days to earn the interest on tens of millions of dollars (which would be a sizeable sum) or a percentage of an improbably large transaction. Whatever it is, many of the 419 scams operate on the basis that the person who will ultimately be victimised is prepared to do something dubious because of the high rewards offered.

Once a person is caught within a 419 scam it is not uncommon for them to be in denial about the fact that they are the victim of a scam, and they will continue to pay money in the hope that they will ultimately get the vast rewards promised (Glickman, 2005:468). These payments will often be in respect of professional services. For example, it may be claimed that the bank needs commission in advance for the transfer, or a lawyer needs to draw up a contract for the 'safety' of the individual. It is easy to create a website that purports to be a legitimate law firm, meaning that the victim believes that the transaction fee is legitimate and indeed potentially validates the initial scam.

Another common issue with 419 scams is that it can lead the victims to recognise that they themselves are acting in a morally dubious manner, meaning that they are perhaps less likely to report any fraud. Classic 419 scams will include people trying to hide multi-million pound funds from tax collectors, smuggling illicitly gotten profits out of a country or an attempt to evade customs charges (some are discussed in Glickman, 2005). These scams work on the basis that the victim is prepared to do something that could be construed as illegal and certainly would be construed as morally wrong. Therefore the victim is perhaps more likely to acquiesce to 'security' and 'confidentiality' that would allow the victim and offender to build up trust whilst at the same time the offender is preparing to spring the scam.

### Romance frauds

A relatively new form of 419 frauds are romance frauds. Of course the reality is that this is not really new since, as was noted above, the original 419 fraud was based on romance (the 'Spanish prisoner'). However, there has been a resurgence in recent years where people have been targeted through romance websites.

As is well known, one of the biggest growth areas in recent years has been dating websites. These range from the generic to the very niche but they all operate on the premise of allowing people to meet people who wish to form a relationship. It has been known for many years that the internet has allowed people to communicate with one another in a romantic way and people are turning to these sites to find romance. However, this same technology and desire allows people to be defrauded, sometimes out of tens of thousands of pounds. Indeed, in their 2012 Annual Report the US IC3 agency (the Internet Crime Complaint Center is a federal agency that supports law enforcement and analyses fraud trends) stated they received over 4,000 complaints concerning romance fraud with losses totalling US$55 million (IC3, 2012:16).

The growth of e-dating has meant that 'fraudsters can cast their nets wider' than they perhaps traditionally would (Rege, 2009:498) and the growth in (legitimate) dating websites means that would-be fraudsters have a list of potential victims. Some people will have registrations on multiple sites showing that they particularly desire to meet someone and therefore are potentially vulnerable to people offering them a romance.

The scam will normally begin with a person pretending to be interested in developing a romance. Rather than being a local contact the person will state that they reside some distance away and thus the initial stages of the romance will take place via email, text messages, etc. This can be a powerful way of developing a relationship because, in essence, the internet allows for a degree of anonymity that simply would not exist in real life. This can be true even of photographs. The internet has thousands of photographs of 'desirable' people irrespective of whether they are actually looking for romance or not. Rege provides the example of Robert Frost, a professional race-car driver, who was surprised to learn that his picture had been used in over 90 web-sites through multiple personalities (2009:501). Obviously people will wish to receive photographs of those they are interested in, but the internet allows people to create a series of images that they can put forward as themselves (or another) with the victim being unlikely to detect the fact that the image is, in fact, false.

Once the romance has begun to develop, a variety of different scams may occur. With some, there may be a series of meetings where a 'real' romance begins but where the person requests financial assistance to facilitate travel, etc. As the romance builds the person may state that they cannot see the victim anymore because they have lots of debt and therefore will need to move to another country to work (unless, of course, the victim could lend him the money to pay off the debt). They may try to persuade them to part with money to make home improvements so that their house can be sold before moving in with the victim. In all those instances, of course, when the money is given the person will disappear.

Not all romance frauds are the same and where the relationship remains distant it is quite possible that the fraudster may request 'gifts' to help them stay in communication (because, for example, an expensive smartphone or laptop has been stolen and they can't afford to get a new one meaning that they won't be able to stay in touch). It may also involve someone posing as a lawyer to say that the person has been arrested by a corrupt police officer, or a 'doctor' claiming that the loved one has been seriously injured but that as nobody is paying the bills he cannot have any treatment (Buchanan and Whitty, 2014:261). In extreme cases there have been examples of people going to African countries to meet their loved one only for them to be kidnapped and held for ransom (Buchanan and Whitty, 2014:262).

Whilst all frauds will sometimes leave victims feeling foolish or embarrassed that they were duped, romance frauds have the potential for significant emotional impact (Buchanan and Whitty, 2014:279), this is because not only does the victim realise that they have been conned out of money but also that the perpetrator faked their emotions. In other words there is the distress that is caused by the betrayal resulting from the pretence that there was an emotional attachment. To that extent it can be said to be a much more sinister fraud than other types of online fraud.

## Phishing

Perhaps one of the most common types of fraud is that of phishing. Along with 419 frauds, virtually everyone who has an email account will at some point have received a phishing email.

There are different ways in which phishing may occur. The 'traditional' method is to ask someone to 'confirm' their personal details. This will often either be their bank details (including log-in credentials) or their email credentials (so that the phisher can access confidential information and/or send spam from the account). It has been noted that a variation on this is where a spoof email is sent but it requests that a person conducts security by telephoning a certain number (Clough, 2010:193). This is a clever scam as it will make people believe that they are calling their bank to verify that the email is, in fact, correct and they are therefore more prepared to confirm their bank details.

Phishing has become more sophisticated in recent years. No longer is there the plain-text email that purports to be from your bank even though the 'from' address shows that obviously it is not. Phishers are now spending considerable time ensuring that the emails look almost identical to legitimate emails, including providing information that would seem to include warnings about phishing. One that the author recently received included the message, 'How do I know this is not a Spoof email? Spoof or "phishing" emails tend to have generic greetings ... Emails from [us] will always address you by your first name'. This provides reassurance therefore that the email is genuine, especially in combination with the official-looking images and even a link to the real site (two links were contained in the email, one to security on the (legitimate) site and one that asked me to complete my bank details (which was not on the legitimate site). It looked genuine and it would be easy to believe that it was legitimate. This particular email had only one flaw. I do not have an account with that bank. However, it shows the level of sophistication that phishers are developing. No longer can we state that only the naïve are the subject of phishing scams because the level of detail paid to the trickery is increasing.

A variation on phishing is that instead of sending a fake email requesting that financial details are verified, the email will purport to show that a payment has been made (see, for example, Aleem and Antwi-Boasiako, 2011:150). This is usually in the context of auction frauds. The scam operates by arranging to purchase something through an auction website. For this to work the transaction will have to take place away from the auction site (as discussed earlier) but the buyer will offer to use, for example, PayPal to ensure that it remains a 'safe' transaction. A fake email is then sent which purports to come from PayPal which shows that a payment has been made by the correct person and for the correct amount. If the seller does not check their PayPal account (or their bank account) and instead just relies on this email then they may believe that the money has been released (when it has not) and will then send the item to the purchaser, meaning they lose out.

### Pharming

Clough suggests that allied to phishing is the phenomenon of pharming which is where a fake website is created instead of fake emails (2010:194). Pharming is quite a sophisticated fraud because it occurs where a person believes they are trying to reach a legitimate site but are instead diverted to a rogue site. Ordinarily this would be achieved by 'polluting' the technical processes of a computer so that the Domain Name lookup Server (DNS) which allows a user to navigate to a particular site will direct the user instead to a fake site (Karlof *et al.*, 2007:58). The most usual way of doing this is through the provision of malware (Brody *et al.*, 2007:47) and the principal difficulty with pharming is that the user will probably not know that the site they are accessing is not legitimate, and will feel safe because they took precautions by, for example, entering the website for the bank or online clearing facility direct.

Another popular (and less technically sophisticated) way of pharming is to rely on what is popularly known as 'fat finger syndrome'. Many of us are accustomed to typing these days and can be quite quick. However, unless one is a professional touch-typist it is likely that occasional mistakes will be made when typing. The second form of phishing relies on this happening. The person operating the scam will create a duplicate site but one which contains a spelling mistake (e.g. paypla.com instead of paypal.com) (Brody *et al.*, 2007:48). How many people check the URL displayed in their internet browser? If you type an address for a site and a site appears that looks like the one you wish to access most people will probably trust that it is the correct site and not check the spelling of the URL. Where the site is for banking or other forms of transactions this can be dangerous as it will record the log-in credentials whilst returning a page saying something like 'Our servers are busy now, please try again later'. Again, this is unlikely to worry an individual and provides the scammer with valuable time to conduct rogue financial transactions.

## Legal responses to fraud

Now that the key themes of fraud have been set out it is necessary to consider how the law has responded.

### Reporting of fraud

One of the most notable aspects of fraud is its reporting. It is commonly thought that fraud is chronically under-reported (Clough, 2010:199). It will be remembered from the previous sections that I postulated that nearly everyone with an email address will have received an email that constituted an attempt at either a 419 fraud or a phishing email. How many will have reported these emails as potentially fraudulent? It would be amazing if most people did more than just press the 'delete' button.

Even where a fraud does occur there would seem quite clear evidence that fraud is under-reported, and this could be for a variety of reasons including the fact that it is a small amount of money, the victim may feel embarrassed, may wonder whether they themselves are complicit or do not know to whom they should address a complaint (Yar, 2013:90). The latter point is particularly interesting, especially within England and Wales. If, for example, V bids for an item on eBay but the item is not delivered, would it be possible to report the matter to the police? It is unlikely that the police would consider this a crime and they are more likely to regard it as a civil matter. Indeed, eBay itself provides a dispute resolution service which effectively allows matters to be dealt with rather than report the matter to the police. The same is true of small-scale frauds relating to bank statements. If, for example, there is a rogue debit card transaction that is obviously fraudulent, to whom should this be reported? It is unlikely that the police would accept this as a crime and, for example, the Metropolitan Police website specifically states that reports should not be made and instead a referral should be made to 'Action Fraud' (http://content.met.police.uk/Site/reportingfraud).

Action Fraud is a national reporting mechanism that was created by the City of London Police to provide a single point of contact for fraud. Whilst it will allow users to report the matter and will provide a crime reference number, it will not actively investigate cases (www.actionfraud.police.uk/ about-us/who-we-are) and it will not provide an update on any case. In fact, the vast majority of small-scale cases such as the hypothetical case discussed above will be resolved by the banks. Contrast this with the position where person X takes a £20 note from person Y's purse. There the matter would not only be reported as a crime but would probably be investigated and there would be police action. The lack of police action and the determination to push such matters to, for example, auction sites or banks has in effect created the privatisation of fraud, where it is not really considered a criminal justice concern but rather a civil matter. Whether this is helpful is perhaps more open to question.

### Cybercrime Convention

The first issue to consider is how the Cybercrime Convention deals with fraud. Unlike in respect of attacks on computers or data the provisions are arguably more vague here. The most notable provision is Article 8 of the Convention ('computer-related fraud') but in respect of some of the frauds discussed here it is likely that Article 7 ('computer-related forgery') would also be of assistance.

## Article 8 (fraud)

Article 8 of the Convention states:

> Each party shall adopt such legislative and other measures as may be necessary to establish as criminal offences under its domestic law, when committed unintentionally and without right, the causing of a loss of property to another person by:
>
> (a) any input, alteration, deletion or suppression of computer data,
>
> (b) any interference with the functioning of a computer system, with fraudulent or dishonest intent of procuring, without right, an economic benefit for oneself or for another person.

It can be seen that this is very broad and lacks the detail that many other provisions contain. This can be seen on the one hand to be an advantage as it means that it can be considered flexible enough to cope with new forms of fraud, but it can also be a disadvantage in that it will be for nation states to translate this into domestic legislation, meaning that there could be very different definitions. It will be remembered from Chapter 2 that jurisdictional challenges can arise where there is incompatibility between national legislations, partly because of the requirement that exists in some countries for dual criminality.

Article 8 deals with fraud that is undertaken through the manipulation of data. Therefore, arguably, it does not apply to simple scams such as auction frauds where, for example, there is non-delivery of goods. This is presumably partly because it is thought that this is not a cybercrime *per se*, in that the Cybercrime Convention is primarily focused on crimes that take place entirely within cyberspace. There is also probably the belief that it is unnecessary to include this within the Cybercrime Convention because domestic law would ordinarily include it.

## Article 7

Article 7 of the Convention may also be pertinent. This states:

> Each party shall adopt such legislative and other measures as may be necessary to establish as criminal offences under its domestic law, when committed intentionally and without right, the input, alteration, deletion, or suppression of computer data, resulting in inauthentic data with the intent that it be considered or acted upon for legal purposes as if it were authentic, regardless whether or not the data is directly readable and intelligible. A party may require an intent to defraud, or similar dishonest intention, before criminal liability attaches.

Unlike Article 8, this is a little more specific although there are still defini-
tional issues that are left to the discretion of member states, including most
notably the definition of the fault element. It has been confirmed that Article
7 could be useful in respect of phishing where data is manipulated to make
it appear that it is authentic, something that is confirmed by the *Cybercrime
Convention Committee* (T-CY, 2013). It is also noted that many of the offences
that we considered in Chapters 3 and 4 (most notably in relation to hacking
and malware) will also apply, and therefore it can be said that the Cybercrime
Convention does seek to tackle fraud.

## Fraud Act 2006

The principal UK legislation is contained within the *Fraud Act 2006* although
other offences will apply (including those relating to computer misuse).
However, for our purposes we will consider the key themes of fraud as they
are most pertinent to what is being discussed in this area.

### Pre Fraud Act 2006

Until the *Fraud Act 2006* came into force there was not a specific offence of
fraud and instead it was dealt with by a variety of offences, most notably
the deception offences under the *Theft Act 1968* and *Theft Act 1978* and the
common-law offence of conspiracy to defraud. The Law Commission were
asked to consider the issue of fraud and their report (Law Commission, 2002)
ultimately led to the change in the law. The Law Commission believed that
the law was ripe for change, not least because the common-law offence of
conspiracy to defraud was unusual in that there was no substantive offence
of defrauding (Law Commission, 2002:5) whereas usually inchoate offences
would have a matched substantive offence.

One of the main concerns that the Law Commission had was in respect of
computers. This was in 2002 when e-commerce was beginning to be noticed
and the Commission noted that where deception was required there was a
fatal flaw:

> A machine has no mind, so it cannot believe a proposition to be true
> or false, and therefore cannot be deceived. A person who dishonestly
> obtains a benefit by giving false information to a computer or machine is
> not guilty of any deception offence.
>
> (Law Commission, 2002:21)

This did not mean that the person necessarily escaped all liability because
it was likely that the offence of theft would have been committed where the
object of the trickery was to obtain property (including money), but where
the object was a service then no alternative existed.

### General fraud offence

The basic framework of the offence is set out in s.1, *Fraud Act 2006* which states that the offence of fraud can be committed in one of three ways:

- Fraud by self-representation (s.2).
- Fraud by failing to disclose information (s.3).
- Fraud by abuse of position (s.4).

Technically this means that a person is charged under s.1 which is unnecessary since ss.2 to 4 could have been stand-alone offences in their own right (Ormerod, 2011:873) and certainly they are presented in this way in the Act.

### Common features

There are some features that are common to all forms of the fraud offence. These primarily relate to the fault element (the *mens rea*). The first of these is dishonesty: all forms of the fraud offence require that person D does something dishonestly. The term 'dishonest' is not defined in the Act and this is because Parliament was content to know that the term was defined clearly in the common law through *R v Ghosh* [1982] 1 WLR 409. However, it has been suggested that this may mean that defendants are more likely to proceed to trial because the nature of the *Ghosh* test is such that they might as well 'try their luck with a jury' (Ormerod, 2011:875).

The *Ghosh* test consists of two parts, an objective part and a subjective part:

1. Would reasonable and honest persons consider the actions of the defendant to be dishonest?
2. If so, does the defendant appreciate that reasonable and honest persons would consider his actions dishonest?

The phrasing of the second question is important. It is not that D must consider his actions to be dishonest, he must know that reasonable and honest people consider his actions to be dishonest. Whilst s.2, *Theft Act 1968* provides three circumstances under which a person is not to be classed as dishonest, no similar negative definition of dishonesty exists under the *Fraud Act 2006* and it has been suggested that this is a mistake (Ormerod, 2011:876–877). Prosecutorial discretion may ensure that no prejudice arises as a result of this omission, although it is unlikely many defendants would place too much reliance on prosecutorial discretion.

The second common fault element is that the fraud must be done with intent to gain or cause loss or to expose to a risk of loss. This is set out in s.5(2) as:

'gain' and 'loss'

(a) extend only to gain or loss in money or other property;
(b) include any such gain or loss whether temporary or permanent;

and 'property' means any property whether real or personal (including things in action and other intangible property).

Section 5(3) and (4) expand on what 'gain' and 'loss' mean by saying a gain includes keeping what one has and a loss includes 'not getting what one might get', which is obviously important in terms of auction frauds where it will be remembered that a common tactic is not to send purchased goods.

### Fraud by false representation

The first of the three ways of committing fraud is by false representation under s.2, *Fraud Act 2006*. The offence is committed where a person dishonestly makes a false representation and intends to make a gain for himself or a loss to another. A statement is false if:

(a) it is untrue or misleading, and
(b) the person making it knows that it is, or might be, untrue or misleading.

(s.2(2), Fraud Act 2006)

Thus falsity is both a matter of fact (that it is untrue or misleading) and a matter relating to the fault element (that the person knows it is untrue or misleading or knows it *might* be). The requirement that the defendant need only know that it *might* be untrue or misleading makes this a wide offence. It has been suggested that it will almost certainly blur into the requirement for dishonesty (Ormerod, 2011:899) and this must be correct. How will a jury react when they are faced with someone who has 'taken a chance' and mislabelled something when they were not sure of its provenance? Will they consider the defendant to be dishonest? The rationale for not simply relying on knowledge is that it would be very difficult in many instances for a person to *know* whether something is actually false or misleading and it would allow for cleverly worded statements to perhaps evade the law. However, the formulation of 'might be' is perhaps taking things a little too far in the opposite direction.

At its simplest this offence can be used for most basic cyber-frauds. A good example is *R v Ullah* [2009] EWCA Crim 2397 where a person used eBay legitimately for a number of months to get a good reputation. Once the reputation was established he then offered high-value goods that he had no intention or ability to deliver. He pleaded guilty to fraud offences relating to the offering of goods worth £229,000 and receiving over £32,000 as a result of the fraud and was sentenced to two years and eight months' imprisonment. A similar result occurred in *R v Clifford* [2013] EWCA Crim 1715 where the appellant sold a Range Rover car over eBay that it transpired was stolen. Whilst he was acquitted of handling stolen goods (and this was the subject of the appeal as he argued that it was inconsistent to acquit him of this charge and yet convict him of fraud, something rejected by the Court of Appeal) he was convicted of the offence of fraud under ss.1 and 2, the representation being that he was entitled to sell the car. These cases demonstrate the flexibility s.2 can bring in respect of these offences.

The wording of s.2 is important because it notes that, unlike with theft, there is no requirement that there is an actual loss. The wording of the statute is that fraud occurs where a person makes a false representation with the appropriate *mens rea*. This could be key in auction frauds where there would be no requirement to prove that the transaction actually occurred, it would be sufficient to show that the representation was made. Let us take an example:

> D offers a car for sale on eBay. The car is described as being in 'excellent condition', has 25,000 miles on the clock and has had one careful owner. In fact, D knows that the car has had a replacement engine and whilst that engine has only driven for 25,000 miles the actual car has been driven for 130,000 miles, with D adjusting the milometer. He also knows that it was written off by an insurance company after the owner caused a serious accident that required extensive repairs, most of which were carried out in a way contrary to manufacturer's guidance.

This would seem a classic scam. It would also appear to meet the threshold of s.2. A representation has been made (both express and implied) and D knows that it is false. It is not necessary to wait for V to purchase this car and complain to the police. As s.2 is triggered by the *making* of a false representation the fact that it is posted on eBay would suffice for liability, assuming that this was identified by the authorities before the transaction occurred. This is a significant weapon in the fight against auction fraud and it is easy to think of a number of items where this advantage could be used.

It will be remembered that one of the concerns that led to the change of the law of fraud was that under the old law a computer could not be deceived. The *Fraud Act 2006* puts beyond doubt this issue in respect of representations when s.2(5) states, 'a representation may be regarded as made if it … is submitted in any form to any system or device designed to receive, convey or respond to communications'. Again this is potentially very significant when it comes to online purchases. If something is to be purchased from an online merchant then it is highly unlikely that a human will take all the details, it is more likely that this will be automated. However, presenting credit card details represents that (a) they are yours and (b) you are entitled to use them. Where a person uses unauthorised card details (e.g. because they were gathered by phishing) then s.2(5) means that person may still be convicted of fraud even though it is an automated process.

The flexibility offered by s.2 means that it is the most likely charge in respect of many internet frauds. The issue of auction fraud has already been considered but it is likely that it will apply equally to 419 frauds and romance frauds. Taking 419 frauds first, it is clear that this is a classic example of representation fraud. The whole basis of 419 frauds is that a person is pretending to be someone they are not and they make a representation that is false or misleading, meaning s.2 is the natural charge. Romance frauds are the same. As noted above, many romance frauds will involve D pretending that something has happened or needs to happen. This would be a representation and if it is done dishonestly (which is highly likely) and is false or misleading then s.2 would apply.

### Failure to disclose information

The second form of fraud is contained within s.3 which is where there has been a failure to disclose information. The offence occurs where '[he] fails to disclose information to another person, which he is under a legal duty to disclose' and this is done dishonestly and with the intention of making a gain or causing a loss to another.

It is important to note that s.3 is restricted to those situations where a person is under a legal duty to disclose and not where there is a moral duty. The genesis of this offence can be seen from the Law Commission report which identified a range of situations where a person would have a legal duty to disclose information including from company law, contract law and fiduciary duties (Law Commission, 2002:64). Ormerod provides a good example which could be relevant for our purposes. Where a person takes out life insurance they must disclose any pre-existing medical conditions. If they do not do so then the policy is void but they may also be liable for fraud under s.3 (Ormerod, 2011:902). This could apply to internet fraud where insurances are frequently purchased over the internet. Presumably the same would apply to car insurances where the disclosure of penalty points or previous accidents could lower a premium (indicating 'gain') and therefore s.3 could apply.

There does not appear to be any requirement that D is aware that he is under an obligation to disclose information although presumably this will be a factor when deciding whether D acted dishonestly.

### Fraud by abuse of position

The third form of fraud is where the fraud occurs through abuse of a position. Section 4(1) defines this offence as:

A person is in breach of this section if he

(a) occupies a position in which he is expected to safeguard, or not to act against, the financial interests of another person,

(b)  dishonestly abuses that position, and
(c)  intends, by means of the abuse of that position

(i)   to make a gain for himself or another, or
(ii)  to cause lose to another or to expose another to a risk of loss.

The key to this offence is the question as to whether a person is in a position where he is expected to safeguard, or not act against, the financial interests of another person, but it has been noted that this was not defined in the Act nor was any clarity introduced during the Parliamentary debates (Ormerod, 2011:905). The government did state that it goes beyond a mere fiduciary duty and the Law Commission suggested that it could include fiduciary duties, directors, professional persons, employer/employee and partnerships (Law Commission, 2002:67). It has been noted that this could include the situation where, for example, the employee of a software company creates a clone of software that the firm sells (Ormerod, 2011:905). Potentially this could be of assistance in respect of phishing and pharming where it is believed that some offenders are 'internals', i.e. employees who use their position of responsibility to create sites that certain people are referred to. It could also be of relevance to online commerce.

> D (an employee of an antiques dealer) sells a valuable antique to X, his friend, for a low price claiming (wrongly) that it was a forgery.

or

> X places a (fake) antique on the internet but it attracts few bids. Y (an employee of an antiques dealer) pays over the odds to buy it and tells his employer that it is genuine (when it is not). X and Y agree to split the profits equally.

In the second example, X would be liable for fraud using s.2 (fraud by representation) but Y could be liable through s.4.

### Obtaining services dishonestly

The general fraud offence (s.1) is not the only offence created by the *Fraud Act 2006* which may be relevant to internet fraud. Section 11 creates the offence of obtaining services dishonestly, which was intended to be a direct replacement for the old offence of obtaining services by deception (s.1, *Theft Act 1978*).

The offence applies where D performs a dishonest act and 'obtains services for himself or another' in circumstances that breach s.11(2). Before considering these circumstances it should be noted that unlike with s.2 fraud, which simply requires a representation to be made, the wording of s.11 is clear that the service must be *obtained*. That said, of course, the *Criminal Attempts Act 1981* can be used in appropriate circumstances where a person has put in place the fraud but, for whatever reason, it was either not successful or was not completed.

The circumstances set out in s.11(2) are that services:

(a) are made available on the basis that payment has been, is being or will be made for or in respect of them,
(b) he obtains them without any payment having been made for or in respect of them or without payment having been made in full, and
(c) when he obtains them, he knows

    (i) that they are being made available on the basis described in paragraph (a), or
    (ii) that they might be, but intends the payment will not be made, or will not be made in full.

Potentially this is a useful offence in respect of certain online frauds. For example, it could apply whereby a person obtains a licence for software through dishonest means. This could include, for example, hacking into a computer to make it look as though payment had, in fact, been received. Other forms of internet-based services would include newspaper subscriptions, subscriptions allowing access to pay-for-view services or even the purchase of a travel ticket (whilst the ticket itself is (tangible) property, the entitlement to travel is a service; where the ticket is, for example, a self-print ticket then there would be no tangible property).

Ormerod has noted a potential flaw where a false credit card is used to procure a service. If the payment is made (and in automated transactions it would be notwithstanding that the victim may later have the money refunded) then s.11 cannot apply because there is a requirement that the service is procured 'without any payment having been made for or in respect of them' (s.11(2)(b), *Fraud Act 2006*) and this would not be satisfied because payment will have been made (Ormerod, 2007:664). However, the conduct would still be culpable under s.2 (as D has represented that he is entitled to use the credit card details provided), but crucially the victim here would be the bank (who will ultimately lose the money as they are obliged to repay the holder of the account for the fraudulent activity) and not the person who provided the services.

An example of how s.11 could be used in the context of communications is given in *Mikolajczak v Poland* [2013] EWHC 432 (Admin) where the appellant was seeking to avoid extradition. The law relating to extradition is irrelevant for our purposes but the conduct is helpful. The appellant accessed a telephone exchange and used the telephone numbers of three people to obtain credit on his mobile SIM card. The Divisional Court held that this would amount to an offence under s.11 because it is done dishonestly, a service was obtained (the use of the telephone network) and he had avoided payment. Interestingly this is also an example of how the law would not have worked under the *Theft Act 1978*, as there would have been no deception since the SIM credit was achieved automatically and, as has been noted before, a machine could not have been deceived.

### Conspiracy to defraud

This common-law offence has been criticised as being 'excessively broad, vague and criminalizes conduct by two or more people that would not be criminal or even tortious when performed by an individual' (Ormerod, 2011:448). Despite the fact that the Law Commission (amongst others) has sought to have the offence repealed (Law Commission, 2002:86) the offence continues to survive and be used, including in circumstances relevant to us.

The classic statement on the offence was provided by Viscount Dilorne in *Scott v Metropolitan Police Commissioner* [1975] AC 819:

> it is clearly the law that an agreement by two or more by dishonesty to deprive a person of something which is his or to which he is or would be or might be entitled and an agreement by two or more by dishonesty to injure some proprietary right of his, suffices to constitute the offence of conspiracy to defraud.
>
> (at 1039 and see Ormerod, 2011:448)

As an inchoate offence there is no requirement that the plan is actually put into place, there need only be the agreement to commit the fraud and an intention to carry it out. That said, it is not clear that it is the conspirators that need to undertake the fraud, only that they agree and intend that someone will do so (see, for example, *R v Hollinshead* [1985] AC 975).

An example of how conspiracy to defraud has been used in respect of cyber-fraud is provided by *R v Wellman* [2007] EWCA Crim 2874. The appellant and four others undertook a complicated fraud whereby they hacked into servers operated by various companies to identify personal information about employees. Using those details they then applied for bank accounts and credit cards and used these to obtain high-value goods and currencies (at [4]). After being arrested for this activity the appellant then purchased compromised credit card details off others and deployed a Trojan virus to capture the log-in credentials for personal accounts which he would then refer to others (at [6]). The appellant was originally sentenced to two terms of six years' imprisonment to be served consecutively as the offence was committed on bail (thus making a total sentence of twelve years' imprisonment). This was reduced to a total of ten years' imprisonment by the Court of Appeal, but they noted that 'it is hard to imagine a more sophisticated and determined course of criminal conduct in this sphere of offending' (at [12]) and there was no doubt in their minds that conspiracy to defraud was properly used for this activity.

The offence was also used in *R v Jabeth and Babatunde* [2014] EWCA Crim 476 which concerned phishing. The appellants, together with a number of others from around the world, sent a series of emails purporting to be from a bank and to which a number of victims responded, giving their bank details. In other words, it was a classic example of phishing. In respect of appellant Jabeth the sophistication was taken to another level. Jabeth identified the victim's bank details and after using a pre-paid mobile telephone contacted the bank pretending to be the victim and requested a security code that would allow online access to the accounts. After securing the code she then accessed the sites online and transferred over £1 million out of the accounts.

These cases show that notwithstanding the fact that the conspiracy offence is subjected to considerable criticism, it remains potentially useful in respect of cyber-fraud cases, and this is particularly true because the internet (as noted in Chapter 2) allows for criminals from all over the world to co-operate and work with each other. English law has responded to these jurisdictional challenges (see s.5(3), *Criminal Justice Act 1993*) and conspiracy to defraud is therefore an important tool in the armoury for such cases.

## Suggested further reading

Glickman, H. 'The Nigerian "419" advance fee scams: Prank or peril?' (2005) 39 *Canadian Journal of African Studies* 460–489.
*This is a good introduction to the 419 scams and discusses whether they should be taken seriously as a crime. Whilst there is a growing body of literature on 419 scams this continues to be an important reference work.*

Law Commission. *Fraud* (Law Comm. 276) (2002, London: HMSO).
*This is the Law Commission report which considered the reform of fraud law, including ensuring that the modern law would be able to tackle cybercrime. It is a detailed analysis of the law at that time and an insight into why the law was changed.*

Snyder, J.M. 'Online auction fraud: Are auction houses doing all they should or could to stop online fraud?' (2000) 52 *Federal Communications Law Journal* 453–472.
*This article is beginning to show its age but it is a useful summary of one of the more popular forms of cyber-fraud and it also raises issues in respect of the balance between the criminal law and private industry.*

Chapter 5 of Yar, M. *Cybercrime and Society* (2nd ed.) (2013, London: Sage Publishing).
*This short chapter puts many of the scams and frauds into context. It provides a useful history of the scams and also discusses the impact that such frauds can have.*

# Chapter 7

# Virtual property

This chapter will examine two topics which are quite different, but which are related by one concept, that of property. It may appear strange to think about property on the internet since it is simply a network of computers but property is a source of live debate. One type of property is intellectual property. This would encompass, for example, computer programs, art or books but perhaps most notably in this context music, television shows and movies. It will be seen later in this chapter that the internet has led to new ways of evading copyright and this chapter will examine how the law has reacted to that.

The second type of property is personal property, but what is meant by that in the digital age is open to question. Certain programs and games allow for users to interact with each other and procure items such as swords, currency and other forms of objects. A question of live debate is whether such virtual objects amount in law to property. If so, then in the context of cybercrime the question would arise as to whether such objects could be stolen.

## Virtual objects

The first issue to consider is the issue of virtual property. There are different ways in which property can exist but this book will focus on one type, that of objects that exist only within the context of an online environment. There are two particular situations where this commonly occurs: computer games and virtual environments.

The internet has led to a growth in multiplayer games. Whereas traditional computer games were played either alone or by two or more people connected to the same device, the internet allows this to be expanded beyond the living room. Using an internet connection it is possible for developers to create so-called 'virtual worlds' where people can meet, play and interact. A new term has been coined for these, 'massively multiplayer online role-playing game' (MMORPG). This is a good summary of their features. The internet allows for thousands of people to interact in the same game, each person creating a representation ('avatar') which they control and use to interact with others and the game itself. Perhaps the most famous example of these games is 'World of Warcraft' which is estimated to have approximately 7 million players registered worldwide.

Outside of games, virtual spaces are also being developed which again allow for large-scale interaction. Perhaps the most famous of these is 'Second Life'. This markets itself as a 'virtual world' and indeed it does take on that role. It allows users to create a plot of land, interact with each other and do most things that can be done in the 'real' world. Second Life has indeed created a crossover between real and virtual worlds, with mainstream churches, banks, shops and even established universities creating a Second Life presence.

Both the MMORPG and virtual worlds share a question regarding property. In Second Life there is a currency (the Linden dollar) and it is possible to buy things, including virtual objects within the virtual world (although it is not restricted to this, and real goods and services can be purchased for delivery/use in the 'real' world). In MMORPGs there are virtual objects that can be created or found. So, for example, in MMORPGs these will normally be weapons, currency, potions, etc. These will allow characters to be stronger or do more things. In other online games (such as simulations) the virtual objects could include vehicles, buildings or furniture. Do these objects amount to property? If so, does that mean they can be stolen or damaged?

### The Theft Act 1968

The starting point would be to consider the definition of theft to see whether the issue is in doubt. Section 1(1), *Theft Act 1968* (TA 1968) states:

> A person is guilty of theft if he dishonestly appropriates property belonging to another with the intention of permanently depriving the other of it.

As is probably well known, ss.2–6 then provide a definition for each element of the offence, with s.4 defining property. Section 4(1), *Theft Act 1968* defines property as including 'money and all other property, real or personal, including things in action and other intangible property'. The reference to the fact that it *includes* those items and that it refers to 'other intangible property' would seem to indicate an expansive meaning should be adopted. Indeed this could perhaps be supported by the fact that ss.4(2)–(4) list items that cannot be stolen. It could be argued, therefore, that Parliament intended a wide meaning to be given to these terms and attempted to cater for those situations where an expansive definition could cause problems by providing exceptions.

Notwithstanding this argument, we know that some things cannot be stolen. In *Low v Blease* [1975] Crim LR 513 it was held that it was not possible to steal electricity. In *Oxford v Moss* (1979) 68 Cr App R 183 the Divisional Court famously held that it was not possible to steal confidential information. This was a case where a student found the proof of an exam paper and copied its contents (but returned the original). Rather than dealing with the matter by way of university discipline the student was prosecuted for theft, the argument being that the exam was confidential information which amounted to intangible property. The Divisional Court held that confidential information was not property capable of being stolen. This is perhaps one of the most important cases on the meaning of property within theft and it continues to have a major impact on the issue under our consideration.

Can virtual objects constitute property? As they are not physical we can only be looking at intangible property. Section 4 refers to two forms of such property: 'choses in action' and 'other intangible property'.

### Choses in action

A 'chose in action' is considered to be a right of property that can only be claimed or enforced by (civil) action, not through taking physical possession (*Torkington v Magee* [1902] 2 KB 427). It is unlikely that virtual objects within games can be considered choses in action because they probably cannot be claimed or enforced by civil action. Most games will introduce 'terms and conditions' of playing and there is invariably a clause that states that disputes are settled by the producers of the game (or, in some instances, the players themselves). The terms and conditions probably also state that the right to play the game, etc., is left to the discretion of the developer and therefore a civil action would be unlikely to succeed.

### Other intangible property

Helpfully, the TA 1968 does not define what intangible property is. It is known that intellectual property constitutes intangible property (see s.30, *Patents Act 1977* and ss.1, 213, *Copyright, Designs and Patents Act 1988*) but this would not assist us. Even if the creation of a virtual object could amount to a design that is worthy of protection (and this, by itself is questionable) it is unlikely that the player of the game (or user of the virtual world) would hold this intellectual property, as the holder would almost certainly be the developer of the game who created the object (or created the mechanism by which the object could be designed) in the first place.

What then constitutes intangible property? It has been noted already that confidential information does not constitute (intangible) property and presumably understanding why this is the case could assist us in understanding what does constitute intangible property. However, the difficulty with *Oxford v Moss* is that the case is remarkably unhelpful. One can speculate whether the facts were of more relevance to the court's decision than the law. In other words, did the Divisional Court believe that it was a case that should never have been prosecuted and thus ruled accordingly? The consequence of

*Oxford v Moss* is that it has been accepted that it is not possible to steal the words on the paper and this can be presumably be extended to other forms of content. The judgment itself provides no clue as to why the court ruled in the way that it did. Smith J, giving the lead judgment, simply rehearsed the facts and then concluded, 'in my judgment, it is clear that the answer to the question [whether confidential information on paper is capable of being property] must be no. Accordingly, I would dismiss the appeal' ((1979) 68 Cr App R 183 at 185). Wien J simply stated 'it is shown in this case that the right to confidential information is not intangible property within the meaning of section 4(1) of the Theft Act 1968'. Neither judge therefore explains *why* confidential information is not intangible property or what would constitute intangible property, something singularly unhelpful.

Perhaps some light can be shed by reference to the Scottish case of *Grant v Allan* 1987 JC 71. Although the Lord Justice-Clerk decided that the decision in *Oxford v Moss* was not 'helpful' because it referred to theft (at 78) this is because of the specific issue the High Court of Justiciary were being asked to consider (which is of relevance only under Scots law). However, whilst *Oxford v Moss* may not have been helpful to the Lord Justice-Clerk it is quite possible that his judgment is helpful to us in understanding *Oxford v Moss*. The circumstances of *Grant v Allan* were that an employee had made copies of confidential information relating to the customers of the company he was employed by. His intention was to sell this information to another company. He was charged with 'clandestinely taking and without his employers' authority making and detaining copies of these computer printouts with the intention of selling them'.

The High Court of Justiciary held that this was not an offence known to Scots law. It is their logic that could assist us. The Lord Justice-Clerk stated the conduct was best thought of as a civil wrong and not a criminal wrong (1987 JC 71 at 77). He stated 'difficult questions might well arise as to whether that crime could be committed by an employee who did no more than memorise the information and subsequently commit it to writing' (at 77) and questioned what happened when an employee (legitimately) acquires confidential information in the course of their employment, commits it to memory and then sometime later leaves the company by mutual consent. If he then used this information for the benefit of his new employer (or himself if he became self-employed) would that become theft? It would be difficult to argue that it should.

This uncertainty of the gathering and use of confidential information perhaps allows us to understand *Oxford v Moss*. The exam paper may not lose its confidential status after it has been taken. Not every university releases their papers or all of their papers. If confidential information could be stolen would that mean that a student who remembers the questions, writes them down after the exam and then, the following year, sells those questions to a new student would be committing a criminal offence? It would be a harsh law that said so and perhaps it was the concern that confidential information was too transient that led to the decision in *Oxford v Moss*. That is not to say there is no wrongdoing here, but that it is perhaps best left to civil rather than criminal law or to lead to the creation of offences relating to the *use* of the confidential information rather than its gathering (which occurs in respect of some forms of intellectual property situations as discussed below).

What then does amount to intangible property? One important case is *Attorney-General of Hong Kong v Chan Nai-Keung* [1987] 1 WLR 1339, a Privy Council decision. The facts of this case are complicated but can be summarised as relating to the trade of export licences. At that time the export of certain goods was subject to quotas and this was effected through a licence system. If a company could not meet their quota they were entitled to sell all or part of their quota either on a temporary or permanent basis. A healthy market was established to trade these quotas.

The defendant was a director of a company and he then created a second company. He sold the quotas owned by the first company to the second company for a heavily reduced price and at a time when the main shareholder was away from Hong Kong. The Privy Council held that this amounted to theft and Lord Keith of Kinkel, giving the lead opinion, said:

> the definition of 'property' in the English Theft Act 1968 ... was intended to have the widest ambit. It would be strange indeed if something which is freely bought and sold and which may clearly be the subject of dishonest dealing which deprives the owner of the benefit it confers were not capable of being stolen. The Lordships have no hesitation in concluding that export quotas ... although not 'things in action' are a form of 'other intangible property'.
>
> (at 1342)

This is an interesting case for two reasons. The first is that it provides authority that perhaps Parliament did intend the meaning of property to be expansive and therefore there should only be limited exceptions. The second reason it is interesting is because it perhaps demonstrates a difference between this case and *Oxford v Moss*. There was no indication in *Oxford v Moss* that the property had any commercial value, it was stolen simply to allow the student to cheat in an examination and it is unlikely that anyone from outside of that particular cohort of students would wish to purchase the paper, as there is no commercial market in past examination papers. It is not just the commercial value that makes it property but also the fact that it could be openly traded. Some *thing* must be traded if money is changing hands and it is not unreasonable for the law to seek to protect against the dishonest acquisition of this commodity by considering it as property.

Where does this leave us? On one level virtual objects could be considered to be information and therefore not capable of being stolen. The objects have no physical presence and exist only as digital data, i.e. ultimately just binary data (0s and 1s). The data is a series of instructions and so it is the ordering of that data which is important and this must mean that it is information – it is something that allows the computer to perform. If so, then that would mean that it cannot be property that is capable of being stolen, which would at least be consistent with other forms of information, including expressive works.

However, this is only the position because, in England, the case of *Oxford v Moss* continues to apply. Could it be argued that technology has overtaken the law and we need to reconsider whether virtual objects should be protected by being classified as property?

### Virtual objects as property

A growing body of literature has begun to consider whether we should begin to recognise virtual objects as a form of property that can be stolen, and this should be considered briefly here. To assist us in this area, not least because it is relatively complex, let us take an example:

> X is playing a MMORPG. X takes the form of a virtual representation (an 'avatar') and plays the game. The game allows a user to find objects that can be of assistance, including weapons, potions and money. After playing for several months X has managed to collect some important and useful objects.

> Y, another user, hacks into the MMORPG account of X and transfers the objects that X possesses to Y's avatar, therefore giving Y all the extra powers and status this brings.

At the outset it should be noted that (a) this is not the only way that such objects can be taken and (b) that some criminal liability would arise in the example above. At the very least, the actions of Y would constitute an offence under the *Computer Misuse Act 1990* and this will be discussed further below. However, the more interesting question is whether the offence of theft is engaged in this scenario?

It may seem odd to think that something which exists only on a computer could be considered 'property' but it has been noted that we may think very differently about other online resources, 'it is not hard to imagine in the near future a virtual world that would store your digital assets, such as your photos, emails … documents, books, music, movies, phone message' (Rumbles, 2011:355). In fact, such a 'world' already exists: the cloud. Cloud storage has become routine (and indeed has been for some time) and many of us use it to store our documents, photographs, movies and music. Even if we do not know that it is the cloud, if we use iTunes or a Kindle then we are using the cloud because our music and books are stored in the cloud and not just on our local storage. Do we feel differently about those? We probably do because we purchased these and we perceive them as being the equivalent to tangible objects. However, as the law currently stands it is unlikely that they could be capable of being stolen because even if they do constitute property (see the discussion on intellectual property in the second half of this chapter) it is not owned by us – the purchaser. We merely receive a licence to play or read the work. If the file is taken (e.g. through duplication) it does not prevent us from using the book itself. Even if the file was deleted it could be downloaded again so there would appear to be no loss.

What of virtual objects within a game? There is unlikely to be a licence here (the licence is to play the game not in respect of each object) and so we are reliant on finding a construction of virtual objects as property. Should gaming objects be considered 'property'?

### Virtual objects as chattels

Fairfield who probably first championed the idea that virtual property should be considered 'property' within the meaning of theft, noted that the difficulty with code amounting to property is that it is essentially just one step up from thought, something that cannot be stolen (Fairfield, 2005:1048). By this he means that the code – like writing – could just be considered a product of the mind and therefore should be protected as intellectual property. However, the code for the objects differs from the game. It produces an object that can be controlled and which interacts with the user and so the question is whether this makes it property that can be owned by the user and not the developer.

Clearly digital data can constitute property but only under limited circumstances. It will be seen later in this chapter that there is a proprietary interest in music although not by the purchaser. The same is true of software. A person (usually) does not own software (e.g. the operating system of a computer such as Microsoft Windows or Apple iOS) but rather you have a licence to use the product. However, a licence is considered to be a property interest in its own right.

Of course what is being discussed here is not whether the whole code is property but whether a particular part of the software can be property. There is no doubt that the game itself is (intellectual) property, but do the objects within the game constitute property? This is a contested area but some believe that they do and that they can be equated to property in the real world, this requiring three characteristics (Fairfield, 2005:1053):

- Rivalrousness (the ability to exclude others from using an owned object).
- Persistence (it does not fade once created but has a permanence to it).
- Interconnectivity (the fact that property can influence more than one person).

Fairfield gives the (non-digital) example of a pen to demonstrate this. He argues that if he has a pen then he has it and the other does not. If he leaves the pen in a room it does not disappear, it remains, and it is interconnected because with his permission anyone can use the pen (Fairfield, 2005:1054). The argument is that this applies also to a virtual object (e.g. a sword). Only one person at a time can have that *particular* sword (there may be multiple swords but there will be a finite number, and therefore at that time only one person can have it), when the person ceases to play the game (because, for example, they go to sleep) it does not disappear, it is there when the person next logs on. The final issue, interconnectivity, is perhaps best demonstrated in that the sword can be used to attack others or, more accurately, the representation ('avatar') of the other within the game.

Others have developed Fairfield's ideas but suggest that there are more than three properties:

1.  Possession, or the right to possess.
2.  The use or enjoyment of the item.
3.  The ability to transfer the item.
4.  Exclusion of others from the item.
5.  No durational limit to possession so long as the necessary fees are paid.

(Rumbles, 2011:361)

It is perhaps interesting to note that there is no suggestion that ownership is one of the characteristics of a chattel. Ownership is an interesting issue because whilst the lay-person often thinks of ownership as being a fundamental part of property (Nelson, 2010:285) a lawyer realises that it is more complicated. The law of property is not simply concerned with ownership rights but recognises other forms of proprietary rights and interests (Smith, 2014:4). In other words it is irrelevant that a person does not own the item so long as they are considered to have an appropriate interest in it.

So can these characteristics apply to virtual objects? Some of Rumbles' factors link to the three characteristics of property identified by Fairfield. Thus the ability to exclude others from using the item is the same as rivalrousness, and the same is true of durational limit which is the same as persistence. The interconnectivity factor identified by Fairfield is perhaps demonstrated by the use or enjoyment of the item. What of the others, however? The issue of transference is interesting. Of course this means legal transfer rather than physical transfer. Most games will allow for users to transfer objects (either willingly or otherwise) and this includes through trade, barter or co-operation. Not only does the ability to transfer show that an object must be a possession (in that some *thing* is being transferred from X to Y) it is also considered to be a key element of property rights, as it is asserting the right to dispose.

Perhaps the key factor is that of possession, or the right to possess. What does possession mean? Given that it is a virtual object it cannot mean physical possession because it is intangible in nature. Therefore the test for possession becomes the ability to exercise control. This is obviously linked to the concept of exclusivity discussed above – the right to exclude others – arguably it goes beyond this as it is more about whether the person claiming possession can exert control.

Can it be said that a person exercises control of a virtual object? Rumbles believes that the answer is 'yes' (Rumbles, 2011:369) and this would seem to be supported by Fairfield:

> If I own a building in a virtual world, I own it regardless of the intellectual property inherent in the underlying code. I own it regardless of the physical chattel used by another person to experience it. I own it, control it, can invite people to be in it, hold meetings in it, work there, invest in it, and sell it to other people who might want to do the same.
>
> (Fairfield, 2005:1078)

Presumably the same could apply in respect of in-game objects such as swords, etc. A person can use the sword, choose to give the sword to someone else (for a specific task or otherwise) or cast the sword aside. However, does the user really have control? The creator of the game sets the parameters in which the object can be used. So, for example, the creator may decide that the sword cannot be used against person X or in situation Y. There is nothing that the user can do to breach that restriction because the code for the virtual object will not permit this. In real life if a person is told not to use a (real) sword against person X there is no physical way of preventing the sword being used against that person. It may not be lawful but the person possessing the sword has control of it.

Even if we decide that this aspect of control is irrelevant because the object is being given to the user within specified parameters (which is perfectly lawful, there is nothing to say that only one person can have a property interest in an object at the same time, and lesser rights can be created which, if appropriated, would amount to theft). The question becomes whether a person who controls a virtual object within a defined virtual environment can be said to control it (as Fairfield asserts). It would seem that the answer is 'yes' because of the reasons articulated by Fairfield. Only one person can possess that particular object (there may be duplicates within the game but they are finite so not everyone will necessarily have that object) and that person will control its use. They can choose to deploy the object or not. They can decide to sell it, trade it or even dispose of it. Therefore it could be argued that they have control.

However, do they? What control does the user actually have? If the game operator decided that, for whatever reason, the player should be excluded from the environment then nothing could be done by the user to prevent that. Similarly if the creator of the game decided to 'reset' all the characters so that they lost all their weapons, etc., there would be nothing that could be done. Realistically what control does the person have? Other than the ability to create the avatar and to operate the character within the parameters the game-owner set, very little. Can that be sufficient to establish property rights?

### Acquiring rights

Of course part of the question that must be answered is how does one acquire the property right? To some this is the key question and demonstrates the arguments both for and against virtual objects constituting property. Initial objects are likely to be given by the creator of the game. Assuming that they did amount to property then this would be unobjectionable because the creator is the person who is most likely to have original property rights, and a fundamental rule of property is that chattels can be given away. Of course the creator will not know who she has given the property too but that is probably unnecessary, it suffices that the creator realises she is giving away the property to a person or persons unknown.

If trade is possible – and it will be seen that this is not uncommon – then an alternative way of obtaining the object would be through buying it. Again, if the object is considered property then that would be a good way to accrue property rights as the purchase of an item will usually be considered a legal transaction that transfers a property right from person X to person Y (Smith, 2014). It will be remembered that the ability to openly trade export licences was one reason why the Privy Council considered them to be property in *Attorney-General for Hong Kong v Chan Nai-Keung* [1987] 1 WLR 1339.

What of the person who simply accrues objects through playing the game (finding them, winning them, etc.)? Some have suggested that the property rights are gained through effort. That the principal method of gaining the objects – and therefore the property – is to work hard and to play the game so that rewards come and that these rewards belong only to the player. However, Nelson (2010) is scathing about such arguments. He draws an analogy to a blacksmith forging a sword. The blacksmith could mine the ore, smelt it and forge it into a sword. The sword would belong to the blacksmith because of the efforts that he has undertaken to extract the ore and forge the sword. Alternatively he could purchase the ore, smelt it and forge the sword. In such a case, according to Nelson, the title to the sword arises not because of effort (as it was the miner who extracted the ore who produced that effort) but through title, the purchasing of the ore (Nelson, 2010:291). Nelson believes that a person whose character is developed through gameplay is in the same position. It cannot be said that it is their efforts that led to the object, but rather it was the efforts of the creator of the game who created the circumstances in which the object could be acquired.

Of course the counter-argument to that is that in many instances people pay to play the game. They must first of all purchase the game which allows them to join the MMORPG environment. If that is the case, is that not the equivalent of the blacksmith purchasing the ore? Surely the creator of the game has been rewarded for her work and thus the player's efforts can now be rewarded? The difficulty with this approach is the nature of the property rights. In the blacksmith example the blacksmith acquired the absolute title to the ore whereas the purchaser of the game merely purchases a right to play the game according to the rules and limitations imposed by the developer. Whilst the right to play a game could in itself be considered a proprietary right, it is difficult to see how that could lead to objects being found within the game to constitute property.

The major difficulty with the argument that one can obtain property rights by effort is the fact that this has never been recognised by the courts (Nelson, 2010:293; Smith, 2014:63 et seq.). Thus it remains a theoretical argument and one that has as many critics as it has supporters, and therefore it is unlikely to assist our analysis.

What are other relevant ways by which property rights could be acquired? One possibility would be through finding. In English law there is no doubt that finding an object can provide title to it (Smith, 2014:63–68). The general rule would appear to be that things found on a person's land can be claimed by the owner of the land but they must first exercise control over that land (see, for example, *Parker v British Airways* [1982] QB 1004). Given the nature of a game – the objects are deliberately placed so as to be found – then it could be argued that even though the game-creators own the game (due to the licensing issue discussed above) it would seem likely they intended finders of the objects to possess or control them. Accordingly, perhaps acquisition happens through finding, although it should be stressed that this of itself does not justify a property right, it merely explains how a property right could be acquired. If the virtual object does not constitute property in the first place then finding becomes irrelevant.

### Commercial worth

Rumbles, who is an advocate of virtual objects being recognised as property, argues that where there is no commercial element (which he defines as being able to replace the object at limited cost) then there cannot be any property rights (Rumbles, 2011:362). The argument here is that it is the ability to trade (either through barter or commerce) that is an essential part of property rights. In the context of the discussion on chattels above this is inextricably linked to the notion of transfer. However, why should the fact that it can be replaced at 'limited cost' matter? Indeed what amounts to 'limited cost'? Even items of trivial value would constitute property if they were tangible. The theft of them may not be prosecuted but that is a matter of prosecutorial discretion rather than a question of law. Why should the absence of value be relevant to intangible property? Surely if one can point to a virtual object and show that the principles of control, exclusivity and transferability are satisfied then it should constitute property.

Some games will allow for real-world or in-game trades to occur and thus this would demonstrate a commercial value. Even when legitimate trade is not permitted a grey market invariably develops. The trade in virtual in-game objects is big business, with it being estimated as being worth up to US$5 billion in 2011 (Rumbles, 2011:358), and it is likely to have increased significantly since then. Thus when we are talking about virtual objects we should not think of them as cartoonified swords, potions and currency but a fundamental part of real-world commerce. Indeed it is thought that in some places a 'battery' type environment of gamers (the analogy being to hens) has grown up where gamers are forced to play for long hours on very little pay so as to procure the objects that can then be traded (Rumbles, 2011:358).

If the game does not recognise the trade in objects does this mean it has no value? As noted above, a 'grey market' arises and it is very difficult to prevent sales. Let us take an example:

> X wishes to purchase a particular object of power. On an online auction site he sees this object listed and buys it. Y, the seller, arranges to meet X 'in game' and transfer the property to him. They both log on at the appropriate time and the avatar of X meets the avatar of Y. The avatar of Y gifts X the object (as games will invariably allow objects to be cast aside).

The owners of the game will not know that this is a commercial sale (whilst they will inevitably know that commerce happens they will not know which particular 'swaps' are for commercial reasons especially with millions of players) and X now has the object. Does it have value? It must do, not least because it was acquired for value. The user licence will almost certainly render such transactions illegal (under civil law) but it has been held that for the purposes of theft it is irrelevant whether illegal material is stolen, it is still property (*R v Smith* [2011] 1 Cr App R 30).

### Legal consequences

There has, in fact, been a case in England and Wales concerning the stealing of in-game objects; however, it was not dealt with as a case of theft. Steven Burrell was successfully prosecuted for hacking into 'RuneScape' (a popular MMORPG) and stealing items that had been accrued before selling them on an auction site (see, for example, *Daily Telegraph* (2013), December 6). However he was prosecuted not for theft (or indeed fraud) but for an offence under the *Computer Misuse Act 1990*. Presumably this was, in part, because there were doubts as to whether the in-game objects amounted to property.

This case demonstrates that even if virtual objects are not considered as property there could still be consequences. As the majority of 'stealing' would appear to involve hacking then the computer misuse offences considered in Chapter 3 may be more appropriate. The difficulty with this approach is that it does not necessarily reflect the conduct of the offender. This is not just a case of unlawful access, it is hacking and then taking something that another values. That sounds as though it should be a property offence but, of course, this returns us to the question of whether virtual objects are property.

The omission of this type of virtual property from the TA 1968 also causes difficulties for the computer misuse offences. Only the offence under s.1, CMA 1990 can be committed and not the aggravated form under s.2. This is because s.2 requires the intent to commit another offence and if it does not come within the TA 1968 then what is the subsequent offence? One possibility would be to rely on the *Fraud Act 2006* (discussed in Chapter 6) but that would depend on a particular set of facts. Where it may apply is:

> D hacks the profile of V within an online role-playing game and takes the power-ups, magic tokens and money of V's avatar. He then goes onto an online auction site and sells these items for real money.

In the instance above it is quite possible that a fraud offence is committed. The property being defrauded is the (real) money, with the implied representation being that D was allowed to sell these objects when that is not true (as they were gathered inappropriately). However, where there is no commercial transaction, then it is unlikely that the offence could be used. Whilst it could be said that the game amounts to a 'service' (potentially raising issues under s.11, *Fraud Act 2006*) it cannot be said that the objects allow that service to be accessed, it is the purchase of the game that provides the service. Thus the central question remains whether virtual objects are property (in which case the example above could be dealt with under s.2, *Fraud Act 2006*). In the absence of this then only the simple offence under s.1, CMA 1990 could apply, irrespective of the fact that the hacker had the intention to steal virtual objects or indeed did so.

There is also the difficulty where there is no hack. Rumbles questions what happens where user X gives user Y an in-game sword for a specific task but Y then refuses to return it and instead uses it for his own purposes (Rumbles, 2011:373). There could be no liability under the CMA 1990 as in this instance there would be no unlawful access. If the object constituted property then it could be theft as it is possible to commit theft by keeping (ss.1, 6(1), TA 1968), but if it is not property then there would seem to be no liability.

Other countries have criminalised the stealing of virtual property. In 2009 it was reported that Dutch judges had criminalised the stealing of virtual objects from an online game (Strikwerda, 2012) although it is not clear that this was dealt with as theft. The particulars of that case were that the perpetrators procured the log-in credentials of the victims through deception. Therefore, this could be considered to be a matter of unlawful access (aka hacking) rather than theft, and so within the discussion set out in Chapter 3. However, in 2012 the Dutch Supreme Court unequivocally upheld a conviction for theft of a 'mask' and 'amulet' within RuneScape after a 13-year-old was threatened with violence until he transferred the objects to the defendant (Wolswijk, 2012:459). The Dutch Supreme Court held that these virtual objects were 'goods' within the meaning of the Dutch penal code and therefore were capable of being stolen.

The Court held that the key test was whether an object was capable of being removed from the control of another (Wolswijk, 2012:461) and that in this case it had. The Court specifically rejected the defence argument that virtual objects were mere data and therefore could not be stolen. Perhaps the court was influenced by the fact that the user was compelled by threat of force to transfer the property and therefore it seemed more serious than other examples. The court noted that the compulsion transferred control of the object to the assailant. However, as has been noted before, does the user actually have control? She has local control in that she can influence what the object does, how it is to be used, etc., but she does not have overall control in that if the owner of the game chooses to end the game/environment or delete the character then there is nothing that can be done about that. Whilst it may be going too far to say that a person must have exclusive control over an object, surely there should be a minimum level of control?

## Consequences of virtual objects being property

If virtual objects were to be classed as property then it would mean that they could be stolen, meaning theft would become possible, but this may have unfortunate consequences. Could a person become liable for theft as a result of playing a game? Nelson provides the example of the rules of the game permitting a person to be robbed or killed, with the assailant being permitted to take the possessions of the victim (indeed this is one of the more popular ways of accruing additional objects). He suggests that this would amount to stealing the object, in essence because the property has been taken without consent (Nelson, 2010:300). Whilst consent is not strictly relevant under English law (see, most notably, *R v Lawrence* [1972] AC 626) it is easy to see Nelson's point, at least in respect of the *actus reus*.

What is less clear, however, is that the *mens rea* for theft is satisfied (something that Nelson concedes by reference to his 'qualified model'). In the context of English law then where the taking is within the rules of the game being played, it is difficult to see how this could amount to theft as there would be no dishonesty, even where trickery was involved. Indeed, games are subject to rules and these rules are normally set out in the 'Terms and Conditions' of the licence/permission to play the game. Where a person does something within the rules of the game then they must presumably have the belief that they have the right in law (contract law presumably) to do as they did, and thus if this was honestly held they cannot be dishonest (s.2(1)(a), *Theft Act 1968*).

If virtual objects were to be classified as property then presumably they can not only be stolen but also be damaged. Again, this has potential consequences. If user X 'knocks down' a virtual building that he has created within a game would that be criminal damage? Unlike a virtual object such as a sword, etc., the building may not have any attributes other than being a building, i.e. it does not give the user any additional benefits within the game. Should we criminalise such demolition as criminal damage? Perhaps the answer is to say that a virtual object without value is not property, but even in games such as SimCity there have been real-world commercial trades of buildings and building designs. Therefore, there could be value attached to the object although perhaps no value (other than effort) has been expended, but value is not necessarily relevant for the purposes of criminal damage (other than in respect of mode of trial).

A further difficulty with classifying virtual objects as property is that criminal damage can be committed recklessly (s.1, *Criminal Damage Act 1971*) and this could be a step too far. Presumably there are many ways that within a MMORPG 'property' could be damaged, and imposing criminal liability on someone who unintentionally damages virtual property would seem harsh. However, there is no easy way to avoid this situation. If virtual objects were to be constructed as property it would probably be through judicial interpretation rather than statutory amendment and thus all the statutory provisions would automatically flow. Parliament could decide to write an exemption into criminal law (Parliament did this to overrule *R v Whiteley* (1991) 93 Cr App R 25 (discussed in Chapter 4), see s.10(5), *Criminal Damage Act 1971*) although this would take time.

It would seem that classifying in-game objects as virtual property could cause numerous difficulties, including unintended consequences. The reasoning behind excluding such objects from the definition of intangible property is perhaps sound, especially when one notes that in the vast majority of situations an offence under the CMA 1990 would occur. Theft is a serious offence and it is unlikely to be appropriate in these circumstances. However, the CMA 1990 would not apply where there is no hack and therefore consideration could perhaps be given to whether a new (summary) offence is required for those types of cases although they will be relatively rare. The alternative (which has a number of attractions) would be to leave this to the civil law, although again conceptions of property may cause problems.

## Intellectual property

The second type of property to consider is that of intellectual property (IP). Unlike virtual objects there is no doubt that this constitutes property, but the question is how the criminal law operates to protect it.

### Identifying intellectual property

The first issue to consider is how we define intellectual property for our purposes. Under English law there are four principal types of IP: patents, copyright, registered designs and trade marks (MacQueen *et al.*, 2011:4–5). Each of these types could be relevant to cybercrime. The technical specifications for a device that is patented could be distributed through the internet, circumventing their protection. However, more than this, some software can be patented and therefore unlawful copying could be a factor. The same is true of registered designs, where there is a burgeoning trade in illegal copies of designs.

Trade mark violations are perhaps one of the most significant forms of cybercrime. It was noted in Chapter 6 that there are lot of fake items that are available to buy on the internet. Whilst these are sometimes passed off as genuine when they are not, it can also be the case that some people will deliberately seek out 'fake' goods knowing that some of the reproductions will have the same appearance as the genuine article but for a fraction of the price. This will not be considered here because this section will focus primarily on the issue of piracy, which is one of the key themes of IP theft, but it should be recognised that false merchandise is an important aspect of cybercrime. Where material is being passed off as legitimate then that is fraud (discussed in Chapter 6) but it is also a crime against the owner of the trade mark, as it is when the goods are being sold (openly) as fake (on this see MacQueen *et al.*, 2011:974–975).

The issue of most relevance to our debate concerns copyright. Digital technologies have completely transformed the manner in which copyrighted material is being traded. This is particularly true of the creative arts such as music and the film industry but can also include other performing arts such as the theatre and music concerts, where people record footage and immediately upload it to the internet. The issue of copyright violation is the one we will consider in the remainder of this chapter.

### Intellectual property 'piracy'

The language of IP-related crime is interesting as we normally refer to the illegal copying or distribution of material as 'piracy' rather than 'theft'. However, defining what piracy actually entails has proven difficult (Yar, 2005:678). It has been suggested that the contemporary definition is 'the unauthorized copying and distribution (often, though not necessarily, for commercial gain) of copyright content' (Yar, 2005:679). However, it must be accepted at the outset that this is not something that is unique to cybercrime. It has been noted that there has been a long and (in)glorious history of copying content, dating back to the 1970s (Yar, 2007:96). If we refer back to Chapter 1 we could describe this as being an example of a pre-existing crime that is *radicalised* by the internet.

Internet piracy probably came to prominence in the late 1990s with the creation of Napster, a file-sharing platform (in essence a peer-to-peer network). Users who downloaded the software would allow the central database to search the music they had on their computer (through, for example, loading CDs onto their machine) and this listing would then be stored on the central server. Users could then search this listing and identify files (music) that they wanted and if a person was online with that file it would put the two in contact and the music could be transferred. The site became immensely popular (with estimates suggesting upwards of 70 million users: Yar, 2007:98) but was obviously alarming to the music industry (and later the movie industry) because it allowed people to access material for free. The site was ultimately involved in litigation worth millions of dollars which led to its closure. It later re-opened legitimately but it set the scene for the beginning of a series of replica sites.

Why is this type of behaviour known as piracy rather than theft? In England it could be, in part, because the definition of theft would not be met as copyrighted material cannot be stolen (*Oxford v Moss* (1979) 68 Cr App R 183), but that would not explain its global usage. It has been suggested by some that it is used to try and imply the behaviour is somehow a serious wrong and not simply a trivial matter (Yar, 2007:101). The echo is to a group of individuals spurning lawful authority and plundering what they wish. However, it could presumably do the opposite, with modern media representations of pirates being rogues rather than hardened criminals, so does the language and analogy now stand up?

Whilst Napster arguably led the way, internet piracy has become big business and is extremely common. Digital technologies have revolutionised the manner in which reproductions occur. It has been said, 'the ability to digitally copy, transfer or transmit the expression of ideas in the form of code has enabled the perfect reproduction of such content, without deterioration or degradation' (Wall and Yar, 2010:257). This is an important point. Think about a book or an article. If you photocopy that book the first copy will be (generally) quite a good reproduction. However, if you then photocopy that photocopy the quality is reduced, with the quality reducing with each reproduction. The same was true of tape recordings and vinyl records. However, digital technology differs in that it is just binary data, so repeated reproduction does not affect its quality; ones and zeros are easily copied. The consequences of this are that the copying can become more widespread (rather than copying from an original, copies will be made of copies and distributed to others who will make further copies and distribute them to others) and thus the potential number of illegal copies that are in circulation will grow exponentially.

The proliferation of IP piracy is perhaps symptomatic of a wider issue, that being the way in which online piracy is perceived. Certainly there is considerable evidence that IP piracy is perceived quite differently from other crimes, including other forms of cybercrime. It has been noted that people, particularly adolescents, will view the illegal downloading of an album very differently than shoplifting the album (Wingrove *et al.*, 2011:271), yet is there realistically much difference between them? In both situations the content of an album has come into a person's possession without them paying for it. What is the difference? Obviously morally and psychologically there is the perception that shoplifting is *theft* whereas sitting in front of a computer screen would seem to be less like criminal activity. Consider your own actions. Have you ever swapped music with a friend? Have you, for example, borrowed a friend's CD and loaded it onto your computer or downloaded a music file from the internet knowing it was pirated. If so, do you consider yourself a criminal?

A common suggestion is that IP piracy is a victimless crime (Morris and Higgins, 2009:175) yet the music industry would disagree, suggesting it inflates prices and causes revenue losses with potential loss of jobs and recording opportunities (Weijters *et al.*, 2013). Indeed it is not uncommon to see reference to the creative industry losing billions of dollars per year through piracy, but it has been suggested that this figure must be questioned. For those losses to be true it must follow that each person who has the illegal material would have purchased it lawfully. If they would not have done so, then arguably there is no loss of revenue (Yar, 2013:73, citing Drahos and Braithwaite). In other words, if a person decides that they like a product but are not prepared to purchase it then arguably there is no loss of revenue caused by the pirating. There is undoubtedly a misuse of property – in that someone other than the purchaser is using the property – but it does not follow that this should be a criminal rather than civil matter. It would be naïve to suggest that everyone who downloads music or films would not buy them, but a number would not and therefore the estimates of industry losses are perhaps higher than they truly are.

What is the rationale for criminalising IP piracy? A common suggestion is that IP piracy is analogous to theft but this has been challenged (Yar, 2013:74–75). The theft of tangible property interferes with the possessor's rights. Generally only one person can use a tangible object at the same time but the same is not true of a program or of music. Let us take an example. I have an iPad. That is a tangible object and only one person at a time can use it. Whilst I may allow others to use it (for example, my partner or my stepchildren) it remains an object that I control (as I decide who can use it and when). If someone takes this object then they deprive me of that use even if it is only for a temporary period. So, for example, person X takes my iPad from my office at work for five days and returns it. That taking has interfered with my rights. It prevented me from using it myself or allowing others to use it (of course whether that amounts to a crime depends on the nature of the 'borrowing': see Ormerod, 2011:836–837).

On my iPad is Microsoft Office. The licence that I have for this package allows me to install it on numerous machines. Microsoft could not realistically know whether I have installed it on my machine or someone else's. More to the point, however, installing the software on computer X does not stop me using it in any way on computer Y. Whilst Microsoft have a method of limiting the number of computers that can have the software installed, there is a black market in licenses that will trick it into allowing it to be installed on extra machines. If the software is loaded onto computer Y does this affect my use of it on the iPad or my laptop? No. I can still use the software, I can still type on it and do everything I need to on it. Of course this argument contains a flaw. Whilst I own the iPad, I do not own the software. I own a licence but Microsoft ultimately own the software. However, that does not assist us in demonstrating the fallacy of an analogy to offline taking. My using the software does not deprive Microsoft or anyone else from using it. They may lose revenue by another using it, but that is not the same as saying that a person has been deprived of its use.

The point of this example is just to help you focus on what the difference between virtual and traditional theft is, particularly in respect of IP. It is relatively difficult to conceive what theft is in respect of this type of IP, other than it being the deprivation of potential revenue. Is this something that should be dealt with by the criminal rather than civil law? Ordinarily, using something without permission would not be a criminal matter but would instead be something considered a tort, a civil matter. Is there any reason why it should be different for copyright? There is no damage or loss of enjoyment, with the only negative effect being a (speculative) loss of revenue with an even lower causal connection to a loss of jobs, etc., in the creative industries. This would not normally feel like a criminal matter but rather a civil dispute. The fact that IP piracy is so widespread is perhaps a factor for considering it a criminal act – that only through criminal sanctions could the misconduct be deterred – but there are lots of widespread civil disputes where they never trouble the criminal law. At least one reason is the political power of the creative industries who put pressure on governments to tackle IP piracy (including through threatening to close down production which would have an impact on employment and tax revenues) through the criminal law.

An additional reason for considering IP piracy to be a criminal act is that it tends to be easier to harmonise criminal rather than civil law. As will be seen, global reach in the protection of IP is considered important.

### Legal solutions: international law

Having considered IP piracy it is now necessary to consider the legal solutions to this. Unlike with virtual objects this is an area where there are both international and domestic legal instruments.

As in previous (and indeed following) chapters the Cybercrime Convention will be considered first although other instruments also address this issue. Article 10 of the Convention states:

1.  Each party shall adopt such legislative and other measures as may be necessary to establish as criminal offences under its domestic law the infringement of copyright, as defined under the law of that Party pursuant to the obligations it has undertaken under the Paris Act of 24 July 1971 revising the Bern Convention for the Protection of Literary and Artistic Works, the Agreement on Trade-Related Aspects of Intellectual Property Rights and the WIPO Copyright Treaty, with the exception of any moral rights conferred by such conventions, where such acts are committed wilfully, on a commercial scale and by means of a computer system.

2.  Each Party shall adopt such legislative and other measures as may be necessary to establish as criminal offences under its domestic law the infringement of related rights, as defined under the law of that Party, pursuant to the obligations it has undertaken under the International Convention for the Protection of Performers, Producers of Phonograms and Broadcasting Organisations (Rome Convention), the Agreement on Trade-Related Aspects of Intellectual Property Rights and the WIPO Performance and Phonograms Treaty, with the exception of any moral rights conferred by such conventions, where such acts are committed wilfully, on a commercial scale and by means of a computer system.

3.  A Party may reserve the right not to impose criminal liability under paragraphs 1 and 3 of this article in limited circumstances, provided that other effective remedies are available and that such reservation does not derogate from the Party's international obligations set forth in the international instruments referred to in paragraphs 1 and 2 of this article.

This is probably the most user-unfriendly piece of text that is reproduced in this book. Why include it? To demonstrate that one of the difficulties of IP is its complexity, particularly in the international arena. The Cybercrime Convention needs to take account of a number of international instruments that govern the protection of IP, and this does not include regional instruments such as EU legislation or international treaties that have been signed subsequent to the Cybercrime Convention coming into force. Why the complexity? Given that IP can include design rights to technology it is imperative that there is global protection. Few companies would be able to spend tens of millions of pounds on research and development if they thought that three weeks after their latest product was launched it could be legally copied and distributed by a company based in another country. Therefore IP requires global protection.

The international treaties that are referred to in Article 10 are too complicated to review in detail here. Reference should instead be made to specific texts on IP law (an overview is provided by MacQueen *et al.*, 2011:25–28).

However, the purpose behind Article 10 was undoubtedly to ensure that signatory states to the Cybercrime Convention commit to ensuring that their obligations under these other instruments will be implemented within the context of IP piracy. Of course the Cybercrime Convention was drafted over a decade ago and therefore does not include the most recent agreements, and it does not include EU legislation (for a useful discussion see O'Sullivan, 2014).

### Legal solutions: domestic solutions

What of domestic law? Whilst the UK has signed a number of treaties these obligations must be transposed into English law and this has been done in a number of different ways. The most relevant for our purposes is those offences that exist under the *Copyright, Designs and Patents Act 1998* (CDPA 1998).

Section 107, CDPA 1998 creates a series of offences that are of direct relevance to us. The principal offence is set out in s.107(1):

> A person commits an offence who, without the licence of the copyright holder
>
> (a) makes for sale or hire, or
> (b) imports into the United Kingdom otherwise than for his private and domestic use, or
> (c) possesses in the course of a business with a view to committing any act infringing the copyright, or
> (d) in the course of a business
>
>> (i) sells or lets for hire, or
>> (ii) offers or exposes for sale or hire, or
>> (iii) exhibits in public, or
>> (iv) distributes, or
>
> (e) distributes otherwise than in the course of a business to such an extent as to affect prejudicially the owner of the copyright,
>
> an article which is, and which he knows or has reason to believe is, an infringing copy of a copyright work.

An early example of how s.107 could be applied is *R v Lewis* [1997] 1 Cr App R(S) 208 where the appellant was convicted of an offence under s.107 when he operated a bulletin board (the predecessor to peer-to-peer networks) that allowed people to distribute computer games. He was charged under s.107(d)(iv) in that he distributed the material by operating the site. Interestingly, there is no evidence that the 'business' was a commercial entity (see the first paragraph of the judgment where HHJ Crawford QC, giving the judgment of the court, stated 'what the business, if we can use that expression') and the court seemed satisfied that this condition was satisfied simply because there was proof he ran the site. If 'business' is interpreted in this way then the potential reach of s.107 becomes very wide.

What of those situations where the perpetrator is not the operator of the site? It can be seen that s.107 is drafted broadly and s.107(1)(e) covers non-commercial distribution, albeit subject to the *de minimis* rule. A good example of this provision is *R v Nimley* [2011] 1 Cr App R(S) 120. The appellant used his telephone to record three movies at a local cinema. He then uploaded the footage to a website where others could download and view the material. He was charged, *inter alia*, with three counts under s.107(1)(e) by distributing the copyrighted material. The case does not end there however. The appellant was also convicted of offences under s.6, *Fraud Act 2006* in that he possessed an article for use in connection with fraud, that being the mobile telephone he used to record the footage (at 701). This introduces a further offence that can be used to combat piracy where even legitimate objects – mobile telephones – can be considered illegal where they are used inappropriately.

Further offences contained within s.107 include the making of an article 'specifically designed or adapted for making copies of a particular copyrighted work' or possessing such an article where he knows or has reason to believe it will be used to make infringing copies for sale or hire (s.107(2), CDPA 1998). It is also an offence for a person to communicate copyrighted work to the public (s.107(2A)) or the public performance or playing or showing of a sound recording or film (s.107(3)).

Section 107(1) is a serious offence in its own right and attracts a maximum penalty of five years' imprisonment (s.107(4), CDPA 1988). Ordinarily the more serious penalties would be restricted to situations where there has been a commercial element to the offence (*R v Nimley* [2011] 1 Cr App R(S) 120) but any conviction is likely to be problematic, especially if forfeiture of equipment (s.143, *Powers of Criminal Courts (Sentencing) Act 2000*) or civil restitution proceedings follow thereafter (something made easier because a criminal conviction means there is a presumption of culpability in civil proceedings).

### Enforcing the law

Of course establishing criminal laws is only one step, and they have to be enforced. It will be remembered from Chapter 6 that many cyber-frauds are not actioned by the police and it may be thought that the same would be true of IP piracy. However, this is not the case because of the way that the industry treats these matters, where they have, in essence, taken the lead on policing it. A good example of this is when they established FACT (Federation Against Copyright Theft). You may have seen adverts for FACT in the cinemas because this was one of the original reasons for FACT being created: people would use a portable video-recorder in a cinema to record the latest blockbuster and then distribute it (indeed this still happens: in 2014 Philip Danks used a camcorder to record *Fast and Furious 6* before uploading it to a website, allowing others to download it. He was sentenced in August 2014 to 33 months in gaol). However, FACT has grown and covers the principal forms of internet piracy, including the music industry. It uses its resources to gather evidence of piracy and passes these details on to the relevant authorities, pressing for prosecutions where appropriate. It also (financially and technically) supports law enforcement, ensuring their capability increases.

FACT and other bodies see education as one of the key planks in piracy protection, and this includes identifying the consequences of piracy. It has become common in recent years for celebrity artists, particularly musicians, to note the effect piracy has on their careers and the industry as a whole in an attempt to persuade people that piracy is wrong (although this does not always work, with some artists stating they understand why illegal downloading happens).

It would be naïve to suggest that every person who downloads illegal material will be the subject of criminal penalties, but there is, at the very least, an attempt to tackle those who are behind the distribution of pirated material. However, the industry does not rely solely on the criminal law and it has increasingly sought to use other forms of enforcement, including pressuring Internet Service Providers (ISPs) to act against those websites that host material. For example, the EU e-commerce directive (Directive 2000/31/EC of the European Parliament and of the Council on certain legal aspects of information society services, in particular electronic commerce, in the Internal Market (2000) OJ L178/1) requires ISPs to remove content when required to do so by an administrative or judicial authority where it is necessary to do so to prevent an infringement (Article 12(3)), and this has been interpreted to mean that ISPs should block access to sites that are known to be hosting pirated material (O'Sullivan, 2014:577). The logic behind this is that the hosting of pirated material means that copyright infringements exist each and occurs every time the material is downloaded by someone else, and that both the owners of the site *and* those who provide access to the site are liable or have a duty to prevent illegal sharing (*EMI Records Ltd v British Sky Broadcasting Ltd* [2013] EWHC 379 (Ch) cited and explained in O'Sullivan, 2014:578).

Denying access to sites is, however, something that is easier said than done. A similar approach is adopted in respect of child pornography, although in some jurisdictions (including the UK) this is done without judicial mandate, something that is considered by some to be controversial (McIntyre, 2013). Serious doubts exist over whether blocking and filtering can be effective (McIntyre, 2013:299–301), although this is contested by others (most notably the Internet Watch Foundation (IWF) who undertake the blocking of child pornography in the UK). Concern has also been raised, within the context of IP piracy, as to whether this is a disproportionate response, in part because it is ineffective (O'Sullivan, 2014:580–581). The Court of Justice of the EU appears alert to these arguments and it has, for example, held that an injunction that does not refer to specific sites but instead simply requires the ISP to generally monitor content for inappropriate material is not appropriate

(*Scarlet v SABAM* [2011] ECR I-11959 discussed in O'Sullivan, 2014:583). However, denying access is seen by the industry as being one of the most important ways of tackling IP piracy.

## Suggested further reading

Arias, A.V. 'Life, liberty, and the pursuit of swords and armor: Regulating the theft of virtual goods' (2008) 57 *Emory Law Journal* 1301–1345.
*This is a good article that summarises many of the key issues that surround the issue of treating in-game objects as virtual property.*

Gillen, M. 'File-sharing and individual civil liability in the United Kingdom: A question of substance or abuse?' (2006) 17 *Entertainment Law Review* 7–14.
*This is an interesting article that considers how civil law is being used in preference to the criminal law in respect of those who share copyrighted material. This raises interesting questions about the purpose of the civil and criminal laws.*

Strikwerda, L. 'Theft of virtual items in online multiplayer computer games: An ontological and moral analysis' (2012) 14 *Ethics and Information Technology* 89–97.
*This is an interesting piece that considers the issue from a philosophical and moralistic point of view. It raises key challenges for the reader in understanding how virtual objects can be construed as property.*

Taylor, A. and Taylor, C. 'Pirates ahoy! Publishing, the internet and electronic piracy' (2006) 17 *Entertainment Law Review* 114–117.
*An interesting introductory piece to some of the issues surrounding electronic piracy and how domestic law can apply to it.*

# Part 3

# Illicit content

# Chapter 8

# Hate and harm

This chapter considers two issues that are separate but arguably on the same spectrum. Yet, as will be seen, the law adopts very different approaches to them. The first issue that will be considered is so-called 'hate speech', a form of odious expression whereby people are targeted on the basis of their race, colour, sexuality, religion or other physical characteristics (including disability). The second issue that will be examined are 'harm' websites or, more properly, 'self-harm' websites, i.e. those websites that seek to encourage or glorify the actions of an individual that could cause harm to themselves. This includes suicide websites, cutting websites and those related to eating disorders.

Both hate speech and harm sites are linked by the fact that they relate to content and not physical contact. What is being discussed in this chapter is therefore not sites that perhaps glorify physical attacks on another but rather those that simply present content that is undoubtedly, from a moral perspective, both offensive and unpleasant. However, as issues of content they undoubtedly raise issues concerning freedom of speech/expression and the extent to which it is permissible for the state to decide what a person may say.

## Hate sites

The first issue to consider is that of hate sites, i.e. those that constitute content that could be considered to be a hate crime. The concept of 'hate' is one that is heavily contested and therefore identifying what is 'hate speech' is similarly contested (discussed in Gillespie, 2014c:490 et seq.). That said it is necessary to attempt to identify a definition before then going on to consider the different type of sites that exist and what occurs on these sites.

## Defining hate speech

Hate speech is undoubtedly a derivative of hate crime but this, by itself, does not necessarily help us, because what is hate crime? The natural meaning of the words would seem to be a crime motivated by hatred towards another but this does not really capture the essence of a hate crime. This is partly because many crimes (including crimes of violence) may be committed through hatred (e.g. two people who have been known to each other for many years and who have developed hostility to each other). Hatred in this sense can almost be said to be an individual hatred – i.e. the hatred is directed towards the individual victim. Hate crime normally differs because the hatred is more general, as it pertains to a class of persons. However, concentrating on hatred can be difficult in its own right as defining what hatred is can itself be problematic.

It has been suggested that the 'hatred' element involves the 'intentional selection of a victim based on a perpetrator's bias or prejudice against the actual or perceived status of the victim' (Craig, 2002:86). Interestingly, of course this does not refer to hatred but instead bias or prejudice, arguably very different emotions. Iganski has suggested that hatred is a very specific form of emotion and notes that it differs from mere anger in that it is a 'resilient state of mind' (Iganski, 2008:2), but again that does not necessarily help us to understand what hatred is, particularly in this context.

It is notable that some believe that instead of hatred what is required is the concept of bias or prejudice (Goodall, 2013) and this perhaps tallies with the dictionary definition of hatred which, *inter alia*, is 'to feel intense dislike for or a strong aversion towards' (*Concise Oxford English Dictionary*), the latter part of which – strong aversion – is perhaps not dissimilar from the concept of prejudice.

The key aspect of hate speech is that the hatred (however it is to be constructed) must be directed towards a group rather than an individual. Most of the literature is dedicated towards hatred on the basis of racism or xenophobia and this is perhaps understandable because this remains one of the key forms of hate crime. It was only in the latter half of the twentieth century that countries such as the USA and the UK adopted laws that prevented discrimination on the grounds of race, and even a rudimentary search of newspapers demonstrates that there continue to be many incidents where prejudice on the basis of race seems apparent. However, hate speech, particularly hate speech on the internet, is not restricted to racial hatred and there are sites that target people on the basis of their religion, gender, sexuality, disability or even lifestyle (e.g. there is a considerable amount of 'anti-goth' material).

The notion that there could be hate crimes against lifestyle choices (as distinct from other factors such as race, religion, gender or sexuality) has proven to be extremely controversial. Greater Manchester Police made headlines when it announced that it was prepared to accept attacks against goths to constitute hate crime (see, for example, Evans, 2013) but it has been argued by some that this is not unreasonable. Indeed it has been put forward that whilst the type of attacks and type of damage inflicted are less than, for example, in race hate crimes there are some similarities, and that community perceptions and selection of victim are comparable to 'hate crime' (Garland and Hodkinson, 2014:625). However, the authors note that extending the definition to encompass such lifestyle choices could be problematic, in part because this extension is not recognised in law (Garland and Hodkinson, 2014:626). There is also undoubtedly the problem of perception about what hate crime is ultimately about. Some have suggested that hate crime is about recognising the power that the majority have over those communities that have been historically oppressed (Taylor, 2002:354) and if that were applied then it would be difficult to argue that goths (who are invariably white and middle class: Garland and Hodkinson, 2014:627) would meet this criterion.

If hate crime is about power – and historically that has been seen to be the case – then excluding goths from the definition would seem correct. That is not to state that attacks (including through content) on those with alternative lifestyles will not be extremely distressing and, in some instances, constitute a crime. However, they are materially different to existing hate crimes and so perhaps should be treated in that way.

For the purposes of this chapter hate crime will carry an even more restricted definition because, to facilitate analysis, only a single type of hate speech – racism and xenophobia – will be considered. Racism and xenophobia remains the most common type of hate speech websites and so it is perhaps the most logical form to examine.

## Growth of hate sites

In common with other forms of illegal content there appears to have been an increase in hate speech sites detected. The Simon Wiesenthal Center, perhaps the World's leading organisation dedicated to tackling anti-Semitism, started to notice the use of the internet as a tool for hate even when it was in its technical infancy. In 1995 there was a single site, albeit one that was very organised (Cooper 2012:21), yet by 2000 the number had grown to approximately 500 sites (McNamee *et al.*, 2010:258) with the suggestion that by 2012 this had risen to over 14,000 sites that were being monitored by that one centre (Cooper, 2012:21). Of course the difficulty with ascertaining the number of sites is that few can necessarily agree on the definition of hate crime and the fact that it is impossible to 'catalogue' the internet. The internet is a space that constantly changes with sites appearing, disappearing and morphing almost constantly. There is also the difficulty that many sites are mirrored in multiple locations which may lead to questions as to double-counting. We will never know the reality of the number of sites that do exist but there seems little doubt that extremist and hate-speech sites are increasing.

## Characteristics of hate websites

For the same reasons that it is not possible to know how many hate sites exist, we similarly cannot know the characteristics of all websites in existence.

However, some studies have looked at the characteristics of websites and some common themes can be detected. An early study suggested that the largest single-issue type of hate site was white supremacy followed by skin-head, Christian identity and Holocaust denial (Gerstenfeld *et al.*, 2003:33). It is not known whether this remains true today. Certainly since that time Islamophobia has increased and therefore it would seem likely that more sites dedicated to this will be apparent, although it could be said that these would fall within the pre-existing labels (as white supremacist and Christian identity sites are unlikely to be 'pro' Islam).

The majority of the sites identified by Gerstenfeld *et al.* were English-language based (Gerstenfeld *et al.*, 2003:34) although this is perhaps less than surprising given (a) the origins of the internet and (b) the methodology adopted by the users. This is not to say that non-English-language sites do not exist because clearly they do, although ascertaining their prevalence is difficult. Where non-English-language sites existed they tended to fall into groupings that perhaps were not unexpected. So, for example, there were a number of neo-Nazi hate sites that contained German language (Gerstenfeld *et al.*, 2003) and recently there has been an upsurge in similar sites in the Russian and Greek languages, perhaps reflecting the growth of extreme right-wing parties within their political systems.

Whilst some sites will be blatant in their form because, for example, it is obvious that they are a hate site against a particular community, this will not always be the case. Some seek to distort what their true purpose is. Indeed it has been noted that, for example, some will seek to present themselves as patriotic rather than subversive and the content may seem ostensibly plausible (McNamee *et al.*, 2010:258). Similarly, some may try to characterise themselves as a political movement, seeking to exploit the tradition that politics in most democracies covers a wide spectrum of beliefs. An interesting phenomenon is that many sites will expressly state that they are *not* a hate site, often trying to blame the group that they target as the 'perpetrator' of the 'myth' that they are a hate site (Tsesis, 2001:834). Some studies have also shown that sites will list other sites that they argue are 'true' hate sites and with which they would refuse to associate themselves (McNamee *et al.*, 2010:272).

One aspect of the internet is that it is possible for sites to appear respectable relatively easily. Groups can cast off their 'rough edges' through the production of slick websites. Free web design is commonplace but even a small amount of knowledge allows for interactive sites that look commercially respectable. Indeed the anonymity of the internet means that groups can pretend to be bigger than they really are. It is simplicity itself to create content that would seem to imply a large organisation operating internationally when the truth may be that it is a small number of individuals operating out of a house.

### Purpose of the sites

It may be thought that hate sites would be just that: a site that is a diatribe against a particular group of persons, but it is not that simple. The internet has become much more than a mere information repository and has become perhaps the most important (remote) social tool. Sites are often not used simply to put out a message of hate but used for more complex reasons. It has been noted the internet is attractive to extremists because as a communication tool it is fast, easy and inexpensive (Gerstenfeld *et al.*, 2003:37). However, it also has an international appeal meaning that the reach of an organisation is considerably greater than it would otherwise be if they were reliant simply on offline methods. It will be remembered from Chapter 1 that the international dimension of the internet is such that it can be difficult for (local) laws to apply, and this will be of particular importance later in this chapter where the issue of free expression will be considered.

There are numerous purposes behind the creation of a hate website but the principal ones are:

- Publicising the message.
- Education.
- Recruiting members.
- Social interactions.

Of course it would be naïve to suggest that each site has only one purpose and it is more likely that sites will have numerous purposes.

### Publicising the message

Perhaps the most obvious reason for creating a website is to publicise the 'message' of the group. Some sites will therefore simply be a repository of hate or distorted opinions. As the internet is multimedia then it is possible to include speeches, text, video, etc. All of this material can be placed onto the internet for others to see. Some sites will try to present themselves as repositories of information and therefore will encourage people to upload their own material so that the amount of material (and ultimately therefore the message) can be spread.

A feature of the internet is that it allows extremist organisations to communicate with the general population without the need to rely upon the media, who would probably ask difficult questions of the group. This is perhaps best encapsulated by the National Director of the Ku Klux Klan: 'we don't really need the media any more ... the only thing we need is the internet' (cited in McNamee *et al.*, 2010:258). Indeed, advances in technology mean that extremist groups can create their own media, including news stations. Internet radio allows people to broadcast globally and there is no doubt that some extremist groups have adopted this technology (Conway, 2007), allowing them to shun what they will portray as 'mainstream' or biased media and put forward their media services as the only true or authentic services.

### Education

A number of hate websites will purport to be educational (McNamee *et al.*, 2010:266), often suggesting that they are presenting a 'true' version of events to correct the lies and misleading statements of others. Perhaps most notably this is done in respect of the denial of the Holocaust (McNamee *et al.*, 2010:266) where sites will make claims that they put forward as verifiable facts. The internet is an ideal resource for this as its multimedia format and the ability to post information without evidence means that it can present distorted views in a way that appears plausible. Think about conspiracy theories. Whilst they have existed for a long time (perhaps the most notable being conspiracy theories surrounding the assassination of the US President John F. Kennedy) the internet has allowed for them to flourish, partly because it is possible to provide 'proof' of the conspiracies through uploading files, looking at microscopic inconsistencies, etc. (Wood *et al.*, 2012 provide an illuminating analysis of the psychology of conspiracy theories). The same, as will be seen, applies to hate speech on the internet where sites purport to show various 'truths' (a good example would be the hundreds of sites that can be returned from a simple internet search on Holocaust denial or related keywords).

The danger of 'educational' sites is that they can influence certain groups. It is perhaps notable that a number of groups connected to hate speech have included material aimed specifically at children. They make clear that the site is educational and is designed to 'answer questions' and they present their content in a way that sounds convincing, including providing a plausible narrative. This can be a powerful technique as it has been shown that narrative and storytelling is an important way of communicating messages in a way to increase believability, particularly in respect of the young (Lee and Leets, 2002). Potentially this means that by putting forward this alternative history they will begin to change the way that people view those whom the sites target.

### Recruiting members

One key reason for operating a hate site is to recruit members. It has been noted that extremist organisations sometimes suffer from high turnover of individuals and that this poses a threat to their sustainability (Blazak, 2001). It is easy to see why this might be the case with offline groups, where there may be difficulties in persuading people to openly support the stance of the group because they will often be considered socially unacceptable and, quite often, legally problematic.

Using a website to recruit members carries with it significant advantages in that there can be anonymity on the internet, meaning that people can join the group without, for example, their work colleagues knowing about it. As noted already, websites do not respect international borders and therefore a group can recruit people from across the globe which potentially increases the scope of sites, making people believe that their views are shared across the world (or a particular racial group) thus 'validating' (in their minds) the views of individuals.

Where groups have an offline presence (e.g. a number of Ku Klux Klan groups continue to have a physical presence) then the website can be used as a way of showing the social aspect that joining such a group brings (McNamee *et al.*, 2010:276). Thus the site may show pictures of meetings that will invariably just show people having 'fun' through camps, having a meal, etc. In this way the group can present itself as normal, thus implying that joining the group is not a deviant practice but rather a social activity.

### Social interactions

As noted above, the social dimension of the internet is also sometimes exploited by those creating hate sites. One study noted that a white supremacist site stated that they were a 'fraternal organisation, a family of friends and a circle of support' (McNamee *et al.*, 2010:268). This also allows them to down-play the extremist or hate elements of the site and instead present themselves as a friendly organisation.

As will be seen in the next part of this book ('Offences against the person') the anonymity of the internet allows for users to interact in a way that they feel is safe. To an extent this was also seen from Chapter 6 where it was shown that romance frauds have flourished as a result of the internet. Interactions on the internet can mirror offline friendships but with the benefit of anonymity. From the point of view of an extremist organisation this carries with it great benefits as it may be that offline meetings will be subject to attention from law enforcement agencies, etc. However, an online site will likely evade some of this overt surveillance (although where there is cause for concern about their activities it is likely that some sites will be placed under electronic surveillance) and certainly this means it is easier to talk to people. Also, as has already been noted, there is an international dimension to the internet which allows social interaction to occur across territorial borders.

### Legality of hate sites

The legality of hate sites is not an easy question to answer. To an extent the most interesting questions relate to the concept of the intersection between the law and freedom of speech/expression which will be considered in a later section of this chapter. However, unlike self-harm sites – which will be discussed momentarily – there are potentially crimes that are committed through the creation of hate websites and, in some instances, in participating on those sites. This section will briefly outline the relevant offences although the critical discussion is left until the discussion of freedom of expression laws.

### Council of Europe

Before turning to domestic law it is worth noting that there is an optional Protocol to the *Council of Europe Convention on Cybercrime* which seeks to tackle racist and xenophobic material which is described as:

> written material, any image or any other representation of ideas or theories, which advocates, promotes or incites hatred, discrimination or violence, against any individual or group of individuals, based on race, colour, descent or national or ethnic origin, as well as religion if used as a pretext for any of these factors.
>
> (Article 2(1))

This is a wide definition but it is notable that religion *per se* is not covered and thus, for example, sectarian hate groups within Northern Ireland would probably not be covered by this definition. However, an anti-Islamic site may well fall foul of it because there is invariably a link between such sites and derogatory comments about a race (e.g. Arabs).

As a Protocol to the Cybercrime Convention it applies only to material that exists on computers or related internet devices. An important part of the Convention is to require signatory states to introduce a series of criminal offences relating to:

- Dissemination of racist and xenophobic material through computer systems (Article 3).
- Racist and xenophobic motivated threat (Article 4).
- Racist and xenophobic motivated insult (Article 5).
- Denial, gross minimisation, approval or justification of genocide or crimes against humanity.

(Article 6)

The latter offence is particularly interesting and this will be returned to later when considering freedom of expression. Article 6 requires states to criminalise the distribution (including through making it available) of material which 'denies, grossly minimises, approves or justifies acts constituting genocide or crimes against humanity', and this specifically includes the Holocaust (Article

6(1)). Holocaust denial is a particular feature of anti-Semitic websites and it is more than just a denial of a terrible incident in human history; it arguably strikes at the dignity of the Jewish people, particularly where the denial is coupled with the belief that it is a Jewish conspiracy, as this seeks to twist the victim into the perpetrator, a form of victimisation (for a discussion see Gillespie, 2014c:501–502).

Of course questions can be raised as to what constitutes denial or gross trivialisation. Would an academic study that suggests that the total number of victims is fewer than official figures infringe this provision? It is unlikely because the offence applies only where it is committed 'intentionally and without right', but who decides what is right and wrong? An academic paper published in a respectable journal may be 'by right' because of academic freedom (Karran, 2007, discusses this concept), but what about where a person simply presents 'academic' research in a non-peer-reviewed way? The internet allows for non-traditional publishing to occur and for it to be presented in a way that appears to be legitimate. Under these circumstances applying the offence could perhaps be more difficult.

A difficulty with the Protocol is that, whilst it will be remembered from Chapter 1 that there are concerns over the number of countries that have signed the Convention itself, even fewer countries have signed the Protocol. This is partly because there are some concerns as to how this relates to free expression or because some countries believe their law already covers the issues.

### Domestic law

In terms of domestic law there are a number of offences that could be relevant. It is not necessary to consider all of them or indeed any of them in detail. However, it would be prudent to name some of the offences to show how they could be applied in practice. The most relevant are:

- Racial hatred offences.
- Religious hatred and hatred on the grounds of sexual orientation.
- Communication offences.

The religious hatred and hatred on the grounds of sexual orientation offences mirror many of the offences that will be considered momentarily in respect of racial hatred. The new offences are contained in Part 3A, *Public Order Act 1986* (POA 1986) which was inserted by the *Racial and Religious Hatred Act 2006*. Religious hatred is defined as 'hatred against a group of persons defined by reference to religious belief or lack of religious belief' (s.29A, POA 1986) with hatred on the grounds of sexual orientation being defined as 'hatred against a group of persons defined by reference to sexual orientation (whether towards persons of the same sex, the opposite sex or both) (s.29AB, POA 1986). Part 3A significantly widened the legislation (a useful commentary on the religious hatred provision is given by Hare, 2006) although it remains controversial as a potential infringement of free speech (Bailin, 2011, and discussed further below).

The communication offences will be considered elsewhere (Chapter 11 in particular) and therefore will not be considered here, although it is worth noting that they could apply. It has been suggested that the communication offences pose a danger to free speech (see, perhaps most notably, Rowbottom, 2012) and certainly it is easy to see how this could apply to an offence based on race. The interference between these offences and free expression will be considered later in this chapter.

This leaves the racial hatred offences. A brief outline of these will be given for context, although as the primary focus of this chapter is on content and free expression it is not necessary to consider them in depth. The principal offences are contained within Part III of the POA 1986 and are divided into two principal classes. The first deals with acts that are intended or are likely to stir up racial hatred (ss.18–22, POA 1986) and the second is possession of racially inflammatory material (s.23, POA 1986).

In terms of the first group of offences a number are potentially applicable in cyberspace. Section 18 criminalises the displaying of 'written material which is threatening, abusive or insulting' where it is intended to stir up racial hatred or where in all the circumstances it is likely to do so. Placing material on the internet would inevitably be classed as 'written material'. Indeed the same offence also applies to the use of 'words' and it is quite likely that where, for example, a person is leaving a message on a website that allows discussion that this could also apply.

Section 19 applies to the publishing or distribution of written material which is threatening, abusive or insulting where it is intended to stir up racial hatred or where in all the circumstances it is likely to do so. It will be remembered from Chapter 2 that this offence has already been considered in the context of cyberspace (see the discussion on *R v Sheppard and Whittle* [2010] 1 WLR 2779). Placing material on the internet is considered to be publishing it and English law adopts the approach that material is published where it is uploaded or downloaded (*R v Waddon* (2000, unreported) approved of in *Sheppard and Whittle*) meaning that this becomes a wide offence.

Section 21 prohibits the 'distributing, showing or playing a recording of visual images or sounds which are threatening, abusive or insulting' where it is intended to stir up racial hatred or where in all the circumstances it is likely to do so. Given the multimedia nature of the internet it is quite possible that this offence could apply, including through placing a video online (where a section of the public could thereby see it) or a sound-clip of, for example, racist speech. If the person himself gives the speech and then places it online he would commit the offence of s.18 (words inciting racial hatred) *and* s.19 because they are two separate offences (speaking the words and distributing, showing or playing them) (see, for example, *R v El-Faisal* [2004] EWCA Crim 456).

Section 23 introduces a possession offence although it is not an offence of strict possession. Its wording is:

(1) A person who has in his possession written material which is threatening, abusive or insulting, or a recording of visual images or sounds which are threatening, abusive or insulting, with a view to

(a) in the case of written material, its being displayed, published, distributed ... whether by himself or another, or
(b) in the case of a recording, its being distributed, shown, played ... whether by himself or another

is guilty of an offence if he intends racial hatred to be stirred up thereby, or having regard to all the circumstances, racial hatred is likely to be stirred up thereby.

This is an important offence because it would include a person who was preparing material for a hate website (as that would be the intention, *inter alia*, to distribute) but it would also include someone who has stored such material in a peer-to-peer space, which would allow someone to take that material (whilst a technical argument could be made that this is also the substantive act of publishing it would perhaps be easier to prosecute for possession with the intent to distribute). That said, it would presumably be necessary to show that the defendant knew the material could be taken from the shared folder and that at least one of his purposes for using such software was for this to happen (see *R v Dooley* [2006] 1 WLR 775).

## Human rights

At the heart of the issue of hate speech is its relationship with human rights. This is also an area where there is a significant discrepancy between USA and Europe. The USA has traditionally adopted the approach that hate speech is (generally) protected under the First Amendment (see Gillespie, 2014c:503) and so there are few laws that govern its production and dissemination. Within Europe, Article 10 provides the Freedom of Expression but it is notable that it is a qualified rather than absolute rule. More than this, however, Article 17 of the ECHR prevents someone from using a Convention right in such a way as to deny the rights and freedoms of others (in this context see, for example, *Garaudy v France* Application No. 65831/01 (2003)). The position in Europe (including the UK) has therefore been that it is not possible to rely on human rights arguments where the purpose of the hate speech is to increase prejudice against others (Gillespie, 2014c:506).

## Self-harm sites

There are a number of different types of self-harm websites but the common versions are:

- Suicide websites (i.e. those that glorify or encourage suicide or provide instruction on how to commit suicide).
- Self-injury websites (i.e. for those who, for example, cut themselves, burn themselves or deliberately poison themselves).
- Eating disorder websites (i.e. those that seek to glorify or encourage eating disorders).

There are other types, for example those that relate to alcohol or drug addiction, but there is a question as to whether these are truly self-harm. Whilst alcohol and drugs are undoubtedly harmful it can be questioned whether their use represents conscious decisions to harm one's own body rather than an addiction. Whilst other types of self-harm behaviours may have addictive qualities this is different from a chemical addiction. Whilst most self-harming behaviours are considered to be a medical psychosis (see, most notably, DSM-V published by the American Psychiatric Association) it will be seen that this is questioned by some who query whether it is a lifestyle choice.

In keeping with the nature of this book – key themes and debates – it is not intended in this section to cover all types of self-harming behaviour because that could constitute a book in its own right.

### Suicide websites

Of the three principal types of websites considered above, there is a material difference between the latter two types (physical and self-harm) and the former (suicide). Not only is suicide a rather more permanent type of self-harm it is also something that the law regulates, or at least does so in part. Until the twentieth century suicide was a crime. It was often referred to as 'self-murder', something that undoubtedly arose from the religious tradition of most of our laws. The term 'murder' is interesting because taken literally it could be justified – murder is the deliberate killing of a person – and so 'self-murder' would be the deliberate killing of oneself. However, murder is a particularly emotive term and it is therefore unhelpful and indeed hurtful for that term to be used.

Suicide was not only a crime; it was at one time a capital crime. Therefore, the oddities of the English criminal justice system were such that if one attempted suicide and were detected, you could be stopped, arrested, prosecuted and, if found guilty, sentenced to be hanged. Something of a waste of resources! Even if suicide was successful the stigma attached to suicide was such that getting a 'decent' burial was problematic. Part of that stigma remains and even today there are special rules that apply to inquests that limit the circumstances in which a verdict of suicide can be returned (Dorries, 2014). The *Suicide Act 1961* decriminalised suicide but it created an offence of aiding, abetting, counselling or procuring suicide (*Suicide Act 1961*, s.2(1)). This was amended by the *Coroners and Justice Act 2009* to encouraging or assisting suicide (reflecting the language of the *Serious Crimes Act 2007*) and is an offence punishable by up to 14 years' imprisonment. One of the stated purposes of these amendments was to cater for suicide websites and the author has previously considered this issue in detail (Gillespie, 2013a). For this reason – and the fact that the law appears to ostensibly apply – the issue of suicide websites will not be considered further.

This leaves physical self-harming behaviours. These pose difficult issues for the law, particularly in respect of balancing any legal regulation with free speech/expression.

### Self-injury

Physical self-harm sites devoted to self-injury undoubtedly exist but they would seem to be less common than eating disorders websites. It has been noted that tales of self-injury have entered mainstream media such as films and sparked media attention (Adler and Adler, 2012:59). As with eating disorders (discussed below) there appears to be an over-representation of adolescents and young adults who self-injure (Lewis *et al.*, 2011:e553) although the reason for that is not clear.

Studies have shown that self-injury sites go beyond community or discussion boards and can include the uploading of videos online (Lewis *et al.*, 2011), even where doing so would almost certainly infringe the terms of service of the content site. It is not known why these videos are uploaded. Sometimes it would seem to be 'instructional' but often it is simply presented as the behaviour of the individual. This does raise the issue about whether such postings could be said to be the expressions of an individual, although it is known that there are many reasons for self-injuring behaviour (Hawton *et al.*, 2002) and so there are likely to be underlying reasons too.

It would seem that some users are self-aware in terms of the 'risk' that their content may influence others. It was reported in one study that many videos posted online would include warnings that their content could include 'triggers' for those who self-harm (Lewis *et al.*, 2011:e555). Given this, it would be interesting to note why such videos are posted The nature of YouTube is such that it is unlikely that it can be said to have a discursive element to it, and indeed it is likely to open up the user to negative comments which could aggravate the underlying reasons for self-harming. It is interesting to speculate whether it is thought to be an expression of their individualism and behaviour. If so, this potentially raises human rights issues that need to be addressed in any legal framework.

The issues in respect of self-injury sites would seem similar to eating disorder sites. As there is a greater body of literature for the latter this chapter will, for reasons of space, concentrate on eating disorders. However, it is worth noting that the issues discussed below, in terms of community and expression, are likely to apply equally to self-injury sites not least because self-injury is not a criminal act in its own right, and nor, unlike suicide, is encouraging or assisting self-injury a criminal act.

## Eating disorders

The remainder of the chapter will therefore concentrate on eating disorders (EDs). Whilst it would seem that there are a lot of these sites it is difficult to quantify the exact number, not least because some are closed down. A number of EDs exist but two have most prominence, both in society and on the internet:

- Anorexia (*anorexia nervosa*) which, in lay terms, is the condition where a person will eat considerably less than they should, including deliberately fasting, with the intention of making themselves as thin as possible.
- Bulimia (*bulimia nervosa*) is also related to weight but is where a person will engage in binge eating and purging (either through making themselves sick or using laxatives).

Most of the literature discusses both eating disorders at the same time although clinically there are differences between them. There is some logic to treating them together since what is being discussed is not the technicalities of the disorders but rather the literature is about those who glorify or encourage participation in EDs. The difference between anorexia and bulimia is less relevant in that context as both are, at least medically, harmful.

### Language and personification

It has been seen already in this book that it is not uncommon in cybercrime for language to develop. This was particularly apparent in Chapter 3 where the issue of hacking was discussed and a whole series of names were used to discuss the different types of behaviour. The same is true here, but interestingly in respect of EDs a thing (the disorder) becomes personified so that many sites and people with an ED will talk about it as though it were a person.

Anorexia is shortened to ANA on the internet and increasingly to Ana. Whilst it can be said that this is a simple abbreviation it is perhaps notable that Ana is also a female name. It is known that women, particularly young women, are distinctly over-represented in those with an ED (Boero and Pascoe, 2012:33) and therefore the choice of a female name is perhaps significant. Bulimia is shortened to MIA or Mia. Again, whilst serving as an abbreviation it is also a female name and thus when it is being discussed it is easy for dialogues to form around the idea that the ED is a living representation.

This personification can be seen in some of the literature where people with an ED refer to Ana not only in the feminine but as a personality. So, for example, one user says 'I live with Ana every day … She is in my life' (Brotsky and Giles, 2007:99) and another, talking about the way that sites may be closed down, says 'the sites come and go, but Ana is always there, waiting for us to find her' (Crowe and Watts, 2013:3). Indeed this personification almost becomes a mantra:

> You may call me Ana. Hopefully we can become great partners. In the coming time, I will invest a lot of time in you, and I expect the same from you.
>
> ('letter from Ana' adduced by Crowe and Watts, 2013:2)

and in some cases takes on an almost religious character who acts as a protector (ibid.). This personification undoubtedly influences how some of those with an ED react to their condition, with it being not uncommon for them to talk about being in a relationship with their ED.

The use of language also extends to those who do not 'fit in', with it being noted that derogatory terms will be used against those who are not thought appropriate to join the online community. It will be remembered from Chapter 3 that the 'newbie' was treated with disdain by the hacking fraternity and the same is true of the 'wannarexic', i.e. somebody who is accused of being a 'wannabe anorexic'. Such people are normally treated with disdain because they do not have the commitment to the lifestyle required for those with an ED (Boero and Pascoe, 2012:39). The status of wannarexic is such that it can cause people to be reticent to join a community for fear that they are considered not to have a 'true' ED. This is then taken further and people worry that if they do not lose weight they will be labelled as a wannarexic and experience hostility directed towards them (Yeshua-Katz and Martins, 2013:505; Boero and Pascoe, 2012:42). This potentially means that they are prepared to lose more weight than they would necessarily choose to. Not all sites operate on this premise, however, and some are more welcoming, with more established users ensuring that those first-joining a site are protected from insults (Brotsky and Giles, 2007:100).

## Types of ED sites

It has already been noted that it is impossible to estimate the number of ED sites that are in existence and thus, perhaps understandably, there are many different types. Most attention has been paid to pro-ED sites although it is clear that anti-ED sites exist, including some that are full of what can only be considered hateful speech against those who have an ED. However, identifying what is a pro-ED site is not, by itself, easy and this is crucial in terms of how the law can react.

Recent years have seen almost a glut of research on ED sites but they do tend to suggest similar patterns. Sites will vary in design but will rarely be information-only and usually they will be high on participatory elements. Indeed it has been surmised that engendering a sense of community is the primary purpose of the sites, with it being said that ED sites allow 'women separated by geography, age, and lifestyle … to share their struggles, goals, triumphs and failures in living a[n ED] lifestyle' (Boero and Pascoe, 2012:29). This has been confirmed by others who believe that the primary motivation for those who participate in ED sites is social support (Yeshua-Katz and Martins, 2013:503). Interestingly, this support will exist for both pro-ED and pro-recovery sites. In both types the participants are seeking acceptance by those who know what they are going through, something that they do not get in the offline world (outside of medicalised therapy).

Unlike some forms of 'problematic' content (although the term is used here in a non-judgmental way to signify content that society may consider inappropriate), there is sometimes little attempt at disguising what the sites contain. Whilst some are clearly clandestine because of the fear of being closed (something discussed extensively below) the majority are in plain sight when one knows the relevant language. Whilst dated, one of the most comprehensive qualitative analyses of ED sites (and which more recent literature continues to validate) found that over 50 per cent of sites had a disclaimer to warn users of the content (Norris et al., 2006:445). The same study showed that three-quarters of the sites stated what their purpose was (e.g. pro-ED, supporting those with EDs, pro-recovery, etc.) and the vast majority of them were readable and user friendly. This latter point has been specifically confirmed in other studies which, for example, have noted that those who run ED websites tend to be very knowledgeable on the effects of EDs, exercise and food (see, for example, Brotsky and Giles, 2007; Yeshua-Katz and Martins, 2013).

An interesting issue is to what extent it can be said that 'recovery' sites differentiate themselves from pro-ED sites. Whilst presented as a method of helping people to recover they could act as a smokescreen for pro-ED messages. Indeed, it could be asked why anyone would need to create a pro-recovery site as it may be thought that recovery would be something best dealt with by medical practitioners. However, it is not that straightforward. It has been argued that it is not always possible to seek health-care support because there are specified criteria for the diagnosis of an ED and there are thresholds that must be reached before treatment will be offered (Dias, 2003:39), in part presumably because of budgetary pressure. Indeed, Dias noted that the imposition of a threshold can actually deter people from seeking help because they worry that they will be told they are not thin enough for treatment which, due to their disorder, could be interpreted as being told that they are fat, effectively entrenching their ED. Therefore, leaving matters to medical practitioners is not always possible.

In any event, it is known that support assists in the recovery process and one of the difficulties of having an ED is the feeling that nobody 'normal' understands:

> All my friends and teachers and pretty much everyone knows about it but I can't go up to them and say, 'oh, I had a really bad today because I ate too much' or 'I had a great day today'.
>
> ('Mary' presented in Yeshua-Katz and Martins, 2013:503)

ED sites therefore present themselves as people who understand. It is one of the reasons why many sites will make clear what type of site they are so that a person entering the site will know, for example, if it is pro-ED or pro-recovery, as 'support' will mean something very different in those contexts. However, it is not always that simple. One investigation on users of ED sites (which is very interesting because it was done covertly so there were a number of thought-provoking ethical questions raised: see Brotsky and Giles, 2007:95–96) showed that users were not really glorifying EDs but rather acting as a support for those who wanted to be involved. When the investigator ended her covert observation her 'internet presence' would announce that she was seeking in-patient therapy to try and 'beat' the ED. It was noted that the messages were almost universally supportive, including messages of hope that she 'beat' the ED (Brotsky and Giles, 2007:101). If pro-ED sites were seen as glorifying or attempting to sustain EDs this would be a strange attitude to adopt. The reality is that it shows how complex pro-ED sites are, as indeed are those who have an ED. It is not that they believe everyone should have an ED or even that they should encourage others to have an ED but are largely trying to sustain a sympathetic community for those who have an ED. This is replicated in other research which shows that unlike many other types of content sites the issues are not a binary divide of 'positive/negative', 'right/ wrong' or 'harmful/heathy'.

The lack of a simple distinction works both ways, however, and this is why pro-recovery sites can still be considered by some to be problematic. Dias refers to an interview with a site owner who says:

> by far ... the most triggering site I've been to, is made by an EX-anorexic and it's a RECOVERY site. I learned more from that site than any PRO site could offer.
>
> (Dias, 2003:39, emphasis in original)

Thus even pro-recovery sites can be used as a source of assistance for those who have an ED. Recovery sites will frequently detail common symptoms and strategies (so that people know when they 'relapse') and thus there is no simple way of differentiating between helpful and harmful sites.

## Harm?

It has been noted that some of the attention paid to pro-ED sites has taken on the characteristics of a moral panic (Pollack, 2003:247). Certainly when it is mentioned in the mainstream media it is rarely presented as anything other than a real cause for concern. For example, the *Daily Mail*, a popular UK tabloid, has stories saying, 'Menace of the internet sites urging teenagers to starve' (2008, April 7) and 'Girls boasting of starvation diets. Grotesque images of jutting bones. In this chilling investigation, we reveal the truth about anorexia websites' (2008, November 27). The latter has many of the hallmarks of a moral panic – 'truth', 'harm' and 'epidemic' (the story saying 'Within the past year, YouTube was found to have 2,500 examples … while other social networking sites have thousands more'). Are the sites harmful?

Whilst Bardone-Cone and Cass, in a pilot study, suggested that for even 'normal' women 'viewing pro-anorexia websites has negative affective cognitive effects on women' (2006:259) there is perhaps some cause to question this. Their study involved only a small sample of women (24), which admittedly they acknowledge (Bardone-Cone and Cass, 2006:257), but perhaps more importantly the sample were students on an introductory psychology programme. Whilst psychological testing on psychology students is not uncommon it can be questioned whether such students may be more prepared to report 'feelings' because they will believe either that such things might happen or be more susceptible to what feelings there are (in a way that others may not).

There is also the point that if this was true then would it be ethical for the people conducting the research to do the study? Interestingly, this is a question that is specifically addressed by Brotsky and Giles who discuss the fact that Sarah Brotsky conducted the primary research by posing as someone with an ED and examining the interactions that pro-ED sites brought. They note that the possibility that the principal investigator could be influenced by the material was a 'chief ethical concern' (Brotsky and Giles, 2007:97) and their solution was to ensure that there was a support network to which Brotsky could turn at regular intervals to ensure that she was not influenced by the material. Does that support the contention of Bardone-Cone and Cass or is it a case of being 'careful'? The truth is that, as with most types of content, it is impossible to quantify to what extent viewing causes people to *do* something (an issue picked up in the following chapters on sexual content) or whether it is only people who are susceptible to influence that are swayed.

If you read articles from the medical sciences then it will be rare to see EDs being described as anything other than harmful or, at the very least, potentially harmful. However, if social science articles are consulted then a different picture begins to emerge. Whilst the majority of the literature continues to perceive EDs as harmful, there is an emerging argument that EDs could be considered to be a lifestyle choice, this article particularly featuring in some feminist literature.

Crowe and Watts argue that pro-ED sites 'are socio-cultural spaces that offer legitimate context for agency' (Crowe and Watts, 2013:4). Agency, as a concept, recognises free will, and it has been suggested that it is the 'ability of an individual to make a semi-autonomous decision to act in a particular way' (Weare, 2013:338). Semi-autonomous is used as recognition of the fact that nobody truly acts in an autonomous way because of societal expectations, etc. By using the term 'agency' the suggestion is that the pro-ED sites recognise that some people with an ED take the conscious decision to act in the way that they do. It has been suggested that an ED lifestyle could be a feminist reaction to society's views on what the ideal female body is (discussed in Pollack, 2003:247, and see Boero and Pascoe, 2012:33 who discuss the link between EDs and societal definitions of femininity) and that a person should have the right to sculpt their body as they wish. Certainly there is some evidence that shows that at least some pro-ED sites adopt this approach, with Pollack providing an illuminating example of a site where the owner expressly rejects the medical diagnosis of anorexia by juxtaposing it with a dictionary definition of 'bullshit' (Pollack, 2003:247–248).

The notion of an ED being a choice is based on the idea that it is a reaction to cultural norms, and thus it can be a person expressing their identity. It has been suggested, for example, that Ana can be seen as 'a discourse that actively resists the dominant cultural norms regarding 'healthy eating' (Crowe and Watts, 2013:6). In other words, anorexia may not be a medical condition where a person acts in a non-normal way but a rejection of societal norms which determine who is 'appropriate' and 'not appropriate'. Rejecting the concept of 'appropriateness' is certainly something that is seen throughout feminist discourse in respect of, for example, behaviour and clothing, and thus supporters of the suggestion that ED can be a lifestyle choice could point to this as a potential justification.

Whilst the notion of ED being a lifestyle choice is controversial in the literature, it is similarly controversial on the websites with users disagreeing amongst themselves:

> It is a disease, and disorder. But it is not a lifestyle. Whoever claims an Eating Disorder is a lifestyle, agh! It makes me want to cry.

> Sorry, but you DO CHOOSE to continue having an ED. And yes, I CHOSE to stick my fingers down my throat when I became bulimic. I didn't catch any anorexic/bulimia virus. Take some personal responsibility people.
> (Brotsky and Giles, 2007:102, emphasis in original)

Of course this is slightly skewed because the second comment refers to physiological issues rather than psychological issues. A virus is something that you catch and is often (but not always) unrelated to lifestyle, but psychological issues are very different. If, as some believe, this is a psychiatric disorder then these comments would resonate with existing literature on mental health problems where the issue of not being able to 'catch', for example, depression is not uncommon. To other users the distinction is irrelevant:

> I live with Ana every day – if she's a disease, disorder, or lifestyle. She is in my life and, for me, it is often a love/hate relationship.
> (Brotsky and Giles, 2007:99)

This reinforces the personification of an ED but it also demonstrates that the person arguably does not care whether anorexia is considered a disease or a lifestyle, it is something that defines their existence. This could provide for both sides of the argument. Those suggesting that it is a medical problem will consider that this is evidence of cognitive distortion whereas those advocating it as a lifestyle choice will argue that it shows agency and a clear statement that the ED is part of that individual's personhood.

When considering harm it is not just about the debate between disorder and lifestyle, it is also about whether the existence of sites will cause people to develop an ED. As with most content crimes, there is no evidence of a causal link between ED sites and the development of an ED, as there are often underlying issues. What is interesting, however, is that there is some recognition of the possibility of this and even though users may be pro-ED it is notable that many do not welcome the thought that they may encourage others to develop an ED (as distinct from supporting those who have an ED). This can be seen from the fact that most sites will contain a warning and clear indication as to the purpose of the site (see, amongst others, Norris *et al.*, 2006) but also from the words of the users themselves. Perhaps an illustrating comment is by 'Billie':

> I always worry that impressionable teenage girls ... who are concerned about their body or weight will visit my blog and read about my hatred for my body and take tips or inspiration from my restrictive diet. I would never want to encourage anyone to start dieting or thinking in the damaging way that I do.
> (Yeshua-Katz and Martin, 2013:505)

### Legalities of ED sites

Unlike with hate speech there is *prima facie* no illegal act in respect of ED sites. Self-harm is generally not a criminal offence and therefore publicising or glorifying self-harm sites will not be criminal either. There are two potential types of criminal offence that might apply: communication offences and obscenity legislation.

As has been noted already, communication offences will be discussed elsewhere (Chapter 11) but it is worth noting here that s.127, *Communications Act 2003* criminalises the sending of an obscene, indecent, grossly offensive or menacing communication. Could the content of ED sites be considered grossly offensive? Arguably, the best definition was provided by Sedley LJ in *DPP v Collins* [2006] 1 WLR 308 where he said '[w]hat is offensive has to be judged ... by considering the reaction of reasonable people ... by the standards of an open and just multicultural society' (at 311: note the decision itself was reversed on appeal ([2006] 1 WLR 2223)) but the definition was not criticised, merely its application. Realistically it would probably be stretching the language of the Act too far to apply this to ED sites, not least because there are already concerns about the compatibility of the offence with the *Human Rights Act 1998* (Rowbottom, 2012).

The *Obscene Publications Act 1959* would seem an unusual choice of possible offence but it does not apply only to sexual material but also to other material that depraves and corrupts (see, for example, *John Calder (Publications) Ltd v Powell* [1965] 1 QB 509 which concerned drug taking). That said, it would be difficult to see how ED sites would meet the threshold of obscenity (see *R v Anderson* [1972] 1 QB 304 and see Ormerod, 2011:1058 et seq. on the correct standard for obscenity). Even if it were possible to make out an argument that ED sites came within the obscenity definition, the Crown Prosecution Service would need to carefully consider whether a prosecution would be compatible with the HRA 1998 and so realistically the OPA 1959 would not work in this field.

There have been Parliamentary calls for ED sites to be recognised as dangerous (see Early Day Motion 973 of the House of Commons, tabled 20.02.08) and France famously proposed to ban ED sites before deciding that this was not feasible. However, there continue to be some who call for this, particularly in the media, but to do so would require a careful balance with the freedom of expression.

## Suggested further reading

Brotsky, S.R. and Giles, D. 'Inside the "pro-Ana" community: A covert online participant observation' (2007) 15 *Eating Disorders* 93–109.
*This is a fascinating and extremely important article. It concerns original research where a researcher entered a number of pro-anorexic websites to understand how they operate.*

Crowe, N. and Watts, M. 'We're just like Gok but in reverse: Ana girls, empowerment and resistance in digital communities' (2013) *International Journal of Adolescence and Youth* (currently online pre-publication: DOI: 10.1080/02673843.2013.856802).

*This article shows that there has been a 'push back' by a number of people with eating disorders who see themselves as exercising a lifestyle choice. This article considers this viewpoint and provides some good illustrations of the competing interests at play here.*

Garland, J. and Hodkinson, P. 'F\*\*king freak! What the hell do you think you look like?' (2014) 54 *British Journal of Criminology* 613–631.

*This is a very good piece that looks at the experiences of goths and questions whether this amounts to a hate crime. As part of the article the meaning of 'hate crime' is critiqued with an analysis made of what its unique properties are.*

McNamee, L.G., Peterson, B.L. and Peña, J. 'A call to educate, participate, invoke and indict: Understanding the communication of online hate groups' (2010) *Communication Monographs* 257–280.

*This is a very interesting piece that looks at online hate groups and analyses how they operate and what this can tell us about their purposes and indeed how to tackle them.*

# Chapter 9

# Sexualised content I

## Adult pornography

This chapter is the first of two chapters on sexualised content. Most attention has traditionally been paid to so-called 'child pornography' and, as will be seen, this is the issue that international law traditionally focuses on. However, increasingly attention has returned to the issue of 'adult pornography', i.e. pornography that features only adults. Cases such as the 'Lady Chatterley's Lover' trial had led many to believe that adult material was, in essence, no longer a matter for the law, but the advent of the internet has changed that.

This chapter and the next will seek to explore some of the key debates surrounding sexualised content. Even in two chapters it is impossible to consider all the provisions in detail (and indeed in respect of child pornography the author has already written a complete book just on this: Gillespie, 2011) and so the analysis will be looking at the important aspects of the debate instead of detailed analysis of the provisions. The two chapters together should serve as an introduction to these areas, allowing you to consider where to look next in terms of considering whether the law should regulate sexualised content.

There are three issues that need to be considered here:

- Obscene publications.
- Extreme pornography.
- 'Revenge porn'.

All three are interlinked and some would argue that the second and third categories are simply a derivative of the first. To an extent this is true but they certainly have an 'added' value to them which makes them worthy of consideration in their own right. The second type – extreme pornography – is also interesting in that it is the only one of the three identified types where it is illegal to possess the material. Criminalising possession was, until recently, restricted to child pornography but that was extended to extreme pornography. The final type – revenge porn – has only recently been (expressly) criminalised by the law and a brief discussion will be presented to show why Parliament legislated.

### Criminalising pornography: feminist perspectives

Before considering how the law criminalises forms of pornography, it is perhaps worth briefly considering the debate that exists over whether any laws should be made in this area. Pornography is an extremely controversial subject that divides commentators. The divide does not only exist between male and female but also, as will be seen, between feminist scholars themselves. Whilst so-called 'second-wave feminists' (led most prominently by Andrea Dworkin and Catharine MacKinnon) believed that pornography was not just a moral wrong but a question of real harm against women, more recent scholars (who have created the so-called 'third-wave feminism') have pushed back against this, with some even suggesting that pornography can be empowering.

The literature in this area is both powerful and fascinating. As part of a single chapter the following text cannot possibly do justice to the debates and arguments put forward by both sides. However, it is possible to give a flavour of the debate as it is important to note that the law in this area does not operate in a vacuum.

Perhaps the starting point of the debate is to consider the work of Dworkin and MacKinnon who became perhaps two of the most well-known advocates for change in the regulation of pornography. These powerful advocates wrote separately on this issue but their collective work was perhaps the most significant, with it being developed into a model law ('ordinance') that could (and indeed was) passed by cities (see Dworkin and MacKinnon, 1988). These laws were ultimately struck down by the courts as being unconstitutional as they conflicted with the First Amendment to the US Constitution, but their passing demonstrated the fact that, for a large section of society, pornography is inappropriate.

As noted above, Dworkin and MacKinnon did not believe that pornography was simply morally wrong, they believed that it was harmful. MacKinnon summarised it thus, 'pornography, in the feminist view, is a form of forced sex, a practice of sexual politics, an institution of gender inequality. In this perspective, pornography is not a harmless fantasy or a corrupt and confused misrepresentation of an otherwise natural and healthy sexuality' (MacKinnon, 1987:197). MacKinnon was therefore rejecting the notion that opposing pornography is simply about morality but was instead a matter of protecting women. She saw pornography as a crime of violence, not only through its production but also through its consumption.

Dworkin agreed that pornography was about violence and the domination of the woman by men and was simply another way that men used their power to subjugate women (Dworkin, 1981). This notion of harm was carried forward to include not only a perceived link between pornography and sexual violence (something that continues to be argued today (Flood, 2010:174 et seq.)) but also the belief that pornography meant that men see women as sexual objects and that it dehumanises women (Dworkin and MacKinnon,

1988). Much of this rests on the 'effects doctrine' which is the notion that a person can be affected by the media that they consume. However, the effects theory is of questionable empirical merit and has attracted critics who believe that it not only skews but even distracts from the anti-pornography message (Boyle, 2000:187, 192).

Easton, in a very interesting chapter, discusses many of the ways that pornography can cause harm and includes the potential that it could cause victims of sexual offences to have their credibility doubted (Easton, 1994:20) although she concedes that the causal link may be too remote to justify criminalisation. It is an interesting argument, however, and is based on the premise that pornography may lead to the greater acceptance of rape myths, etc. More research would be required to substantiate any such link but even then it could be questioned whether this justifies the criminalisation of pornography or rather requires responses to combat these myths and/or credibility, including judicial training and the issuing of more appropriate jury directions (a useful reference work on the effect of rape myths is Ellison and Munro, 2009).

Before considering the response of third-wave feminists it is worth noting that the desire of Dworkin and MacKinnon to ban pornography was not universally supported. In 1984 the group 'Feminist Anti-Censorship Taskforce' (FACT) was created to challenge the assertions that Dworkin and MacKinnon had put forward. FACT, as a liberal movement, was deeply suspicious about any form of censorship which they believed could allow the state to usurp fundamental rights. However, they also argued that the pro-abolition arguments had led to women who had (heterosexual) sexual desires feeling ashamed (Crawford, 2007:139).

It is perhaps this latter point that has been most taken on board by third-wave feminists. They reject the anti-sex discourses of second-wave feminists and believe that they are reclaiming sex, considering it something that is both fun and desirable. Third-wave feminists do not consider that issues should be framed by 'women's issues' but instead they look towards issues that interest them. An offshoot of this is the recognition that womanhood suffers as many differences of opinion as do the differences between men and women (Crawford, 2007:119). Thus there is not 'a line' or 'message' that should be adopted on an issue but instead the recognition that there could be divergence of views. Whilst second-wave feminists would consider issues such as dress and make-up as part of the political battle against male domination, third-wave feminists believe that it is about choice (Crawford, 2007:120). If they wish to wear make-up or fashionable clothes then that is a matter for them and not a political decision.

Pornography and indeed sex is an issue where there is a marked difference between second-wave feminists and some third-wave feminists. It has been suggested that third-wave feminists will often advance one (or more) of the following four points:

1. Pornography is a form of sexual expression.
2. Pornography is a type of performance that is subject to different interpretations.
3. Pornography is not unique in the way that women are socially and economically exploited.
4. Pornography is part of a sex-positive agenda.

(Crawford, 2007:140)

The third point – exploitation – is interesting because it shows not a general belief that pornography is harmless but rather that it is perhaps just one more example of the sexual discrimination that a woman can receive in society. However, third-wave feminists reject the notion that this is a *harm per se* but rather just see it as another aspect of a patriarchal society.

Perhaps it is the final point that most separates second- and third-wave feminists. To (some) third-wave feminists, sex and indeed pornography can be pleasurable (Doyle and Lacombe, 1996:189). This can be contrasted with the views of MacKinnon who rejected the notion that a woman can choose to participate in pornography or indeed to sexual activity with a man. To her, this is the response of a survivor, that instead of it being true empowerment or the claiming of a sexual identity, it is simply a strategy to avoid the recognition that she is the victim of sexual abuse and sexual objectification (MacKinnon, 1987:149).

The debate between second- and third-wave feminists has not finished and it is punctuated by constant revision. One of the difficulties in this area is the fact that everything is contested and both sides rely on spurious data. It has been suggested that pro- and anti-pornography activists have been cursory in their approach to using empirical data to substantiate their arguments (Weinberg *et al.*, 2010:1390), which is almost certainly true. However, it is also the case that much of the data can be interpreted to support either side. Perhaps the most notable example of this is the effect that pornography has on those who consume (view) it.

There would appear to be cogent evidence to suggest that pornography must act as a normalisation process when it is used frequently (Weinberg *et al.*, 2010:1391). The premise of the argument is that pornography is viewed to sexually stimulate an individual and the more times it is watched the more normal it seems, and the natural conclusion to this argument is that participants would start to act out those scenes. However, this argument is neutral in that the fact that participants may engage with pornography will be positive or negative depending on the stance of the individual and whether there is true consent (the latter point is perhaps the most contentious). Certainly some will argue that the use of pornography can be positive and indeed some feminists have argued that it is only through pornography that they have found their sexual identity (perhaps one of the more extreme examples of this is Minkowitz, 1995, but others exist and an interesting series of essays can be found in Part II of Johnson, 2002).

Similarly the research suggests that pornography has led people to change their sexual behaviour (Weinberg *et al.*, 2010:1398) but this can be interpreted in different ways. Pro-pornography advocates are likely to be able to point to some of the results to suggest that pornography has allowed women to find their sexual identity and explore what makes them sexually excited. Anti-pornography advocates are likely to be able to point to some of the results to show that women are being expected to change their sexual behaviour, going beyond what was considered 'normal' to please the man.

Where there is perhaps more consensus concerns the impact that view-ing pornography can have on adolescents. Some believe that the normalisa-tion effect is causing problems for young people who believe that the more extreme features of some pornography – including group sex – is normal and that adolescents feel inferior when compared to the 'stars' of pornography (Owens *et al.*, 2012:116). There remains, however, contention as to what the implications of this are and whether it should be allowed to lead to a complete ban on pornography.

In the USA restrictions were put in place to try and limit access to pornog-raphy by children. The most obvious move was the *Child Protection Internet Act* passed by the US Congress to require public libraries and schools to install pornography filters so as to ensure children could not access pornogra-phy. The US Supreme Court ruled that such a process was constitutional and rejected an argument that it breached the First Amendment (*US v American Library Association Inc* 539 US 194 (2003)) although this was partly because the filters would be turned off if an adult requested it. There was no doubt that an outright ban or wider restriction would have been ruled unconstitu-tional and it is notable that this Act only applies to *public* libraries and pub-licly funded schools (as the justification is that Congress can limit the purpose of the funds it provides).

## Obscene publications

Now that the feminist debates have been reviewed it can be noted that regard-less of who is correct, there appears to be no likelihood that all pornography will be banned in the near future. Therefore, what must be considered is the approach that the law currently adopts to the regulation of adult pornogra-phy. The analysis will be restricted to the UK since, at present, there is no international instrument that has sought to regulate adult pornography.

Until recently, adult pornography was principally regulated by the *Obscene Publications Act 1959* (OPA 1959). At one point it was thought to have almost fallen into disuse because of a number of high-profile prosecutions that had led to acquittals, perhaps the most notable being the prosecution in respect of the publication *Inside Linda Lovelace* which contained pictures of hard-core pornography. Not only had such prosecutions failed they had arguably had the reverse effect of what was intended. It has been noted that before the trial only a few thousand copies of the book had ever been bought, partly because it probably did not enter the consciousness of society. However, after the trial the sales figures had risen to over 600,000 with one leading commentator suggesting it demonstrated the futility of trying to censor material (Robertson, 1993:213). The internet has led to an increase in prosecutions under the OPA 1959 which perhaps demonstrates the reality that the internet is now the major instrument for the trading of pornography (Brigham, 2014:47).

Section 2(1), OPA 1959 creates two offences. The first is publishing an article for gain or not, and the second offence is having an obscene article for publication for gain (whether gain to himself or another), this being introduced by the *Obscene Publications Act 1964*.

### Defining the offence

There are three elements to the offence:

- Obscene.
- Article.
- Publishes or has in possession with a view to publish.

#### Obscene

At the heart of the Act is the notion of obscenity. The common-law definition of obscenity was set out in *R v Hinks* (1868) LR 3 QB 360 as the tendency to 'deprave and corrupt those whose minds are open to such immoral influences' and this was carried through to the OPA 1959. Section 1(1), OPA 1959 defines obscenity 'if its effect ... is, if taken as a whole, such as to tend to deprave and corrupt persons who are likely, having regard to all relevant circumstances, to read, see or hear the matter contained or embodied in it'. The statutory definition usurps the ordinary dictionary definition and the latter should not usually be referred to (*R v Anderson* [1972] 1 QB 304).

What does 'deprave and corrupt' actually mean though? The classic definition was provided by Byrne J in the 'Lady Chatterley's Lover' trial:

> To deprave means to make morally bad, to pervert, to debase or corrupt morally. To corrupt means to render morally unsound or rotten, to destroy the moral purity or chastity, to pervert or ruin a good quality, to debase, to defile.
>
> (see *R v Penguin Books Ltd* [1961] Crim LR 176 at 177)

Thus the link to morality is immediately noted (a useful discussion on the controversies of the moral concept of 'obscene' is provided by Johnson,

2010) and the reference is to making someone morally bad or corrupting them by destroying their moral purity. Of course this raises the question about what happens if they are already morally bad or have no moral purity? The answer would appear to be that it is possible to be *further* corrupted and therefore there can be no excuse that the likely reader is already perverted (see *DPP v Whyte* [1972] 3 All ER 12). However, it has been held that where the material is so obscene that no-one would be depraved and corrupted by it (because, for example, they are so shocked) then the offence cannot be made out (*R v Calder and Boyers Ltd* [1969] 1 QB 151, although it has been noted that it will be a difficult argument to sustain (Ormerod, 2011:1059).

The question of who should be depraved or corrupted has entertained the courts for many years (Ormerod, 2011:1062) but the position is perhaps slightly more straightforward in respect of our content because the internet makes it generally available. One of the few cases to have specifically addressed this issue was *R v Perrin* [2002] EWCA Crim 747 where the Court of Appeal noted that the trial judge said:

> you may think there are many people of all ages who sit possibly in their bedrooms at home surfing the internet. Therefore, it is a question for you to decide, having regard for all the circumstances, who might read [or see] … the matter contained or embodied in this material which you are considering.

(at [10])

Interestingly the jury convicted the defendant in respect of material that was available as a 'preview' site and they acquitted him in respect of material that was hosted behind a 'pay wall' that required the production of a credit card (at [12]). This, the Court of Appeal, thought could be of significance (at [27]) because, in essence, what the prosecution were alleging is that children could access the material which is available as a 'preview' whereas the requirement for a credit card means that it is less likely a child would be able to access the material (as the usual age for a credit card would be 18).

The significance of this proposition is perhaps illustrated, albeit obliquely, in the prosecution of Darryn Walker. Walker was prosecuted under s.1, OPA 1959 for writing a blog that described the members of the pop group 'Girls Aloud' being raped, murdered and dismembered. The blog was entitled 'Screams Aloud'. Counsel for the prosecution tried to argue that because it was on the internet it was likely that it could be read by children who would be depraved and corrupted. The defence adduced evidence that it would in fact be extremely difficult to find this particular page on the internet, in part because of the number of sites that existed in respect of this group. In light of this evidence the prosecution conceded that it could not continue the prosecution (Hughes, 2009).

*Article*

The second element of the offence is that it must be an article. Usually this will not be problematic in the context of the internet. Section 1(2), OPA 1959 defines an article as:

> any description or article containing or embodying matter to be read or looked at or both, any sound record, any film or other record of a picture or pictures.

It would be possible to critique each word within this definition but in *Attorney-General's Reference (No 5 of 1980)* [1981] 1 WLR 88 the Court of Appeal said, 'the object of subsection (2) was to bring all articles which produced words or pictures or sounds within the embrace of the Act' (at 95 per Lawton LJ). In other words, it is not necessary to consider the precise terms, they are in essence mere interpretative assistance to reach the overall conclusion that anything that embodies words, pictures or sounds will come within the provision. In *Attorney-General's Reference* this included a video cassette and in *R v Fellows and Arnold* [1997] 1 Cr App R 244 the Court of Appeal held that data on a hard disc amounted to an 'article' and rejected any suggestion that an article had to be restricted to technology within the mind of Parliament when passing the legislation (at 256).

The broad definition of 'article' under the OPA 1959 means that all forms of pornography are covered. Whilst it will obviously include photographs and movies, it will also include text (and indeed the OPA 1959 is littered with the scars of the battles fought over the written word), sound and any other type of representation. It is perhaps one of the widest definitions of types of material and this is deliberately so. Where Parliament identifies a potential gap in the definition of 'article' it has tended to legislate (so, for example, in *Straker v DPP* [1963] QB 926 the Court of Appeal held that negatives could not be kept for publication (as they were instead being used for making prints) and so Parliament legislated through s.2(1), *Obscene Publications Act 1964*. Computer data was expressly brought within the OPA 1959 by the *Criminal Justice and Public Order Act 1994*).

*Publishes*

The first form of offence contained within s.1, OPA 1959 is to publish an obscene article. 'Publish' is defined in s.1(3)–(6) but for our purposes we need only consider s.1(3) which states that a person has published an article where he:

(a) distributes, circulates, sells, lets on hire, gives or lends it, or who offers it for sale or for letting on hire, or

(b) in the case of an article containing or embodying matter to be looked at or a record, shows, plays, or projects it or, where the matter is data stored electronically, transmits that data.

It is clear that there are different ways that publishing can occur. The reference to 'sells, lets on hire, gives or lends it' all encompasses a form of distribution that can take place to a single person (*R v Barker* [1962] 1 WLR 349). Whilst the Court of Appeal, probably *in obiter*, have suggested that publishing to a single person is possible for all forms (*R v Smith* [2012] 1 WLR 3368 at 3375) it is not necessarily that clear, because *Barker* did not state whether non-commercial distribution or the showing or playing has to be to be to more than a single person (see Gillespie, 2014b:353). However, for our purposes it is not strictly necessary to decide this because in the context of cybercrime it will always be data that is published. Therefore, s.1(3)(b) is relevant which states, *inter alia*, that 'where the matter is data stored electronically [publication takes place when she] transmits that data'.

It will be remembered from Chapter 2 that one of the reasons why jurisdiction can be secured in England and Wales in respect of cybercrimes is the manner in which the territorial principle has been applied in some contexts. In respect of obscenity it was held in *R v Waddon* (2000, unreported) that:

> there can be publication on a website abroad, when images are there uploaded; and there can be further publication when those images are downloaded elsewhere.
>
> (at [12])

The implications of this were considered in Chapter 2 but in essence it means that publication can be an offence capable of being tried in England if either:

(a) X, residing in England, uploads an obscene photograph to a website hosted in America, or
(b) Y, residing in France, uploads an obscene photograph to a website hosted in America and it is shown that this image is accessible to residents of England.

In example (a) the position of X is relatively straightforward because the publication – the transmission – takes place in the territory of England and Wales. In example (b) the position is a little more complicated. Y can only be prosecuted if he comes into the jurisdiction of England. However, if he does enter the jurisdiction then Y could be prosecuted under the OPA 1959 because if publication takes place when material is downloaded, then it means that when the person accessing the images downloads that image Y has published the photograph to him. Hirst argues that the finding is incompatible with the wording of the Act, '[s.1(3)(b)] provides that data may be published by transmitting it, but that does not mean (nor even does it suggest) that the act of publication occurs where the transmission is received' (Hirst, 2003:190). The argument here is that as a verb 'transmit' would suggest the sending of a signal, and therefore if the website is based abroad then the data is sent/transmitted *from* outside the country and therefore would not be within the jurisdiction. The only potential argument in favour of this decision is that transmission implies the conveying of a signal *to* another and so long as that person was within the jurisdiction then this may mean that part of the transmission took place within the territory of England (Gillespie, 2012:169). That said, the position is not straightforward and it was not discussed in depth in either *Waddon* (where it was arguably *obiter dicta*) or *Perrin* and therefore it perhaps deserves fuller attention by the courts.

### Having an obscene article for publication

The second form of the offence under s.2 is to have an obscene article for publication. Unlike the 'publish' variant of the offence this is therefore a possession offence but not one of simple possession as it must be 'for publication' and, perhaps most importantly, 'for gain'. The latter is an important condition and the prosecution must prove not only that D has the items in his possession but that he has them for gain (*R v Levy* [2004] EWCA Crim 1141). Section 1(5), OPA 1964 states that 'gain' includes 'consideration for the publication or in any other way' but 'gain' itself is not defined, although it implies commercial reward.

Reference to 'having' means 'ownership, possession or control' (s.1(2), OPA 1964). 'Possession' ordinarily means 'custody or control' and so the question is realistically whether the material is within the person's custody or control. In the context of cybercrime this would include the material being found on a storage device that is controlled by a person. However, it will be remembered that possession itself is not sufficient, it must be 'for publication' and this would mean that there must be the intent or knowledge that it would be published (including through transmission). Potentially this includes storing the material in an accessible manner, meaning either a peer-to-peer network or through providing a password to access a virtual library (see *R v Fellows and Arnold* [1997] 1 Cr App R 244). However, this is subject to the point discussed above that it must be 'for gain'.

### Public good

There is a defence to publishing an obscene publication that being 'that publication of the article in question is justified as being for the public good on the ground that it is in the interests of science, literature, art or learning, or of other objects of general concern' (s.4(1), OPA 1959). Expert evidence on the merit of these objectives is expressly permitted (s.4(2), OPA 1959) and ordinarily such experts would be introduced.

It is not necessary to consider this provision in depth here as much of the material on the internet would be difficult to bring into these sections (for a general overview see Ormerod, 2011:1069–1071). However, it is to be noted that the defence of public good has been used in a number of instances, particularly the written word, where it has been used successfully to suggest that an otherwise obscene book is considered a literary work (perhaps the most obvious example of this being the book *Lady Chatterley's Lover*).

## Extreme pornography

The second offence to be examined is a relatively new introduction to English law. It is the offence of possessing an image that constitutes extreme pornography. Much of the literature appears to draw a distinction between extreme pornography and obscenity, in part because the legislation was apparently passed partly because of a belief that the OPA 1959 was no longer fit for purpose (Rackley and McGlynn, 2013:401). However, it should be noted that the offence relating to extreme pornography is not a replacement for the OPA 1959. As will be seen, the extreme pornography offence is a possession offence. The OPA 1959 offence it will be remembered was not. Thus if extreme pornography is being distributed then (technically) the OPA 1959 should be used for this, although anecdotal evidence suggests that the extreme pornography offence is being used because, as will be seen, it is simpler.

### Background to the offence

The offence is inextricably linked to a single incident. In 2003 Graham Coutts was convicted of the murder of Jane Longhurst. During the trial it was alleged that Coutts had been motivated by a sexual fetish relating to strangulation and death. Media reports suggested that the killing was preceded by him watching extremely violent pornography and that this 'led' to him murdering Jane Longhurst (see, for example, Pritchard and Dhaliwal, 2004). In fact there was no evidence that watching pornography caused him to kill Longhurst, and in a way it is a strange argument to put forward: that it was not the responsibility of Coutts who deliberately killed a young woman but instead it was the responsibility of the pornography industry. Putting forward this line almost allows the killer to distance himself from his responsibility.

The media, particularly the *Daily Mail*, began a campaign to 'clean up' the internet and to criminalise extreme pornographic images. This (inevitably) received support from the government (as supporting such material would be unpopular) and draft legislation was published. The focus of the legislation became, as will be seen, the fact that images had to be both obscene or 'disgusting', which chimes with the emotional nature of the campaign that led to its introduction.

Not everyone was persuaded that the fact the images were grotesque justified their criminalisation. It has been noted that Lord Faulkner and the Joint Committee on Human Rights (a key Parliamentary pre-legislative scrutiny body) both argued that the fact that material was unpleasant was not sufficient to justify criminalisation (Johnson, 2010:150). Certainly this would accord with ordinary understandings of the justifications for criminalising mere content. It has long been thought that only harm can be used to justify restrictions on content (perhaps best articulated by J.S. Mill), although it must be conceded that not everyone agrees with this and some believe morality can justify the imposition of criminal law.

The government sought a 'Rapid Evidence Assessment' (REA) (Itzin et al., 2007) and this purported to show that there was harm. The REA concluded that there were 'negative, psychological, attitudinal and behavioural effects on adults who access this material' (Itzin et al., 2007:26). They concluded that the production of such material involved 'physical assault, sexual assault and rape and death' even though there remains significant scepticism as to whether so-called 'snuff' videos exist. They ultimately concluded:

> Pornography raises complex moral and political issues and strong feelings amongst those with opposing views. Advances in the available analytical methodologies have made it possible to evaluate the pornography effects research independent of these issues. Taken as a whole, the empirical and theoretical evidence of harmful effects associated with extreme pornographic material suggest a need to focus on those who are harmed by it, including the damage it does to the attitudes, beliefs, fantasies, desires and behaviour of those who use it.
>
> (Itzin et al., 2007:29)

However, the REA was not universally welcomed and some have questioned whether it was a 'loaded' document: 'the REA was authored by three academics known for their anti-pornography views. That the authors should be partisan is a problem endemic to this kind of research exercise but that their research should have been presented as conclusive is unacceptable' (Attwood and Smith, 2010:175). This view is shared by others who suggest that the 'extent to which the REA supports the contention that the consumption of extreme pornography has a causal effect is far from convincing' (Carline, 2011:317).

Perhaps not surprisingly the debate shifted away from harm – which was difficult to prove – and onto the more emotional aspects. During the initial consultation period the Home Office had stated that the type of material to be prohibited '[has] no place in our society' (Home Office, 2005:6) and Parliamentary debates began to focus around the 'horrible, nasty and unpleasant' material that was to be outlawed (Carline, 2011:322). Reference was made to the fact that the public would not approve of such material, which raises interesting questions regarding the right to free speech where, it will be remembered, it was held that the right was supposed to include material that others considered offensive. The offence became unquestionably one about moral judgment (Johnson, 2010) and this has led some to question whether 'minority sexualities remain bothered and silenced' (Carline, 2011:322).

### The offence

The offence is set out in s.63, *Criminal Justice and Immigration Act 2008* which criminalises the possession of an extreme pornographic image (s.63(1)), this being defined as an image that is both pornographic and extreme (s.63(2)).

The term 'image' is defined as a 'moving or still image (produced by any means) or data (stored by any means) which is capable of conversion into [such] an image' (s.63(8)). At first sight this would seem a very broad definition and would encompass, for example, drawings and cartoons. However, the legislation requires the images to be 'explicit and realistic' (s.63(7)) which limits the type of material. The requirement that they be 'realistic' does not mean that they have to be a photograph and it could, for example, include morphed or manipulated photographs (discussed more extensively in Chapter 10 in respect of so-called pseudo-photographs of a child). The Explanatory Notes to the legislation state that the wording 'has the effect of excluding animated characters, sketches, paintings and the like' (paragraph 459, *Explanatory Notes*) but it may not be that simple. The Explanatory Notes accompanying an Act are not a legislative guide to the meaning of the words, which remains a matter solely for the courts. Whilst sketches will not be realistic it is quite possible that some computer-generated images will be realistic and they could come within the law. Accordingly, if computer-generated or computer-manipulated images are within the statute then arguably this takes this legislation even further away from harm and closer to a recognition that this is a moral judgement.

### Pornographic

The first aspect that must be proven is that the image is pornographic. This is defined as meaning an image that is 'of such a nature that it must reasonably be assumed to have been produced solely or principally for the purpose of sexual arousal' (s.63(3), CJIA 2008). Where there is more than one image then the position becomes more complicated as the context of that image in the entirety of the images must be considered (s.63(4)), and if it forms one of a narrative then the image will not be classed as pornographic if the images as a whole were not such that 'they must reasonably be assumed to have been produced solely or principally for the purpose of sexual arousal' (s.63(5)). In other words, if one image amongst a series is pornographic then it does not follow that the offence has been committed if the creation of the whole was not solely or principally for the purpose of sexual arousal.

Potentially this could be of significance for some types of material. A book or electronic slideshow may, for example, depict one or two images that could, if considered separately, be considered pornographic, but taken as a whole unless it can be shown that it was produced solely or principally for the purpose of sexual arousal then the offence will not be established. This, it is submitted, is a high threshold because, for example, it could be argued that it was prepared for the gratification of narrative or for literary reasons. Whilst there is no defence of 'public good' (as there is with obscenity legislation) it is for the prosecution to prove that the image or images are pornographic. Therefore, they must prove beyond all reasonable doubt that they were produced solely or principally for the purposes of sexual arousal and not for other reasons.

### Extreme

The second element of the offence that must be met is that the image is 'extreme'. This has two elements to it:

(a)  that it falls within s.63(7), and
(b)  that it is 'grossly offensive, disgusting or otherwise of an obscene character'.

(s.63(6))

Taking the second element first, it would seem unusual to use within a statute the term 'disgust'. The term 'disgust' will mean very different things to different people although it has been noted that at least some jurists have suggested that it can be an appropriate emotion to take when deciding the propriety of something (Johnson, 2010:152, citing Devlin who was perhaps the best known advocate for legislating on the basis of morality).

What is perhaps more interesting about this definition, however, is that it adopts a different test of obscenity than used in the OPA 1959. It will be remembered that the test for obscenity under the OPA 1959 did not rest on offensiveness or disgust but instead on corruption and depravity. It was noted above that articles could be disgusting or offensive without being depraved or corrupting. Given that this offence was supposed to apply to the same material as that contained within the OPA 1959 it appears unusual to use a different test. The test of 'otherwise of an obscene character' will also not lead to the OPA 1959 definition being used, because that is a statutory definition.

Outside of the OPA 1959 the usual test for 'obscene' is by reference to contemporary standards of decency (see, for example, *R v Stamford* [1972] 2

WLR 1055). At first sight it would seem that this involves a lower threshold than that which is contained within the OPA 1959; this is perhaps balanced out by the fact that the extreme image must depict certain actions. The logic of this offence is presumably that these actions are so extreme that they would otherwise be considered depraved or corrupting. Of course this neglects the 'aversion theory' discussed above. Whilst something may be so obscene so as not to be depraved or corrupting under the OPA 1959, the opposite conclusion would apply under this offence. Such an image would inevitably satisfy limb (a) and if it depicts one of the actions set out below then it is illegal. This produces the rather odd situation that a person may not, in law, be guilty of publishing the image but guilty of possessing it. Given that publishing is generally thought to be more serious, this would seem an odd consequence.

It will be remembered that the second limb is that it must satisfy the requirements of s.63(7) which prescribes the following images:

(a) an act which threatens a person's life,
(b) an act which results, or is likely to result, in serious injury to a person's anus, breasts or genitals,
(c) an act which involves sexual interference with a human corpse, or
(d) a person performing an act of intercourse or oral sex with an animal (whether dead or alive).

These would appear extreme actions but it has been noted that actually not all of these actions are themselves illegal (McGlynn and Rackley, 2009:246). Indeed, if conducted substantively, there are a number of these actions that would not be illegal, including actions that threaten a person's life (which is different from a threat to kill), sexual interference with a corpse (as only the penetration of, or by, a corpse is illegal) and the performance of oral sex on a dead animal. Perhaps more illogical is the reference to bodily harm. McGlynn and Rackley complain that depicting serious injury to certain parts of a body but not others is 'potentially ludicrous' (McGlynn and Rackley, 2009:249). Certainly there could be some strange inconsistencies. There is a fetishism in respect of amputees (acrotomophilia). Let us pose a hypothetical example:

> X downloads a movie that shows Y, a 19-year-old female, being forcibly stripped before Z produces a machete and cuts the hand of Y off. Z then proceeds to have sex with Y.

Possession of this movie would be perfectly lawful under this statute. Whilst it would unquestionably shows an act that shows serious injury to the person, it is not to the anus, breasts or genitals. Thus it does not fall within s.63(7). The answer may be to say that 'ah well, it would be life-threatening' but what if the film shows Y receiving medical attention in the intervening period? It is an absurd example but it does show the fact that the law does not seem to address what its underlying purpose is supposed to be.

### Possession

The offence here is one of possession and whilst 'possess' is not defined it is a term that is found throughout criminal law. It has been questioned whether this is an appropriate test for computers, with accessibility suggested as perhaps being more appropriate (Ormerod, 2006:750). Certainly it has been held that where an image has been deleted then it is no longer in the person's possession (*R v Porter* [2006] 1 WLR 2633). This could cause problems for prosecuting offenders if it cannot be proven, prior to deletion, whether the person was in custody and control of the machine when the image was downloaded.

### Defences

There are few defences to this offence. Unlike the OPA 1959 there is no defence of 'public good' and it has been noted already that this could create a paradox whereby a defence exists to the more serious action (publishing) but not to the lesser offence of possession. The rationale for this omission is difficult to understand but its inclusion was resisted during the passage of the legislation.

Section 64 introduces a defence whereby the material has been classified by the British Board of Film Classification (BBFC). This is a sensible provision that is designed to ensure that something that is certified for public release is not later classed as criminal when it is possessed. However, s.64 then has an unusual clause within it, as it states that an image will not be excluded if it is separated from the classified images where the purpose of its separation was for sexual arousal (s.64(3)). It has been noted that this defence has been the subject of ridicule (McGlynn and Rackley, 2009:254) because it does not alter the fact that the original work has been certified for public release so why should an extract be considered criminal? Prohibiting it when it is for the purposes of sexual arousal is also problematic given that some restricted yet classified films will themselves have been created for sexual arousal (the so-called R18 category) which makes the exception even more problematic.

In terms of substantive defences, three are set out in s.65(2) although it should be noted that it is for the defendant to prove the existence of the defence (s.65(1)), thus creating a reverse burden of proof. The three defences are:

(a) that D has a legitimate reason for being in possession of the image,
(b) that D had not seen the image and had no reason to suspect it to be an extreme image, and

(c) that D

    (i)   was sent the image without asking for it, and

    (ii)  did not keep it an unreasonable length of time.

These defences are modelled on those that exist in respect of the possession of child pornography (discussed in the next chapter) and are largely uncontroversial. Given the terms bear the same definition as under s.160, CJA 1988 reference should be made to the substantive discussion in the next chapter as what is said there will apply equally to this offence.

### Images of rape

McGlynn and Rackley believe that the extreme pornography laws are flawed because the law is based on moral judgments as to what is wrong rather than on the harm that is caused. They do not necessarily object to the inclusion of certain forms of the material but believe that it misses the point: 'we suggest that as the Government came under pressure, it lost sight of the nature of the harm it was seeking to legislate against and reverted to the weakest possible justification for action, disgust' (McGlynn and Rackley, 2009:256). They believe that the legislation should have been inextricably linked to harm and, most notably, included the depiction of rape (McGlynn and Rackley, 2009; Rackley and McGlynn, 2013). *Section 37, Criminal Justice and Courts Act 2015* amended s.63 to include rape or a realistic depiction of rape (s.63(7A)). Proving the latter could be difficult as a lot of material would seem to be simulated. To advocates of this change, the inclusion of simulated footage of rape is necessary to ensure that all footage of rape is captured and because the portrayal of rape is itself demeaning to women. To others, however, the inclusion of simulated rape will mean that the law is further removed from direct harm and raises concerns over free expression. It is likely to place greater emphasis on the BBFC exemption because the media portrayal of rape is not uncommon in films.

## Revenge porn

The issue that has most recently been the subject of legislative attention is that of 'revenge porn'. This is an issue that has risen to prominence in recent years and is a direct result of digital technology. Whilst in the pre-digital era it was necessary to take a film into a shop (usually a chemist for some reason) to get photographs developed, digital cameras allowed photographs to be stored without anyone else seeing them (the only precursor to this was the Polaroid camera which took individual photographs). Personal video cameras had begun to be developed immediately before the digital revolution (with the images stored on a tape) but once again digital technology transformed this and it meant that video cameras became inexpensive, but also mobile telephones started to have cameras built into them that allowed both still and moving images to be recorded.

Inevitably the fact that images could be produced without oversight from anyone else meant that sexual photographs and movies began to be produced. This is unsurprising since there has been a strong link between sex and photography for many years. However, digital media undoubtedly has increased the number of people who are recording themselves having sex. Before considering the legal implications of this it does perhaps return us to the discussion at the beginning of this chapter concerning feminist critiques of pornography. An interesting question as regards the filming is to what extent both participants give true consent to the recording? Indeed, there is a question about whether the partner always knows that they are being recorded or whether some footage is obtained covertly (voyeurism).

The recording of participants engaging in sexual activity is perhaps not unsurprising as it can be considered to be a form of sexual expression (although it is conceded that many would question this statement and ask whether this is another example of the pornification of sex). As noted already, people have been recording themselves in intimate poses for many years and so the growth of this behaviour is not unsurprising. In some countries such behaviour has even been recognised as a constitutionally protected form of expression of the individual (*R v Sharpe* 2001 SCC 2).

Where the material has been gathered without the consent of an individual then this must be considered an important breach of the personal integrity of an individual. The law would already protect against this (see s.67, *Sexual Offences Act 2003*) and it submitted that the police and Crown Prosecution Service should treat such matters seriously. Where, however, the material is gathered consensually then the most obvious issue where problems could arise is where the couple split up or, for whatever reason, one partner decides to share the material with a third-party without the permission of the other. An aggravated form of this behaviour is where a person deliberately posts the footage onto a public website that has been created specifically for the purpose of allowing people to take revenge on their former partners. A number of sites exist for this and it has become a growing problem.

### Victim impact

What are the consequences of revenge porn? Little is known about this because, whilst there is increasing literature being published on revenge porn, they tend to be from a crimino-legal stance rather than looking at victim impact. Whilst it is known that in some tragic cases there have been suicides following disclosure this is not routine, and we should be careful to ensure that this is not extrapolated beyond the isolated cases. However, it can be readily postulated that, at the very least, a degree of distress could accompany the release of intimate images.

Whilst it would be easy to draw a parallel to how victims of child pornography are harmed by its production, the analogy is not strictly accurate. As will be seen from the next chapter, images of child pornography are (largely) criminalised because they are pictures that show a crime taking place. As children under the age of consent cannot consent to sex then a picture of a child under that age depicting them in sexual activity is the picture of a crime. However, in respect of revenge porn the same is not true. Whilst the recording may not be consensual (although in many instances it will be) the sexual activity itself is lawful. Therefore the pictures are not depicting a crime.

Perhaps a better approach would be to look at the issue of voyeurism where there may be parallels. It has been suggested that voyeurism can often lead to a double victimisation, the first being when the material is gathered and the second when it is disseminated (Calvert and Brown, 2000:488). Whilst the first issue is not present in all forms of revenge porn the second part would be and therefore this may help us understand some of the effects. At the heart of this debate is the concept of privacy (Rothenberg, 2001) but which could as easily be rephrased as the personal integrity of the individual. The display of these images infringes the essential privacy and integrity rights of the individual.

It has been postulated that in Western society one of the fundamental aspects of privacy is the right to 'control the exposure of one's body' (Rothenberg, 2001:1135). Whether the concept of nudity is, as some would argue, distorted by Victorian senses of prudishness, it cannot be doubted that this statement is correct. Few would wish everyone to see them naked or engaging in sexualised behaviour, and indeed many would consider that choosing who can see them naked and limiting this to those they are intimate with is an essential part of personal integrity. The voyeur – or, in our case, the person posting revenge porn – is interfering with that right, therefore, by exposing the body of the person to all, removing the right of the individual to control her body.

In an echo of the feminist arguments discussed earlier, it has been suggested that voyeurism dehumanises a woman and dismembers her so that it is the sexualised parts of her body that are the focus of the attention and dissemination (Calvert and Brown, 2000:501). The same could be said of revenge porn. The person is not putting a photograph of the other on the website, they are putting a photograph or movie on the website that accentuates the sexual identity of the victim. They are therefore stripping away the right of the victim to control her body and indeed control her sexuality and instead it is placed on the internet for all to see. This is the degrading of an individual and must be considered to be not merely the imposition of distress but of harm. It is a harm against the integrity of the individual.

### Legal solutions?

There is an argument that revenge porn is a civil wrong and therefore could be addressed through the law of tort (see, for example, Richardson, 2012, on how this could occur). Whilst this is true, it is submitted that the harm that is caused by this behaviour is such that it can justify the invocation of the criminal law. This is true even without considering the issue about whether victims suffer emotional harm (which would be actionable in its own right). The degradation the victim suffers can make this a question of harm and not mere morality and therefore justifies a criminal response.

It has been noted already that where the footage was gathered without the knowledge of the victim then this would constitute the offence of voyeurism (s.63, SOA 2003) which has a maximum sentence of two years' imprisonment where tried on indictment. However there was doubt as to whether the criminal law applied where a person released footage obtained with ostensible consent. Whilst, it will be seen, some in the legislature thought the answer was 'no' it would seem to be covered by the *Protection from Harassment Act 1997*, s.127 of the *Communications Act 2003* and s.1 of the *Malicious Communications Act 2003*.

During the passage of the *Criminal Justice and Courts Act 2015* (CJCA) a Lords Amendment was introduced that would lead to the express criminalisation of revenge pornography. The offence is set out in s.33 which prescribes the disclosure of a private sexual photograph with the intention of causing that person distress (s.33(1)). No offence is committed where the disclosure is to a person who features in the photograph (s.33(2)) which is obviously designed to ensure that couples are free to exchange photographs of each other. But it does potentially leave a loophole where, for example, person X wishes to remind person Y that the photograph exists (which they may, for example, have previously agreed to destroy).

The photograph needs to be both private and sexual. 'Private' means it depicts an act not normally seen in public (s.35(2)) which may exclude topless sunbathing. 'Sexual' means that it depicts:

- an individual's exposed genitals or pubic area,
- it shows something that a reasonable person would consider to be sexual because of its nature, or
- its content, taken as a whole, is such that a reasonable person would consider it sexual (s.35(3)).

This is a broad definition and would cover what most people would consider to be sexual and certainly the behaviour identified above that constitutes revenge pornography. To that extent the provision can be largely welcomed.

Perhaps the most important aspect of the offence will be the fault element (*mens rea*). This requires the intention to cause distress (s.33(1)) but s.33(8) states that a person is not to be taken to have this intent where it was merely the natural and probable consequences of doing so. This wording is somewhat unusual (cf s.8, *Criminal Justice Act 1967*) and could be taken to mean that oblique intent will not apply, and that the intent to cause distress must be through direct intent. If that were to be the case, it would severely limit the offence. There may be a number of reasons why a person would disclose a photograph, including to cause embarrassment, the end of a relationship or a loss of employment. Each of these may ultimately cause distress but it is not their primary purpose. If s.33(8) means direct intent is required, then for each of the reasons above, D would not be guilty even if it was virtually certain the disclosure would cause distress. This would be deeply unfortunate and allow a number of offenders to escape liability.

There are a limited number of defences to the disclosure. The first is that the suspect reasonably believed that the disclosure was necessary to prevent, detect or investigate crime (s.33(3)) which is perhaps uncontroversial. The second defence is that the disclosure was made in the course of publishing journalistic material and it was in the public interest to do so (s.33(4)). This is perhaps more questionable since it does not form part of a wider 'legitimate reason' defence, (which perhaps would have been more understandable), but is perhaps a reflection of the backlash against the 'Leveson report' and the belief that journalists do not have sufficient protection from the law. The final defence is that D believed that the photograph had already been disclosed for reward, and he had no reason to believe this earlier disclosure occurred without consent (s.33(5)). This is a somewhat niche defence and it is difficult to see under what circumstances it would be used.

The offence is punishable by a maximum sentence of two years' imprisonment (s.33(9)) which is akin to the other adult pornography offences. S.32, CJCA 2015 raises the maximum sentence for an offence contrary to s.1, MCA 1988 to two years' imprisonment. Arguably prosecuting under the MCA 1988 would be easier and so it must be questioned whether this will impact prosecutorial policy on cases relating to revenge pornography.

## Freedom of expression

It is perhaps briefly worth noting the impact that freedom of expression has on adult pornography. The concept of freedom of expression was introduced in the previous chapter but it is perhaps simpler in respect of obscenity. In the context of the USA the Supreme Court has struggled with the concept of obscenity. Perhaps one of the most notable statements of the historical approach it took was given in *Roth v United States* 77 S.Ct. 1304 (1957) where it was said, 'we hold that obscenity is not within the area of constitutionally protected speech or press' (at 1309). This ruling denied the protection of the First Amendment to matters of obscenity, meaning that it could be criminalised easily.

Eventually the Supreme Court was called upon to reconsider the strict approach it had adopted, in part because of the way that moral standards changed in the USA itself. The matter returned in the landmark case of *Miller v California* 93 S.Ct. 2607 (1973). The defendant in the case had sent obscene material through the US mail service (a Federal offence). The Supreme Court began to distance itself from its earlier decisions, especially *Roth* although it began from the same starting point, i.e. that it was legitimate for state and the Federal governments to legislate to restrict obscenity. However, the Supreme Court stated that even explicit sexual content could come within the First Amendment if it has a 'serious literary, artistic, political, or scientific value' (at 2616). The court noted that the essence of the First Amendment was to protect such values irrespective of whether 'the government or a majority of the people approve of the ideas these works represent' (at 2620). The court also noted that the definition of obscenity had to be based on 'contemporary community standards' rather than 'national standards' (at 2622) which accepts that standards will change and the law needs to adapt to that. The result of *Miller* was that pornography became more prevalent because it became easier to class material as 'artistic' or 'expressive'. The USA is now one of the biggest producers and hosts of pornography and that is partly because pornography has been brought within First Amendment protections. Further decisions have focused extensively on children and these will be discussed in the next chapter.

Of more direct relevance to us is the *European Convention on Human Rights* and, in particular, Articles 10 and 8. In respect of Article 10 (expression) one of the legitimate aims that is contained within Article 10(2) is the protection of morals and the European Court of Human Rights has traditionally extended a large measure of discretion (known as the margin of appreciation) to states in respect of obscene material.

Perhaps the first and most notable of the cases is *Handyside v United Kingdom* (1979–80) 1 EHRR 737, which concerned the *Little Red Schoolbook*. This was an English translation of a book that was widely in circulation across Europe, and indeed had also been circulating in parts of the UK without prosecution. The book, written by two Danish teachers, called upon teenagers to question societal norms and it included chapters on drugs, alcohol and tobacco. It also contained 26 pages on sex, including instructional aspects. Following a media campaign the book was referred to the Attorney-General who pressed the Director of Public Prosecutions to institute a prosecution against Handyside (who had distributed the English-language version) under the OPA 1959. Following conviction (for which a fine of £50 was imposed) the book was amended to remove certain passages and was re-published. The Director of Public Prosecutions stated that he would not bring any prosecution in respect of the revised edition.

Handyside petitioned the European Court of Human Rights (ECtHR) alleging that his prosecution amounted to a breach of Article 10. The ECtHR rejected this argument and stated that 'it is not possible to find ... a uniform European concept of morals' (at 753), partly because the concept of morality will change as society progresses but also taking account of the different standards adopted by society. The Court noted that 'State authorities are in principle in a better position than the international judge to give an opinion on the exact content of these requirements as well as the "necessity" of a "restriction" or "penalty" intended to meet them' (at 753–4). In other words, the ECtHR was happy to defer to the national courts' understanding on the need and necessity to protect morality, although this will be subject to an analysis of proportionality.

The deferential approach was carried forward to *Müller v Switzerland* (1991) 13 EHRR 212 which concerned an art exhibition which included three paintings considered obscene that depicted sexual activity between humans and animals. The exhibition was open to all and without admission charge. The gallery owner was prosecuted under Swiss obscenity law and was fined. He petitioned the ECtHR alleging that the prosecution breached Article 10. Once again the ECtHR rejected the petition. They noted that the fact that the exhibition was open to all meant that children could see the material (at 227) and also noted that the domestic courts were in the best place to decide the necessity of any measures to protect morality. The same has been held in respect of non-sexual material (see *Wingrove v United Kingdom* (1997) 24 EHRR 1 which concerned blasphemy) and therefore it can be seen that countries have a wide discretion in this area.

What of extreme pornography? It might be argued that possessing material is more to do with private life than expression (in that the courts have held that the sexual identity of an individual is part of the private life: see, for example, *Dudgeon v UK* (1982) 4 EHRR 149). However, it is unlikely that this would make any difference. Article 8(2) similarly permits an interference with the right for the legitimate aim of, *inter alia*, the protection of morals. Whilst there is a material difference in that the extreme pornography provisions relate to the private possession of material rather than its distribution or exhibition, it is unlikely that the ECtHR will shift away from the stance that it has previously adopted. The lack of a direct link to harm would seem to be an obvious reason to consider the proportionality of restrictions (something that will be discussed in the next chapter in respect of so-called 'virtual child pornography') but there is no evidence; however, the fact that the ECHR permits restrictions on the basis of morality would seem to undermine that argument. Certainly there is no indication that the ECtHR appears to be retreating from its stance and therefore the compatibility of the provisions is probably secure (for a contrary view see Easton, 2011).

## Suggested further reading

Crawford, B.J. 'Toward a third-wave feminist legal theory: Young women, pornography and the praxis of pleasure' (2007) 14 *Michigan Journal of Gender and Law* 99–168.
*This is a very good introduction to the debates surrounding the origins of third-wave feminist thinking and, in particular, how it applies to pornography.*

Dworkin, A. and MacKinnon, C. *Pornography and Civil Rights: A New Day for Women's Equality* (1988, Minnesota: Organizing against Pornography).
*It is not possible to consider these issues without looking at the work of either Dworkin or MacKinnon because their work continues to influence so much of the debate (both by those who agree with them and those who fundamentally disagree with them). Virtually any of their writing could be chosen but I suggest you read this as it puts forward their ideas of how the law could be used to tackle pornography.*

Easton, S. 'Criminalising the possession of extreme pornography: Sword or shield?' (2011) 75 *Journal of Criminal Law* 391–413.
*This is an interesting article that considers the provisions of the Criminal Justice and Immigration Act 2008 and, in particular, considers its compatibility with the ECHR.*

Glass, K. 'How to stamp out revenge porn' (2013) *The Sunday Times*, June 30.
*A very good article that shows how some women are developing strategies to combat 'revenge porn'.*

# Chapter 10

# Sexualised content 2

## Child pornography

The second type of sexual content to consider is that of 'child pornography'. It was seen from the last chapter that in the 1960s and 1970s there was a gradual relaxation of the laws relating to pornography. About this time there began to be a concern that this was leading to an increase in so-called 'child pornography' causing harm to children. Therefore, laws began to be introduced that drew a distinction between adult and child sexualised content and they developed in a different way, with a lower threshold for child sexualised content.

As technology advances new forms of child pornography have begun to exist and since the turn of the millennia the focus has turned to so-called 'virtual child pornography', i.e. computer-generated images of children depicting sexual abuse. These raise different issues and therefore this chapter will draw a distinction between these forms.

## Photograph-based material

The first type of material to be discussed is that of photograph-based material. This remains the most common form of child pornography and is certainly the most damaging in terms of victims. This chapter will consider why we need laws for child pornography before considering the definition of child pornography and then finally looking at how domestic and international laws have sought to tackle this behaviour.

### Rationale for criminalising child pornography

The year 2014 was unusual because suddenly there was considerable discussion in the media of the 'Paedophile Information Exchange' (PIE). This was an organisation that existed in the 1970s and sought to campaign for the reduction (or abolition) of the age of consent and the legalisation of child pornography. Whilst the activities of PIE had occasionally featured over the years in media discussions, there was renewed examination of its activities in 2014. The central focus of much of the attention was by the *Daily*

*Mail* and its sister publication the *Mail on Sunday* who sought to argue that three prominent Labour politicians had somehow facilitated or supported the activities of PIE (see, for example, Adams, 2013, and McKinstry, 2014) and then expanded their denunciations to include leading judicial figures (see, for example, *Mail on Sunday*, 2014, and Beckford, 2014). The stories are interesting because they conflate a particular issue – the fact that PIE existed as a campaigning group in the 1970s – with innuendoes. For example, the Labour figures stated that far from supporting the activities they actively sought to campaign against them, and the judicial figures were attacked for either providing legal advice or representing members of PIE even though the Barrister Code of Conduct expressly requires lawyers to provide legal advice to those who consult them, something considered to be a fundamental part of an independent legal system.

However, there was no doubt that PIE did exist and some believe that it continues to exist today. PIE was not unique, other countries also had/have similar groups and perhaps the best known of these is NAMBLA (North American Man/Boy Lovers Association) which similarly campaigns for the reduction/abolition of the age of consent and the legalisation of child pornography. To PIE and NAMBLA, paedophilia is simply a minority sexual identity and therefore should be treated as such (in the same way that homosexuality would become recognised as a legitimate expression of minority sexual identity, although many campaigners for Gay and Lesbian rights find any analogy to be, quite rightly, repugnant). In the 1970s the human rights/ civil rights organisations were beginning to develop and it is perhaps unsurprising that campaigns such as PIE could put forward what we would think of as abhorrent ideas.

Whilst society has distanced itself from such campaigns, it remains the case that some continue to argue that child pornography amounts to 'just photographs'. However, it will be seen that this is far from the case and the concept of harm is at the heart of the need to criminalise this material, both in its primary sense and in its secondary sense.

### Primary harm

The first reason for criminalising child pornography is that harm is caused to the participants. It is this that lies at the heart of the desire by some to avoid the use of 'child pornography' (and instead terms such as 'child abuse images' are used: see Gillespie, 2011:3–4). It will be seen below that there are different types of child pornography but a considerable amount of material depicts what would, in law, amount to a sexual assault. This has now been slightly altered by the fact that in some countries (including the UK) the age of a child for these purposes is above the age of consent. However, the majority of images continue to depict a sexual assault (on the basis that a child below the age of consent cannot give valid consent in law to sexual acts).

The first way in which primary harm can be caused is in its production. There are a variety of ways in which child pornography can be produced, including self-production (known as sexting). Whilst adult pornography is invariably a commercial enterprise the same is not necessarily true of child pornography. Whilst it will be impossible to quantify the amount of commercial child pornography available (because the amount of material available is also not known, contrary to what some authors purport to suggest) there is no question that it can bring big money, with a single notable website (Landslide Productions) reported to have had receipts of over US$1 million per month (Taylor and Quayle, 2003:5). The commercial incentives are therefore great and it is perhaps not surprising that people are prepared to engage in this behaviour irrespective of the harm that it causes.

Alongside commercial production is the small-scale production by individuals or small collectives. It has been noted that whilst most commercial producers are not sexually interested in the material the same is not true of the small-scale producers, indeed the majority of small-scale producers filmed themselves engaging in sexual acts with their victims (Wolak *et al.*, 2005:39). In such instances the harm is clear but is the harm caused by the production of the child pornography or the sexual assault? The answer is both, because there is *additional* harm caused by the production of child pornography.

Studies have shown that children suffer psychological harm from the production of child pornography (Quayle *et al.*, 2006:48). This harm comes from the knowledge that the activities are being recorded and that they will be used by the person creating them to relive the abusive experiences but also the concern that they will be distributed and seen by others. Victims are afraid that people who see them will believe that they consented to the abuse (Palmer, 2005:63) or that they may be recognised by people later in their life (for example, when they attend university or start employment).

This additional harm can also be used to justify criminalising the distribution of child pornography. If the psychological harm is caused by the distribution of material or the fear of distribution then obviously the person who does the distribution is contributing to that harm. Ost argues that whilst distribution is one step removed it is undoubtedly influenced by the primary harm: 'he is only able to perpetrate his acts of distribution because of the creator's primary harm' and that criminalising distribution is 'justified on the basis of him underwriting and profiting from the primary harm of the creator' (Ost, 2009:107). Clearly therefore there is a link to harm and it is possible to justify the criminalisation of such material on that basis.

### Secondary harm

What of possession or viewing? It was seen in the previous chapter that it is unusual to criminalise possession of pornographic material and some have suggested that it is inappropriate to criminalise it in respect of child pornography too (Williams, 2004:257), but the then UN Special Rapporteur on the sale of children, child prostitution and child pornography has been adamant that criminalisation of possession is required to criminalise 'each participant in the chain' (Petit, 2004:10).

It is difficult to identify how a possessor can be the cause of primary harm in that they are not the person who abused the child and nor are they responsible for the production of the material. Perhaps one of the most common policy justifications advanced for the criminalisation of possession is that it leads to people sexually abusing children. However, the reality is that there is no proof that this is true. For every study that shows there is a link there is another study that shows there is no link (discussed in Gillespie, 2011:34–37) and realistically it can be said that the research is so inconclusive as to preclude using it as a justification for criminalising possession.

It has been noted that some argue that possession must be criminalised so as to ensure that the market for imagery is reduced, although not everyone is convinced about the validity of such an approach (Ost, 2009:113–118); some have postulated that an alternative theory would be to suggest that one justification would be that the possessor is benefiting from the illegal acts and harms of the creator (Baker, 2007:387), and given possessors know that the material is illegal this would mean that their actions can be considered illegal for contributing to the chain of illegality and harm.

However, the stronger argument is that possession contributes to the *continuing* harm of the child, something often known as secondary victimisation. This suggestion has been recognised by the courts, perhaps most famously in *R v Beaney* [2004] EWCA Crim 449 where the Court of Appeal recognised that a child can suffer psychological harm by the knowledge that 'people out there [were] getting a perverted thrill from watching them forced to pose and behave in this way' (at [8]). Certainly this would seem to accord with psychological evidence that suggests re-victimisation occurs through the images being kept perpetually alive (Taylor and Quayle, 2003:24).

This justification does raise an interesting ethical dilemma though. Ost agrees that the harm arises where the child is aware that their image is being circulated (Ost, 2009:123) but what does this mean in the context of those who are not aware of the harm? For example, where the material was gathered in a covert way or because the child was too young to understand what was happening? Should the authorities inform the victim that they are portrayed in child pornography? It may be necessary to do so in order to interview them as to subsequent offending or safeguarding, but are the authorities then causing the harm? Does it matter if the victim is told some considerable time after the events occurred? The harm undoubtedly continues to exist (Gillespie, 2011:38) and thus the issue of harm, albeit in its secondary sense, can justify criminalising the possession of child pornography.

## The international dimension

In 2001 an editorial in *The Lancet* said, '[child pornography] is surely precisely this sort of borderless problem that requires firm action from one of the international agencies' (357 *The Lancet* 569). This is a pertinent point. It will be remembered from Chapter 1 that cybercrime is a global phenomenon that is marked by, amongst others, its spread. That is certainly true of child pornography where the internet and related digital technologies have revolutionised the way that it is produced and disseminated (Taylor and Quayle, 2003). The jurisdictional challenges of this have been noted already in Chapter 2 but international co-operation can help facilitate the prevention, detection and prosecution of this crime.

Given that at the heart of child pornography is the abuse or exploitation of a child, it is an area where many countries at least agree on the need to do something to combat child pornography. Within the global context one of the most important provisions is the *Optional Protocol to the UN Convention on the Rights of the Child on the Sale of Children, Child Prostitution and Child Pornography* (OPSC). The *Convention on the Rights of the Child* (CRC) is one of the most important international documents that is designed to given an overarching system of rights to children (see Buck, 2014 for a detailed commentary on the CRC) but it has few provisions relating to abuse and nothing specific on Information and Communication Technologies (ICT) based child pornography. It was always intended that a specific instrument seeking to tackle sexual abuse would be created and the OPSC was drafted and opened for signature in 2000.

The OPSC is designed to cover three forms of sexual exploitation (Article 1), one of which is directly relevant for our purposes as it concerns child pornography. Given that it was written in 2000 when the internet had begun to achieve popular subscription it is perhaps surprising that more attention was not paid to the issue of ICT-based abuse. As will be seen, however, this did not happen and it can be argued that the OPSC is starting to show its age.

It will be remembered from Chapter 1 that the *Convention on Cybercrime*, whilst drafted by the Council of Europe, was intended for a wider audience and it has been adopted by numerous countries across the world. The only offence relating to sexual exploitation contained within the Cybercrime Convention relates to child pornography. Given its inclusion in a treaty governing cybercrime it was obviously designed to tackle the growing importance of ICT in this area, although a criticism of the Convention is that it does not cover other forms of child sexual exploitation committed online (considered further in Chapter 11). Reacting to this criticism the Council of Europe designed a new treaty that is designed specifically to tackle all forms of child sexual abuse and exploitation, known as the *Council of Europe Convention on the Protection of Children against Sexual Exploitation and Sexual Abuse*, also known as the 'Lanzarote Convention'.

As a treaty that covers all forms of child sexual exploitation the Lanzarote Convention encompasses matters relating to child pornography but it is a much wider treaty and it includes other forms of sexual exploitation. The Convention also goes further than other instruments in that it does not simply prescribe minimum offences that must be enacted by signatory states but it also provides requirements for police co-operation and support for victims (see Gillespie, 2014b). This is an important issue that is sometimes missed within legal instruments that, perhaps naturally, focus on criminality rather than support.

Alongside these key instruments others are beginning to emerge. At the supranational level, the European Union has, for some time, been involved in the fight against child pornography (Gillespie, 2014b:360–361) and this has culminated in the legally binding *Directive 2011/92/EU of the European Parliament and of the Council of 13 December 2011 on Combating the Sexual Abuse and Sexual Exploitation of Children and Child Pornography, Replacing Council Framework Decision 2004/68/JHA*. As a legally binding instrument this differs greatly from most international instruments that are not enforceable. Changes brought about by the Lisbon Treaty mean that the Court of Justice of the EU will have a role in enforcing this legislation which could have a major impact on the EU.

Outside of Europe other bodies are also looking at this area. The African Union has passed the *African Charter on the Rights and Welfare of Children* which includes reference to the sexual abuse of children, including through child pornography. The African Union is also in the process of passing a Cybercrime Treaty (which currently exists in draft form) and which will include specific reference to child pornography. The Commonwealth of Nations (formerly the 'British Commonwealth') has also created a model code for dealing with cybercrime and this includes a commitment to work on the sexual exploitation of children, including child pornography.

It can be seen, therefore, that child pornography is an important issue that is recognised as requiring international co-operation. However, rather ironically it will be seen that this multitude of treaties arguably disguises a lack of effective action. It is easy to sign a treaty but it is a very different thing to actually commit to implementing it. More than this, however, it is not clear what countries are supposed to do. For example, the UK is a signatory to the CRC, OPSC, Cybercrime Convention and the Lanzarote Convention. It has also exercised its opt-in right in respect of the EU Directive on combating sexual abuse. Therefore, it is a signatory to most of the instruments that have been mentioned in this section. However, the treaties do not all say the same thing. Whilst we want international co-operation, a difficulty appears to be that there are different standards being exercised in this area (Gillespie, 2010). Perhaps this is not surprising because treaties will deal with different types of countries, but it perhaps undermines the call by *The Lancet* for international co-operation. If each is adopting a different standard then confusion can reign and no standard is achieved. This is perhaps just a reflection of international law – that countries are starting from different points – but it would be helpful if they there was agreement as to at least *minimum* standards that could be reached. This is perhaps what the point of the OPSC was. However, if standards are set too low then it is perhaps unsurprising if other countries seek to build on this. Nevertheless, this should not be at the expense of raising everyone to a standard minimum requirement and international co-operation should be based around this: i.e. adopting a minimum standard and a 'higher' standard. For this to work it is likely that a truly global resource is required. Unfortunately, as will be seen, the OPSC is perhaps the weakest of all the instruments and therefore perhaps it is time to overhaul this treaty. The OPSC was introduced almost 15 years ago and technology has advanced exponentially since that time, as has our understanding of offender behaviour, and therefore a new global standard may be required.

The exact differences between these instruments will be discussed in the next section that looks at the definition of child pornography.

### Defining child pornography

How is child pornography defined? There are three components to any definition:

- What is a child?
- What type of material is covered?
- What is it about the material that causes it to be classified as child pornography?

Each raises slightly different issues.

#### Meaning of 'a child'

Obviously a crucial element to define is the meaning of 'a child'. This may seem an unusual question but there is rarely an agreed definition of what constitutes a child. For example, in England and Wales there are a variety of ages at which a person may do something (at ten they achieve the age of criminal responsibility, at 14 may start employment, at 16 may ride a motorbike or have an alcoholic drink whilst having a meal at a public house).

How does one define a child? Perhaps one way would be to consider whether there is a physical definition. The most obvious physiological difference between a child and an adult is the process of puberty. Puberty marks the point at which the body is capable of sexual reproduction and this has sometimes been considered to be a point of (physical) maturity. However, there are difficulties in using puberty as a definition. The first is that puberty is not something that happens overnight: it is something that occurs over a series of years. At what point do you decide that a child is pre- or post-puberty? The most obvious sign for females would be menarche but that is not something easily identified from a photograph. What about males? The main sign is usually the first ejaculation but again this is not something that would be easily identifiable from a photograph, and given that few victims are identified (Palmer, 2005) then asking the victim is not a realistic option in many instances.

Another alternative would be to consider psychology but the same problem arises. Paedophilia is a clinical term even though it has undoubtedly also taken on a wider, colloquial societal definition. Clinical paedophilia is best described as the sexual preference for pre-pubescent children (Seto, 2004:322) and given that puberty marks the point at which a body is capable of reproduction then it can be argued that a sexual interest in children before that point is against nature. However, this continues to have the same problems as above. It is difficult to ascertain puberty from a photograph, although it is conceded that it would be possible in many instances to note whether the individuals are clearly pre-pubescent or clearly post-pubescent because of the physiological changes puberty brings. However, this would cause problems for children going through puberty. The other difficulty is that there is some indication that children are progressing through puberty earlier and just because the body is physically capable of reproduction does not mean that the child is emotionally ready for sex or that it is societally acceptable for sexual contact to occur.

The narrow definition of paedophilia has led others to suggest that there may be other psychological disorders, with the most commonly cited being hebephilia. This is a term that was developed in the 1950s (Blanchard *et al.*, 2009:336) and is designed to encapsulate those who have a sexual interest in children post-puberty but under the age of consent. The difficulty with this is that the age of consent is an arbitrary choice. It is set by each country according to the standards that they think appropriate at the time. Can you have a psychological disorder that relates to an arbitrary age? Certainly not everyone seems to think so and hebephilia is not universally supported (discussed in Gillespie, 2011:14) and it is perhaps notable that after prolonged debate DSM-V (Diagnostic and Statistical Manual of Mental Disorders published by the American Psychiatric Association) does not include hebephilia.

Thus it would seem that neither physical nor psychiatric factors are appropriate in defining 'a child' and therefore the most appropriate method would be to prescribe age. This has the simplicity of being consistent across individuals and is also comparable to substantive sex offences where there is ordinarily an age prescribed, and if a person has sexual contact with a child below that age then they are guilty of an offence.

If an age is to be prescribed then two questions immediately arise. First, what age should be prescribed, and secondly how is that age ascertained? In terms of the age chosen, until comparatively recently the age chosen was the same as the age of consent. The logic behind choosing this is obvious. If, as was noted above, a reason for criminalising child pornography is that it depicts illegal sexual activities then choosing the age at which the activities cease to be illegal is an obvious choice. However, some NGOs began to argue that a child is not able to consent to being depicted within pornography and that therefore the age of 'a child' should be raised to 18 (discussed in Gillespie, 2011:17). This began to be reflected in international instruments. Whilst the OPSC does not specifically address age it is known that the CRC considers 18 to be the (ordinary) age of majority and therefore the same applies to the OPSC. The Cybercrime Convention defined a child for the purposes of child pornography to be 18 but permitted signatory states the right to reduce this age to no less than 16 (Article 9(3)). The same position arises in respect of the Lanzarote Convention (Article 20(3)) but the EU Directive requires the age of 18 to be chosen (Article 2). The fact that international treaties required this meant that ultimately the UK chose to comply with their (new) legal obligation and the *Sexual Offences Act 2003* amended the age of 'a child' for the purposes of child pornography to 18 for the offence in England and Wales.

The fact that there is now a difference between the age of consent (16) and the age of a child for the purposes of child pornography (18) means that a slight paradox has been created. It is perfectly lawful for A to have sexual intercourse with B (a 17-year-old girl) but if he takes a topless picture of her then he commits an offence.

## Type of material

The second issue to consider is the type of material. Whilst we may think of photograph-based material as being the most obvious form of material, the original meaning of pornography was writing rather than pictures (Ost, 2009). In terms of child pornography three principal forms are known to exist: visual depictions (including photographs, drawings and pictures), written depictions and audio depictions (sound files).

The OPSC has perhaps the widest definition of child pornography in that it refers to:

> any representation, by whatever means, of a child engaged in real or simulated explicit sexual activities or any representation of the sexual parts of a child for primarily sexual purposes.
>
> (Article 2(c))

The reference to 'by whatever means' clearly encompasses all forms of material although few countries would appear to have criminalised all forms (a rare example is Ireland which does criminalise all forms: see *Child Trafficking and Pornography Act 1998*). All the other instruments simply focus on visual depictions. Whilst considerable attention has been focused in recent years on so-called Virtual Child Pornography (discussed later in this chapter) it is clear that the main focus of attention remains photographs or photograph-based material.

### Nature of the material

Perhaps the most difficult question to answer is what is it about the images that justifies it being described as child pornography? This is an issue where there is a lack of consensus in the international instruments, potentially causing some forms of confusion.

The starting point is that research with sex offenders has shown that offenders will use a broad range of material for the purposes of sexual gratification (Tate, 1990:15; Taylor and Quayle, 2003). Taylor and Quayle have suggested that there are three broad types of material:

1. Indicative.  Material depicting clothed children which suggests a sexual interest in children.
2. Indecent.  Material depicting naked children which suggests a sexual interest in children.
3. Obscenity.  Material which depicts children in sexual acts.

(Taylor and Quayle, 2003:27)

This broadly reflects legal understandings of pornography. It will be remembered from the previous chapter that obscenity is considered a relatively high standard and is the usual threshold for action to be taken in respect of pornography. However, the harm that is caused by child pornography is generally thought to justify a lower threshold for action, although that would not normally encompass the first level of material, indicative.

In terms of international instruments there are a variety of approaches. The most common is to identify certain aspects that are always classed as child pornography. The most obvious of these is 'sexual activity' which is contained within all instruments (Gillespie, 2010:218). This is perhaps unsurprising given the mischief behind the instruments. Where disparity exists is over what else should be covered. The OPSC specifically refers to the exhibition of the female breast whereas other instruments mention the sexual organs of a child which may not include the breast. It is in the description where matters get more complicated. The Cybercrime Convention refers to material being 'lascivious' which is a term that is most commonly used in America and which is not easily defined (Gillespie, 2010:219). The OPSC and the Lanzarote Convention prohibit the depiction of sexual activity or the depiction of the sexual organs of a child for a primarily sexual purpose. This, it is submitted, is a clearer definition because it is easy to identify precisely what renders an image illegal.

In England and Wales the approach that is adopted is one of indecency (s.1, *Protection of Children Act 1978*). The term 'indecent' is not defined in the statute and therefore it has been left to the courts to establish the term. In *R v Stanford* [1972] 2 QB 391 it was said, albeit in a different context, that obscenity and indecency were on opposite ends of the same scale. This reinforces the point that the law is prepared to accept a reduced threshold due to the harm that is caused to children by this material.

As with obscenity, 'indecent' is an objective concept where the jury is asked to consider the issue applying ordinary standards of decency. The context of the images is ostensibly irrelevant as it should be an objective issue. In *R v Graham-Kerr* [1988] 1 WLR 1098 the appellant had been convicted of taking pictures at a nudist swimming event. He sought to argue his motivation for taking the photographs should be taken into consideration but this was rejected by the court who said that the issue of indecency was simply a question for the jury to consider in isolation when examining the photographs. In *R v Smethurst* [2002] 1 Cr App R 6 the same issue was brought before the Court of Appeal but this time the appellant, who had downloaded material from the internet, sought to argue that the objective test was incompatible with Article 6 of the ECHR (right to a fair trial). The Court of Appeal emphatically rejected this contention and stated that the objective standard was the only one applicable. The Court was concerned that if a subjective element was introduced this would cause difficulties when a person came into possession of an image for legitimate purposes but later people did not (at p.58).

It has to be questioned whether the Court of Appeal was right to be concerned about this point because by rejecting context it arguably creates more problematic concerns. Let us take an example:

> X is the mother of an 18-month-old baby (Y). She takes a picture of Y when she is in the bath but when she takes the picture Y falls back with her legs in the air. Thinking it is funny she sends it to Z, X's brother, and the uncle to Y.

It may be thought that this is a perfectly normal scenario. Is it child pornography? It is certainly not what we would think of as being child pornography but if Y's genitals are exposed then depending on how child pornography is defined, it could be so classified. Now let us develop the scenario.

> A breaks into Z's house and steals his tablet computer. When looking though its contents he sees the photograph above. A knows that B is a person with a sexual interest in children and he sells the photograph to B. B uses the photograph to masturbate to and sends it to C and D, people he believes share his outlook.

Let us look at this photograph again. Ignoring the objective element does the subjective element tell us anything? It is submitted that it does. X and Z have the photograph for a legitimate purpose, Y belongs to their family unit. The mere fact that they are family does not render the photograph non-indecent because it is known a majority of sexual abuse takes place within the family so such a rule would be dangerous. However, in the scenario above, X and Z have a perfectly legitimate reason for having the photograph of Y and indeed it is a typical photograph that many family members may be sent. It should not constitute child pornography.

What of B, C and D? This is more difficult. Consider the example. Do you feel happy that B, C and D have that image? If not, why not? Is there a difference between B having this image and Z? There obviously is but according to *Graham-Kerr* and *Smethurst* this cannot be taken into account. The Court of Appeal is stating that the object of the legislation is the photograph itself and therefore it should *always* be indecent or not, but it is submitted that this is wrong. The short title of the Act is the *Protection of Children Act 1978* and therefore child protection should be relevant. Does any harm accrue to Y in the first example? The answer can only be 'no'. What of the second example? Here the answer would seem to be that there could be harm. It would seem to be secondary harm but it is possible to argue that harm could be caused to Y when she finds out her image is being used in this way.

If, as suggested, there is a material difference between X and Z, and B, C and D then should this not be reflected in the legal test? If the test is purely objective then the answer is 'no' but if we took a subjective element into account then the answer would be 'yes'. X and Z should not be at risk of prosecution. The police and Crown Prosecution Service (CPS) may argue that they would not be at risk of prosecution because of prosecutorial discretion but the treatment of Julia Sommerville – a then famous newsreader – suggests that this is not necessarily correct. Sommerville and her partner were arrested and questioned over a photograph of her child taken in the bath. Whilst she was not prosecuted she was subject to the investigatory process over an innocent family photograph.

What is the solution? In *Smethurst* the appellant tried to argue that child pornography offences should follow the House of Lords judgment in *R v Court* [1989] AC 28, later enshrined in statute as the test of sexual in s.78, *Sexual Offences Act 2003*. The test (in the wording that could be applied to this context) would be:

An image is indecent if:

(a) whatever its circumstances or person's purpose it is considered indecent, or
(b) because of its nature it may be indecent and because of its circumstances or the purpose of any person in relation to it, it is indecent.

If this were to be applied then some forms of child pornography would always be indecent. This would include, for example, photographs showing obscene acts (including sexual activity) and clearly posed images. However, others – such as the first example above – are *capable* of being indecent (because, for example, it shows the genitalia of the child) but then the context needs to be taken into account. In respect of X and Z their context is perfectly legitimate and therefore it should not be considered indecent. There is no sexual intent to anything that they have done and it is, in that context, a perfectly legitimate photograph. What of A, B, C and D? Here the context changes. It is still *capable* of being indecent and this time the context is problematic. A knows that B will find the image sexually interesting and B, C and D do. In this instance they are using the image for sexual gratification and therefore it is being used for an indecent purpose. It is submitted that there is no reason why this should not be classed as indecent. The image is being used in a materially different way than X and Z are using it and the objective test does not distinguish this. It should.

Notwithstanding the criticisms above, the objective test has primacy. Not only did it survive domestic challenges in *Graham-Kerr* and *Smethurst* but it was also challenged before the European Court of Human Rights (*O'Carroll v United Kingdom* (2005) 41 EHRR SE 1). O'Carroll, a former leading member of the Paedophile Information Exchange, had been convicted of importing child pornography into the UK (contrary to s.170(2)(b), *Customs and Excise Act 1979*). The images were naturist and after unsuccessfully challenging the definition of indecency in the English courts (*R v O'Carroll* [2003] EWCA Crim 2338) he petitioned the ECtHR alleging that this was a breach of Articles 8 and 10. The ECtHR refused permission stating the case was unarguable and thus the objective test, for all its flaws, remains intact.

## The offences

Now that child pornography has been defined what are the actions that are criminalised? The main offences are contained within the *Protection of Children Act 1978* (PoCA), s.1(1) of which states:

It is an offence for a person

(a) to take, or permit to be taken, or to make, any indecent photograph or pseudo-photograph of a child; or
(b) to distribute or show such indecent photographs or pseudo-photographs; or
(c) to have in his possession such indecent photographs or pseudo-photographs, with a view to their being distributed or shown by himself or others; or

(d) to publish or cause to be published any advertisement likely to be understood to be conveying that the advertiser, distributes or shows such indecent photographs or pseudo-photographs, or intends to do so.

Alongside this sits s.160, *Criminal Justice Act 1988* which prescribes an offence of simple possession. For the purposes of this section the only focus will be on photographs because the concept of pseudo-photographs will be considered later.

### Taking or making

The first offence is that of taking or making. 'Taking' is an easy term to define and in the context of photographs, it is simply the act of taking a photograph or recording a moving image file from, for example, a video camera. The more interesting term is 'making' which was, at one point, thought to only refer to pseudo-photographs. However, in *R v Bowden* [2000] QB 88 it was noted that when one downloads an image from the internet a file now exists on the computer that did not used to exist, in other words it had been made. The implications of this are that, following *DPP v Atkins* [2000] 1 WLR 1427, if the user is aware that the image is automatically stored (and most people are now aware of that) then the offence under s.1, PoCA 1978 is made out and not just the offence of simple possession (discussed below).

The way that browsing the internet (ordinarily) works is such that the logic of *Bowden* could be applied to the viewing of an image. In *R v Jayson* [2003] 1 Cr App R 13 it was held that even if the image was not stored in the cache the image might still be 'made' by calling the image up on the screen. This would be a much wider term and it is difficult to accept the logic of this. The court stated the image was created when it was called up on the screen, but was it? Making must mean that there is some substance – it must exist somewhere. By calling it up to the screen it is not really in existence. A copy of it is being *displayed* but that does not mean it is in existence on the local machine. Where it is copied in the cache then it is in existence but where it is only displayed on the screen – and it is now possible to disable the cache function – then it is only to be found in the RAM of the computer and this is not really in existence, it is simply the display of an existing file. To that extent it is submitted that *Jayson* is wrong.

Interestingly, the problem with viewing images rather than downloading them is increasingly found in international instruments. With super-fast internet speeds why should a user run the risk of downloading the images when she could look at the material online just as quickly, potentially without leaving a forensic trace. It is for that reason that some instruments are suggesting criminalising the *access* to indecent photographs and not just their downloading (see, most notably, Article 20(1)(f) of the Lanzarote Convention).

The advantage of this is that it is not necessary to consider the technical processes of computers to decide whether an image is made, downloaded, viewed or anything else. Accessing the images becomes culpable and thus it would also include, for example, the viewing of streamed images (Gillespie, 2011:40). This is to be preferred to the fiction of *Jayson*.

When first drafted there was no defence to an offence under s.1(1)(a). However, the *Sexual Offences Act 2003* inserted two new provisions into PoCA 1978 (s.1A and s.1B) both of which introduce a defence for this conduct. The first (s.1A) is a rather unusual defence regarding children aged 16 or over. The defence decriminalises the taking of these images but only if the two 16-year-olds are married or living together in an 'enduring family relationship' which is not defined. However, note they must live together. If they don't live together then the defence does not apply. The picture must also not show anyone else in it, again a slightly unusual precondition. In essence the defence will never be used and is pointless. However, attacks on it to widen the defence beyond living together have failed (see *R v M* [2011] EWCA Crim 2752).

The second defence (s.1B) introduces a defence where it is necessary to take or make the photograph in order to prevent, detect or investigate crime or as part of the duties of the security services (aka MI5 and MI6). The defence is a pragmatic one because, for example, the police and CPS would be routinely breaking s.1(1)(a) when they investigated or prosecuted child pornography offences as they would invariably need to look at or download the evidence, including the image. The defence is not limited to such persons and it would include defence lawyers (who will similarly need to look at the material) and even the Internet Watch Foundation (IWF) who operate the hotline through which illegal content can be reported (and who will therefore need to look at it to see if it was illegal). Previously this conduct would have been dealt with through prosecutorial discretion (i.e. it would not have been in the public interest to prosecute such conduct). It seems somewhat odd that Parliament decided it could not trust the CPS to continue such discretion and it does raise again the question about whether parents who take (legitimate) photographs of their children can similarly rely on prosecutorial discretion.

### Distribution

The second category of offence is distribution. For our purposes this will encompass two forms: actual distribution of material (s.1(1)(b), PoCA 1978) and possessing with a view to their being distributed (s.1(1)(c)). In the context of the internet both are important and interconnected.

Distribution is obviously at its most simple when X sends Y an indecent photograph. This would be the natural meaning of the term distribution and it is easily proven. Where X is based in England it is irrelevant where Y is based because the distribution takes place from within the territory and therefore there are no jurisdictional issues. However, distribution need not only be this simple and s.1(2), PoCA 1978 defines it as including circumstances when D 'parts with possession of it to, or exposes or offers it for acquisition by, another person'. This makes the offence potentially much wider as the mere exposure of material would constitute distribution. However, it does raise a question as to what the difference between this and s.1(1)(c) is.

Law enforcement and the courts do not necessarily appear to appreciate the meaning of s.1(2). In *R v Fellows and Arnold* [1997] 1 Cr App R 244 the Court of Appeal was asked to consider whether a defendant who had created a password-protected electronic archive was guilty of possessing material with a view to distribution when he supplied passwords to others to access those images. The appellant argued that he did not actively distribute them, he simply acted passively by allowing others to take images and therefore he could not be culpable. The Court of Appeal rejected this arguing that creating the password and supplying the log-in credentials were positive acts and therefore he could be culpable (at 255). However, is this not a very long-winded way of deciding this? It would surely have been better for the defendant to be charged with distribution, applying s.1(2). By creating an archive and allowing others to see the material he must have exposed or offered them for acquisition. This would have avoided the overly technical approach of the Court of Appeal.

A similar difficulty arose in *R v Dooley* [2006] 1 WLR 775 where the appellant used a peer-to-peer network. He was convicted of possessing images with a view to them being distributed because the material was found in his 'my shared folder'. However, he sought to argue that the mere presence of them in that folder did not constitute 'with a view to them being distributed' because material that was copied from elsewhere in the network would also be stored there, and he had simply failed to move them into a (non-shared) folder. The Court of Appeal quashed his conviction saying that whilst 'with a view to' was different from 'with intent to do so' it was higher than mere foresight which would not suffice (at 779). The court held that at least one of the purposes for the images being in the folder must have been to allow others to access them and the prosecution had not proven that.

It has been suggested that proving knowledge of how peer-to-peer operates would defeat the argument put forward in *Dooley* (Ormerod, 2006:646) and this receives support from a Scottish case that considered a similar provision (see *Peebles v HM Advocate* (2007) JC 93). However, if the offender had been charged with distribution – through the material being exposed for acquisition – the position would have been simpler. Whilst following *Dooley* it is clear that s.1(1)(c) has *mens rea* it has been held that the offence of s.1(1)(b) is one of strict liability subject to defences (see *R v Price* [2006] EWCA Crim 3363). The defences would not have applied to the defendant in *Dooley* and therefore it would have been a much simpler offence.

Section 1(4) provides two defences for those who are accused of distributing or having images in their possession with a view to distribution. The first is that he had a 'legitimate reason' for doing so (s.1(4)(a)) and the second is that 'he had not himself seen the photographs ... and did not know, nor had any cause to suspect, them to be indecent' (s.1(4)(b)). These are both very similar to defences that are found below in respect of possession and so they will be discussed there. However, it is worth noting that the absence of 'legitimate reason' is what required the introduction of s.1B discussed above. Where the police send a photograph to the CPS as part of the evidence file they are technically distributing an indecent photograph of a child. However, they have a legitimate reason for doing so and thus are not culpable. Before the introduction of s.1B, however, they would have had no defence for duplicating the photograph.

### Possession

Section 160, CJA 1988 creates an offence of possession. Unlike the offence under s.1(1)(c) it is an offence of simple possession, i.e. there is no need for an ulterior intent. Possession means custody or control and in *R v Porter* [2006] 1 WLR 2633 the Court of Appeal held that where someone had deleted an image in such a way that they could not recover it then that person was no longer in possession of it even if it could be recovered using specialist recovery tools. This is a sensible decision because if possession is about custody or control then where the material is placed beyond their access then they cannot be considered to have it in their custody or in their control.

It is possible to circumvent this ruling however. The first way is that it is possible to charge the person possessing it the day before the image was deleted. This would require the prosecution to prove that the offender possessed the storage medium (which may be easier than proving he downloaded it as there is nothing within the CJA 1988 that requires D to be in *exclusive* possession of it) but if this is possible (for example, D admits he has owned the computer device for a period of time) then this would be possible. Indeed, by deleting the image it could show that D is in control of the image (because he is claiming the right to dispose of it: see the Canadian case of *R v Chalk* 2007 ONCA 815). The person could also be charged with making, to which *Porter* does not apply.

There are a number of defences to simple possession which is one of the reasons why the decision in *Bowden* discussed above is so controversial. Setting aside the rather absurd 'young person' defence that was discussed above (which applies equally here: s.160A) there are three of relevance:

(a)  that D had a legitimate reason for having the photograph,
(b)  that D had not himself seen the photograph and did not know, nor had any cause to suspect, it to be indecent, or

    (c)  that the photograph was sent to him without any prior request made
        by him and he did not keep it for an unreasonable length of time.

                                              (s.160(2))

It is clear from *R v Collier* [2005] 1 WLR 843 that s.160(2) imposes a reverse
burden of proof onto the defendant, i.e. D must *prove* the existence of the
defence and it is not left to the prosecution to disprove it. As with all reverse
legal burdens, the standard of proof placed on the defence is the preponderance of probabilities rather than the higher standard required by the
prosecution.

    'Legitimate reason' is not defined in the Act and is designed to cover those
situations where it is accepted that a person may need access to material
that constitutes an indecent photograph of a child. Obvious examples would
include the police and prosecutors but it could also include educational purposes. A student studying paediatrics may need (legitimate) photographs of
the genitalia of a child. However, the courts have been clear that they will
put a person to strict proof on the *necessity* of having the material. In *Atkins
v DPP* [2000] 1 WLR 1427 the appellant was a lecturer in English and he
sought to argue that he had possession of the material for academic purposes.
This was disbelieved by the trial judge and the Divisional Court agreed with
that finding saying,

> the central question … will be whether the defendant is essentially a
> person of unhealthy interests in possession of indecent photographs in
> the pretence of undertaking research, or by contrast a genuine researcher
> with no alternative but to have this sort of unpleasant material in his
> possession.

                                            (at 1435)

In respect of the second defence the requirement that D does not know
'they' are indecent means indecent photograph *of a child* not merely indecent
images. In *R v Collier* [2005] 1 WLR 843 the defendant had ordered CDs
featuring adult pornography. Unbeknown to him one of the CDs contained
four indecent photographs of children. The court at first instance declined
to allow him to run the defence on the basis that he had ordered material
which was clearly indecent (but he thought it related to adults). The Court
of Appeal, however, quashed the conviction saying that it was not enough
that he ordered indecent images, he must have ordered indecent images *of
children*. That, it is submitted, has to be the correct interpretation.

    The final defence is where material is sent unsolicited and it is not kept for
an unreasonable period of time. It is submitted that 'unsolicited' will need to
be construed in the same way as *Collier*. Let us take those facts as an example.
If C had viewed the CD, seen the images, been repulsed by them and threw
the CD out then he could not use the defence under s.160(2)(b) because he

would have *seen* the images. Nor, on a literal interpretation could he use the defence in s.160(2)(c) as he did ask for the photographs (not knowing what they contained) and so he cannot fulfil the literal criteria. The logical response would be to say that the unsolicited request for indecent material means an unsolicited request for indecent photographs *of children* (as is the position under s.160(2)(b)) as to do otherwise leaves a person open to prosecution for otherwise lawful behaviour.

## Virtual Child Pornography

The second type of material that needs to be discussed is Virtual Child Pornography (VCP). This will be discussed slightly more briefly due to requirements of space but it is important to note that it represents a major shift in recent years and something that has been brought about by advances in digital technology.

### Defining Virtual Child Pornography

The first issue to consider is the definition of VCP. Some writers will use the term 'pseudo-photograph' interchangeably with VCP and yet this is not strictly true. The legislative changes introduced by the *Coroners and Justice Act 2009* (CJA 2009) have significantly complicated the position, as it means that spread across three statutes (PoCA 1978, CJA 1988 and CJA 2009) are three classes of material:

- Photographs (which we have considered already).
- Pseudo-photographs.
- Prohibited images of children.

The two latter categories are arguably *capable* of being considered VCP although possibly only the latter fully meets the criterion.

The principal distinction that needs to be drawn for our purposes is between computer-*manipulated* images and computer-*generated* images. In essence it is the latter that can properly be considered as VCP.

### Computer-manipulated images

This is a non-statutory term but is useful in helping us to understand what VCP is. Technology allows us to manipulate and alter images. The power of Photoshop, a well-known graphics manipulation program, is renowned. It allows editors not only to 'improve' images but also to create an image that has never existed. A classic example of the former is that of 'air-brushing'. It has become almost standard practice in the fashion and PR industries to alter an image to improve the aesthetic quality of the subject. This may take the form of smoothing out wrinkles or adjusting hair but in extreme cases can be used to alter body styles, something that famously occurred to Kate Winslet, an actress, whose appearance was dramatically altered for a photoshoot (Davies, 2003).

The same technology can also, however, lead to photographs that never actually took place. In 1998 the media gave an insight into how two tabloid newspapers managed to 'recreate' a picture of Diana, Princess of Wales embracing her then-lover (McCann and Watson-Smyth, 1998). The difficulty is the picture never existed, it was a manipulation of other images. Similarly, in 2007 it was reported that a minister, James Purnell MP, had his image digitally inserted into a group photograph because he was late for a photoshoot. The resultant image therefore reflects an untruth. No longer is a picture showing something that has happened. Whilst the minister was present at that location he was not there at the time the photograph was taken. Therefore the 'photograph' does not reflect reality but is instead a fiction.

Can the image of the minister in a group shot be properly called a photograph? Arguably, it does not reflect what a photograph is naturally considered to be – capturing a moment in time – since, as has been noted, that moment never existed. However, can it really be said to be a virtual image? Arguably not, because it does use photographs, it simply involved splicing two photographs together to create a third image. What is the resultant image however? It is a pseudo-photograph because it has the characteristics of a photograph and is derived from a photograph. In the context of child pornography, a pseudo-photograph would include altering an (adult) pornographic image to depict the face of a child (therefore suggesting that this child is engaged in sexual activity) or an image such as in *R v H* [2005] EWCA Crim 3037, which involved the defendant manipulating a photograph to include semen onto the faces of children he had photographed at school, the resultant image suggesting that they had engaged in oral sex.

Pseudo-photographs cannot properly be considered to be VCP because they are derived from a photograph. The definition was extended by the *Criminal Justice and Immigration Act 2008* to include tracings and other images that are derived from photographs (s.69, CJIA 2008). This would include, for example, mobile phone applications that produce an outline line drawing or cartoon-based image of the subject. Both would be derivatives of photographs and therefore if it can be forensically ascertained that the image is derived from a photograph then it would be classed as a pseudo-photograph.

Pseudo-photographs are treated as though they were a photograph and therefore everything that was discussed in the previous section concerning indecent photographs would apply equally to pseudo-photographs.

### Computer-generated images

The more relevant issues for our purposes are those images that are generated or created by a graphics package. In other words the image is not a photograph or a derivative of a photograph. It is this which is arguably the basis of VCP.

The definition of a pseudo-photograph included an image that 'appeared to be a photograph' (s.7(7), PoCA 1978) and this means that pseudo-photographs could actually be wider than mere manipulations. If the image is of such good quality that a person would need to look carefully to decide whether it is a photograph or not then it is quite possible/likely that this would meet the definition of pseudo-photograph, notwithstanding the fact that it could represent a completely fictitious image. If it does amount to a pseudo-photograph then it would be treated in the same way as a photograph (discussed above) even though it is clear that the overarching aim of PoCA 1978 and the CJA 1988 is the protection of children. When it is a computer-generated image, however, there is not necessarily a child that is in need of protection.

### Criminalising VCP

It will be remembered that the principal purpose of criminalising photograph-based child pornography was because it caused harm to a child. This was true of even possession, where it was remembered that it could be said that this causes secondary harm to the child and some would argue it exacerbates primary harm.

If there is not a real child then what is the basis of criminalising VCP? The first point to note is the first word of the preceding sentence. *If* there is no child. Some commentators on VCP operate on the basis that VCP never refers to a real child but, of course, that need not be the case. A person can produce a drawing of a real child. It has been done for hundreds of years (the art of portraiture) and technology simply provides new opportunities for doing so. It is submitted that we need to draw a distinction between those situations that involve a real child and those that do not.

The mere fact that an image presents a child does not automatically mean that there is harm because of course it is simply a picture. Therefore, it does not depict the actual sexual assault of a child, and so can it be argued that there is harm? The answer to that must be a qualified 'yes'. A child is likely to be extremely embarrassed, hurt and disgusted if they are portrayed doing a sexual act that they have not done, with a person that they would not do it with. Think about how you would feel if someone showed all your friends a picture of you engaging in sex with someone you do not like. You would be outraged. Is outrage, embarrassment and disgust sufficient reason to outlaw such an image? Some would argue 'yes' and perhaps one of the best articulations of this is by Ost who suggests that real harm is caused to children who are depicted in VCP (Ost, 2010:240).

What of those images that do not portray a real child? What justification is there for criminalising these images? The UK government, when introducing laws on VCP, suggested there were three principal justifications put forward:

- It reinforces negative views and feelings towards children.
- It could be used by offenders to groom children.
- It was frequently found alongside 'real' child pornography

(MoJ, 2008:6).

The difficulty is that these reasons are largely unpersuasive. The suggestion that VCP reinforces negative views and feelings was considered in the previous chapter in respect of adult pornography. Whilst obviously the argument is stronger in the context of children (who should not be viewed as a sexual object) it does not alter the underlying principle that it is not convincing as it relies on moralistic/paternalistic principles.

The suggestion that VCP could be used to groom children would seem, at first sight, to be convincing. It is known that some offenders do use material to convince children to acquiesce to sexual acts as VCP could normalise such activity (Taylor and Quayle, 2003:23; Gillespie, 2011:108). For this reason it could be said that criminalising such material could be justified; however, in *Ashcroft v Free Speech Coalition* 122 S.Ct. 1389 (2002), perhaps the leading judicial analysis of VCP, the US Supreme Court noted that many innocent activities were by themselves capable of being useful to groomers but that this did not justify their criminalisation (at 1402). This is undoubtedly true. Whilst it is possible for VCP to be used to groom children, the answer to this is to criminalise grooming not the mere possession of such material (Gillespie, 2011:109).

The third justification – that VCP is found alongside real child pornography – is the weakest. There is lots of material that can be found alongside child pornography and it does not follow that they should be criminalised. The mere fact that material could be of interest to sex offenders is not sufficient justification to criminalise material. Even underwear catalogues are of interest to child sex offenders (Taylor and Quayle, 2003:27) and yet few would suggest they should be criminalised. It cannot be argued that VCP is indistinguishable from 'real' child pornography because technologically it is possible to differentiate between them and, as has already been noted, if the quality of the image was indistinguishable visually from a photograph then it would, in any event, be considered a pseudo-photograph and thus illegal.

In *Ashcroft* the US government sought to argue that criminalising VCP could be justified as such material could 'whet' the appetite of sex offenders (122 S.Ct. 1389 at 1403). The US Supreme Court had little truck with such arguments noting that there was no causal proof of this. It has already been noted that there is no concrete proof that VCP, or indeed any child pornography, leads to sex offending and therefore this justification must fail too. If causal proof did exist then this would perhaps be the strongest argument for criminalising VCP, but there is no indication that such proof is likely to be found in the immediate future.

The conclusion of many authors is that VCP is, in effect, criminalised on the basis of morality (see, for example, Ost, 2010). Is this problematic? It was seen in the previous chapter that the ECHR adopts the approach that regulating sexually explicit material to safeguard morality can be justified. Whilst many theorists would doubt the appropriateness of banning material on the basis of morality, it does not seem that such an approach is likely to be adopted by the ECtHR, at least presently. The position in Canada is very different. The Canadian constitution has very similar provisions relating to private life and freedom of expression (Articles 2(b) and 7 of the *Canadian Charter of Right and Freedoms*). In *R v Sharpe* 2001 SCC 2 these were discussed in the context of non-photograph-based forms of child pornography of a non-identifiable child.

Sharpe was accused of possessing material that constituted child pornography although this was in the form of stories. Under Canadian law the definition of child pornography is wider and even covers text (s.163.1 of the Criminal Code and see Gillespie, 2011:77). Any justification for criminalising text-based child pornography must be the same as for VCP since, in essence, it could similarly depict something that is fictitious. The Supreme Court ruled that two exclusions be read into the criminal law, one of which is directly relevant here. The Court held that 'self-created works of the imagination, written or visual, intended solely for private use of the creator' should be exempted because there was no convincing justification and it was, in essence, criminalising thought (2001 SCC 2 at [108]).

There is, however, no indication that *Sharpe* will be followed by the ECtHR and indeed to do so would involve a departure from existing jurisprudence. Therefore, at least initially, it would seem that a challenge to criminalising VCP under the ECHR and/or HRA 1998 would not succeed.

## Coroners and Justice Act 2009

The government moved to criminalise VCP under the *Coroners and Justice Act 2009* (CJA 2009). This introduced the concept of 'prohibited image of a child' and is an offence of simple possession. As will be seen the threshold for this offence is obscenity (rather than the lower standard of indecency required for photograph-based child pornography) and therefore distribution of the material should (theoretically) be prosecuted under the OPA 1959. However, the reality is that, as with extreme pornography, it is likely to prove simpler to prosecute for the offence of possession.

### Defining a prohibited image of a child

The first issue is what amounts to a prohibited image of a child? As with extreme pornography the exact definition is somewhat complicated. Section 62(2) states that a prohibited image is an image that is:

(a) pornographic,
(b) falls within subsection (6), and
(c) is grossly offensive, disgusting or otherwise of an obscene character.

Importantly, the image may not be a photograph or pseudo-photograph (s.65(3)), and the obvious intent of this is to ensure that images that constitute photograph-based child pornography are not brought under this provision because the maximum sentence is significantly shorter (three years' imprisonment instead of the five for possession of an indecent photograph or ten for making, taking, etc.).

'Image' is defined widely to include any moving or still image and also includes data capable of conversion into such an image (s.65(2)). It then caters for the impossible. As has been noted, VCP includes non-real persons and the Act states that reference to 'a person include references to an image of an imaginary person' and this includes a child (s.65(7), (8)). More than this, a person can be considered a child even if 'some of the physical characteristics shown are not those of a child' (s.65(6)). This is where it can be strange. There is a whole genre of material available on the internet that shows fairies or pixies in child-like ways but drawn in a sexualised way or engaging in sexual conduct. Is that a criminal offence? Have we reached the point where we now criminalise the sexual depiction of fairies or pixies? A literal reading of s.65 would mean the answer is 'yes'.

There is obviously a requirement that the prohibited image be of a child and this is defined as someone under the age of 18 (s.65(5)), but this is subject to the point noted above and the fact that an image is to be treated as an image of a child if 'the impression conveyed by the image is that the person shown is a child' (s.65(6)). Not only does this therefore raise the 'pixie-porn' question noted above, it raises questions in terms of anime, etc. Pokemon is a popular example of the Japanese art form Manga. Some forms of Manga can be sexually explicit (known as Hentai). However, it is difficult to 'age' the characters. Whilst they are obviously portraying humans, their facial and body features are usually drawn in a way that is not really representative of human biology. To that extent how does one decide whether the image is 'of a child'? Presumably it is a question of fact and therefore ultimately for the jury or magistrates to decide but will expert evidence be admissible? Whilst this is not permissible for photograph-based images, it is submitted that expert evidence may well be required for these types of images.

It will be remembered that the image must be 'pornographic' and 'grossly offensive, disgusting or otherwise of an obscene character'. These terms are defined in the same way as they are for extreme pornography (as considered in Chapter 9) and the criticisms and critique mentioned previously apply equally here. One of the purported reasons for introducing this offence was to try to deal with Hentai material but it is submitted that this may not happen.

As 'pornographic' requires the *primary* purpose to be sexual gratification, a loophole is potentially created. It can be argued that the primary purpose of Hentai is entertainment rather than sexual gratification and that many forms are representing violence rather than sex. If this was shown (and, once again, it is submitted that it is inevitable that expert evidence must be required for this) then the threshold would not be met and the defendant would be acquitted.

Not only must the image be pornographic and meet the obscenity test but it must meet the requirements of s.62(6) which states that it must either 'focus solely or principally on a child's genitals or anal region' (s.62(6(a)) or depict an activity contained in s.62(7). Reference to 'anal region' instead of 'anus' is peculiar language. Is the bottom of a child within the anal region of a child? The risk that s.62(6) could be too expansive is perhaps militated slightly by the fact that the image must be grossly offensive, disgusting or obscene. Therefore, the mere depiction of a bare bottom would not suffice.

The acts contained within s.62(7) are:

(a)  the performance by a person of an act of intercourse or oral sex with or in the presence of a child;
(b)  an act of masturbation by, or involving or in the presence of a child;
(c)  an act which involves the penetration of the vagina or anus of a child with a part of a person's body or with anything else;
(d)  an act of penetration, in the presence of a child, of the vagina or anus of a person with a part of a person's body or with anything else;
(e)  the performance by a child of an act of intercourse with an animal (whether dead, alive or imaginary);
(f)  the performance by a person of an act of intercourse or oral sex with an animal (whether dead, alive or imaginary) in the presence of a child.

It must be remembered that where 'child' or 'person' is said this *de facto* means a non-existent child. Given that acts undertaken in the 'presence' of this non-existent child become culpable it does demonstrate that the justification for this offence can only be one of morality and not harm. The position is even worse thanks to (e) and (f) where *imaginary* creatures are within the scope of this offence. Coupled with the 'pixie-porn' debate above this creates a position far-removed from harm:

> D is charged with the possession of an image that shows a fairy-like creature that has some of the features of a child (notwithstanding the fact that, for example, it has wings, etc.) watching as a man has sexual intercourse with a dragon.

Such an image would seem to meet the criteria required of the CJA 2009 and yet it is difficult to see what harm this can possibly involve.

## Certified images

As with extreme pornography, those images that have been certified by the British Board of Film Classification are excluded from the definition (although subject to the same slightly unusual wording as regards extracting images out of context). Everything that was said in Chapter 9 on this applies equally here.

## Possession

The offence is one of simple possession and the term 'possess' must be constructed in the same way as s.160, CJA 1988. Indeed, it is clear that the offences of possessing extreme pornography and prohibited images of children were both modelled on s.160 and therefore the same definition must be used. However, this does raise a problem in respect of deleted images. It will be remembered that in *R v Porter* [2006] 1 WLR 2633 it was held that where a person has deleted an image and it is no longer possible to recover that image without the use of specialist software, he cannot be said to still be in possession of it. The 'work-around' for this in the context of photograph-based child pornography is to instead charge the offence of 'making' but there is no equivalent of this under the CJA 2009. Accordingly, the prosecution would need to prove actual possession and/or charge possession immediately before deletion where this could be proven. It also raises issues where a person is not in custody or control of the cache (e.g. where D is viewing the images at a cyber-café). Presumably in those instances there is no possession (as they do not control the computer) and therefore no offence.

## Defences

Three defences are created (s.64) and these are an almost carbon-copy of the defences contained within s.160(2), CJA 1988 and therefore everything that was said in respect of those defences applies equally to this type of material.

## Suggested further reading

Gillespie, A.A. 'Defining child pornography: Challenges for the law' (2010) 22 *Child and Family Law Quarterly* 200–222.
*I make no apologies for selecting my own work as much of my work is on how the law can seek to protect against child sexual exploitation, particularly where it is facilitated by Information and Communication Technologies. This piece demonstrates the fact that international law and a number of the major countries in the world cannot agree how to define child pornography.*

Gillespie, A.A. 'Adolescents, sexting and human rights' (2013) 13 *Human Rights Law Review* 623–643.

*It will be remembered from this chapter that the age of 'a child' was raised from 16 to 18 as a result of international pressure. This has consequences for children aged 16 or over who are lawfully allowed to engage in sexual activity but not record themselves doing so. This article considers the implications of this, particularly where so-called 'sexting' is seen as sexual expression. The article is also of interest in respect of 'revenge porn' discussed in Chapter 9.*

Ost, S. 'Criminalising fabricated images of child pornography: A matter of harm or morality?' (2010) 30 *Legal Studies* 230–256.

*This is an excellent piece that critiques the introduction of the so-called 'Virtual Child Pornography' laws. It demonstrates the weakness of some of the stated arguments but puts forward suggestions as to how certain forms of VCP could be criminalised.*

Taylor, M. and Quayle, E. *Child Pornography: An Internet Crime* (2003, Abingdon: Routledge).

*Most of what we know about child pornography comes from this book and the research that accompanied it. Taylor and Quayle were two of the most important scholars in this field (and Quayle continues to be) and this is an excellent, approachable book that details not only how child pornography should be constructed but also how offenders use the material and how it impacts victims.*

# Part 4

# Offences against the person

# Chapter 11

# Offences against the person

The previous three chapters considered the issue of illicit content. This chapter will shift the focus to show how it is possible for offences against the person to take place on the internet. There are a variety of different ways in which harms can occur to people on the internet. With some forms this is where people produce material that is illegal (for example, material that could be considered child pornography) and this could be either through trickery or consent (see Gillespie, 2013c). However, it is also possible to consider other ways that harm can be caused to those who use the internet and in this chapter two forms will be considered. The first relates to cyberstalking and the second relates to sexual actions.

As with all the other chapters this will simply introduce the concepts and debates because an entire book could be produced in respect of both of these topics. However, it will help us draw a comparison to illicit content.

## Cyber-harassment

The first issue to consider is 'cyber-harassment'. This a term that can cover a variety of different forms of behaviour although they arguably all feature within a wider sub-set. Perhaps the key distinction that exists is between cyber-bullying and cyberstalking. Whilst some believe that these terms can be used interchangeably it will be seen that some literature does differentiate between them. An interesting question is the extent to which the 'cyber' variants differ from their 'offline' or traditional forms. Some authors believe that the cyber-form is simply a variant of existing forms (Yar, 2013:128) whereas others believe that it is a distinct form of behaviour (Bocij *et al.*, 2002:3). It is perhaps notable that the latter belief is perhaps more predominantly found in the earlier literature, and later studies began to show that there were differences although they were perhaps not as profound as some believed, and that the activities could be best described as parallel forms of behaviour (Sheridan and Grant, 2007). Certainly one of the challenges for the law has been to ensure that the 'offline offences' are capable of being used to combat the electronic versions and this has led to some legislative changes.

### Defining cyber-bullying and cyberstalking

The first issue to consider is how cyber-bullying and cyberstalking are defined. It is common to see references to 'cyber-bullying' where the victim is a child or adolescent. 'Cyber-harassment' tends to be used where the victim is an adult, and the term 'cyberstalking' tends to be used in regard to adult victims too. Realistically this is not a good distinction to be drawn. Bullying has existed for centuries and all too often potentially criminal or harmful actions are written off as being 'just playground bullying', and schools over the years have treated such matters as trivial when realistically they should be taken more seriously (Smith *et al.*, 2008). It is a little patronising to adolescents to dismiss something as bullying whereas it is considered harassment for others.

Bullying and harassment are often considered to be different to stalking although there is some crossover between them. However, it is worth, at least initially, considering them separately to identify what, if any, differences there are.

### Bullying and harassment

The first type of behaviour to consider is that of bullying and harassment. This is often considered to be individualised negative behaviour where someone deliberately acts in an aggressive or hostile manner with the intent of intimidating the victim. There are a variety of different types of behaviour that can constitute bullying or harassment but they typically include:

- Flaming (the posting of provocative or abusive posts).
- Malware (the deliberate sending of a virus or other software in an attempt to cause damage to a computer or otherwise; or signing someone up to spam, etc., so that their email system is clogged up).
- Outing (the posting or misuse of personal information).

In many instances the behaviour is not unique and can be combined. These types of behaviour can be committed across all forms of communication, including email, internet sites, text messages and telephone calls.

The first type of behaviour – flaming – is perhaps relatively well-known and so will require little explanation. It is where offensive or provocative statements are routinely made. In the days before social media this not infrequently took place in chatrooms and could involve a person deliberately following their victim from one location to another so that the bullying and harassment never ceased, effectively bullying a person off the internet (O'Connell *et al.*, 2004:14). Social media has changed the mechanisms under which flaming occurs but the behaviour remains. In recent years there have been numerous high-profile incidents of flaming that take place on, for example, Twitter or Facebook. The term 'troll' now appears affixed to such behaviour although that is a departure for a term which has been used on the internet for some time. The term originally meant someone who would deliberately be provocative on, for example, message boards or chatrooms. Frequently they were annoying rather than harmful, simply raising futile or illogical points to provoke exasperation.

The second typical form of bullying concerns the distribution of malware. This will not be discussed in this chapter because any criminal liability for this will be based on the same principles that were discussed in Chapter 3. The motivations for installing malware can be various including trying to damage the computer, scare the user (Clough reports an instance where an offender gained control of a computer to demonstrate his power: Clough, 2010:384) but could also include planting spyware onto the computer so that the perpetrator can monitor the activities of the victim. Where the malware leads to the offender gaining access to the computer of the victim the consequences could be significant where, for example, an online calendar is used (as this would allow the victim's movements to be known) or where emails could be deleted or faked (to isolate the victim from their social circle). There have also been reports that people have accessed the webcam of a user through malware, meaning that the user may not know that they are being recorded, and this could include gaining intimate pictures of the user (Southworth and Tucker, 2007) which could later be released.

The third form of behaviour – outing – can vary dramatically. It can be used as a tool to increase the harm or distress caused by 'traditional' bullying (where, for example, a mobile phone picture is taken of a child being tied up or humiliated and then distributed) or it can be used to distribute sensitive information, including contact details. The material need not solely feature the victim and indeed it can sometimes be more effective when it does not. For example, if a person places an advert showing a sexualised photograph of a woman but then lists the contact details of the victim, then even though the image is not of the victim the results can be significant. People will not know who the victim is and believe that the picture is an open solicitation for sexual contacts (Parsons-Pollard and Moriarty, 2009:437). Other examples have included the posting of the home details of children with the suggestion that they are willing to have sex or the posting of the family telephone number on child sex sites (Bocij et al., 2002).

A form of outing could be the posting of sexualised photographs of former partners in the hope of causing fear, harm or anger. This was discussed in Chapter 9 as it is encapsulated by 'revenge porn'. Whilst some have suggested creating sexual offences to counteract revenge porn, it is perhaps more appropriate to label it as a matter of harassment rather than a sex offence, as the motivation for the posting of the images is not sexual but rather a desire to hurt the victim. Therefore, it is not realistically a sexual offence (which are invariably either objectively or subjectively sexual in character) but a crime of harassment. That is not to downplay the seriousness of the offence, because the consequences of such outing can be extremely serious, with suicides reported following such actions, but rather it is about identifying an appropriate way in which the law can react. By labelling it as a matter of harassment then it becomes easier to criminalise the posting of such material, as it is an action directed at harm or embarrassment and a fault element directed towards those motivations should be easily proven.

Concern has been raised about whether the internet allows for anonymous bullying (Yar, 2013:135) but it does not seem that this is always the case, especially in respect of adolescents where it is not uncommon for the victim to know their abuser (Srivastava and Boey, 2012:305). In terms of victimisation it would also seem that those who are the subject of bullying or harassment in the offline setting are likely to suffer cyber-bullying (Beran and Li, 2006:271), something that is not readily seen for adults or in cyberstalking. This perhaps raises again the question whether, at least for adolescents, cyber-bullying is a different form of abuse or whether it is simply a new form of existing behaviour.

### Cyberstalking

Whilst some aspects of cyberstalking may be similar to cyber-harassment, it can also form an individual behaviour that is categorised in a very similar way to (offline) stalking. Identifying a precise definition is not easy because the term covers a broad range of activities.

Its different types are perhaps encapsulated in the issue of the connection between the perpetrator and victim. It has been said that cyberstalking is 'more likely to remain mediated and at a distance' rather than involve direct face-to-face contact (Yar, 2013:134) although realistically that is perhaps only one form of cyberstalking. As other forms of cyber-harassment exist, including the use of technology to propagate offline stalking, it cannot be said that it is always this simple. Again, however, this is probably just a reflection of the complexity of stalking (including cyberstalking) and reinforces the fact that the difference between stalking and cyberstalking is not easily explained. As with other forms of cybercrime, some crimes will exist only online but others will use technology to facilitate offline behaviour. Cyberstalking is perhaps a classic example of this.

So what are the characteristics of cyberstalking? It has been suggested that it will typically involve the following behaviours:

- Communicating with the victim (including both passive and aggressive forms).
- Publishing information about the victim (similar to 'outing' above).
- Targeting the victim's computer (especially to gain personal data).
- Placing the victim under surveillance, including cyber-surveillance.

(Clough, 2010:375)

Apart from the final factor there would not seem to be much difference between these behaviours and cyber-bullying. MacEwan has suggested that there are five factors, four of which are roughly similar to those set out by Clough. However, MacEwan believes that outing can be broken into two distinct sub-groups: the publication of false information (as discussed above, although outing can include the disclosure of true (albeit embarrassing) information, something that MacEwan neglects) and impersonating the victim (MacEwan, 2012:773). This latter point is important and sometimes missed by other commentators. There may be various reasons why an offender would impersonate a victim, including to post false information (as earlier in the context of outing) or to break down social relationships with others.

As three of the four factors have been discussed already, it is not necessary to discuss them in detail. That said, it is worth noting that the first factor – communication – can include repeated and unwarranted messages, including abusive content (Yar, 2013:133), and so is similar to flaming discussed above. However, the communication need not involve abusive communications and could include communications that were originally innocuous and indeed amorous, with online dating being a fertile breeding ground for cyberstalking (McFarlane and Bocij, 2003).

The factor that has not been discussed so far in this chapter is the one that concerns surveillance. Perhaps the inclusion of surveillance is unsurprising since in the offline form of stalking it is not uncommon for a person to track the movements of the victim and/or follow her (Finch, 2001 remains one of the most comprehensive discussions on stalking). This perhaps reinforces the notion of stalking and cyberstalking being parallel behaviours. It has been suggested that there are broadly two types of cyber-surveillance used, the first is where technology is used to gain information about the victim and those connected to the internet (Clough, 2010:385). The intention here could be partly to show that the perpetrator is familiar with the victim's area (thus an attempt to build up a rapport) or to scare the victim into believing that nowhere is safe because he knows where she will be, including areas that the victim may perceive as 'safe'. The second type of surveillance would be the more traditional meaning of surveillance, i.e. the use of technology (including computers) to monitor the victim's activities. This could include the planting of a 'bug', accessing a mobile telephone or tablet's GPS information or installing tracking software (such as keyloggers). Whilst these may seem extreme examples an early study showed that 7–10 per cent of people had experienced such behaviour (Spitzberg and Hoobler, 2002:83–84), and this behaviour may be more prominent now in light of the further development of tracking technology.

As cyberstalking covers a wide range of activities its victim impact will also be broad. This could range from someone simply being annoyed by what is happening to psychological harm or distress being inflicted on an individual (Parsons-Pollard and Moriarty, 2009:437–438). One study on cyberstalking has noted that whilst traditional stalking may lead to changes in employment, online stalking is more likely to lead to a loss of family or friends (Sheridan and Grant, 2007:636) which the authors suggest is difficult to understand. Certainly the loss of family is perhaps more difficult to explain but the loss of friendship is perhaps not if the cyber-stalking causes someone to limit their use of the internet. A considerable amount of social activity now takes place through social networking sites (e.g. Facebook, Twitter, etc.) and if a person ceases to participate in those activities it may be more difficult to maintain social ties. This reinforces that cyberstalking is far from trivial as, at the very least, it can cause significant disruption to the personal life of an individual.

### Legal solutions to cyber-bullying and cyberstalking

Now that the definitions of cyber-bullying and cyberstalking have (briefly) been discussed it is necessary to consider how the law can react to them. The first point to note is that cyber-bullying and cyberstalking are good examples of behaviours that show that the *Convention on Cybercrime* is ageing, as this type of behaviour does not feature. This is partly because our knowledge of cyberstalking was not fully understood at the time the convention was written. Of course certain forms of cyberstalking (e.g. the sending of malware) will be caught by its provisions but not all forms (including, for example, harassment and surveillance) are covered.

The latest international treaty is the draft cybercrime convention that has been developed by the African Union. Sadly this convention does not consider either cyber-bullying or cyberstalking and this must be considered a missed opportunity. A comprehensive cybercrime convention should seek to cover the main forms of abusive activities that occur, and this should include cyberstalking.

With the omission of cyber-harassment from international law we can move straight on to domestic law. There is no specific offence of cyberstalking (and indeed until recently there was no offence of stalking) and as the behaviours that constitute cyber-bullying and cyberstalking are similar, this section will consider both offences rather than separate out the behaviours. This will also help demonstrate that there are a broad range of offences that could be used to tackle this behaviour, which should allow for flexibility and the ability to cover all its forms.

This section will not consider issues relating to hacking a victim's computer or the distribution of malware as these have been discussed elsewhere in the book (Chapter 3) and reference should be made to that chapter in respect of these types of behaviour.

### Offensive comments

The first type of offence to consider is that which relates to offensive comments. There are two offences here that need to be considered; s.127, *Communications*

*Act 2003* (CA 2003) and s.1, *Malicious Communications Act 1988* (MCA 1988). They are very similar offences, which does make one wonder why Parliament decided that there was a need for two near-identical offences.

Section 127(1), CA 2003 states:

A person is guilty of an offence if he

(a) sends by means of a public electronic communications network a message or other matter that is grossly offensive or of an indecent, obscene or menacing character; or

(b) causes any such message or matter to be so sent.

Section 1(1), MCA 1988 states:

Any person who sends to another person

(a) a[n] … electronic communication … which conveys

(i) a message which is indecent or grossly offensive;
(ii) a threat; or
(iii) information which is false and known or believed to be false by the sender; or

(b) any … electronic communication … which is, in whole or in part, of an indecent or grossly offensive nature,

is guilty of an offence if his purpose, or one of his purposes, in sending it is that it should … cause distress or anxiety to the recipient or to any other person to whom he intends that it or its contents or nature should be communicated.

It can be seen therefore that the offences are very similar in nature, although there is an express *mens rea* in respect of s.1, MCA 1988 whereas there is no express *mens rea* on the face of s.127(1). In *DPP v Collins* [2006] 1 WLR 2223 Lord Bingham accepted the proposition that the *mens rea* is, at least in respect of grossly offensive messages, that the person must either intend the messages to be grossly offensive or is aware that they are (at 2228), and the same would seem to be true of the other forms of the offence (see *DPP v Chambers* [2013] 1 WLR 1833 at 1844).

In *Collins* Lord Bingham also set out the difference between the two pieces of legislation, suggesting that the difference lies in their mischief. The purpose of the MCA 1988 is to 'protect people against unsolicited messages which they may find seriously objectionable' whereas the purpose of the 2003 Act is 'to prohibit the use of a service provided and funded by the public for the benefit of the public … which contravenes the basic standards of our society' (at 2227). Whilst this may be true it does not alter the fact that the CA 2003 would seem, on the face of it, to be able to tackle the same mischief. The absence of the intent to cause distress or anxiety must make this offence easier to prove as the *mens rea* requirement for s.127 is simpler.

All four forms of s.127 could be relevant for cyber-harassment. The terms 'indecent' and 'obscene' should be given their ordinary meanings (see *DPP v Collins* [2006] 1 WLR 308, DC, which was reversed by the House of Lords but not on that point) and these terms were considered in earlier chapters. As it was noted that some offenders will seek to disseminate sexualised images of their victims, it is quite possible that they will be relevant.

'Grossly offensive' is a question of fact that must be decided according to contemporary standards and the 'words must be judged taking account of their context and all relevant circumstances' (*DPP v Collins* [2006] 1 WLR 2223 at 2228). The fact that context can be taken into account is important because it could mean that some words or phrases that perhaps have a double meaning can be examined with the purpose of the sender in mind. That said, it must be noted the test is one of *gross* offensiveness not simple offensiveness. Gross means 'very serious' and thus it shows there is a threshold before this offence is triggered.

The meaning of 'menacing' is slightly more complicated. The Divisional Court in *Collins* had stated that 'menacing' meant 'a message which conveys a threat – in other words, which seeks to create a fear in or through the recipient that something unpleasant is going to happen' ([2006] 1 WLR 308 at 311), which would accord with the dictionary definition of the term. However, in *Chambers* a different constitution of the Divisional Court decided that this was too simple and held that the threat must be credible and that it must cause the recipient, or someone likely to be the recipient, fear or apprehension ([2013] 1 WLR 1833 at 1842). Whilst it is easy to see why the court so ruled – especially in the context of the particular circumstances of that case, which was a case that should never have been prosecuted in the first place – this would seem to blur the distinction between the CA 2003 and the MCA 1988 and indeed it could cause an unusual position.

> D sends a threatening message to V hoping that it will cause her distress or anxiety. In fact V thinks the message is preposterous and just dismisses it out of hand.

Under the ruling in *Chambers* there can be no liability because V is not menaced by it even though the House of Lords in *Collins* had expressly noted that there was no requirement for a message to even be received, and that the offence was complete at the time the message was sent ([2013] 1 WLR 1833 at 2227). This would seem to contradict the ruling in *Chambers* that the effect of the message is relevant to its *actus reus*. However, D would be liable under s.1, MCA 1988 as it was his *intent* to cause distress or anxiety. This perhaps demonstrates once again the belief that the overlap between the MCA 1988 and CA 2003 is obscure.

The existence of the MCA 1988 and CA 2003 offences has proven to be extremely controversial because it is thought that they can interfere significantly with human rights (an important consideration of these principles is given by Rowbottom, 2012). The Crown Prosecution Service (CPS) introduced guidelines to ensure that these offences were not used in a way that could breach Article 10 (www.cps.gov.uk/legal/a_to_c/communications_sent_via_social_media/). That said, in the context of cyber-harassment the human rights values are arguably more nuanced. It will be remembered that Article 10(2) permits interference 'for the protection of the reputation or rights of others', and Article 17 will be relevant which would prohibit a person from relying upon Article 10 to attack the rights and freedoms of another (also discussed in Chapter 8). Indeed the ECtHR has held that Article 8 includes the right to physical and mental integrity (*X and Y v Netherlands* (1986) 8 EHRR 235) and therefore the balance of human rights arguments should be in favour of the victim rather than the perpetrator. This is reflected by the CPS in its guidance but it is an important point to note.

Sections 1 and 127 are wide enough given those terms themselves but other provisions within the legislation make them even wider. Section 1(a)(iii), MCA 1988 refers to false information and this is replicated in the CA 2003 by s.127(2):

> A person is guilty of an offence if, for the purpose of causing annoyance, inconvenience or needless anxiety to another, he
>
> (a) sends by means of a public electronic communications network, a message that he knows to be false;
> (b) causes such a message to be sent; or
> (c) persistently makes use of a public electronic communications network.

Sections 1(a)(iii) and 127(2) would, on the face of it, be potentially very useful offences in the context of both cyber-bullying and cyberstalking because, as was seen, a common behaviour is the posting of false information. However, can it be justified to criminalise mere false information? At least s.1(a)(iii) requires the ulterior intent of causing distress or anxiety which would make it more justifiable, whereas s.127(2) does not and probably only requires the message to be sent intentionally with D knowing that the content was false or was likely to be false.

It would seem odd that the mere sending of intentional false information should by itself be criminal as this would normally be dealt with under the tort of defamation. Where there is an intent to cause distress or anxiety then it becomes analogous to an offence against the person (with psychological harm being recognised in *R v Ireland* [1998] AC 147), but without that intent it would seem disproportionate to criminalise false information by itself. The alternative way of dealing with false information would be to consider it as a part of a course of conduct for harassment (discussed below) and this would perhaps be more justifiable.

### Harassment

The second offence to consider is that of harassment. The *Protection from Harassment Act 1997* (PfHA 1997) was introduced as a result of a number of stalking and harassment cases and at least one of its purposes was to tackle stalking (see *Thomas v News Group Newspapers* [2001] EWCA Civ 1223 and *R v C* [2001] EWCA Crim 1251). Interestingly the PfHA 1997 was amended by the *Protection of Freedoms Act 2012* to introduce a new specific offence of stalking (discussed extensively by MacEwan, 2012) and this is discussed below. The stalking offence is a constructive form of harassment and therefore it is first necessary to consider the PfHA 1997.

The PfHA 1997 is unusual in that it creates a definition of harassment (s.1) which can either be a crime (ss. 2 and 4) or a tort (s.3). The definition of harassment is:

A person must not pursue a course of conduct

(a) which amounts to harassment of another, and
(b) which he knows or ought to know amounts to harassment of the other.

(s.1(1), PfHA 1997)

A second definition applies where there are two or more victims (s.1(1A)) but this is not particularly relevant to our purposes. What does 'harassment' mean though? It is said to *include* causing alarm or distress to a person (s.7(2)) although the fact that it is an inclusive definition would mean that it can be wider than this. A person 'ought to know' that it amounts to harassment if a reasonable person with the same information would think the course of conduct amounted to harassment (s.1(2)).

One of the key terms is 'course of conduct' and this is defined as 'conduct on at least two occasions in relation to that person' (s.7(3)(a)), although this includes the actions of another where it was aided, abetted, counselled or procured with appropriate knowledge (s.7(3A)). Thus before the PfHA 1997 can be triggered there must be conduct on two or more occasions, but it has been held that this is not simply a question of maths as there must be a proximate link between the events and therefore the fewer there are and the further apart they are, the less likely it will be considered a *course* of conduct (*DPP v Lau* [2000] 1 FLR 799; *DPP v Ramsdale* [2001] EWHC Admin 106).

The requirement that there be separate acts can cause difficulties in the context of online communications. In *Kelly v DPP* [2002] EWHC Admin 1428 (Divisional Court) the defendant had sent three abusive telephone messages to the victim. However, they had not been picked up and were thus recorded on voicemail. All three messages were listened to at the same time and the defendant sought to argue that this should only amount to a single act as they were all listened to at the same time but this was rejected, in part, because they were sent separately. However, the decision is somewhat dubious because the three messages were sent within five minutes of each other and so it must be really questioned whether they were truly separate or part of one transaction. The Divisional Court expressly stated that emails could be considered separate communications (at [23]) but given contemporary internet sites it is possible to have email conversations almost as quickly as instant-messenger services (although there is no guarantee with email that there will not be delay). Consider the following situation:

> D sends an abusive email to V.
> V responds to say 'stop'.
> D replies no and adds other abusive comments.
> V again asks for D to stop or that she will report D to the police.
> D replies he doesn't care and sends another abusive email.

Assuming that the replies were sent immediately the emails were received, can it truly be said that D undertook three acts or is it more likely that it constitutes a single act? What would the position be in respect of instant-messenger services? In the context of obscenity the Court of Appeal has held that each message can amount to a distinct 'article' (*R v Smith* [2012] 1 WLR 3368) although that decision has been questioned (Gillespie, 2014b) but surely it could not be suggested that each message is 'conduct'? Surely the conversation must amount to a single instance of conduct?

The reality is that in many instances it will not be problematic to find two communications. However, it will be remembered that whilst the definition of harassment is given in s.1 this forms the basis of either a tort or a crime. The criminal offences are contained in ss.2 and 4, PfHA 1997. Section 2 is the simpler offence and criminalises a person who pursues a course of conduct that amounts to harassment. No further *mens rea* is required because it has been seen that the course of conduct contains a fault element in any event. The offence is triable only summarily and punishable by a maximum sentence of six months' imprisonment.

The more serious offence is contained in s.4:

> A person whose course of conduct causes another to fear, on at least two occasions, that violence will be used against him is guilty of an offence if he knows or ought to know, that his course of conduct will cause the other so to fear on each of those occasions.
>
> (s.4(1))

The question of whether a person ought to know it would put the victim in fear is to be decided by the reasonable man in the same way as with s.1 (s.4(2), PfHA 1997). Note the person must be placed in fear on at least two occasions. This does not mean on each occasion in the course of conduct (so, for example, if there were ten acts in the course of conduct but three caused V to fear harm then this would suffice) but even with this it remains a significant threshold.

Perhaps unusually the fear of violence must be against the person and not someone close to him (including a spouse or child) which may seem odd as threats against another can be effective (Finch, 2001:263).

A potential difficulty with s.4 is that whilst nothing in the Act requires the person to fear immediate violence (cf. the position in respect of assault) it has been held that the violence *will* happen and not that it *might* happen (see *R v Ireland; R v Burstow* [1998] AC 147 at 153 per Lord Steyn). This is certainly a more difficult proposition, particularly in respect of cyber-stalking where the perpetrator may be anonymous or located some distance away.

### Stalking

Whilst it has been seen that the PfHA 1997 appears to cope relatively well with harassment, including stalking, the government in the *Protection of Freedoms Act 2012* introduced two new offences into the PfHA 1997 (s.2A and s.4A) which are both expressly designed to tackle stalking. It is not uncommon for politicians to announce the creation of a new offence even though existing offences can tackle the behaviour, partly because politically it can look as though the government is doing something to tackle a perceived inadequacy of the law. Even taking this into account, however, the new offences of s.2A and s.4A are unusual.

The new stalking offences are constructive offences in that they remain expressly based on the existing definition of harassment but that it must also involve 'stalking' (see, for example, s.2A(1), PfHA 1997). 'Stalking' is defined in s.2A(2) as where:

(a) it amounts to harassment of that person,
(b) the acts or omissions involved are ones associated with stalking, and
(c) the person whose course of conduct it is knows or ought to know that the course of conduct amounts to harassment of the other person.

This is a strikingly odd provision since apart from paragraph (b) these are just the same terms as required by s.1. As noted already, one of the principal purposes of the original PfHA 1997 was to tackle stalking, so what does paragraph (b) add? Section 2A(3) provides a list of acts or omissions that are associated with stalking:

(a) following a person,
(b) contacting or attempting to contact, a person by any means,
(c) publishing any statement or other material

(i)  relating to or purporting to relate to a person, or

(ii)  purporting to originate from a person,

(d)  monitoring the use by a person of the internet, email or any other form of electronic communication,

(e)  loitering in any place (whether public or private),

(f)  interfering with any property in the possession of a person,

(g)  watching or spying on a person.

Each of these is undoubtedly capable of being a characteristic of stalking but they were equally capable of being caught under the original wording of the PfHA 1997. Where does that leave us? MacEwan has argued that the new offences will be used instead of the original offences when seeking to prosecute someone for cyberstalking (MacEwan, 2012:774) but it is far from clear that this will be the case. Given that the maximum sentence for the basic offence (s.2A) is the same as for the s.2 offence and there is a requirement to prove an additional element for s.2A (the stalking element) it must be questioned why the CPS would use this offence. Surely it would be easier to simply rely on the base offence (which is required by s.2A(1)(a) and (c)) rather than risk a case by proving additional elements? It perhaps shows the fallacy of introducing new offences without repealing the earlier ones.

Will the offences cover cyberstalking? MacEwan believes that there could be loopholes. He believes that the requirement that there be two actions or omissions is problematic and that it should be reduced to one (MacEwan, 2012:780). He bases this argument on the belief that there must be victim impact in respect of *both* acts (or more where two would not suffice). The logic is based on the notion of covert activity and the belief that if a person is acting covertly then the victim cannot be harassed (i.e. caused alarm or distress), and D cannot have the required fault element because he cannot know, or ought to know, that V will be harassed because he thinks she will never know. However, it is far from clear that this logic holds. In respect of the first point – victim impact – there is no requirement that V has to find out at the time the surveillance is carried out and it suffices if they find out when, for example, the police tell them (see *Kellett v DPP* [2001] EWHC Admin 107). MacEwan believes there may be a coincidence point there, but it is not clear that there would since it is unlikely that it can be said that the stalking has stopped merely because the police have intervened. In any event, there is only a requirement that at least one act causes alarm or distress and it is unlikely that the police would discover the covert surveillance unless other actions led the victim to believe that she was being stalked (and there is no requirement that V need to know *who* is stalking her).

Whilst wholly covert surveillance without any further action may not theoretically come within the offence of stalking, it is not clear that it has ever been the intention of Parliament to criminalise covert surveillance (and indeed Parliament expressly refused to do so when passing the *Regulation of Investigatory Powers Act 2000*). The reality is that cyberstalking does not involve the mere passive watching of a person without ever letting them know that they are being watched, it involves a multitude of behaviours as noted above. It is more likely that the covert surveillance would be accompanied by communications (either to the victim or in the name of the victim), gifts, malware or other activities. If the victim was aware of any of those then the offence would be satisfied. Also, once surveillance is detected (and there are a variety of ways that it can be detected even if the person conducting the surveillance is not himself detected) then it has been held that this suffices even if previous instances were undetected (see *Howlett v Holding* [2006] EWHC 41 (QB)).

It is submitted therefore that the PfHA 1997 both in its original guise and with the inclusion of the new stalking offences is likely to be capable of tackling the type of cyberstalking behaviour discussed earlier in this chapter.

## Sexual solicitation of a child

The second form of behaviour to consider relates to the sexual solicitation of a child. The internet provides new opportunities for sex crimes to occur, both facilitating contact offences (where, for example, a person is raped after meeting a person following an online introduction) and crimes that take place almost exclusively online. A good example of the latter is *R v Devonald* [2008] EWCA Crim 527 where a father of a teenage girl tricked the former boyfriend of his daughter into masturbating in front of a webcam so as to embarrass him. There was no physical contact and therefore it is more properly considered to be a cybercrime.

One of the features that has caught the public's attention in recent years is the use of the internet to facilitate the sexual abuse of children. Whilst there are numerous examples of how this occurs, this chapter will consider one form of sexual abuse, that known as the grooming or solicitation of children.

At the beginning of the new millennium there was concern about the 'grooming' of children online (see, for example, Gillespie, 2001; Quayle and Taylor, 2001). The notion of grooming at that time was befriending a child online with the intention of later abusing them. The term 'grooming' is not one that is necessarily universally supported (Craven *et al.*, 2006) but since that time we now understand the term much better and recognise that it covers a much broader range of behaviours (see, for example, McAlinden, 2012). The type of behaviour identified above is perhaps now better known as online solicitation although the term grooming remains used (in part due to the wording of the statute).

### Summarising the behaviour

Grooming or solicitation covers a broad range of behaviours and therefore identifying a definition can be difficult. However, we are looking at a particular form of grooming – online solicitation – and the author has previously argued that this can be defined accordingly:

> The process by which a child is befriended by a would-be abuser in an attempt to gain the child's confidence and trust, enabling them to get the child to acquiesce to abusive activity. It is frequently a pre-requisite for an abuser to gain access to a child.
>
> (Gillespie, 2002:411)

This simple definition won support from other academics (Craven *et al.*, 2006:288) partly because it sought to define a particular pattern of behaviour. It was recognised even before the internet that this form of grooming is cyclical in nature (Howitt, 1995:92) and it was quickly realised that online behaviour adopted the same approach. Academics started to identify a so-called 'cycle of abuse' or 'grooming cycle' that explained the stages through which the offenders travel (see, for example, Terry and Tallon, 2004). The definition above hints at this and notes that it is a *process* of conditioning and therefore there are many different ways that this pattern can be followed.

The 'typical' form of behaviour depicted was the situation whereby a man (as the defendant was invariably male) would seek to persuade a teenage girl (as the victims were invariably female) to fall in love with him. Once love was established the next natural step would be sexual contact, not least because teenagers are going through puberty and are more conscious and intrigued about sex, including its interrelationship with love. Different cyclical models were developed but nearly all begin with the perpetrator suffering from regression and lack of self-worth (Terry and Tallon, 2004:21). The solution to this would often be fantasy, including fantasising about sex with children (which often could be the reason for the regression in the first place).

The internet brought about new opportunities for offenders to meet children. One offender noted that, 'you can't go up to [a child] in the street and say ... do you fancy having sex ... whereas you could online' (Quayle and Taylor, 2001:602). The internet thus provided an available means by which children could be contacted through chatrooms, social networking sites, etc. In the early days concern was raised about offenders lying about their age (and pretending to be adolescents) but it was gradually realised that whilst a number of perpetrators did this a number did not and would be open about their age. This mattered little in some instances because teenagers were often in their rebellious phase or wished to be treated like an adult and here was an adult who, unlike their parents, 'got it'.

The internet allowed for a rapport phase to begin. This is where the user would spend considerable time talking to the victim and would begin to gain her trust. They would talk about lots of things, generally (but not always) innocuous. It is relatively easy to come across as good natured and friendly on the internet, especially when it is text-only and there is the ability to be anonymous. Communication technologies allow people to feel disinhibited (both perpetrator and victim). Indeed, a victim can feel safe because although they are talking in ways they would not do in public, nobody can see their reaction and they can feel safe. They are in a house, with their parents downstairs, so they are safe, and thus free to go further than they may do ordinarily.

After a while the communication will progress into the exclusivity stage where the victim will spend increasing amounts of time speaking *only* to the perpetrator. This will increase the sense of kinship and friendship and will mark the beginning of the 'wooing' phase. Whilst the conversation may already be sexual in places (because teenage chatrooms frequently discuss sex in the same way that conversations about school are common), if it is not the conversation may start to turn sexual now. Initially this will be to talk about whether the victim has ever been kissed, touched, touches herself, etc. (O'Connell, 2003:9). Small steps will be taken to ensure that she is not scared off. Gifts may also be given at this stage.

By the end of this stage the child will begin to think of herself as in a relationship with the perpetrator and the conversation will be increasingly sexual, discussing what a relationship would be like, and could also include engaging in cybersex (Quayle and Taylor, 2001:601–603). This marks the final stage where the child is ready to acquiesce to sexual contact.

It should be stressed that this is *one* form of grooming/solicitation and whilst most attention was spent on this form in 2000–2005 our understanding of this behaviour is now significantly improved. Alongside internet grooming sits institutional grooming (McAlinden, 2012) and group localised grooming, which has involved gangs of people exploiting vulnerable young females (Mooney and Ost, 2013). It is also known that sometimes the befriending is not of the child but of the parent to gain access to the child (a contemporary example of this can be seen in *R v Day* [2013] EWCA Crim 1648). However, this type of online solicitation continues to exist and therefore it is worth considering how the law has sought to tackle it.

### Legal solutions: international law

The issue of online solicitation is perhaps another good example of a behaviour that shows the age of the Cybercrime Convention. At the time the convention was drafted the concept of online solicitation was not really understood and so it was not included even though offences relating to child pornography were. However, the *Council of Europe Convention on the Protection of Children against Sexual Exploitation and Sexual Abuse* (the 'Lanzarote Convention') is a more modern instrument and also one that is designed specifically to tackle child sexual exploitation, and it expressly covers the issue of child sexual exploitation.

Article 23 of the Convention states:

> Each party shall take the necessary legislative or other measures to crimi-
> nalise the intentional proposal, through information and communication
> technologies, of an adult to meet a child who has not reached [the age of
> consent] for the purpose of committing [a child sex offence] against him
> or her, where this proposal has been followed by material acts leading to
> such a meeting.

This provision has been obviously influenced by the UK legislation (discussed below) which, for one of its main offences, requires communication
with a child, and the meeting or travelling to meet a child for the purposes of
sexual abuse (see s.15, *Sexual Offences Act 2003*). Article 23 is very similar.
It is notable that it applies only to intentional proposals to a child and there
must be 'material acts' leading to such a meeting so that mere online invita-
tions and discussions will not suffice. The argument here is undoubtedly
because some raised concerns about the probity of criminalising mere solicitations but there is a danger that this requirement could now be overtaken by
technology. Let us take the following example:

> D, aged 41, is talking to V, a 14-year-old girl. D is pretending to be a 17-year-
> old boy. After repeated online contact the conversation turns sexual.
>
> *Scenario A*
> D persuades V to take off her top and bra and to sit in front of the
> webcam so that he can see her topless.
>
> *Scenario B*
> D persuades V to masturbate whilst they are talking and to tell him what
> it feels like and when she climaxes.

In neither situation would the above example come within Article 23. There
is no meeting and so the provisions would not be captured. In both scenarios
do you think that D should be criminally liable?

In scenario A if D records the footage (which is, of course, technically
feasible) then it would constitute the production of child pornography and
therefore it would infringe Article 20, but if he does not then it is quite possible that no offence is committed. In Scenario B it is quite possible that no
offence is committed within the purview of the Lanzarote Convention. Whilst
Article 18 does criminalise 'engaging in sexual activities' it is not clear that this
can be committed online rather than face-to-face. Even if it is, does D engage
in sexual activity with V or does he induce V to engage in sexual activity with
herself? There is sufficient doubt to show that the Lanzarote Convention did
not necessarily consider online-only solicitations. That said, compared to the
Cybercrime Convention the Lanzarote Convention is a major step forward.

### Legal solutions: domestic law

The balance of this chapter will consider domestic law, i.e. the law in England and Wales. The *Sexual Offences Act 2003* (SOA 2003) introduced a major reform of sexual offences in England and Wales and one of the primary purposes behind it was to ensure the law was capable of tackling modern threats (see the *Explanatory Notes to the SOA 2003*).

The primary offence to tackle child solicitation is s.15, SOA 2003. Whilst this is sometimes referred to as the 'grooming offence' it is not accurate to call it this. Indeed, as will be seen, the offence is labelled within the statute as 'meeting a child *following* grooming, etc.' (my emphasis) which reinforces the fact that the grooming has already happened. The SOA 2003 actually creates a patchwork of offences that could be used to tackle such solicitation. In this section a brief outline of the key offences will be given.

### Section 15

As noted already the first offence is that of s.15. This has been through several amendments but the latest version is set out in s.15(1):

A person aged 18 or over (A) commits an offence if:

(a) A has met or communicated with another person (B) on at least two occasions and subsequently

    (i) A intentionally meets B,

    (ii) A travels with the intention of meeting B in any part of the world or arranges to meet B in any part of the world, or

    (iii) B travels with the intention of meeting A in any part of the world,

(b) A intends to do anything to or in respect of B, during or after the meeting mentioned in paragraph (a)(i) to (iii) and in any part of the world, which if done will involve the commission by A of a relevant offence,

(c) B is under 16, and

(d) A does not reasonably believe that B is 16 or over.

It can be immediately seen that this is a good example of the difficulties of defining cybercrime that were considered in Chapter 1. Is this a cybercrime? It is certainly not solely a cybercrime as there must be a physical (rather than virtual) meeting. Nor does it necessarily ever amount to a cybercrime since the *actus reus* elements identified above could be committed wholly offline (through, for example, meetings), but texts devoted to cybercrime will mention this as an example of an offence (Clough, 2010; Yar, 2013) although this could, in part, be because the reality is the vast majority of uses of s.15 have involved technology.

The principal *actus reus* elements of the offence are:

- A either meets or communicates with B on at least two occasions (and this is either/or so it could be one meeting and one communication).
- After those two events:
  - A meets B (so, if this were only done by meetings this would have to be the third meeting),
  - A travels or arranges to meet B in any part of the world,
  - B travels to meet A in any part of the world.
- B is under the age of 16.

The *mens rea* elements are:

- A intends to do something to B which would amount to a criminal offence.
- A either knows that B is not aged 16 or over or does not reasonably believe that B is aged 16 or over.

The *actus reus* elements are relatively straightforward. 'Meeting' and 'communication' are broad terms and are easily defined. The Act is not clear on what constitutes separate communications and therefore it is quite possible that the discussion about whether instant-messenger conversations are separate communications (or SMS messages for that matter) would equally apply here. Some have questioned the need for more than one communication and periodically there is the suggestion that this should be reformed. The *Criminal Justice and Courts Act 2015* has not introduced this change (s.36), although it must be questioned whether this will make any difference as there has not been a single reported instance of someone not being able to be prosecuted for only a single meeting or communication, in part because the grooming process is likely to take longer.

When originally enacted s.15 only criminalised meeting with B or travelling to meet with B. This created two potential loopholes:

- Where A arranged to meet B. So, for example, A asks C to pick up B and drive to location X. At what point could it be said that A was travelling to meet B? Probably when A sets off to location X. However, if C had already picked B up at this point then the child was potentially at risk.
- Where A asked B to travel to him. In that instance A does not travel to meet B and so logically the only time culpability would have arisen is when A and B meet, which again places the child in danger.

The revised wording of s.15 helps tackle this weakness and is to be welcomed.

It is not enough that D meets and communicates with a person under 16 there must be the intention at that meeting to commit a relevant sex offence. This means an offence within Part 1 of the *Sexual Offences Act 2003* which potentially leaves a loophole where the intention is to photograph the child. As noted already, that is an offence under s.1, *Protection of Children Act 1978* (PoCA 1978) ('taking an indecent photograph of a child') and not *prima facie* an offence under the SOA 2003. There are two potential ways of avoiding this possible loophole. The first would be to argue that persuading a child to remove their clothing so as to produce a photograph would be 'sexual activity' and therefore culpable under s.9, SOA 2003 which is within Part 1. The other alternative is to rely on s.48, SOA 2003 which criminalises, *inter alia*, inciting child pornography. Under s.48 inciting B to become involved in pornography (which means, in this context, an indecent photograph of a child – see s.51(1), SOA 2003). The difficulty with this approach is it relies on incitement (which would include asking the child) so if the intention was to gather voyeuristic images without the knowledge of the child then s.48 would not work. It would have been much simpler to list PoCA 1978 as a relevant sexual offence and it is slightly odd that this has never been done when amending s.15 at other times. The one reason for not doing so is that it could be brought under other offences, most notably s.14, SOA 2003 but it would be simpler to use s.15.

When must the intent be formed? It is clear from the wording of the statute that it must be at the time of the relevant meeting. It was held in *R v G* [2010] EWCA Crim 1693 that where the intent was formed *during* that meeting then this would not suffice. Again, this is unlikely to cause too many problems, and indeed did not in *G* because the Court of Appeal accepted that there was considerable evidence to show that the offender in that case had formed the intent when he arrived at the meeting (not least because he brought condoms.

At the time of drafting the offence there was concern that it would not be easy to prove intent (Khan, 2004) but this has proven not to be the case. Whilst the precise number of prosecutions for this offence is not known, a simple search using legal and newspaper indexes demonstrates that it is in the hundreds. The police continue to support its use and believe that it is an effective tool in their armoury to protect children from sexual abuse.

The main drawback with s.15 is that which was identified for Article 23 of the Lanzarote Convention, i.e. that it does not apply to solicitations that take place *only* online. Let us remind ourselves of the two examples:

> D, aged 41, is talking to V, a 14-year-old girl. D is pretending to be a 17-year-old boy. After repeated online contact the conversation turns sexual.

> *Scenario A*
> D persuades V to take off her top and bra and to sit in front of the webcam so that he can see her topless.

> *Scenario B*
> D persuades V to masturbate whilst they are talking and to tell him what it feels like and when she climaxes.

Clearly s.15 cannot apply here as there is no physical meeting, so what other offences could be used?

### Section 10

The second potential offence is s.10, SOA 2003 which tackles 'causing or inciting a child to engage in sexual activity'. The basic offence is set out in s.10(1):

A person aged 18 or over (A) commits an offence if

(a) he intentionally causes or incites another person (B) to engage in an activity,
(b) the activity is sexual, and
(c) either

    (i) B is under 16 and A does not reasonably believe that B is 16 or over, or

    (ii) B is under 13.

The mode of trial for this offence differs depending on the activity. Where it involves the penetration of the vagina or anus (whether of B or by B), the penile penetration of B's mouth or the penetration of another's mouth by B's penis then the offence is triable only in the Crown Court (s.10(2), SOA 2003), otherwise it is triable only summarily.

'Incites' is a common word and simply means to encourage an act. The key issue in this offence is whether there is an activity and whether it is sexual. The term 'sexual' bears a particular definition within the SOA 2003:

[an] activity is sexual if a reasonable person would consider that

(a) whatever its circumstances or any person's purpose in relation to it, it is because of its nature sexual, or
(b) because of its nature it may be sexual and because of its circumstances or the purpose of any person in relation to it (or both) it is sexual (s.78, SOA 2003).

This test is derived from *R v Court* [1989] AC 28 and is very flexible. It can be seen that there are two limbs. Paragraph (a) is a purely objective test, i.e. a reasonable person would look at the activity and decide that it is obviously sexual. Masturbation would be a classic example of this. A reasonable person would not think that this could be anything other than sexual. Paragraph (b) is designed to tackle those situations where behaviour is *capable* of being considered sexual but it is not *obviously* sexual. In those instances a subjective element is introduced which is to consider the circumstances or purpose of the individual. If that is sexual then the activity is sexual. A good example of this would be spanking someone. There may be different reasons for spanking but if D is spanking V because he receives sexual gratification from spanking then it would be considered sexual.

The test under s.78 must be clearly understood. Paragraph (b) does not make the test subjective. Before paragraph (b) can be used it must be objectively considered that the act is *capable* of being sexual. Let us take an example of someone who has a sexual fetish for shoes. D steals the shoes of V and later holds them whilst masturbating. The activity here would be the taking of shoes. However, even though D receives sexual gratification from shoes the act of taking them is not objectively sexual and therefore the taking of the shoes would not be sexual, and therefore inciting a child to give him her shoes would not be an offence contrary to s.10.

For our purposes, however, most activities are likely to come within s.78 and this is certainly true of the two scenarios that were presented above. In respect of scenario A the 'activity' for the purposes of s.10 would be removing her top and posing in front of the webcam. There can be little doubt that this amounts to an 'activity', the ordinary meaning of which simply means performing an action which it obviously is. Applying the s.78 test, it cannot be said that this is anything other than falling within s.78(a) as something that the reasonable person would consider is inherently sexual. Subject to knowledge as to the age of B then the offence under s.10 would be satisfied.

In respect of scenario B it is even easier. There is nothing within s.10 that requires the activity to be on another person or for another person to perform the activity on the victim. It suffices that an activity occurs and that activity is sexual. Inciting a child to masturbate is undoubtedly an action and it must obviously fall within s.78(a) again.

This demonstrates the flexibility of s.10 and also reinforces the fact that s.15 was never intended to be 'the' grooming offence. In the scenarios discussed in this part of the chapter it is highly likely that the child has been groomed in the sense that was discussed above. It would be a fallacy to simply decide that the law should ignore the fact that the sexual activity took place online rather than offline and therefore s.10 is an appropriate response.

## Sections 12 and 14

The final sections to examine briefly are ss.12 and 14 as these arguably help criminalise the grooming process rather than the *result* of the grooming process, something that ss.10 and 15 do. Section 12 criminalises causing a child to watch a sexual act. It has been noted that one strategy in grooming a child is to show them sexually explicit material to 'normalise' sexual activities and encourage children to think that it is appropriate behaviour (Taylor and Quayle, 2003:23). Section 12 was defined to address this behaviour.

Section 12(1) states:

A person aged 18 or over (A) commits an offence if

(a) for the purposes of obtaining sexual gratification, he intentionally causes another person (B) ... to look at an image of any person engaging in activity,
(b) the activity is sexual, and
(c) either—

    (i) B is under 16 and A does not reasonably believe that B is 16 or over, or
    (ii) B is under 13.

Both 'activity' and 'sexual' bear the same meaning as discussed already. In terms of 'image' this includes all forms of visual representations, including holograms and imaginary persons (s.79(5), SOA 2003). Thus this would include showing a child adult, child or virtual child pornography and it is completely irrelevant whether the material is lawful to possess or not so long as it depicts sexual activity. However, note it must depict an activity. Therefore if A sends B images of a topless teenage female then this would not seem to meet the definition within s.12(1). Whilst stripping can be an activity (as for s.10) the still photograph of a topless girl cannot be said to depict an activity (whereas a moving image depicting the girl undressing presumably might as that would be an action, whereas the topless female photograph is depicting the *result* of an action). Less complicated are images that depict sexual conduct between one or more persons since that would be an activity.

It is not enough to show a child an image depicting a sexual activity, the showing must be for the purposes of sexual gratification. The question arises whether it is necessary for the person to gain sexual gratification *at the time* of the showing or later. Whilst the ordinary syntax of the section would imply it should be at the time of the showing (which is when the *actus reus* occurs), the Court of Appeal in *R v Abdullahi* [2007] 1 WLR 225 held that there is no requirement for temporal proximity and that it would suffice if the showing was for later gratification. This is perhaps a surprising decision given the wording of the legislation but it does make it more useful in the context of grooming where the gratification may be later, especially where it is part of the normalisation process.

Section 14 is a very different offence as it is an inchoate offence and if there is an offence that is designed to tackle grooming it is probably this (see *R v Harrison* [2005] EWCA Crim 3458 at [13]). Section 14(1) provides:

A person commits an offence if

(a) he intentionally arranges or facilitates something that he intends to, intents another person to do, or believes that another person will do, in any part of the world, and

(b)  doing so will involve the commission of an offence under any of sections 9 to 13 [of the SOA 2003].

It can be seen that this is both a wider and more restricted offence. It is wider in that it is clearly an inchoate offence that tackles the arranging or facilitating of *anything* that would involve the commission of an offence by someone. It is limited because it makes reference only to ss.9 to 13 of the SOA 2003 but, as was noted above, this may not be overly problematic given that 'sexual activity' within s.9 can be construed widely.

There is an exception to s.14(1) where it is for certain prescribed purposes (see s.14(2),(3)) but these are not particularly relevant to our discussion as the kinds of matters that we are discussing would not fall within this provision. However, it is worth noting that the exceptions are quite controversial in their own right as there are a number of ambiguities contained in the exceptions (Ormerod, 2011:763) and potentially they could be misused by someone seeking to justify their sexualised behaviour.

As the offence is one of arranging or facilitating something for that person to do, or indeed anyone else, it can be a potentially wide offence. There is no need for a physical meeting (in contrast with s.15) and therefore it could involve online encounters. Section 14 can be used where a person is grooming more than one child or is grooming the child to undertake sexual assaults on another:

> D has been speaking to X online for several weeks. Their discussion is sexual and relates to how they both want to have sex with teenage girls. D is aged 40 and X is aged 14. X tells D that he has found a girlfriend (V) and that she has agreed to let him 'touch her'. D supplies a camera to X that is disguised as a book so that he can covertly record the sexual touching and send D the footage.

Here there is no meeting that would involve D but clearly D should be liable. Section 14 is perhaps the easiest offence to prove. D has arranged or facilitated the doing of something, the recording of sexual contact. Will this involve the commission of an offence? Yes. It is an offence under s.1, PoCA 1978 which is not within the remit of s.14 but in order to get the footage, X will sexually touch V which is an offence under s.9 (and therefore s.14). Nothing within s.14 requires that the offence would *only* take place because of the actions of D, it simply requires that an activity is arranged or facilitated which would involve the commission of an offence and this would happen.

Whilst s.14 can be used for grooming situations it can also be used for solicitation, including offline solicitations but which involve the use of technology, and this can be particularly important in respect of 'sting' operations. A good example of this is *R v Glancey* [2011] EWCA Crim 118. The appellant had been arrested for the downloading of indecent photographs of a child but whilst on bail awaiting trial he went online to talk to 'like-minded individuals' who could help him find 'live webcam footage' of young girls engaging in sexual activity. Unbeknown to him he was actually talking to undercover police officers. They discussed the appellant masturbating whilst a child performed in front of him and then ejaculating on the child. Arrangements were made to do this (although, of course, the police never intended to actually do this) and he was subsequently arrested and convicted under s.14.

*Glancey* shows the versatility of s.14 as it allows the police to 'take over' communications and gather sufficient evidence of a person seeking to sexually abuse a child. Of course 'stings' can be controversial (Fulda, 2002) and therefore it is necessary that there must be procedural safeguards to ensure that such operations are conducted appropriately. However, if used properly they can be a useful tool to protect children from abuse.

## Suggested further reading

MacEwan, N. 'The new stalking offences in English law: Will they provide effective protection from cyberstalking?' [2012] *Criminal Law Review* 767–781.
*This article considers the amendments to the Protection from Harassment Act 1997 and, in particular, whether the changes will be useful in combating cyberstalking. It concludes that whilst they will have some impact further improvements are required.*

Gillespie, A.A. 'Cyberstalking and the law: A response to Neil MacEwan' [2013] *Criminal Law Review* 38–45.
*This served as a critique of the points put forward by Neil MacEwan in his article on cyberstalking. You will find it useful to read both articles so that you can see the different arguments put forward on how the law may tackle cyberstalking.*

Ost, S. *Child Pornography and Sexual Grooming: Legal and Societal Responses* (2009, Cambridge: Cambridge University Press).
*This is an excellent book that considers the harm involved in both child pornography and child grooming/solicitation. It also critiques the current law and suggests reforms.*

Craven, S., Brown, S. and Gilchrist, E. 'Sexual grooming of children: Review of literature and theoretical considerations' (2006) 12 *Journal of Sexual Aggression* 287–299.
*This is an excellent article that examined the issue of 'grooming'. It was one of the earlier pieces to note that the term 'grooming' could be problematic and that there is no single grooming behaviour. It draws together a considerable body of literature to suggest ways that the behaviour can be reconsidered.*

# References

Adams, G. 'Apologists for paedophiles' (2013) *Daily Mail*, December 14.

Adler, P.A. and Adler, P. 'Self-injury in cyberspace' (2012) 11 *Contexts* 59–61.

Aleem, A. and Antwi-Boasiako, A. 'Internet auction fraud: The evolving nature of online auctions criminality and the mitigating framework to address the threat' (2011) 39 *International Journal of Law, Crime and Justice* 140–160.

Anderson, R., Barton, C., Böhme, R., Clayton, R., van Eeten, M.J.G., Levi, M., Moore, T. and Savage, S. 'Measuring the cost of cybercrime' in Böhme, R. (ed.) *The Economics of Information Security and Privacy* (2013, Springer) (265–300).

Arias, A.V. 'Life, liberty, and the pursuit of swords and armor: Regulating the theft of virtual goods' (2008) 57 *Emory Law Journal* 1301–1345.

Attwood, F. and Smith, C. 'Extreme concern: Regulating "dangerous pictures" in the United Kingdom' (2010) 37 *Journal of Law and Society* 171–188.

Aust, A. *Handbook of International Law* (2005, Cambridge University Press).

Bailin, A. 'Criminalising free speech?' [2011] *Criminal Law Review* 705–711.

Baker, D.J. 'The moral limits of criminalising remote harms' (2007) 10 *New Criminal Law Review* 370–391.

Bardone-Cone, A.M. and Cass, K.M. 'Investigating the impact of pro-anorexia websites: A pilot study' (2006) 14 *European Eating Disorders Review* 256–262.

Barnett, E. 'Why it just got easier to access your details on Facebook' (2011) *Daily Telegraph*.

Beckford, M. 'New chief coroner is exposed as a paedophile apologist' (2014) *Mail on Sunday*, March 16.

Beran, T. and Li, Q. 'Cyber-harassment: A study of a new method for an old behaviour' (2006) 32 *Journal of Educational Computing Research* 265–277.

Blanchard, R., Lykins, A.D., Wherrrett, D., Kuban, M.E., Cantor, J.M., Blak, T., Dickey, R. and Klassen, P.K. 'Pedophilia, hebephilia and the DSM-V' (2009) 38 *Archives of Sexual Behaviour* 335–350.

Blazak, R. 'White boys to terrorist men: Target recruitment of Nazi skinheads' (2001) 44 *American Behavioral Scientist* 982–1000.

Bocij, P., Griffiths, M. and McFarlane, L. 'Cyberstalking: A new challenge for criminal law' (2002) 122 *The Criminal Lawyer* 3–5.

Boero, N. and Pascoe, C.J. 'Pro-anorexia communities and online interaction: Bringing the pro-Ana body online' (2012) 18 *Body and Society* 27–57.

Boyle, K. 'The pornography debates: Beyond cause and effect' (2000) 23 *Women's Studies International Forum* 187–195.

Brenner, S.W. 'Cybercrime jurisdiction' (2006) 46 *Crime, Law and Social Change* 189–206.

Brenner, S.W. and Koops, B. 'Approaches to cybercrime jurisdiction' (2004) 41 *Journal of High Technology Law* 1–46.

Brigham, J. 'Sex in context: Space, place, and the constitution of images' (2014) 27 *International Journal of Semiotics and the Law* 47–63.

Brody, R.G., Mulig, G. and Kimball, V. 'Phishing, pharming and identity theft' (2007) 11 *Academy of Accounting and Financial Studies Journal* 43–56.

Brotsky, S.R. and Giles, D. 'Inside the "pro Ana" community: A covert online participant observation' (2007) 15 *Eating Disorders* 93–109.

Buchanan, T. and Whitty, M.T. 'The online dating romance scam: Causes and consequences of victimhood' (2014) 20 *Psychology, Crime and Law* 261–283.

Buck, T. *'International Child Law'* (3rd ed., 2014, Routledge).

Caldwell, T. 'Ethical hackers: Putting on the white hat' (2011) 7 *Network Security* 10–13.

Callahan, E.S., Dworkin, T.M. and Lewis, D. 'Australian, UK and US approaches to disclosure in the public interest' (2004) 44 *Virginia Journal of International Law* 879–912.

Calvert, C. and Brown, J. 'Video voyeurism, privacy and the internet: Exposing peeping toms in cyberspace' (2000) 18 *Cardozo Arts and Entertainment Law Journal* 469–568.

Carey, P. 'Data protection: A practical guide to UK and EU law' (2009, Oxford University Press).

Carline, A. 'Criminal justice, extreme pornography and prostitution: Protecting women or promoting morality?' (2011) 14 *Sexualities* 312–333.

Choo, K.R. 'Organised crime groups in cyberspace: A typology' (2008) 11 *Trends in Organised Crime* 270–295.

Clough, J. *Principles of Cybercrime* (2010, Cambridge University Press).

Clough, J. 'Cybercrime' (2011) 37 *Commonwealth Law Bulletin* 671–680.

Cluley, G. 'Sizing up the malware threat – key malware trends for 2010' (2010) 4 *Network Security* 8–10.

Collis, P. 'EU update' (2013) 39 *Computer Law and Security Review* 719–723.

Conway, M. 'Terrorist use of the internet and the challenges of governing cyberspace' in Cavelty, M.D., Mauer, V. and Krishna-Hensel, S.F. *Power and Security in the Information Age* (2007, Ashgate: Aldershot) (95–128).

Conway, M. 'Privacy and security against cyberterrorism' (2011) 54 *Communications of the ACM* 26–28.

Cooper, A. 'From big lies to lone wolf: How social networking incubates and multiplies online hate and terrorism' in Baker, A. (Ed.) *The Changing Forms of Incitement to Terror and Violence: The Need for a New International Response* (2012, Konrad Adenauer Stiftung, Jersusalem) (21–35).

Craig, K.M. 'Examining hate-motivated aggression: A review of the social psychological literature on hate crimes as a distinct form of aggression' (2002) 7 *Aggression and Violent Behaviour* 85–101.

Craven, S., Brown, S. and Gilchrist, E. 'Sexual grooming of children: Review of literature and theoretical considerations' (2006) 12 *Journal of Sexual Aggression* 287–299.

Crawford, B.J. 'Toward a third-wave feminist legal theory: Young women, pornography and the praxis of pleasure' (2007) 14 *Michigan Journal of Gender and Law* 99–168.

Crowe, N. and Watts, M. '"We're just like Gok, but in reverse": Ana girls – empowerment and resistance in digital communities' (2013) *International Journal of Adolescence and Youth* (DOI: 10.1080/02673843.2013.856802).

Davies, H. 'Why there's more to slimline Kate than meets the eye: Lads' mag gives star a digital makeover' (2003) *Daily Telegraph*, January 10.

Deseriis, M. 'Is Anonymous a new form of luddism?' (2013) 117 *Radical History Review* 33–48.

Detica. *The Cost of Cybercrime* (2011, Cabinet Office).

Dias, K. 'The Ana sanctuary: Women's pro-anorexia narratives in cyberspace' (2003) 4 *Journal of International Women's Studies* 31–45.

Dinniss, H.H. *Cyberwarfare and the Laws of War* (2012, Cambridge University Press).

Dinstein, Y. *War, Aggression and Self Defence* (5th ed., 2011, Cambridge University Press).

Dorries, C. *Coroners' Courts: A Guide to Law and Practice* (2014, Oxford University Press).

Doyle, K. and Lacombe, D. *Porn Power: Sex, Violence and the Meaning of Images* (2006, Rutgers University Press).

Dworkin, A. *Pornography: Men Possessing Women* (1981, Penguin Books).

Dworkin, A. and MacKinnon, C. *Pornography and Civil Rights: A New Day for Women's Equality* (1988, Organizing against Pornography).

Dyson, M. 'R v Sheppard: Public order on the internet' [2010] *Archbold Review* 6–9.

Easton, S.M. *The Problem of Pornography: Regulation and the Right to Free Speech* (1994, Routledge).

Easton, S. 'Criminalising the possession of extreme pornography: Sword or shield?' (2011) 75 *Journal of Criminal Law* 391–413.

Ellison, L. and Munro, V.E. 'Reacting to rape: Exploring mock jurors' assessment of complaint credibility' (2009) 49 *British Journal of Criminology* 202–219.

Evans, M. 'Attacks on goths, punks and heavy metal fans to be treated as hate crimes' (2013) *Daily Telegraph*, April 4.

Fafinski, S. 'Access denied: Computer misuse in the era of technological change' (2006a) 70 *Journal of Criminal Law* 424–442.

Fafinski, S. 'Computer misuse: Denial of Service attacks' (2006b) 70 *Journal of Criminal Law* 474–478.

Fafinski, S. 'The security ramifications of the Police and Justice Act 2006' (2007) *Network Security* 8–11.

Fafinski, S. 'Computer misuse: The implications of the Police and Justice Act 2006' (2008) 72 *Journal of Criminal Law* 53–66.

Fairfield, J.A.T. 'Virtual property' (2005) 85 *Boston University Law Review* 1047–1101.

Finch, E. *The Criminalisation of Stalking* (2001, Cavendish).

Flood, M. 'Young men using pornography' in Boyle, K. (ed.) *Everyday Pornography* (2010, Routledge) (165–178).

Fulda, J.S. 'Do internet stings directed at pedophiles capture offenders or create offenses? And allied questions' (2002) 6 *Sexuality and Culture* 73–100.

Furnell, S. 'Hackers, viruses and malicious software' in Jewkes, Y. and Yar, M. *Handbook on Internet Crime* (2010, Willan Publishing).

Furnell, S. and Ward, J. 'Malware an evolving threat' in Kanellis, P., Kiountouzis, E., Kolokotronis, N. and Martakos, D. *Digital Crime and Forensic Science in Cyberspace* (2006, Idea Group).

Furnell, S.M. and Warren, M.J. 'Computer hacking and cyber terrorism: The real threats in the new millennium' (1999) 18 *Computers and Security* 28–34.

Ganor, B. 'Defining terrorism: Is one man's terrorist another man's freedom fighter?' (2002) 3 *Police Practice and Research* 287–304.

Garland, J. and Hodkinson, P. 'F**king freak! What the hell do you think you look like? Experiences of targeted victimisation among goths and developing notions of hate crime' (2014) 54 *British Journal of Criminology* 613–631.

Gerstenfeld, P.B., Grant, D.R. and Chiang, C. 'Hate online: A content analysis of extremist internet sites' (2003) 3 *Analysis of Social Issues and Public Policy* 29–44.

Gibson, M. *Neuromancer* (1984, Ace).

Gillespie, A.A. 'Children, chatrooms and the law' [2001] *Criminal Law Review* 435–446.

Gillespie, A.A. 'Child protection on the internet – challenges for criminal law' (2002) 14 *Child and Family Law Quarterly* 411–426.

Gillespie, A.A. 'Defining child pornography: Challenges for the law' (2010) 22 *Child and Family Law Quarterly* 200–222.

Gillespie, A.A. *Child Pornography: Law and Policy* (2011, Routledge).

Gillespie, A.A. 'Jurisdictional issues concerning online child pornography' (2012) 20 *International Journal of Law and Information Technology* 151–177.

Gillespie, A.A. *The English Legal System* (2013a, Oxford University Press).

Gillespie, A.A. 'Cyberstalking and the law: A response to Neil MacEwan' [2013b] *Criminal Law Review* 38–45

Gillespie, A.A. 'Adolescents, sexting and human rights' [2013c] *Human Rights Law Review* 623–643.

Gillespie, A.A. 'Sexual exploitation' in Buck, T. (ed.) *International Children's Law* (2014a, Routledge) (353–383).

Gillespie, A.A. 'Obscene conversations, the internet and the criminal law' [2014b] *Criminal Law Review* 350–363.

Gillespie, A.A. 'Hate and harm: The law on hate speech' in Savin, A. and Trzaskowski, J. (eds) *Research Handbook on EU Internet Law* (2014c, Edward Elgar).

Glassman, M. and Kang, M.J. 'Intelligence in the internet age: The emergence and evolution of open source intelligence' (2012) 28 *Computers in Human Behaviour* 673–682.

Glickman, H. 'The Nigerian "419" advance fee scam: Prank or peril?' (2005) 39 *Canadian Journal of African Studies* 460–489.

Goodall, K. 'Conceptualising "racism" in criminal law' (2013) 33 *Legal Studies* 215–238.

Gordon, S. (2006) 'Understanding the adversary: Virus Writers and Beyond' *4 IEEE Computer & Security* 67–70.

Gregory, D. 'From a view to a kill: Drones and late modern war' (2011) 28 *Theory, Culture and Society* 188–215.

HAC. *Home Affairs Select Committee: E-crime* (2013, 5th Report of the Home Affairs Select Committee). HC 70.

Hald, S.L.N. and Pederson, J.M. 'An updated taxonomy for characterizing hackers according to their threat properties' (2012, ICAT, ISBN: 978-89-5519-163-9).

Hampson, N.C.N. 'Hacktivism: A new breed of protest in a networked world' (2012) 35 *Boston College International and Comparative Law Review* 511–542.

Hare, I. 'Crosses, crescents and sacred cows: Criminalising incitement to religious hatred' [2006] *Public Law* 521–538.

Hawton, K., Rodham, K., Evans, E. and Weatherall, R. 'Deliberate self-harm in adolescents: Self report survey in schools in England' (2002) 325 *British Medical Journal* 1207–1211.

Hinde, S. 'Cyber-terrorism in context' (2003) 22 *Computers and Society* 188–192.

Hirst, M. *Jurisdiction and the Ambit of the Criminal Law* (2003, Oxford University Press).

Hirst, M. 'Suicide in Switzerland: Complicity in England?' [2009] *Criminal Law Review* 335–339.

Home Office. 'Consultation: On the possession of extreme pornographic material' (2005, HMSO).

Howitt, D. *Paedophiles and Sexual Offences against Children* (1995, John Wiley and Sons).

Hughes, M. 'Blogger who wrote about killing Girls Aloud cleared' (2009) *The Independent*, June 30.

Hunt, A. 'Criminal prohibitions on direct and indirect encouragement of terrorism' [2007] *Criminal Law Review* 441–458.

Hunton, P. 'The growing phenomenon of crime and the internet: A cybercrime execution and analysis model' (2009) 25 *Computer Law and Security Report* 528–535.

IC3. *Internet Report 2012* (www.ic3.gov/media/annualreports.aspx).

Iganski, P. *Hate Crime and the City* (2008, Policy Press).

Iqbal, M. 'Defining cyberterrorism' (2004) 22 *Journal of Computer and Information Law* 397–408.

Itzin, C., Taket, A. and Kelly, L. *The Evidence of Harm to Adults Relating to Exposure to Extreme Pornographic Material: A Rapid Evidence Assessment* (2007, Home Office).

Jewkes, J. and Andrews, C. 'Policing the filth: The problems of investigating online child pornography in England and Wales' (2005) 15 *Policing and Society* 42–62.

Johnson, M.L. (ed.) *Jane Sexes It Up: True Confessions of Feminist Desire* (2002, Four Walls Eight Windows).

Johnson, P. 'Law, morality and disgust: The regulation of "extreme pornography" in England and Wales' (2010) 19 *Social and Legal Studies* 147–163.

Jones, A. 'Cyber terrorism: Fact or fiction' (2005) 6 *Computer Fraud and Security* 4–7.

Jordan, T. 'Mapping hacktivism: Mass virtual direct action, individual virtual direct action and cyber-wars' (2001) 4 *Computer Fraud and Security* 8–11.

Karlof, C., Tygar, J.D., Wagner, D. and Shanker, U. 'Dynamic pharming attacks and locked same-origin policies for web browsers' (2007) Proceedings of the 14th ACM Conference on Computer and Communications Security, 58–71.

Karran, T. *Academic Freedom in Europe: A Preliminary Comparative Analysis* (2007, Higher Education Policy).

Keyser, M. 'The Council of Europe Convention on Cybercrime' (2003) 12 *Journal of Transnational Law and Policy* 287–326.

Khan, A. 'Sexual Offences Act 2003' (2004) 68 *Journal of Criminal Law* 220–226.

Kisiel, R. and Osborne, L. 'They watched me in the bath via my laptop' (2013) *Daily Mail*, June 19.

Klang, M. 'Spyware – the ethics of covert surveillance' (2004) 6 *Ethics and Information Technology* 193–202.

Klimek, L. 'Combating attacks against information systems: EU legislation and its development' (2012) 6 *Masaryk University Journal of Law and Technology* 87–100.

Langer, R. 'Stuxnet: Dissecting a cyberwarfare family' (2011) 9 *IEEE Security and Privacy* 49–51.

Law Commission. *Computer Misuse* (Cm 819) (1989, HMSO).

Law Commission. *Fraud* (Law Comm. 276) (2002, HMSO).

Ledewitz, B. 'Perspectives on the law of the American sit-in' (1995) 16 *Whittier Law Review* 499–574.

Lee, E. and Leets, L. 'Persuasive storytelling by hate groups online' (2002) 45 *American Behavioural Scientist* 927–957.

Lewis, S.P., Heath, N.L., St Denis, J.M. and Noble, R. 'The scope of nonsuicidal self-injury on YouTube' (2011) 127 *Pediatrics* e552–e557.

Li, X. 'Hacktivism and the First Amendment: Drawing the line between cyber protests and crime' (2013) 27 *Harvard Journal of Law and Technology* 302–330.

MacEwan, N. 'The Computer Misuse Act 1990: Lessons from its past and predictions for its future' [2008] *Criminal Law Review* 955–967.

MacEwan, N. 'The new stalking offences in English law: Will they provide effective protection from cyberstalking?' [2012] *Criminal Law Review* 767–781.

MacKinnon, C. *Feminism Unmodified* (1987, Harvard University Press).

MacQueen, H., Waelde, C., Laurie, G. and Brown, A. *Contemporary Intellectual Property: Law and Policy* (2011, Oxford University Press).

McAlinden, A. *Grooming and the Sexual Abuse of Children: Institutional, Internet, and Familial Dimensions* (2012, Oxford University Press).

McCann, P. and Watson-Smyth, K. 'The *Sun* did it. Stalin did it. This is how simple it is to retouch history' (1998) *The Independent*, August 20.

McFarlane, L. and Bocij, P. 'An exploration of predatory behaviour in cyberspace: Towards a typology of cyberstalkers' (2003) 8 *First Monday* (http://dx.doi.org/10.5210/fm.v8i9.1076).

McGhee, J.E. 'Cyber redux: The Schmitt analysis, Tallinn manual and US cyber policy' (2013) 2 *Journal of Law and Cyber Warfare* 64–103.

McGlynn, C. and Rackley, E. 'Criminalising extreme pornography: A lost opportunity' [2009] *Criminal Law Review* 245–260.

McGuire, M. and Dowling, S. *Cybercrime: A Review of the Evidence* (2013, Home Office).

McIntyre, T.J. 'Child abuse images and cleanfeeds: Assessing internet blocking systems' in Brown I. (ed.) (2013, Edward Elgar) (277–308).

McKinstry, L. 'The Left's web of shame' (2014) *Daily Mail*, March 1.

McNamee, L.G. Peterson, B.L. and Peña, J. 'A call to educate, participate, invoke and indict: Understanding the communication of online hate groups' (2010) 77 *Communication Monographs* 257–280.

*Mail on Sunday.* 'Propagandist for paedophile information exchange' (2014) March 9.

Meehan, K.A. 'The continuing conundrum of international internet jurisdiction' (2008) 31 *Boston College International and Comparative Law Review* 345–369.

Mentor, The. 'The hacker's manifesto' (1986) (http://phrack.org/issues/7/3.html).

Minkowitz, D. 'Giving it up: Orgasm, fear and femaleness' in Walker, R. (ed.) *To Be Real* (1995, Bantam Doubleday Dell Publishing Group).

MoJ. 'Consultation on the possession of non-photographic visual depictions of child sexual abuse – Summary of responses and next steps' (2008, HMSO).

Mooney, J. and Ost, S. 'Group localised grooming: What is it and what challenges does it pose for society and law?' (2013) 25 *Child and Family Law Quarterly* 425–450.

Morris, R.G. and Higgins, G.E. 'Neutralizing potential and self-reported digital piracy' (2009) 34 *Criminal Justice Review* 173–195.

Nelson, J.W. 'The virtual property problem: What property rights in virtual resources might look like, how they might work, and why they are a bad idea' (2010) 41 *McGeorge Law Review* 281–309.

Norris, M.L., Boydell, K.M., Pinhas, L. and Katman, D.K. 'Ana and the internet: A review of pro-anorexia websites' (2006) 39 *International Journal of Eating Disorders* 443–447.

O'Connell, R. *A Typology of Child Cybersexploitation and Online Grooming Practices* (2003, UCLAN).

O'Connell, R., Price, J. and Barrow, C. *Cyber Stalking, Abusive Cyber Sex and Online Grooming: A Programme of Education for Teenagers* (2004, UCLAN).

Ormerod, D.C. 'Case comment: Search powers' [2002] *Criminal Law Review* 972–973.

Ormerod, D.C. 'Indecent photograph of a child: Possession of indecent photograph of a child' [2006] *Criminal Law Review* 748–751.

Ormerod, D.C. 'Letter to the Editor' [2007] *Criminal Law Review* 661–664.

Ormerod, D.C. *Smith and Hogan's Criminal Law* (13th ed., 2011: Oxford University Press).

Ost, S. *Child Pornography and Sexual Grooming: Legal and Societal Responses* (2009, Cambridge University Press).

Ost, S. 'Criminalising fabricated images of child pornography: A matter of harm or morality?' (2010) 30 *Legal Studies* 230–256.

O'Sullivan, K.T. 'Enforcing copyright online: Internet service provider obligations and the European Charter of Human Rights' (2014) 36 *European Intellectual Property Review* 577–583.

Owens, E.W., Behun, R.J., Manning, J.C. and Reid, R.C. 'The impact of internet pornography on adolescents: A review of the research' (2012) 19 *Sexual Addiction and Compulsivity* 99–122.

Palmer, T. 'Behind the screen: Children who are the subject of abusive images' in Quayle, E. and Taylor, M. (eds) *Viewing Child Pornography on the Internet* (2005, Russell House Publishing).

Parsons-Pollard, N. and Moriarty, L.J. 'Cyberstalking: Utilizing what we do know' (2009) 4 *Victims and Offenders* 435–441.

Petit, J.M. *Rights of the Child: Report of the Special Rapporteur on the Sale of Children, Child Prostitution and Child Pornography* (2004, UN Economic Social Council) (E/CN.4/2005/78).

Podgor, E.S. 'Cybercrime: Discretionary jurisdiction' (2009) 47 *University of Louisville Law Review* 727–738.

Pollack, D. 'Pro-eating disorder websites: What should be the feminist approach?' (2003) 13 *Feminism and Psychology* 246–251.

Pritchard, L. and Dhaliwal, G. 'It took us less than 24 hours to cripple the two grotesque pornographic websites that drove a pervert to strangle this teacher' (2004) *Daily Mail*, February 8.

Quayle, E. and Taylor, M. 'Child seduction and self-representation on the internet: Assessment issues' (2001) 4 *Cyberpsychology and Behaviour* 597–608.

Quayle, E., Erooga, M., Wright, L., Taylor, M. and Harbinson, D. *Only Pictures? Therapeutic Work with Internet Sex Offenders* (2006, Russell House Publishing).

Rackley, E. and McGlynn, C. 'Prosecuting the possession of extreme pornography: A misunderstood and mis-used law' [2013] *Criminal Law Review* 400–405.

Rahman, M.R., Khan, M.A., Mohammad, N. and Rahman, M.O. 'Cyberspace claiming new dynamism in the jurisprudential philosophy' (2009) 51 *International Journal of Law and Management* 274–290.

Rahman, R. 'Legal jurisdiction over malware-related crimes: From theories of jurisdiction to solid practical application' (2012a) 28 *Computer Law and Security Review* 403–415.

Rahman, R. 'The legal measures against Denial of Service (DoS) attacks adopted by the United Kingdom legislature: Should Malaysia follow suit?' (2012b) 20 *International Journal of Law and Information Technology* 85–101.

Rathmell, A. 'Cyber-terrorism: The shape of future conflict?' (1997) 142 *The RUSI Journal* 40–45.

Rege, A. 'What's love got to do with it? Exploring online dating scams and identity fraud' (2009) 3 *International Journal of Cybercriminology* 494–512.

Reid, A.S. and Ryder, N. 'For whose eyes only? A critique of the United Kingdom's Regulation of Investigatory Powers Act 2000' (2001) 10 *Information and Communications Technology Law* 179–201.

Reidenberg, J. 'Technology and internet jurisdiction' (2005) 153 *University of Pennsylvania Law Review* 1951–1974.

Richardson, J. 'If I cannot have her everybody can: Sexual disclosure and privacy law' in Richardson, J. and Rackley, E. (eds) *Feminist Perspectives on Tort Law* (2012, Routledge).

Richmond, S. 'The internet giant admits it has been collecting data from wireless networks across Britain' (2010) *Daily Telegraph*, October 25.

Robertson, G. *Freedom, the Individual and the Law* (7th ed., 1993, Penguin).

Robertson, H.B. 'The suppression of pirate radio broadcasting: A test case of the international system for control of activities outside national territory' (1982) 45 *Law and Contemporary Problems* 71–101.

Rogers, M. *A New Hacker Taxonomy* (2000) (http://homes.cerias.purdue.edu/~mkr.hacker.doc).

Rogers, M.K. 'A two-dimensional circumplex approach to the development of a hacker taxonomy' (2006) 3 *Digital Investigation* 97–102.

Rothenberg, L.E. 'Re-thinking privacy: Peeping toms, video voyeurs and the failure of criminal law to recognize a reasonable expectation of privacy in the public space' (2001) 49 *American University Law Review* 1127–1165.

Rowbottom, J. 'To rant, vent and converse: Protecting low level digital speech' (2012) 71 *Cambridge Law Journal* 355–383.

Rumbles, W. 'Theft in the digital: Can you steal virtual property?' (2011) 17 *Canterbury Law Review* 354–374.

Sandywell, B. 'On the globalisation of crime: The internet and new criminality' in Jewkes, Y. and Yar, M. (eds) *Handbook of Internet Crime* (2010, Willan Publishing) (38–66).

Schabas, W.A. *An Introduction to the International Criminal Court* (2011, Cambridge University Press).

Schmitt, W.N. 'Cyber operations and the *jus ad bellum* revisited' (2011) 56 *Villanova Law Review* 596–606.

Schmitt, W.N. *Tallinn Manual on the International Law Applicable to Cyber Warfare* (2013, Cambridge University Press).

Seto, M.C. 'Pedophilia and sexual offences involving children' (2004) 15 *Annual Review of Sex Research* 321–361.

Shaw, M. *International Law* (7th ed., 2008, Cambridge University Press).

Sheridan, L.P. and Grant, T. 'Is cyberstalking different?' (2007) 13 *Psychology, Crime and Law* 627–640.

Smith, J.C. 'Tampering with computer software: Whether "tangible" property' [1991] *Criminal Law Review* 436–437.

Smith, J.C. 'Police officers securing access to Police National Computer for non-police purposes' [1998] *Criminal Law Review* 53–54.

Smith, J.C. 'Unauthorised access to computer program or data: Meaning of unauthorised' [1999] *Criminal Law Review* 970–972.

Smith, P.K., Smith, C., Osborn, R. and Samara, M. 'A content analysis of school anti-bullying policies: Progress and limitations' (2008) 24 *Educational Psychology in Practice* 1–12.

Smith, R.J. *Property Law* (2014, Pearson).

Snyder, J.M. 'Online auction fraud: Are auction houses doing all they should or could to stop online fraud?' (2000) 52 *Federal Communications Law Journal* 453–472.

Sommer, P. 'Criminalising hacking tools' (2006) 3 *Digital Investigations* 68–72.

Southworth, C. and Tucker, S. 'Technology, stalking and domestic violence victims' (2007) 76 *Mississippi Law Journal* 667–676.

Spitzberg, B.H. and Hoobler, G. 'Cyberstalking and the technologies of interpersonal terrorism' (2002) 4 *New Media and Society* 71–92.

Srivastava, A. and Boey, J. 'Online bullying and harassment: An Australian perspective' (2012) 6 *Masaryk University Journal of Law and Technology* 299–320.

Stabek, A., Watters, P. and Layton, R. 'The seven scam types: Mapping the terrain of cybercrime' (2010) Second Cybercrime and Trustworthy Computing Workshop, 41–51.

Stohl, M. 'Cyber terrorism: A clear and present danger, the sum of all fears, breaking point or patriot games?' (2006) 46 *Crime, Law and Social Change* 223–238.

Stratford, J. and Johnson, T. 'The Snowden "revelations": Is GCHQ breaking the law? (2014) *European Human Rights Law Review* 129–141.

Strikwerda, L. 'Theft of virtual items in online multiplayer computer games: An ontological and moral analysis' (2012) 14 *Ethics and Information Technology* 89–97.

Tate, T. *Child Pornography: An Investigation* (1990, Methuen).

Taylor, M. and Quayle, E. *Child Pornography: An Internet Crime* (2003, Routledge).

Taylor, R.S. 'Hate speech, the priority of liberty, and the temptations of nonideal theory' (2002) 15 *Ethical Theory and Moral Practice* 353–368.

T-CY. Guidance Note #1: *On the Notion of 'Computer System'* (2012, T-CY, 21).

T-CY. Guidance Note #4: *Identity Theft and Phishing in Relation to Fraud* (2013, T-CY, 8E Rev.).

Terry, K.J. and Tallon, J. *Child Sexual Abuse: A Review of the Literature* (2004, US Conference of Catholic Bishops).

Thierer, A. 'Technopanics, threat inflation, and the danger of an information technology precautionary principle' (2013) 14 *Minnesota Journal of Law, Science and Technology* 309–386.

Trachtman, J.P. 'Cyberspace, sovereignty, jurisdiction and modernism' (1998) 5 *Global Legal Studies Journal* 561–581.

Tsesis, A. 'Hate in cyberspace: Regulating hate speech on the internet' (2001) 38 *San Diego Law Review* 817–874.

Urbas, G. and Choo, K.R. *Resource Materials on Technology-enabled Crime* (2008, Australian Institute of Criminology).

Van Laer, J, and Van Aelst, P. 'Cyber-protest and civil society: The internet and action repertoires in social movements' in Jewkes, Y. and Yar, M. (eds) *Handbook of Internet Crime* (2010, Willan Publishing).

Walden, I. *Computer Crimes and Digital Investigations* (2007, Oxford University Press).

Walker, C. *Terrorism and the Law* (2011, Oxford University Press).

Wall, D. 'Cybercrimes and the internet' in Wall, D. (ed.) *Crime and the Internet* (2001, Routledge).

Wall, D. *Cybercrime* (2007, Polity Press).

Wall, D. and Yar, M. 'Intellectual property crime and the internet: Cyber-piracy and "stealing" information intangibles' in Jewkes, Y. and Yar, M. (eds) *Handbook of Internet Crime* (2010, Routledge) (255–272).

Walton, R. 'The Computer Misuse Act' (2006) 11 *Information Security Technical Report* 39–45.

Wasik, M. *Crime and the Computer* (1991, Oxford University Press).

Wasik, M. 'The emergence of computer law' in Jewkes, Y. and Yar, M. (eds) *Handbook of Internet Crime* (2010, Routledge).

Weare, S. '"The mad", "the bad", "the victim": Gendered constructions of women who kill within the criminal justice system' (2013) 2 *Laws* 337–361.

Weijters, B., Goedertier, F., Verstreken, S. 'Online music consumption in today's technological context: Putting the influences of ethics in perspective' (2013) *Journal of Business Ethics* (DOI: 10.1007/s10551-013-1892-y).

Weinberg, M.S., Williams, C.J., Kleiner, S. and Irizarry, Y. 'Pornography, normalization, and empowerment' (2010) 39 *Archives of Sexual Behaviour* 1389–1401.

Williams, K.S. 'Child pornography law: Does it protect children?' (2004) 26 *Journal of Social Welfare and Family Law* 245–261.

''Wingrove, T., Korpas, A.L. and Weisz, V. 'Why are millions of people not obeying the law? Motivational influences on non-compliance with the law in the case of music piracy' (2011) 17 *Psychology, Crime and Law* 261–276.

Wolak, J., Finkelhor, D., and Mitchell, K.J. *Child Pornography Possessors Arrested in Internet-related Crimes* (2005, NCMEC).

Wolswijk, H. 'Taking a virtual object in RuneScape' (2012) 76 *Journal of Criminal Law* 459–462.

Wong, R. *Data Security Breaches and Privacy in Europe* (2013, Springer).

Wood, M.J., Douglas, K.M. and Sutton, R.M. 'Dead and alive: Beliefs in contradictory conspiracy theories' (2012) *Social Psychological and Personality Science* 767–773.

Yar, M. 'The global "epidemic" of movie "piracy": Crime-wave or social construction?' (2005) 27 *Media, Culture and Society* 677–696.

Yar, M. 'Teenage kicks or virtual villainy? Internet piracy, moral entrepreneurship, and the social construction of a crime problem' in Jewkes, Y. (ed.) *Crime Online* (2007, Willan Publishing) (95–108).

Yar, M. 'E-crime 2.0: The criminological landscape of new social media' (2012) 21 *Information and Communications Technology Law* 207–219.

Yar, M. *Cybercrime and Society* (2nd ed., 2013, Sage).

Yeshua-Katz, D. and Martins, N. 'Communicating stigma: The pro-Ana paradox' (2013) 28 *Health Communications* 499–508.

# Index